THE BAHAMAS FLY-FISHING GUIDE

THE BAHAMAS FLY-FISHING GUIDE

VACATION PLANNING RESOURCE

STEPHEN VLETAS AND KIM VLETAS

The Lyons Press
Guilford, Connecticut
An imprint of The Globe Pequot Press

Copyright © 2005 by Stephen Vletas and Kim Vletas
Photographs copyright © Kim Vletas unless otherwise noted.

The Lyons Press is an imprint of The Globe Pequot Press

Printed in the United States of America

10 9 8 7 6 5 4 3 2 1

Designed by Linda R. Loiewski

ISBN 1-59228-726-3

Library of Congress Cataloging-in-Publication Data is available on file.

CONTENTS

ACKNOWLEDGMENTS

Most of the research that went into this project could not have been accomplished without the tremendous support of the people on the Out Islands—lodge owners, operators and their staffs, fishing guides, taxi drivers, restaurant and service personnel, and everyone else who took the time to make us feel welcome over the years—you are the reason we were able to complete this book. In particular, our many friends on Andros, Abaco, Grand Bahama, Long Island, and Crooked Island are responsible for us thinking of the Bahamas as our second home. Guides such as Charlie Neymour (who was our first guide in 1988), Andy Smith, Frankie Neymour, Barry Neymour, Ivan Neymour, O'Donald Macintosh, James "Docky" Smith, and Tommy Rolle have been valued fishing companions over the years, and have been instrumental in our ongoing efforts to explore and better understand the fisheries.

We would like to extend a special "thank you" to everyone at Tranquility Hill Fishing Lodge, at Treasure Cay Resort and Marina, to Greg Vincent at Pelican Bay Bonefishing, to Jill and Docky Smith at Stella Maris, and to Carter and Heidi Andrews at Pittstown Point Landings. Along with others, you have created that extra special welcome feeling travelers always remember, and want to return to.

For this updated edition, we are in even greater debt to the many traveling anglers and vacationers who took the time to relate their experiences to us. We appreciate the information, the stories, and the friendships that developed out of these meetings and conversations.

On the publishing side, we consider ourselves fortunate to have worked with the people at The Lyons Press, people who share our love of fly-fishing. We also extend thanks to Lisa Purcell for her editorial insights and hard work in putting this manuscript into such fine shape.

We are grateful to Angela Burton, and her extraordinary design skills, for taking raw maps and turning them into the distinctive and informative maps included in the book.

And finally, we recognize and appreciate that we have been extremely fortunate over the past 15 years or so, blessed really, with the ability to visit and explore some of the most magnificent saltwater landscapes in the world. It all started with someone mentioning Andros Island, the possibility of huge bonefish in virgin waters. That turned into a dream to pursue, that turned into planning the trip, and then, arriving in Behring Point.

Now we have a gallery of memories—the "north shore" of Cat Island, the Water Cays of South Andros, Wide Open, Sandy Cay, Jamaica Cay, a 20-pound bonefish hooked and lost, sipping Kaliks with friends overlooking a quiet marina, a magenta sunset with no land in sight—a fantasy slide show that flashes in our minds whenever we summon it.

We hope it can be that way for you, too. Pick a place, plan your dream, and make it come true.

INTRODUCTION

Stephen and Kim Vletas.

Well, it has been a long time coming . . . but we are happy to have this updated edition in your hands now. Thanks to all of our readers for your patience.

This edition was written with the following goals in mind. Number one: the book was designed to assist anglers and adventure travelers through the planning process for a future trip. The information provided here will help you select the destination that is right for you, based on goals you set for your trip. Are you planning a hard-core fishing trip? Will non-anglers join your group? Are you looking for simple accommodations or a luxurious resort with a variety of amenities? We hope the depth and accuracy of the information will point you in the right direction and help you set realistic expectations for your trip.

Number two: the book was designed to help anglers who have already arranged trips on their own or through a travel professional. Once you reach your destination, you can use the maps to find lodges, restaurants, and fishing access points. You can use our tide suggestions to pick the best fishing times during a day. You can use our suggestions to pick a fishing guide, a restaurant, dive shop, or car rental agency, or to extend your vacation and stay at one of the locations we recommend.

Number three: we wanted to make it easy for you to book your vacation on your own, or through a travel professional, for "do-it-yourself" trips. Over the past several years, this has been the number-one request from our readers and Web site visitors. This edition will give you the advice and information you need for self-guided trips throughout the islands.

And for those of you who might be wavering, thinking about maybe going to the Bahamas, or trying a new location in the Bahamas, we hope the book will be an enticement. We hope that somewhere we've written something that touches you, that makes you think, *yep, I've got to go there. I've got to see that. I've got to try that.* If you feel this sort of inspiration while reading these chapters, then we've achieved our ultimate goal, which is to give anglers something that can change their lives, as the Bahamas has changed ours.

Angling travel is by no means just about catching fish. As Yvon Chouinard of Patagonia has said about mountain climbing, "It is the process itself, the opportunity for striving, and becoming a better person." We know from experience that the planning and preparation of a trip can be just as much fun as the trip itself, and in most cases, this process, the daydreaming and anticipation, lasts longer than the vacation.

So, whether you're a serious angler headed to the Bahamas for your tenth time, or planning a honeymoon trip where you may only fish for a few hours in a week, this book was written for you.

Stephen Vletas and Kim Vletas
Jackson Hole, Wyoming

HOW TO USE THIS GUIDE

One of the goals of this book is to make it as easy as possible for anglers and adventure travelers to gather the information they need to plan a trip to the islands. We recommend reading, or at least skimming through, the first three chapters before going on to the island chapters. This will give you an overall perspective of the Bahamas that will enable you to better evaluate the specific information on the islands.

Each island chapter is broken down into the following sections:

Island Introduction: An overview of the island, describing the island's location and geography, population, local atmosphere and culture, adventure activity highlights, and travel tips specific to the island.

Around the Island: A detailed tour of the island, with maps for reference. The tour is for boaters and land-based travelers. Specific information covers the structure of the fishery, fishing access points, boating routes and marinas, ferries and bridges, highways and roads, towns and settlements, lodges, restaurants, and sightseeing opportunities.

Fishing Highlights: Everything you need to know for a general understanding of the gamefish species, habitat, food sources, and tides, including best tides for fishing and specific tidal characteristics. The top gamefish species—bonefish, permit, tarpon, sharks, barracuda, and others—are covered individually. We also discuss the best months for each species, along with our favorite tackle and flies.

Optional Activities: If you're not fishing every day, you'll want to know what else there is to do. Diving, snorkeling, sea kayaking, windsurfing, sailing, eco-tours, wildlife observation, bicycling, golf, tennis, shopping, and other activities are available on the various islands.

Lodging, Guides, and Services: Broken down into Featured Lodges, Additional Accommodations, and Do-It-Yourself Options. This is where you will find specific descriptions of lodges, accommodations, food, service, amenities, suitability for anglers and/or non-anglers, vacation packages, and general pricing information.

Featured Lodges are our top recommendations on each island. What criteria did we use to make these recommendations? We combined our personal experiences with reports from fellow travelers in areas of service, comfort, amenities, food, quality of guiding and fishing, and an overall "experience" factor. The best way to put it is to say that these are places we would want to visit again soon. These resorts and lodges range from properties with elegant accommodations and superior service to simple, rustic destinations where a cold Kalik and a comfortable bed are all you need to enjoy your vacation. They also cover the pricing spectrum from expensive to economical.

Additional Accommodations are locations that are suitable, or not, depending on the type of vacation you want. We've had good experiences at many of them. Some of these options are also appropriate for do-it-yourself vacations.

The Do-It-Yourself Options section is new. These are locations where you are on your own—lodges, hotels, private houses where meals may or may not be provided, where you can cook on your own, hire independent guides, rent a boat or car, fish on your own. You run the show and choose activities at your whim. And now a word of caution: doing things on your own involves many hazards, too many to mention them all here. There are vast areas to explore, but doing so on your own can be dangerous, and navigating the waters throughout the islands requires extensive local knowledge. Proceed at your own risk. Adventurous anglers who understand the risks can have a great time, which will include doing many things wrong that will result in catching no fish. Still, trying on your own is part of the "experience," right? Make sure you understand the risks before you go.

Guides: Many of the best guides on each island are independent. This means that they run their own businesses, set their own rates, make their own policies, own their own boats and equipment, and only work with lodges and accommodation options of their choosing. Generally, independent guides will pick you up at your place of accommodation, but some will require you to take a taxi, or drive yourself, to meet them at a dock or boat launch site. Only a few independent guides have tackle and flies, so you should plan to take all of your own tackle and flies. Some guides fish a standard 8 A.M. to 4 P.M. day, while others will fish to suit your schedule. Most guides do not provide lunch, so you should plan to pack your own. Most guides will have a cooler with ice for you to keep your drinks and lunch cold. Be sure to confirm rates, payment policy, deposit policy, pick-up time and place, fishing area, and fishing preferences (wading or out of a poled skiff) before finalizing your reservation. Most guides only accept cash as payment, though some will accept personal checks or money orders for deposits. Most guides have a "no refund for any reason" policy. It is your sole responsibility to understand all the aspects of booking a trip directly with an independent guide.

Services: Information on marinas, adventure activities, car rentals, taxi services, restaurants, ferries, grocery stores, banks, clinics, and more.

New Developments: New or proposed resorts, lodges, and fishing grounds are being developed all the time. Guides and outfitters create various new programs on a continuous basis. We assess these developments based on our experience and reports from fellow anglers. Updated information on these developments will be available on the BFFG Web site: www.bahamasflyfishingguide.com.

Pricing: It is not possible to provide specific pricing for lodges, guides, and other services. Much depends on packages, time of season, options chosen, and so on. We do, however, include a general guideline for anglers and vacationers to begin their trip planning in the right direction. Our pricing guidelines are as follows:*

$ = inexpensive, $225 to $275 per person per day
$$ = moderate, $275 to $400 per person per day
$$$ = expensive, $400 to $525 per person per day
$$$$ = very expensive, $525 and up per person per day

Rates at bonefishing lodges are usually consistent throughout a given season. The bonefishing season runs from October through May, with some lodges open in June and July. Most bonefishing lodges work on a package plan per person per day (double basis) that includes accommodations, meals, guided fishing, and government taxes. If you are traveling as a single, you will pay the entire guided fishing expense yourself, which means your rate will be significantly higher than the double rate. Your reward is that your guide will devote his full attention to you, and all the fishing time on the deck will be yours.

Independent guides usually charge in the $350 to $450 range for a full day of guided fishing. A few independent guides will do half days, usually in the range of $225 to $300 for a half day of guided fishing. In the Turks and Caicos Islands, guide rates are substantially higher: $500 to $750 for a full day.

Booking a do-it-yourself trip is usually less expensive (in terms of money, not necessarily in terms of your time) than booking a package trip. Accommodation options work out to be more economical, as do the prices of meals.

Please be aware that all prices are subject to change without notice and, in fact, they change regularly. Traveling anglers will be best served by requesting specific lodge and activity pricing for specific dates of travel. This is the only way to obtain accurate prices for the trip you want. The same is true for air travel. Current pricing is available directly from lodges, guides, and airlines, or through a professional travel consultant.

Generally, the winter tourist season runs from mid-December through April. The summer season is the rest of the year. Winter rates are normally the most expensive, with bargains sometimes available in summer and fall. Different lodges have different policies about charging for maid service, air-conditioning, and other services, and these policies change often. Meals can be included or not. Optional activities can be included or not.

* Pricing guidelines are based on double-occupancy rates and include accommodations, all meals, and guided fishing. Other expenses may also be included, such as government taxes and airport transfers. Non-angling rates are available at many of these locations. You must confirm specific pricing at the time of your booking.

THE BAHAMAS—AN OVERVIEW

Stephen and Andros guide Charlie Neymour on a flat in the Middle Bight.

A mere 50 miles off the southern coast of Florida, the Islands of the Bahamas beckon—to anglers and adventure travelers alike. They are sirens singing their ancient irresistible songs promising peaceful relaxation, endless stretches of pristine beaches, glistening turquoise waters, delicious food and drink.

And of course there are a diversity of angling challenges, a chance to match wits and skill with the world's finest gamefish. This total experience is the essence of fly-fishing, and we're all searching for that experience . . . the one that will lighten our souls forever. The islands await.

Fishing has long been an integral part of the Bahamian lifestyle and culture, in no small part due to its physical makeup and geography. The Spaniards called the region Baja Mar, the Shallow Sea, and it is one of the most magnificent saltwater fisheries in the world.

Practically speaking, the fishing opportunities are divided into two distinct types. The most popular with fly-fishers is the shallow-water flats fishery. The blue-water, or offshore, fishery has been recognized as sensational by conventional anglers for years and is becoming more popular with fly anglers with each passing season.

Flats species consist of the big three: bonefish, tarpon, and permit; plus barracuda, lemon and blacktip sharks, jack crevalle, mutton snapper, and mangrove snapper. The most abundant gamefish to pursue over the inshore reefs include cubera snappers, grouper, a variety of jacks, barracuda, numerous species of sharks, sierra and king mackerel, and amberjack.

Many of the best flats regions have been famous for years, while others are just now being explored. Bimini is a legendary flats destination for anglers hunting big bonefish. Look in the International Game Fish Association record books and you'll see that Bimini is well represented. At the East End of Grand Bahama, Deep Water Cay has established itself as one of the premier bonefishing lodges in the world.

On Andros, the North and Middle Bights have been visited by the rich and famous since the 1930s. The Bang Bang Club on Pot Cay in the North Bight was one of the first bonefishing clubs. Treasure Cay, Abaco, serves up fine family accommodations, and delivers anglers to the doorstep of the Marls, a vast mangrove flats region reminiscent of the Everglades. Eleuthera's Windermere Island, once an elegant retreat laced with lavish homes, fell on hard times in the 1980s and 1990s but has now made a comeback. Nearby Savannah Sound is composed of white sand flats suited to anglers who want to fish on their own.

Since the "bonefishing explosion" in 1999, the Bahamas has experienced significant changes on most islands. A government-sponsored program to loan money to Bahamians to develop bonefishing lodges created a building boom, even among locals who knew nothing about bonefishing. Some of these lodges have succeeded, but most failed due to post-9/11 impacts and poor planning.

A notable success has been Chez Pierre on Long Island, more of a vacation eco-lodge than a bonefishing lodge but, nonetheless, a hit with anglers wanting to combine fishing with snorkeling, sea kayaking, and island exploring. Tiamo Resort, in the South Bight of Andros, has become one of the top eco-lodges in the Caribbean, and a haven for fly-fishers who want to wet a line in these famous waters.

Overall, the bonefishing industry in the Bahamas has matured. Successful lodges and guides have realized that service and comfort matter, and that catering to couples and families, as well as serious anglers, is a must. Increasing numbers of anglers are showing a desire to fish on their own without a guide. This has caused crowding on some of the more accessible flats on the islands of Eleuthera, Long Island, and elsewhere, and has created conflict with local guides. Sometimes progress is good, and sometimes not, but the crowding and conflicts are part of the natural evolution in up-and-coming tourist destinations throughout the world.

On the blue-water front, the most popular gamefish species continue to be blue and white marlin, sailfish, a variety of tuna, wahoo, and dolphin. Some of the best-known areas include Walker's Cay in north Abaco, Bimini, Nassau, Port Lucaya/Freeport, and Fresh Creek, Andros, where the Tongue of the Ocean sweeps in against the flats and plummets to depths of 6,000 feet. U.S. Naval buoys off the eastern shore of Andros are phenomenal dolphin and Allison tuna magnets.

Farther south, Cat Island, San Salvador, Long Island, and Crooked Island are remote blue-water havens. Some of the best blue marlin, tuna, and wahoo fishing on the planet can be experienced here.

Renowned billfish tournaments are traditions that continue to flourish. The most popular tournaments include the Hemingway Championships out of Bimini, the Bahamas Billfish Championship Series, as well as others out of Walker's Cay, Green Turtle Cay, Treasure Cay, Marsh Harbor, and George Town. The Bahamas Wahoo Championship Series is held throughout the islands, generating a spirit of lively competition during the winter months.

If you enjoy these tournaments, and you want a rocking party atmosphere, we recommend that you visit the Abaco Beach Resort and Boat Harbour in Marsh Harbour during any tournament. Be sure to make your reservations well in advance.

■

A quality that is foremost in our minds about the Bahamas is its tranquility and charm, especially across the Out Islands. The fact is, there are really two Bahamas. The first exists in the high-profile resort settings of Freeport and Nassau. The other consists of the Out Islands, or Family Islands, where the residents are friendly and welcoming, and change happens at a snail's pace.

Out Island residents make a habit of welcoming guests. Anything you need, no problem, mon. The simple truth is you don't need much—a comfortable room, good food, a cold Kalik, and a place to hang out with friends and maybe tie some flies or rig some leaders. This is one of the best places in the world to relax and just live day to day. "Eat, fish, drink, sleep, eat, fish, drink, sleep," becomes the hypnotic mantra.

A phrase we often use is "How bad can it be in a place like this?" The settings of the Bahamas are sometimes stunning and dramatic, though more often the beauty is simple, subtle, and soothing. Clear aqua-green water, pink sand beaches, lush mangrove cays, cool pine forests, the sound of the surf as it pours over a reef, along with the abundant bird and sea life—these are your constant companions.

While the people are laid-back, they also possess an old-fashioned sense of purpose. As tourism moves into the mainstream, they focus new energy and enthusiasm on developing marinas and resorts. This has been most prevalent on Abaco and Exuma. The Four Seasons Resort at Emerald Bay, Exuma, opened in November 2003.

The impressive Atlantis is like a glitzy Vegas hotel dropped into a tropical paradise.

The ultra-upscale resort and residential community, the Abaco Club on Winding Bay, shifted into high-gear development in early 2004. Both resorts feature championship 18-hole golf courses and have plans for new marinas.

In spite of this, the way of life throughout the Out Islands remains relatively unchanged. Work hard, honor your family, have pride in yourself, and be friendly seems to be the motto. This way of life has persisted for generations. It is the essence of harmony that can seep into your soul and, along with the fishing, it can keep you coming back again and again.

A Brief History

Everyone knows Columbus sailed the ocean blue in 1492, but exactly where he landed first in the Bahamas is a matter of debate. Most people believe he landed on Guanahani, where a native culture had existed for years. Columbus then renamed the island "San Salvador," which is Castilian for Holy Savior. The name the Spaniards gave the present-day Bahamian Islands, Baja Mar, Shallow Sea, is somewhat misleading. The islands are actually mountain plateaus that emerged from the Atlantic Ocean hundreds of thousands of years ago. These plateaus fostered an expanse of sea-strewn coral, which comprises the limestone base of the islands today.

The Lukku-cairi, or "island people" as they called themselves, were the first settlers. It is believed they wandered in boats from South America, through the Caribbean to the Bahamas around the ninth century A.D. Historically, they are known as "Arawaks," but they are usually referred to as "Lucayans," a Spanish distortion of their name. Columbus mistakenly referred to the Lucayans as "Indians" because he believed he had landed in the East Indies when he walked ashore in the Bahamas.

In 1500, in search of gold and other riches, the Spanish conquistadors followed Columbus. They initiated the first slave labor, kidnapping most of the Lucayans to work the gold mines and pearl beds of Cuba and other nearby islands. Enslavement and disease soon wiped out the Lucayans. And once slave labor was no longer available, the Spaniards sailed away, having never settled the islands, though they ruled them for more than a century.

Bahamian history moved into a new era in 1647 when Eleutheran Adventurers arrived from Bermuda. In pursuit of religious freedom, they formed the first British colony on the island of Eleuthera, and were soon followed by other English settlers. A prosperous agricultural economy developed on the island; it is still maintained today.

The geography of the islands attracted many well-known pirates, including Edward Teach, Henry Morgan, and Anne Bonney. Their primary operating method was to lure unsuspecting ships into the treacherous shallow waters, then attack and loot whatever treasure was on board.

Britain claimed the islands in 1670, but remained powerless against the pirate predators for almost 50 years. By 1700, lawless chaos reigned in Nassau. Edward

Teach, the notorious Blackbeard, took Fort Nassau as his residence and harassed the British Royal Navy for years.

The British government actually contributed to the islands' pirating ways by sanctioning privateers. Privateers were essentially pirates who carried a license, a letter of marque, which allowed them to loot and plunder legally. For the most part, these marauders were beneficial to British interests because they preyed on merchant ships of Britain's Spanish, French, and Portuguese enemies. When the opportunity arose, however, many privateers looted indiscriminately, often attacking the Crown's own ships.

In 1718, the British decided to put the pirates out of business forever. They appointed the successful privateer Woodes Rogers as Royal Governor of the colony. Rogers began his campaign by offering royal pardons to pirates who would cease their illegal activities. To make a point, however, Rogers did not offer these pardons to everyone. Instead, he pursued certain pirates to their deaths.

Among those pursued were Blackbeard, Roger Vane, and eight other notorious compatriots. Blackbeard and Vane escaped the initial attacks, Vane by burning a ship to cover his getaway.

Blackbeard was eventually killed off the coast of Virginia in June 1718. An outlaw to the end, he ignored the warnings of his allies and allowed the British ship *Pearl* to trap his vessel near a sandbar. Blackbeard chose to fight rather than surrender. In the brutal hand-to-hand combat that followed, it is said that Blackbeard suffered five pistol ball and twenty cutlass wounds before succumbing.

Roger Vane was apprehended after his ship ran aground. He was then taken to Kingston, Jamaica, where he was tried, convicted, and hanged. The other eight pirates were hanged in Nassau from gallows standing on what is now the Hilton British Colonial Hotel's west beach. Having cleaned up the port city, Woodes Rogers moved into Fort Nassau and lived there until his death a few years later from mysterious causes.

Rogers' victory allowed the Bahamas to emerge as a recognized British colony, though privateering continued when it suited the Crown. Many Spanish ships loaded with treasure stolen from South and Central America were in turn plundered as they came through the islands on their way to Europe. Much of the treasure was lost and has not been recovered to this day.

The art of plundering was not left solely to pirates and privateers. Many people of the Abacos made their living by looting ships unfortunate enough to be wrecked off the islands, either by storm or by help from unscrupulous islanders swinging lanterns off the treacherous sandbars and reefs. This lucrative "wrecking" industry did not stop until the first lighthouse was built in 1836.

During the Revolutionary War, Spain sided with America and briefly regained control of the Bahamas in May 1782. A year later, under the Treaty of Versailles, the Bahamas once again became a British colony.

After Britain's defeat in the Revolutionary War, Southern Loyalists immigrated to the islands with their slaves to grow cotton under the protection of the British Crown.

In 1838 the Crown abolished slavery, which put most cotton plantations out of business and caused a general decline in agriculture.

Turbulent times in America meant prosperity for the islands. During the Civil War years, the North established a naval blockade in an attempt to cripple the Confederacy. Bahamians amassed great wealth running Confederate cotton to English mills and then sending military equipment back to the Confederates.

Tough times hit the Bahamas after the Civil War, and lasted until the Roaring Twenties and Prohibition, when rumrunners used the Bahamas as a base of operations. Cash again flowed into the islands bringing prosperity to many residents. After the repeal of Prohibition, the economy again stagnated.

The arrival of wealthy Americans on luxury yachts was a bright spot in the dark times of the 1930s. Families such as the Mellons spent weeks and even months at various islands, contributing jobs and currency to the local economies. The Middle Bight area of Andros Island was a consistent beneficiary. The Mellons hired local guides from Moxey Town to take them bonefishing, which began a tradition of famous bonefishing guides in the Moxey family.

Still, it was not until World War II, when the United States and Great Britain used the islands for air and sea bases in the Atlantic, that general prosperity reemerged.

In the 1950s tourism was recognized as an emerging industry, which changed business priorities in the islands forever. In 1955, the Hawksbill Creek Agreement laid the groundwork for the creation of Freeport/Lucaya to become the second largest city in the country.

When Cuba was closed to U.S. tourism after the Castro revolution in 1959, the Bahamas again benefited from nearby trouble. Increasing numbers of Americans began traveling to the islands to enjoy the tropical atmosphere.

Great Britain granted the islands self-government in 1964, and then changed the Bahamas' status from colony to commonwealth in 1969. In 1973, the Commonwealth of the Bahamas became independent within the Commonwealth of Nations, but retained Queen Elizabeth II as constitutional head of state.

In 1992 the opposition Free National Movement won the general election, thus ending 25 years of rule by the Progressive Liberal Party. In 1997, Prime Minister Hubert Ingraham and the FNM won a second term.

Prime Minister Ingraham's government brought about many positive changes throughout the islands. The country encouraged greater foreign investment, which stimulated growth and

Andros guide and lodge owner Charlie Smith. Charlie's Haven is across the street from this shack. (Ric Fogel)

improved tourism services in Nassau and Freeport. The formation of local government districts focused attention on improving the quality of life in the Out Islands. New roads, plus better power and telephone service to the Out Islands, raised the standard of living throughout the Bahamas.

In May 2002, the PLP Party regained control of Parliament with a triumph in the general election. The Honorable Perry Gladstone Christie was sworn in as the country's third prime minister, and also assumed the cabinet office of minister of finance.

For comprehensive updated information on the government of the Bahamas, visit their Web site at www.bahamas.gov.bs.

Cultural Notes

The roughly 300,000 people who live in the Bahamas (70 percent of this population lives on New Providence) are predominantly of West African ethnicity, descendants of the slaves brought to the islands to work the cotton plantations. The majority of Caucasian residents of the Bahamas are descended from the British Eleutheran Adventurers or the Loyalists who emigrated from the southern United States.

Religion is an integral part of Bahamian life. Even the tiniest village has a church, which often is the center of community interaction. Music is another spiritual part of Bahamian life. African rhythms, Caribbean calypso, and English folk songs meld into the unique Bahamian musical medium, the Goombay beat. The fast-tempoed goom-bahhh drumbeat can be traced back to the days of slavery and is used both for story-telling and dancing.

Junkanoo is a national festival in the Bahamas, the only place where it holds such an honor. The origin of the word "Junkanoo" is obscure. Some say it comes from the French l'inconnu (meaning the unknown), in reference to the masks worn by the paraders. Others contend the name derived from "John Canoe," the name of an African tribal chief who demanded the right to celebrate with his enslaved people.

It is believed that this festival began during the sixteenth or seventeenth century. Slaves were given a special holiday at Christmas when they could leave the plantations to be with their families. They spent the holiday celebrating with African dance, music, and costumes.

Junkanoo Lounge at the North Eleuthera Airport.

Today you can walk down to Bay Street in Nassau during the early morning hours of Boxing Day, the day after Christmas, and you'll be bombarded with a riot of color and sound. If you miss the Christmas celebration, Junkanoo parades are also held in conjunction with other special holidays such as Independence Day (July 10).

To find out more about Bahamian culture, contact the People-to-People program center at 242-302-2000, or e-mail peopletopeople@bahamas.com. This year-round Ministry of Tourism program gives visitors a genuine and informal view of Bahamian hospitality and culture.

Bahamas National Trust (BNT)

Established by an Act of Parliament in 1959, BNT is a non-profit organization responsible for the preservation of Bahamian places of historic interest and natural beauty. Its patron is HRH the Duke of Edinburgh.

The BNT administers more than 320,000 acres in 12 national parks and protected areas. One of BNT's most noteworthy accomplishments was the saving of the nearly extinct West Indian flamingo, the national bird of the Bahamas. Thanks to BNT efforts, there are nearly 60,000 flamingos on Great Inagua. Ongoing projects include work to prevent the extinction of the Bahama parrot and the green turtle.

BNT maintains close relationships with important scientific organizations throughout the world, all with an eye on protecting the Bahamas' invaluable marine environment, which includes some of the most magnificent living reefs in the world. For anglers, this effort is a key reason the fisheries of the Bahamas remain in such pristine condition.

Donations, membership dues, a small annual government grant, and an endowment fund sustain BNT. Dues and fees paid by U.S. citizens in U.S. dollars to the Environmental Systems Protection Fund are tax deductible. Membership applications and additional information are available from the Bahamas National Trust, P.O. Box N-4105, Nassau, Bahamas; telephone 242-393-1317 or 242-393-2848. Internet: www.bahamasnationaltrust.com. E-mail: bnt@batelnet.bs.

Food and Drink

Although most types of international food are available, it would be a mistake to miss an opportunity to sample the local cuisine. No matter where you are, it's easy to find restaurants or lodges serving Bahamian fare at reasonable prices.

Seafood is the staple of the Bahamas, and conch (pronounced konk) is a specialty. The firm, white, peach-fringed meat comes from a large ocean mollusk. Fresh uncooked conch is often served ceviche-style, cut into small pieces and marinated with lime juice and spices. Most commonly, conch is fried. Conch fritters, served with a rich sauce for dipping and washed down with a cold Kalik beer, is our favorite après-fishing tradition. Conch is also steamed, used in soups, salads, and stews, or made into chowder.

Kim, Pelican Bay Hotel guide Tommy Foley, and Rosie at Rosie's Chicken Nest on Grand Bahama's West End.

The Bahamian rock lobster is a spiny, clawless variety that is tasty served broiled, steamed, minced, or used in salads. The lobster season runs from August 1 to March 31. Other delicacies include boiled or baked land crabs, which are usually caught on the back roads after dark or after a heavy rain.

Fresh fish also plays a major role in Bahamian cooking. A popular brunch is boiled fish served with grits. Stewed fish, made with celery, onions, tomatoes, and various spices, is another local specialty. Pigeon peas and rice, seasoned with spices, tomatoes, onions, and bacon, accompany many dishes. Andros Island has a population of wild boar, as do several other islands, so locals there eat pork regularly. If you get the chance, we highly recommend a meal of pork with peas and rice or black beans and rice, accompanied by warm johnnycake bread.

Peas figure prominently in an array of fragrant Bahamian soups. Pea soup with dumplings and salt beef is one of our favorites. A unique soup is called "the souse." The ingredients are water, onions, lime juice, celery, peppers, and meat. No thickeners are added. The meat added to the souse is often oxtail or pigs' feet, giving the souse a delicious flavor that is new to most visitors. Remember that the cuisine of the Bahamas is rarely bland. If spicy food is a problem for you, be sure to mention this before ordering any local dishes.

For dessert, our favorite island choice is Key lime pie. Chef Iyke Moore, who works on Andros Island at the Mangrove Cay Club, makes the best we've tasted anywhere.

Blended drinks are a Bahamian art form. Bartenders take pride in their own special recipes of rums and fruit juices. Be careful with these concoctions; they usually possess a serious kick.

Kalik, the beer of the Bahamas, is light and wheaty. We don't drink any other beer while we're in the islands, though many imports are available.

The Bahamian refresher of choice is coconut water (not the heavier, fattier coconut milk) blended with sweet milk and gin. Some of our guides spend hours on the flats singing the famous "Gin and Coconut Water" song to hold them over until we return to the lodge for the real thing.

Geography and Climate

The Bahamas are strategically located in the Western Hemisphere, at the crossroads of the Americas. The northernmost islands are only 50 miles from Florida, and the coral archipelago stretches south to the Caribbean Sea. Located along the Tropic of Cancer, the Bahamas are warmed by the waters of the Gulf Stream and cooled by southerly trade winds. Also called the Isles of June, the Bahamas tropical climate is one of the most pleasant in the world. The average year-round temperature is 77°F (25°C), with daily maximum and minimum temperatures differing by about 12 degrees.

There are two distinct weather seasons in the Bahamas: winter and summer. Winter weather patterns generally begin in November, but can be postponed until as late as January. Winter begins with the first cold front, or norther, generated when normal easterly flows of water-tempered air are disturbed by continental high-pressure air. Cold fronts occur throughout winter, and usually begin with the wind veering to the south or southwest. Once the cold front arrives, winds usually shift quickly to the northwest, then north, and blow themselves out from the northeast. These winter cold fronts usually take two to four days to blow through, and winds range from 20 to 35 knots. In general, the more severe the weather in the United States, the colder and windier it becomes in the Bahamas. Once a cold front reaches Florida, it is only 12 hours away from the northern Bahamas.

The summer weather pattern usually begins by May, or after the last cold front. This pattern is governed by easterly flows of maritime air. Winds tend to blow from the eastern side of the compass, with southeast being predominant. Summer winds are usually light, in the five- to ten-knot range, and calm evenings are common. Cotton-ball cumulus clouds mushroom most afternoons, and can turn into thunder and lightning storms. Heavy afternoon rains account for the bulk of rainfall throughout the islands, with June producing more rainfall than any other month. The main hurricane season is August and September, with July and October as shoulder hurricane months. Weather forecasts are available for each island on the Internet at www.bahamas.com or at www.weather.com.

Adventure and Resort Activities

Nassau's Paradise Island and Cable Beach are the centers of resort activity on New Providence. The Atlantis Resort on Paradise Island is spectacular, combining a Las Vegas–style casino and showroom with a playground of swimming pools and water sports, a massive saltwater aquarium, and elegant guest accommodations. Nightclubs, fine dining, tempting beaches, diving and snorkeling excursions, golf, tennis, and duty-free shopping are all available.

Visiting the aquarium at Atlantis is something we highly recommend, even if you just have a few hours to spend in Nassau. Bonefish, permit, tarpon, mutton and other snappers, sharks, barracuda, jacks, and a variety of exotic saltwater fish can be viewed from above or below the water's surface. From an angler's perspective, watching these gamefish is fascinating.

Freeport/Port Lucaya on Grand Bahama is considered the Bahamas' second city. The streets are clean, beautifully landscaped, and traffic is rarely congested. Casinos,

Relaxing in a hammock at Cargill Creek Lodge on Andros Island.

duty-free shopping, diving, snorkeling, golf, tennis, water sports and white sand beaches will keep non-anglers pleasantly occupied, as will sea kayaking excursions through the Lucayan National Park. For those who enjoy a lively nightlife, the Port Lucaya Marketplace and Count Basie Square is one of our favorite hot spots, but beware of the craziness that goes on here during Spring Break.

There are a variety of deluxe accommodations, from hotels to condominiums, and numerous restaurant choices. The Our Lucaya Westin and Sheraton resorts (actually one huge combined resort) include a casino, international convention facilities, a quarter mile of beach, four swimming pools, expansive gym and full-service spa, lighted tennis courts, and the Bahama Reef golf course. A variety of restaurants and bars cover the spectrum from dress-up elegant to beachy casual.

Across the street from Our Lucaya, on the Port Lucaya Marina, the Pelican Bay Hotel creates the best of all worlds for anglers and resort vacationers alike. Pelican Bay operates the best bonefishing program on the island, while providing guests with deluxe hotel accommodations, two swimming pools and a pool bar, and fine dining at the Ferry House restaurant. Pelican Bay guests have reciprocal privileges at Our Lucaya.

Port Lucaya area resorts and hotels receive our highest recommendation for vacationers who want to combine a resort experience with high-quality flats fishing. It is the only place in the islands where these two experiences can be combined without favoring one over the other.

Next door to Pelican Bay, the UNEXSO dive center is one of the best in the Caribbean. They also offer a comprehensive dolphin experience program.

Forget the gambling, shopping, and lots of people, but keep all the other options, and you have the Marsh Harbour, Treasure Cay corridor on Abaco. You can rent a house or condo on a secluded beach, stay in a first-class resort, cruise the offshore cays by boat, or fish the incoming tide on your own on a nearby flat. Golfers will find the Dick Wilson course at Treasure Cay a delight, and the new course at the Abaco Club on Winding Bay, south of Marsh Harbour, is scheduled for completion in December 2004.

Eco-tourism is thriving in the Bahamas. Sea kayaking excursions through the Exuma Cays Land and Sea Park are a top draw. There are countless diving and snorkeling options where enthusiasts can swim over vivid living reefs, explore underwater caverns and blue holes, or descend massive rock and coral walls. Two of the best dive programs are on Andros Island at Small Hope Bay Lodge, and on San Salvador at the Riding Rock Inn and Marina. Nature lovers can visit the national parks and bird sanctuaries, examine more than 40 species of wild orchids, or hike into cool pine forests.

Looking for a romantic getaway? The problem you'll have is deciding which intimate remote beachfront resort to choose. Some of our favorites include the Pink Sands Hotel on Harbour Island, Fernandez Bay Village on Cat Island, Tiamo Resort in the South Bight of Andros, Cape Santa Maria Resort on Long Island, and the Bluff House on Green Turtle Cay, Abaco.

If photography is your pleasure, you'll have a hard time conserving film, though with the advances in digital photography, film might be becoming obsolete. Kim has switched over to mostly digital photography, using a one-gigabyte memory card to store hundreds of high-resolution images. She recommends cameras that can use a polarizing filter to bring out the blues and greens and to create vivid images of released gamefish as they swim away underwater after a gentle release.

When it comes to keeping busy, only your imagination will limit your activities in the Bahamas.

Travel Tips

The English language, friendly people, stable currency, and the acceptance of U.S. dollars combine to make travel to the Bahamas convenient and carefree. The Bahamian dollar is one-to-one with the U.S. dollar.

Bahamasair, American Eagle, US Airways, Delta/Comair, Continental/Gulfstream, ATA, and numerous smaller air carriers and charter companies offer flights daily from the United States. Air Canada, British Airways, Air Jamaica, and others offer additional international service. The most convenient travel to the Bahamas is through the U.S. cities of New York, Atlanta, Charlotte, Orlando, West Palm Beach, Ft. Lauderdale, and Miami.

Nassau is the air hub for Bahamasair and Western Air, with most international flights from the States landing here, and then funneling travelers on to the Out Islands. Direct commercial flights, usually on commuter carriers, are also available from the

Bahamasair: your passport to fly-fishing paradise.

States to Freeport, North Eleuthera, Marsh Harbour, Treasure Cay, Exuma, and Bimini. Charter flights are available from West Palm, Ft. Lauderdale, and Miami to most of the Out Islands. Clearing customs in Nassau or Freeport is relatively convenient at all hours, seven days a week. If you need to clear customs on one of the Out Islands outside of regular business hours, or on weekends, you need to arrange for customs officials to be present, and you will have to pay for this service.

Be aware that all services such as banks, customs ports, rental agencies, and fuel stations do not necessarily operate on American schedules, especially on the Out Islands. Normal banking hours in Nassau and Freeport are 9:30 A.M. to 3:00 P.M., with some banks open until 5 P.M. on Fridays. There are a few ATMs in Nassau and Freeport, but don't count on these conveniences on any of the Out Islands. If you need to get some cash, rent a car, or buy a stamp, make sure you know the hours of operation for the services you need.

The same is true for hospitals and clinics. The quality of the government-run clinics is good, but you have to consider your location. If you're visiting a remote fishing or diving lodge, how long will it take to reach a medical facility? It is your responsibility to know these things, especially if you have a pre-existing condition.

Use common sense in how you pack and in the type of luggage you use. Soft luggage is preferable to hard luggage, especially if you will be traveling in a small aircraft or by boat. Make sure your luggage is clearly marked for easy identification. Some anglers we know use bright orange or yellow tape for this purpose. Pack so you can carry your own belongings. Be aware of where your luggage is at all times, and double-check the transfer of your luggage whenever possible.

With the current TSA regulations and restrictions on carry-on luggage it is no longer possible to carry on all of your fishing gear. These regulations continue to evolve and change. Flies, tools, and any type of sharp objects cannot be carried on. Multi-piece fly rods, as of summer 2004, could still be carried on; however, reels were sometimes allowed as carry-on and sometimes not. A TSA official told us that the fly lines on reels could potentially be used to strangle someone. When checking rod cases and other luggage, remember that TSA requires access to your bags. You should not lock these items. If you do lock your luggage, it may not reach your destination with you.

We still recommend that you carry on all allowed essentials, which can include basic clothing, polarized sunglasses, insect repellent, sunscreen, prescription medicines, toiletries, and other personal items.

Anglers and vacation travelers should always use a travel checklist in preparing for any trip. Specific lists are available for specific destinations from professional booking agents, or you can use our list for all Bahamian travel located in chapter 2.

Clothing

Casual summer clothing can be worn during the day any time of the year. We recommend comfortable and functional outdoor clothing from companies like Patagonia, Ex Officio, Tommy Bahama, Columbia, and others. These companies produce fashionable sportswear and fishing clothing that is attractive, lightweight, cool, easy to pack, and relatively maintenance-free. This type of clothing is easy to wash at night and it will be dry by morning. A light jacket or sweater is recommended for cooler evenings and during cold fronts, especially from December to February. Raingear is essential, especially on the Out Islands. We highly recommend taking a rain jacket and rain pants. There are a number of upscale restaurants in Nassau and Freeport that require appropriate evening attire, which in some cases means a jacket for men.

While the Bahamas is a laid-back country, it is also relatively conservative, with a firm religious foundation. So how does this relate to clothing? It is inappropriate to walk through the streets of Nassau or Freeport in swim trunks or bikinis. The same is true for restaurants, shops, and casinos. This guideline especially applies to the Out Islands.

Customs Regulations and Taxes

It's best for a U.S. citizen to have a passport for entry into the Bahamas, though an original birth certificate and valid photo ID are acceptable. British subjects and Canadian citizens may enter the Bahamas without passports for up to three weeks. Stays of longer than that require a passport.

Upon entering the Bahamas, you must fill out and sign an immigration form. This form is usually supplied on board the commercial aircraft flying you into the Bahamas. If not, you can get the forms at the customs location upon arrival. You need to keep part of the form with your passport, and hand it back in when checking in for departure. An oral baggage declaration is required. This is usually a routine procedure, though customs officials can ask to inspect your luggage.

Each adult visitor is allowed 50 cigars (no Cubans if you are a U.S. citizen), 200 cigarettes or one pound of tobacco, one quart of spirits, and a variety of personal effects, including radio/Walkman, bicycle, cameras, fishing gear, and so on. Upon departure, all visitors are required to pay a $15 departure tax (plus $3 security fee leaving Freeport), though children six years and under are exempt. This tax is normally paid at your commercial airline ticket counter when you check in, though this fee is

The Bahamian flag flutters in the breeze alongside the Stars and Stripes. (Brian Hodges)

included in some ticket fares. If you are flying back to the United States on a charter aircraft, this fee may or may not be included in your rate. Charter flight passengers are also subject to U.S. entry and/or departure fees. It is your responsibility to check on these fees and know what you owe.

Departures to the U.S. from Nassau and Freeport must go through U.S. Customs pre-clearance. U.S. visitors may take home $600 worth of duty-free merchandise. The next $1,000 is taxed at 10 percent. Gifts valued up to $50 may be mailed home duty-free. One liter of wine, liqueur, or liquor may be taken duty-free.

Driving

British rules apply! This means you drive on the left. Be especially careful at those roundabouts, and keep left. You can use your regular driver's license for up to three months, and then you must apply for an international driver's license. Pedestrians need to remember to look right before crossing streets. To be on the safe side, look everywhere.

Electricity

The standard is 120 volts AC. We use all of our American appliances throughout the islands without problems.

Fishing and Diving

The Bahamas is an environmentally friendly country. To protect the marine environment, spearfishing using scuba gear is illegal, and possession of spear guns in the

Islands of the Bahamas is illegal. Cruising boats must clear customs at the nearest port of entry before beginning any diving or fishing activities. A permit is required for visiting vessels to engage in sport fishing. The cost of a permit is $20 per trip or $150 per year for vessels on which not more than six reels will be used. Areas within national parks, such as the Exuma Cays Land and Sea Park, have strict rules against the taking of any natural resources. The Bahamas National Trust administers these parks. It is your responsibility to know where you are and what the laws are. For updated regulations, you can visit the Ministry of Tourism's official Web site at www.bahamas.com.

Shopping

Nassau and Freeport are the shopping meccas, though a number of colorful shops are sprinkled throughout the Out Islands. Bay Street is Nassau's shopping haven, with designer stores from all over the world presenting their wares in enticing fashion. Bay Street becomes a wild scene when one of the giant cruise ships unloads a thousand passengers at one time.

In Freeport, the International Bazaar and Port Lucaya Marketplace are the main attractions. Both combine name-brand stores with local merchants and straw markets.

The better resorts and hotels have specialty boutiques and shops for gifts and tourist necessities. The real draws in the Bahamas are duty-free shopping and bargain prices on many luxury items such as fine perfumes and watches. Be aware that many stores are closed on Sunday.

Spring Break Season

Spring break season normally runs from mid-February to mid-April. Plan ahead for any trip to the Bahamas during this period since airline reservations can be extremely

A straw market next to Nassau Harbour.

tight. Spring breakers normally stay in the bigger resorts on Nassau and in Freeport, so you may want to avoid these areas if you're looking for peace and quiet. The Out Islands usually remain tranquil, though some locations on Abaco and Exuma are now being "discovered."

Taxes and Tipping

This can be confusing, but here are the basics. A 10-percent government tax is added to all accommodations, and/or all room/meal packages. There is no tax charged on guided fishing rates. Many resorts will charge an additional energy tax and a maid service fee. Most resorts and restaurants will add on a 15-percent service/gratuity charge. Take the time to ask what charges will be added on so that you won't be unpleasantly surprised.

Tipping customs are the same as in the United States. Tip according to the quality of service you receive. Bellboys and porters usually receive $1 per bag, while other servers such as waiters and bartenders receive 15 percent. Check your restaurant bill carefully to note whether a service charge has already been added. A professional flats fly-fishing guide normally receives $40 to $50 per day ($20 to $25 per angler based on two anglers per guide), and more if the guide is exceptional. Offshore boats with a captain and mate generally receive $60 to $80 per day given to the captain, and more if the experience was exceptional.

Time Zone

Eastern standard time (EST) is used throughout the Islands of the Bahamas. From the first Sunday in April to the last Sunday in October, eastern daylight time (EDT) is followed, in accordance with U.S. daylight savings time.

Airline Contact Information

Commercial Airlines

American Eagle: 800-433-7300; Internet: www.aa.com
Delta Airlines: 800-221-1212; Internet: www.delta.com
US Airways: 800-622-1015; Internet: www.usairways.com
ATA: 800-435-9282; Internet: www.ata.com
Bahamasair: 800-222-4262 or 242-339-4415; Internet: www.bahamasair.com
Western Air: 242-377-2222; Internet: www.westernairbahamas.com
Air Sunshine: 800-327-8900 or 954-434-8900; Internet: www.airsunshine.com
Continental/Gulfstream: 800-231-0856; Internet: www.continental.com
Southern Air: 242-377-2014
Island Air Charters: 800-444-9904 or 954-359-9942; Internet:
   www.islandaircharters.com
Lynx Air: 888-596-9247 or 242-352-5778; Internet: www.lynxair.com
Major's Air Services: 242-352-5778; Internet: www.thebahamasguide.com/majorair/

Cat Island Air: 242-377-3318; Internet: www.aircharterbahamas.com

Chalks-Ocean Airway: 800-424-2557 or 242-347-3024; Internet: www.flychalks.com

Resort Charters

Deep Water Cay Club, Grand Bahama: 912-756-7071; Internet: www.deepwatercay.com

Fernandez Bay Village, Cat Island: 800-940-1905 or 954-474-4821;
   Internet: www.fernandezbayvillage.com

Tropical Diversions Air, Berry Islands: 800-343-7256 or 954-629-9977;
   Internet: www.tropicaldiversions.com

Greenwood Beach Resort, Cat Island: 242-342-3053;
   Internet: www.greenwoodbeachresort.com

Hawk's Nest Club, Cat Island: 800-688-4752 or 242-357-7257;
   Internet: www.hawks-nest.com

Tom Jones Charters, Cat Island: 242-335-1353 or 954-359-8099

Riding Rock Inn, San Salvador: 800-272-1492 or 954-359-8353;
   Internet: www.ridingrock.com

Small Hope Bay Lodge, Andros: 800-223-6961 or 242-368-2014;
   Internet: www.smallhope.com

Stella Maris Resort, Long Island/Exuma: 800-426-0466 or 242-338-2051;
   Internet: www.stellamarisresortairservice.com

Island Wings, Long Island/Crooked and Acklins: 242-338-2022 or 242-357-1021

Out Island Mail Boats

Inter-island mail boats run weekly to and from most Out Islands. The mail boats provide a leisurely way to cruise through the islands. One-way passage to just about anywhere costs between $30 and $50. Remember that these mail boats run on Bahamas time, which will not always coincide with your watch, or with the published timetables.

The following are the mail boat routes to/from Nassau:

Mail Boat Name	Scheduled Stops
Bahamas Day Break II	Eleuthera: Rock Sound, Governor's Harbour, Harbour Island, The Bluff
Bimini Mack	Cat Cay and Bimini
Capt. C	Ragged Island, Exuma Cays
Capt. Moxey	South Andros: Kemp's Bay, The Bluff, Long Bay Cays, Driggs Hill
Capt. Gurth Dean	Abaco: Sandy Point, Moore's Island, Bullock's Harbour, Berry Islands
Current Pride	Eleuthera: Hatchet Bay and The Bluff

Eleuthera Express	Eleuthera: Governor's Harbour, Rock Sound, Spanish Wells, Harbour Island
Fiesta Mail boat	Grand Bahama: Freeport
Grand Master	Exuma: George Town
Lady D	Central Andros: Fresh Creek, Stafford Creek, Blanket Sound, Behring Point
Lady Francis	San Salvador, Rum Cay
Lady Rosalind	North Cat Island: Arthur's Town, Bennet's Harbour, Orange Creek
Legacy	Abaco: Marsh Harbour, Green Turtle Cay
Lisa J III	North Andros: Nicholl's Town, Mastic Point, Morgan's Bluff
Mangrove Cay Express	Central Andros: Cargill Creek, Mangrove Cay, Lisbon Creek, Driggs Hill
Mia Dean	Long Island: Clarence Town
Sea Hauler	South Cat Island: Smith Bay, New Bight, Old Bight.
Sherice "M"	North Long Island: Salt Pond, Deadman's Cay, Seymour's
Trans Cargo	Mayaguana/Abraham's Bay; Inagua/Matthew Town
United Star	Acklins/Spring Point; Crooked Island/Colonel Hill, Long Cay

Check with the dockmaster's office in Nassau for specific schedules, and then be sure to reconfirm times the day of departure. Call 242-393-1064.

Bahamas Fast Ferries

While travel by mail boat can be an adventure, travel via fast ferry is quick, comfortable, and convenient. A lot of fun too, plus a great way to travel with your car, or to carry important supplies.

The Bahama Ferry Services boats are modern, air-conditioned, catamaran-hulled ships of approximately 35 meters in length. They cruise at a speed of 35 knots (about 40 miles an hour), and carry between 150 and 200 passengers with spacious comfortable seating.

The following are the Bahama Ferries routes to/from Nassau:

M/V *Bo Hengy*	Spanish Wells, Harbour Island, Governor's Harbour
M/V *Seawind*	Andros: Morgan's Bluff, Fresh Creek
	Exuma: George Town
	Abaco: Sandy Point
	Eleuthera: Current, Governor's Harbour

Contact Bahamas Ferries: Bahamas Ferry Services Ltd., P. O. Box N-3709 Nassau, N.P., Bahamas. Telephone: 242-323-2166. Internet: www.bahamasferries.com

Questions that People Frequently Ask Us

1. **How far in advance should I book my trip?** Book as far in advance as possible. Booking a year in advance is sometimes necessary to secure the most popular guides and lodges during prime time. Booking six months in advance in any case is recommended. April and May are the most popular bonefishing months. If you plan to use frequent flier miles, booking six months in advance is a minimum.

2. **What is the procedure for trip deposits and payments?** When booking directly with lodges and guides, you will be required to make a non-refundable deposit. (Large resorts on Nassau and Freeport can be exceptions.) Some lodges accept payment by credit card, usually through their U.S. offices. Many lodges, and all guides will require payment by check or via wire transfer. A 50-percent deposit is typical. Final payment is normally due at least 45 days in advance of your trip arrival date. Remember that payments to most resorts and fishing lodges are non-refundable. Sometimes a lodge will allow you to come another time if you can't make a trip, but you should not expect this. Cash refunds are not given. If these policies are not acceptable to you, you should use a U.S. booking agent who may have different policies. In any case, we highly recommend the purchase of trip cancellation insurance.

3. **How is the drinking water?** You can drink the water from the tap at the major resorts in Nassau and Freeport. Otherwise, each island is different and you should use caution. Andros Island has more fresh water than any Bahamian island, yet we always drink bottled water on Andros. We recommend drinking bottled water at all times, if for nothing else but the taste. As a doctor friend of our says, "Any time you change your water, your system can get upset. Why take a chance on ruining your vacation?" Bottled drinking water is available on all the Out Islands.

4. **Are groceries and liquor available on the Out Islands?** This depends on the island, but all the islands rely on supply boats or aircraft. The smaller the settlement or the more remote a location, the less often it is resupplied. This includes some of the established fishing lodges. It is not uncommon for fresh fruit,

produce, milk, or red meat to run low, or run out. At times, bottled water can run out. Red meat, milk, and eggs are also expensive items in general.

Our motto is simple, "when in doubt, stock up." If we're staying in a rented house, cottage, or whatever, we stock up right away, or as soon as we can, based on available supplies. We also establish a rapport with the local grocery people to find out the resupply days. It pays to be at the store when the boat arrives.

You need to find out ahead of time if liquor is available at local stores, so you can take your own if necessary. If you like particular brands of wine or liquor, we recommend that you take them with you. Kalik, the beer of the Bahamas, is available almost everywhere.

5. **How do payments work on the Out Islands?** Are credit cards and traveler's checks okay? Cash is always accepted and preferred. U.S. dollars are one-to-one with the Bahamian dollar, and both are accepted everywhere. Traveler's checks, credit cards, and personal checks, when accepted, will often be charged a service fee of 2 percent to 5 percent per use. Many Out Island establishments do not accept credit cards, traveler's checks, or personal checks, period. Also, change may not be available for large bills, so be sure to have plenty of small bills. It is your responsibility to know what forms of payment are accepted at each location you visit. Using a professional travel agent is one way to make sure that none of these little details slip by. If you are booking on your own, make sure you know all payment and cancellation policies.

6. **Is medical care available?** Yes, but depending on where you are, it might take hours to reach a clinic or a doctor. National healthcare clinics in the Bahamas are good. In addition to larger facilities in Freeport and Nassau, the Ministry of Health operates more than 100 clinics throughout the Out Islands. As in the U.S., the larger clinics offer more services than the smaller, remote clinics. When additional care is needed, patients are flown to Princess Margaret Hospital in Nassau. For very serious accidents and illnesses, Air Ambulance services can be called to evacuate people to West Palm Beach, Ft. Lauderdale, or Miami. You will be billed for this service, and rates are extremely steep.

Prescription drugs are available in the larger towns and settlements, but supplies can be limited. You should take all necessary prescription medicines with you in your carry-on luggage.

You should always travel with your health insurance card or information. We recommend the purchase of trip cancellation insurance, which can also include trip health insurance. It is your responsibility to know what care is or is not available at any destination you visit.

7. **What about boat, car, golf cart, and other rentals?** All types of rentals are available in Nassau and Freeport. Limited rentals are available on the Out Islands. We recommend booking your rentals ahead of time, along with the rest of your trip.

Booking rentals ahead of time is essential during the prime months, especially in places like Treasure Cay or Elbow Cay, where boats, cars, and golf carts are limited in numbers. Car rentals are generally expensive, between $60 and $80 per day.

8. **Should I bring my own fishing gear?** You should always take your own fly-fishing gear. Very few lodges or guides have equipment for clients to use, though the better guides will have back-up gear if something happens to yours. Some lodges do have rental fly-fishing equipment. You should check this in advance of your trip. Conventional fishing gear is more readily available, though we recommend taking your own if you have it. Most offshore fishing boats provide conventional fishing gear and lures. There is always an additional charge for bait.

9. **Should I take my own snorkeling and diving gear?** The better dive operations will have complete diving and snorkeling gear. You should confirm this before your trip and reserve this gear in advance. We always take our own masks, snorkels, and fins. This way we are sure the gear fits comfortably, and we have the flexibility to use it whenever we choose.

10. **How is the nightlife, including restaurants?** Nightlife rocks in Nassau and Freeport. Everywhere else it is fairly sedate, though special parties and events are held throughout the Out Islands, most commonly on Friday and Saturday nights. As for restaurants, top Nassau restaurants are on par with the finest restaurants in U.S. cities. We suggest making reservations, or at least confirming hours of operation, in all cases. The better Out Island restaurants fill up during prime months, and others may or may not open unless they have confirmed reservations.

11. **Will my cellular phone operate in the Bahamas?** If you must take your cell phone, service will be available in many locations depending on your home carrier. The Bahamas Telecommunications Corporation (BaTelCo) has automatic roaming agreements with many cellular carriers in the United States, Canada, and Mexico. Check with your carrier to see if they have a roaming agreement with BaTelCo. If so, be sure your cellular number is active in the Bahamas, switch your phone to system B, and make your calls.

    Be aware, however, that in remote areas, service may not be available. You can contact BaTelCo at 242-394-4000 or 242-394-7638, or on the Internet at www.batelnet.bs.

12. **Is Internet service available?** Can I check my e-mail? Most resort hotels in Nassau and Freeport have business centers with high-speed Internet service. Internet service is available on most of the Out Islands also, but it can be sporadic. A number of small resorts and bonefishing lodges offer Internet service to their guests. You should check ahead of time with your chosen destination, and then plan ahead. If you need to check your e-mail at an Out Island lodge, talk to the manager to find out the best times to make a connection.

13. **What about bugs?** Yep, lots of bugs live in the Bahamas. The islands with freshwater lakes, such as Andros, have the most "doctor" flies. These big, green-headed flies draw blood when they bite. They generally live around mangroves, so

you'll be most susceptible when you're out fishing. Wearing long pants will pro-tect you, especially when wading because these bugs mostly like to bite legs and feet. Around lodges and on the beaches, mosquitoes and sand flies will be out when the wind is down, and in the evening and early morning. Avon Skin-So-Soft works against the sand flies, while regular DEET-enhanced repellent works against the mosquitoes. If the bugs really like you, wear a long-sleeved shirt, pants, and shoes with socks when you go out to dinner.

14. **How do I get tide information for the Out Islands?** There are specific NOAA tide stations for some locations in the Bahamas, including Nassau, which has the same tides as the east coast of Andros. For locations without tide stations, you will have to make your own calculations, or obtain tide charts from your destination. You can also purchase your own tide software that will calculate tides for you. Call Bluewater Books & Charts at 800-942-2583. Tide sites we use include: http://tbone.biol.sc.edu/tide/sitesel.html, http://tidesonline.nos.noaa.gov/, and www.noaa.gov/ocean.html.

Internet Sites for the Bahamas

www.bahamasflyfishingguide.com. The accompanying site for this book. This site is updated on a continual basis—news, new lodges, lodge reports, fishing reports, and more. We encourage you to e-mail us through this site with fishing reports and updates of your own.

www.bahamas.com. The official site for the Bahamas Ministry of Tourism. This is a reliable means for obtaining additional updated information.

www.bahama-out-islands.com. The official site for the Bahama Out Islands Promo-tion Board.

www.bahamasvg.com. The Bahamas Vacation Guide is a good source of different information on resorts and services not necessarily found on other sites.

http://bahamas.wheretostay.com. An online booking source for condos, villas, and resorts.

www.bahamashomesite.com. Detailed information for fishing, diving, boating, and water sports activities.

www.tcimall.tc, www.provo.net, www.wherewhenhow.com. Specific details and contact information for services and accommodations throughout the Turks and Caicos Islands.

■

Disclaimer: We are not promoting or endorsing any air or water carriers, just listing some of the ones friends and we have used. Select your carriers and methods of trans-portation at your own risk. We recommend that all travelers use a qualified professional travel agent. We also recommend the purchase of trip cancellation insurance, especially if you end up booking your own trip.

All boating references are for descriptive purposes only and are not intended for navigational purposes. Boating navigation throughout the Bahamas and the TCIs requires specific knowledge and experience, and the use of accepted navigational maps and charts. It is your responsibility to make all the preparations necessary for a safe boating trip.

CHAPTER 2

TIPS, TACTICS, AND TACKLE

Stephen with Andros guide Andy Smith, hooking a bonefish.

We have spent considerable time the past 15 years pursuing our saltwater fly-fishing passion. Much of this time has been spent in the Bahamas and in the Turks and Caicos; exploring, hosting groups of clients, working with lodges to improve services, and training guides on many of the islands.

Countless hours have been spent talking with anglers over après-fishing Kaliks or at dinner tables throughout the islands. As fly-fishers, we all want to learn, to improve our skills, to gain an edge for that next day on the water. The following topics are the ones that have been brought up to us most through the years. We hope some of these ideas will be useful the next time you venture onto the flats.

Flats Fly-Fishing from a Poled Skiff

Fishing from a poled skiff is a team sport, and your team needs good communication. When it's your turn on the bow, make sure you and your guide are in sync. Guides will focus your attention on incoming fish by using clock positions and distances to the target. Good guides will add in clock directions for which way the fish is moving. Point your rod at a clock position, and then ask your guide to direct you from there. The guide will say something like, "Go right, stop, a little more right, stop, 40 feet, moving from 11 to 12, cast now." Follow your guide's directions and you will catch fish even when you don't see them. If you have any questions about clock positions ask your guide right away.

A good guide has a plan for the fishing day. This involves running time to the flats in various directions. If you have any special requests, make these known to your guide first thing in the morning, then rely on his judgment of what is possible according to the present conditions and your fishing skills.

Only strip off the amount of line you can cast accurately. Make a few casts so your guide can assess your ability, then have your guide call out the distances of each practice cast. This will help you get in tune with each other, and with true distances. Line handling is just as important as casting. Make some practice strips, varying between short, medium, and long strips, while working with your guide to understand what he means when he uses stripping instructions.

Make sure your fly line is stretched out and in a position on the deck to avoid any obstructions when you shoot line or clear line. Pull at least a full rod's length of fly line out of the tiptop guide. Hold your tippet, just above the fly, in your non-casting hand. Now, assuming a 9-foot rod and 9-foot leader, you could make a simple roll cast and the distance would be about 27 feet. Use this formula to help judge distances accurately.

You shouldn't need to false cast for anything closer than 30 feet. In general, make as few false casts as possible. Flats fish are usually on the move. They are often swimming toward you. You need to present your fly quickly and accurately, before the fish spooks off or changes directions. Your goal should be no more than one false cast for casts to 50 feet. For casts out to 80 feet, your goal should be no more than two false casts.

Once you make your presentation cast, follow your fly line to the water with your rod tip. This will prevent slack from forming in your line, and will allow you to move your fly with your first strip. This is very important. The first strip needs to move the fly because bonefish often eat a fly before the first strip. If it takes two or three strips to remove the slack, you won't be able to set the hook before the fish spits your fly.

Hook-Setting and Presentation Techniques

Set the hook with your line hand first. Do this by making one long strip, as long as your reach allows, or until you feel a solid hook-up. Don't trout set, which is setting by quickly raising your rod tip. Not only will you rarely hook a fish this way, but you will also pull your fly completely out of the fish's feeding zone. If you miss the hook set with a line hand strip, the fly will still be in front of the fish. Chances are good the fish will eat the fly again.

If the fish doesn't eat your fly immediately after your presentation, let it sink to the fish's level, then begin a retrieve. The retrieve is used to attract the fish's attention. Learn to vary your retrieve based on the fish's behavior. More important, learn to let the fish eat the fly. Many people think they need to keep stripping once a fish charges their fly. This is a definite no! When the fish swims for the fly, stop stripping. Let the fish eat it. If the fish stops, make a long strip to set because a fish will rarely stop unless it has eaten the fly.

When casting to moving fish, learn to lead the fish according to water depth and wind conditions. A longer lead is usually required in skinny water, or in low wind conditions. An exception to this can be when you are fishing to tailing fish. At times, a tailing fish is so focused on the area immediately around it, that you have to risk a close cast directly into this feeding zone.

You can present your fly closer to a fish in deeper water or in windy conditions. In deeper water, however, you have to lead the fish enough so that your fly will sink to the proper depth by the time the fish arrives at that spot.

Watch your target carefully. Judge the swimming speed and wind direction. Don't wait too long to cast, especially when fish are swimming toward you. The farther you can cast the better chance you have of getting a second or third shot before a fish gets too close.

Wading the Flats

If wade fishing is your preference be sure to include this criteria in your trip planning. Some locations offer much better and more varied wade fishing options than others. Some of the best wade fishing destinations include South Andros, Exuma, Long Island, Crooked, and Acklins Islands.

The same basics discussed above apply to wade fishing, but there are some differences. You don't necessarily want to strip off as much line as you can cast accurately, especially if you can cast over 60 feet. We recommend stripping off 50 to 60 feet of

Fishing for bonefish on a tranquil Long Island flat. (Brian O'Keefe)

line, then trailing it behind you in one long loop. This will allow you to break the water surface tension on the line and make a good cast quickly. You should still have at least a rod's length of line out of the tiptop guide, and be holding your tippet just above the fly in your non-casting hand.

In general, wading anglers can get closer to fish without spooking them than boat anglers. To balance this out, however, wading anglers are often fishing to tailing fish. Bonefish in skinny water will usually be spookier than fish in deeper water.

It is important to notice a fish's behavior. Is it cruising, stopping occasionally to feed, or is it feeding aggressively? This will tip you on how you should present your fly. We like to cast very close to aggressive fish, especially when they are kicking up mud. Fish feeding sporadically need a longer lead. Cruising fish need the longest lead, especially if they're bunched into large schools.

When we see a school of 10 or more fish in skinny water, tails and fins breaking the surface, we often drop a fly 20 feet in front of them, then just let the fly sit on the bottom. A small Yarn Crab is our favorite pattern for this tactic. As the fish reach the fly, we give the fly just the slightest twitch. This method is extremely effective and often necessary on flats where fish are heavily pressured. The mistake most anglers make is to strip too soon or too long. A longer strip makes too much commotion. You just need a tiny twitch, and patience, patience, patience.

Another tactic we employ when wading is casting directly into the wind. By doing this you will be able to straighten out your backcast, then drive it forward with ease. You can crouch low and use a sidearm cast to avoid most of the wind too. But most of all, the wind will be carrying any sounds or disturbances you make away from the fish.

The last tip is on how to walk when you wade. Shuffling or sliding your feet is a good option when fishing on flats with a lot of stingrays, though there are not many of these in the Bahamas. If you shuffle, be careful to do it slowly and smoothly. Push your feet through the water. Don't slog. You don't want to put up a wake that will alert nearby fish. Our favorite method for sneaking up on fish, taught to us by some long-legged Bahamian guides years ago, is to walk like a heron. Pick your leg up slowly, completely out of the water, then point your toes and ease your foot back down to the bottom. Total silence is the goal here. No splashing. Stealth is critical when stalking tailing bones.

Make Use of Your Fishing Partner

When your partner is on the deck fishing, you should be the line tender. Stretch the line and coil it so it clears from weighted line to running line. Make sure there are no obstacles near the line. Shoes, bags, clothes, and anything else that could catch the line should be out of the way.

Once your partner makes a cast and starts stripping in line, gather the slack in an orderly manner. Coil it on the deck again or in the bottom of the skiff. This is especially important in windy conditions. If a fisherman is stripping line, and the wind is blowing the line in the water or under the boat, recasting will be difficult or maybe impossible. Be alert for the fisherman's recast. Be ready to let go of the line. Watch your feet. Don't step on the line.

You can help with clearing the line when your partner hooks up. Not only will this sort of teamwork produce better results, but it also keeps both people involved and is a lot more fun.

Hunting for Specific Fish—Big Bones, Permit, Tarpon

The hunt for big bonefish often means sacrificing numbers of fish and fishing in deeper water where it is more difficult to see. While it is certainly possible to catch big bones on a variety of flats, your chances will increase dramatically if you make a special effort.

You need to be mentally prepared for this type of fishing. You have to be willing to catch nothing. You have to put in your days. You should fish the islands with the highest numbers of big fish. If we could only fish one island for big bonefish, Andros would be the easy choice. Abaco, Grand Bahama, and Bimini are also top choices. If we had to pick one fly it would be a #2 Clouser Minnow-style fly, a fly that gets deep quick and attracts attention. Tan, gold and Gotcha colors are our favorites.

Part of being mentally prepared is acknowledging that fishing for big bones is like fishing for permit. Big bones look at flies, and treat flies, with the same disdain as permit. Opportunities are what you're looking for. Cashing in on those opportunities is what we all hope to do.

If you're on a permit quest there are only a few places in the Bahamas worth your time, though permit are available throughout the islands. You never know when one might pop up, so being prepared with a permit rod is vital. The best flats for permit run along the West Side of Andros, from Miller Creek to Red Bay. The remote flats around Williams Island hold the highest concentration of permit in this region. Other good locations around Andros include the Joulter's Cays and the ocean-side flats in front of Big Wood Cay and Mangrove Cay.

We have seen decent numbers of permit around Grand Bahama, on the flats between Crooked and Acklins Islands, and around remote cays between Long Island and Exuma. We've caught a few, and been snubbed by many more. Permit fishing is all about getting your shots and shots are relatively few in the Bahamas. If permit are important to you, you should go elsewhere—to Mexico or Belize.

The west coast of Andros holds the largest tarpon population in the islands. There are good numbers of tarpon year-round, tarpon in the 50- to 100-pound class. Larger migratory tarpon run from May through October.

The most experienced tarpon guides work out of Cargill Creek and Behring Point, though there are good ones in Stafford Creek and on Mangrove Cay. Fishing for tarpon involves relatively long runs to the West Side to fish classic clear white sand flats where you can see the magnificent silver kings coming more than a hundred yards away. A shallow water cockroach is usually the only fly you need for these aggressive fish.

Spotting Fish

Spotting fish involves intense concentration and practice. Most anglers find that after a few days they start seeing fish better. Adopt a consistent scanning pattern. Start in close, 20 to 50 feet, and then scan outward looking for obvious signs of movement, mud puffs, or nervous water. Nervous water is a ripple-type pattern on the surface that is different from the natural surface conditions. After scanning outward, return to the closer zone and do it again. Your scanning range should be between 10 and 2 on the clock, with occasional glances out to 9 and 3.

If you can reduce the zone you have to scan, your chances of seeing fish will increase. You do this by understanding the path bonefish will take across flats or along shorelines. At times sun angles and surface glare will limit your areas of vision. A good guide will set you up so you can see the best areas clearly.

Fishing guide netting bait.

Learn the clock directions until you can react instinctively to your guide's instructions. If you have to think about two o'clock before you look or before you cast, you've given the fish an advantage. Learn to judge distances by using your rod. Most rods are 9 feet long. Let's round that off to about 10. Three rod lengths are close to 30 feet. If you know the clock, and know your distances, you'll be able to focus quickly on the area your guide has called out. The sooner you see the correct area, the better chance you have of seeing the fish.

It is common for anglers to catch fish they never see by following their guide's instructions, but when you see the fish yourself, your hook-up percentage will improve dramatically.

Sight Hooking

This is closely related to spotting fish, and is just as important as sight casting. There is no simple way to teach this. This is a skill you develop after spending some time on the water. There are, however, signs you can look for to get started.

We talked before about "letting" the fish eat your fly. This is critical. You spot the fish, make your cast, start stripping, and then watch the fish charge your fly. Stop stripping. Let the fish eat the fly. How do you know when he's got it? When the fish stops, he probably has the fly. Set the hook with a long strip. This is like sight nymphing in a river. You can't see the nymph, but you see the fish move to where the fly should be. You set the hook. You need to have faith. When the fish stops, long strip.

Maybe you can't see the whole fish, but you can see the head and gills. When you see the gills flare, this means the fish has sucked in your fly. Long strip. If the fish tilts downward, long strip. If you see the mouth open, long

Kim with Andros tarpon.

strip. One day you'll see it all perfectly: everything. You'll make a long strip, feel the weight of the fish, and it will be an exhilarating experience.

Or maybe you've seen it many times already. Whatever the case, sight hooking is the ultimate bonefishing experience. When you see the fish eat your fly, chances are he's yours.

Handling Saltwater Gamefish

Saltwater fish are tougher and hardier than freshwater fish, but you still need to handle them with care, and as little as possible. Bonefish, permit, and tarpon all have a protective slime or film that acts as a cloaking device. This slime protects fish from infections and diseases and contains their scent. When the slime is removed by excessive handling, this scent is radiated across the flat. Every shark in the vicinity can then zero in on this fish. Insect repellent and suntan lotion can also burn these fish like acid. Make sure to wash these lotions off your hands before handling fish.

Tarpon are big beautiful monsters, yet they have delicate internal organs that can be harmed if you jerk them out of the water. Treat all gamefish as gently as you can so they can live to fight another day.

Guided Trips vs. Do-It-Yourself

We almost always fish with a guide because we want to give ourselves the best chance to catch fish every day. Even though we fish in salt water many days each year, every

Fishing offshore aboard the *Thunderbird*.

day is precious. If you only have six or seven days a year for flats fishing, you need to make the most of them. The only way to do that is to fish with a good guide.

That said, we understand some people prefer to fish on their own. Do-it-yourself trips have increased dramatically in the past few years. Requests to our Web site for information about self-guided trips are more common than any other request. Part of the reason is that anglers are also trying to save money.

OK. Our advice is to plan your trip to the locations that will give you the best chances for success, and we highly recommend that you fish with a guide at least one day at your chosen destination.

Our favorite islands for do-it-yourself angling are Long Island, Cat Island, Eleuthera, and Exuma. Relatively easy access to the flats, good numbers of fish, and comfortable inexpensive accommodations are the top reasons for choosing these islands. Other islands, including Abaco, Grand Bahama, and Andros, have good but limited do-it-yourself options, though logistics and flats access are more complicated, and the level of angling skill required for success is higher.

With the popularity of do-it-yourself trips increasing, so has the fishing pressure. Many locations that were once little known or rarely fished are now fished hard. Fish are spookier and tougher to catch in these spots. If you expect to have a flat all to yourself for that "idyllic solitary experience," chances are other people will be there with the same expectation. A good example is fishing in Fresh Creek on Andros Island. With easy access and good accommodations and restaurants nearby, this has become a haven for do-it-yourself anglers. While fishing here is still good, you might end up fishing in a crowd.

In planning your trip, carefully research the tides, based on the time of day of the tides. If you wade fish, you will only be able to fish one set of tides per day in most locations. If you hit high tides during the morning, or at midday, you'll have a tough trip due to your limited access. The best locations will be those that allow you to fish different stages of tides by moving from one area of an island to another, by boat or car, in a short period of time.

Anglers cruising the Bahamas in their own sailboat or motor yacht will have a better chance for fishing success on their own than will land-based anglers. With the use of a dinghy or sea kayak, access to many of the best flats, cays, cuts, and creeks is possible. Please see the Around the Island sections of each island chapter for the best fishing options for boaters and do-it-yourselfers.

Tackle Recommendations

Saltwater gamefish tend to be tackle busters. It doesn't make sense to spend a good chunk of money on a trip, then skimp on your rod, reel, line, and flies. Buy the absolute best equipment you can afford. That includes a comprehensive selection of flies; it's better to have too many flies than not enough.

The fly-fishing tackle industry has made great strides in recent years in terms of developing new gear, including inexpensively priced top-quality rods and reels. Virtually every manufacturer has introduced a value line of rods and reels covered by their best warranties. Consult with your local tackle shop to pick out the most appropriate equipment for your needs.

Most Bahamian lodges and guides do not have fly-fishing tackle or flies available for client use. Where fly tackle is available, it is often in poor condition. If you plan to use lodge or guide equipment, be sure to confirm the type of equipment that is available, and the condition it is in. Also confirm the type of flies that may be available.

We recommend medium-fast to fast-action fly rods. You need to generate plenty of line speed for accurate casts in windy conditions. While we enjoy fishing with slower rods at times, they require more patience to cast. If you have an aggressive casting style, slower rods will not work well for you.

If you only have one rod for flats fishing, and for bonefish in particular, we recommend a 9-foot 8-weight in a multi-piece travel model. For women, Kim recommends light, crisp, rods with very little swing weight. Swing weight is how heavy a rod feels as you cast it. Does it drag through the air, or does it move through the air effortlessly? Swing weight is much more important than the actual weight of a rod, and it does not follow that the actual weight of a rod correlates to its swing weight.

You will need at least one back-up rod any time you travel to a remote location. If you want to cover the range of flats fishing, think in terms of an 8-weight, 10-weight, 12-weight triumvirate. The 10-weight will be ideal for permit, sharks, barracuda, dorado, tarpon to 120 pounds, plus general inshore, reef, or creek fishing. The 12-weight will cover larger tarpon and many offshore fishing situations.

Fishing reel.

Bonefish reels must have a reliable disc drag and a capacity for at least 200 yards of 20-pound backing. Go with at least 250 yards of 30-pound backing on the 10-weight rig, and at least 300 yards of 30-pound backing on the 12-weight rig. Our favorite reels are large arbor models with smooth cork drags. These types of reels are reliable, durable, and they retrieve line faster than conventional models.

Fly lines can get complicated if you let them, so keep things simple. Scientific Anglers, Rio, and Cortland all make high-quality lines to suit the spectrum of saltwater fishing conditions. For bonefish we like a WF saltwater taper floating line that is stiff enough to turn over big flies in the wind, yet supple enough not to hold too much memory, or to cause frustrating tangles. Ideal set-ups for your 10-weight and 12-weight would be a WF tarpon taper clear-tip intermediate sinking line and a Teeny Saltwater 350. Once you accumulate lots of tackle, consult with your favorite fly-fishing professional for the best line and head systems for any given situation.

Terminal tackle is critical. Leader butt sections must be stiff to snap over into the wind with heavy flies. Tippets need to be abrasion-resistant around mangroves and coral. Fluorocarbon material, while expensive, is worth the money for strength and stealth. For standard mono, our favorite brands are Ande, Mason, and Maxima. While there are a number of good companies that manufacture tapered leaders, we prefer to tie our own with Ande or Mason tippet material. A 9-foot 10-pound leader is standard for most bonefishing situations. When fishing for larger bones around mangroves or coral, go up to 12- or 15-pound tippet. We recommend that all saltwater anglers buy a good knot book and practice tying knots. One of our favorite books is *Practical Fishing Knots* by Mark Sosin and Lefty Kreh.

A key ingredient in selecting flies for the flats is the sink rate. You need to match the fly sink rate to the depth of the water combined with any tidal flows. The best cast in the world won't do you any good if the fly doesn't sink to a level where the fish can see it. In deeper water, lead eyes are helpful in getting flies down fast, and a sparsely tied offering will sink faster than a bushy one.

Our favorite Andros bonefish fly, especially for big fish, is still a #2-4 Clouser's Minnow in a Gold Shiner or Gotcha color. The original Gotcha color includes a hot pink head, pearlescent body, and tan craft fur wing laced with crystal flash. A #4-6 Clouser's Minnow is our favorite choice throughout the rest of the Bahamas, though colors vary depending on the flats we fish.

That said, you must be willing and able to adapt to specific fishing situations. For tailing bonefish our favorite flies are a #6 Tan Yarn Crab, or a #6-8 Mantis Shrimp. We also like small, #6-8, traditional Gotchas, Bunny Gotchas, Hoovers, and Bone Shrimp. Another favorite for big bones in deep water is a #2-4 Spawning Shrimp. For grassy or crunchy coral bottoms that can hang you up, we like a weedless Greg's Flats Fly or a Snapping Shrimp.

As a general bonefish selection, we recommend the following flies: #2-6 Clouser's Minnow (Gotcha, Gold Shiner, Tan); #2-8 Gotchas; #4-6 Bunny Gotchas; #2-6 Spawning Shrimp; #4-6 Charlie's (gold, pearl); #4-6 Beck's Sililegs; #4-6 Horrors; #4 Bonefish Specials; #4-6 Tan Yarn Crabs, #4-6 Tan Mantis Shrimp; #4-6 Greg's Flats Flies; #4-6 Bone Wigglers (like a Puff, in pink, tan); #4-8 Hoovers (pink, gold, chartreuse); #4 Borski Bonefish Critter; #4-6 Dorsey's Kwan. There are also a number of new patterns tied with rabbit fur. These "bunny" flies, combined with rubber legs, are deadly. Their billowing action in the water makes them effective when stripped, or left still on the bottom.

A tarpon fly selection is relatively simple. Our favorite fly is a #4/0 Shallow Water Cockroach. Your box should also include #4/0 Shallow Water patterns in Black Death, Red/White, and Tan/Brown colors. If you can tie or buy these flies on Owner hooks, so much the better. Clouser's Minnows and surface poppers will also take tarpon, especially in the creeks.

Our favorite barracuda and shark fly is a #4/0 Orange Popovic's Banger. This may seem like a surprising choice, but fishing a popper is the most exciting way to catch both of these aggressive gamefish. Additional shark and barracuda flies should include: #2/0 RM Needlefish; #1/0 Cuda Killer and Kudalicious; #3/0 Cut Bait; #2/0 and #5/0 Deceivers in a variety of colors. Red/Black is our favorite color combination. And if you absolutely want to catch big barracuda . . . forget the fly rod and take a light spinning rig with plenty of fluorescent green tube lures. Barracuda go nuts for these lures, and the action is sensational.

We have caught permit on a variety of flies, and have several favorites, but there is no such thing as one single killer permit fly. If permit were human, they would need years of psychiatric treatment to function in the realm of normality. Yarn Crabs, Clouser's Minnows, Spawning Shrimp, and Swimming Shrimp can all entice permit to eat. Add a couple of Del's Merkins, Captain Crabbys, and Epoxy Crabs to your box, then give it your best shot if a permit materializes. The common denominator with all these flies is their sink rate: they all sink fast.

Packing Tips

A number of companies manufacture high-quality functional warm-weather clothing. Patagonia, Ex Officio, Columbia, and Tommy Bahama are top brands. Ex Officio's Air Strip long-sleeved and short-sleeved shirts are like wearing air, and are now available in "buzz off" bug repellent material. Patagonia's Tropical Fishing shirts, shorts, and pants are best for anglers who prefer a soft cotton fabric. Whatever clothing you choose, it should be lightweight, offer sun protection, dry in minutes, and be maintenance-free. A cool hat that will protect ears and neck is also essential. Footwear should be suitable for wading hard coral bottoms, and it should provide arch support for standing on the deck of a poled skiff.

The highest-quality polarized sunglasses are mandatory, and may be the most important piece of gear you own. The more fish you can see, the more fish you will catch. If you are willing to spend $300 and up for a rod or reel, you should be willing to spend up to $200 on a pair of polarized sunglasses. A number of companies manufacturer high-quality glass lenses. Our favorite brand is Action Optics by Smith, and our favorite all-around lens colors are photochromic amber and photochromic copper. Amber lenses cut blue light from the spectrum and increase contrast so your vision can penetrate the surface and let you see even the slightest movement. Copper lenses cut the sun better on really bright days. Side-shields are also important for a glare-free field of vision and for protecting your eyes from the wind and stray hooks.

Sunscreen, bug dope (Kim's favorite is Off Skintastic), soft durable luggage, a boat bag, first-aid kit, prescription medicine, and other personal items are all necessary for a comfortable trip. Consult with your favorite fly-fishing professional to prepare for your specific destination. The following is the travel checklist we use when preparing for a trip. We do not necessarily take all of these items on every trip, but the list is the best way we know to get organized.

Saltwater Travel Checklist

- ☐ Passport
- ☐ Copy of passport
- ☐ Airline tickets
- ☐ Vouchers/itinerary
- ☐ Wallet/cash/traveler's checks
- ☐ Destination phone numbers

- ☐ Fly rods
- ☐ Fly reels/spools
- ☐ Neoprene reel protectors
- ☐ Extra fly lines/extra backing
- ☐ Leaders/tippet/wire spools
- ☐ Flies/fly boxes
- ☐ Pliers/hemostats/snips
- ☐ Hook sharpener
- ☐ Fly line dressing
- ☐ Stripping basket
- ☐ Leader stretcher
- ☐ Chest pack/fanny pack

- ☐ Guide lanyard
- ☐ Wading booties/shoes
- ☐ Wading socks
- ☐ Snorkel/goggles/fins

- ☐ Laundry bag
- ☐ Long pants
- ☐ Shorts
- ☐ Swimsuit
- ☐ Long-sleeved shirts
- ☐ Short-sleeved shirts
- ☐ Sweater/windbreaker
- ☐ Wide-brimmed hat
- ☐ Updowner hat
- ☐ Tennis shoes
- ☐ Comfortable shoes
- ☐ Underwear/socks
- ☐ Rain gear/pants and jacket
- ☐ Flaps/thongs/sandals

- ☐ Sun gloves
- ☐ Polarized sunglasses
- ☐ Extra sunglasses/glasses
- ☐ Optical cloth/cleaner
- ☐ Sunscreen 20+ SPF
- ☐ Lip balm
- ☐ Insect repellent/DEET
- ☐ Avon Skin-So-Soft

- ☐ Ziploc bags
- ☐ Tupperware
- ☐ Fishing towel/beach towel
- ☐ Camera/film/batteries in a waterproof bag
- ☐ Toiletry kit
- ☐ First-aid supplies/itch balm

- ☐ Band-Aids/alcohol
- ☐ Aspirin/Advil/Motrin/Aleve
- ☐ Caladryl/Benedryl
- ☐ Prescription medicines
- ☐ Dramamine or substitute
- ☐ Travel flashlight
- ☐ Travel alarm clock
- ☐ Boat carry-on bag
- ☐ Water bottle
- ☐ Travel iron/clothesline
- ☐ Waterproof tape
- ☐ Glue/moleskin
- ☐ Reel lubricant
- ☐ Knot book
- ☐ Reading material
- ☐ Notepad/pen

CHAPTER 3

TRAVEL EXPECTATIONS
AND BOOKING A TRIP

Carter and Heidi Andrews fishing from the *Thunderbird*.

Ninety-nine percent of the complaints we have heard over the years from travelers were caused by unrealistic expectations. The best way to avoid this—to start your trip off on the right foot—is to just relax and enjoy the local culture. Engage the locals in conversation, ask them questions, and participate in their way of life. If you hold yourself apart, you will rarely have as much fun.

Traveling anglers need to acknowledge ahead of time that destination travel means encountering different ways of life and different cultures. Passing quick judgments on the differences, or comparing the quality of services to those in the United States, can set travelers up for disappointments.

The most important part of the travel planning process is to define the goals of your trip. So how should you gather the pertinent facts to choose a destination suitable to these goals? The first part of the answer is to establish a list of priorities for a particular trip. Is this a hard-core fishing trip, or will other vacation activities be included? What are the ability levels of the anglers going on the trip? What type of accommodations and services do you expect? Once you have your basic goals in mind, you can begin to ask additional questions that will give you the best chance for planning a successful vacation.

Let's begin with novice saltwater anglers. Bonefishing is the best way to get started for a number of reasons. First, bonefish are plentiful throughout the Bahamas.

Beginning anglers need as many "shots" as possible. You can't get better if you don't get opportunities. Second, bonefish eagerly take flies. In spite of being finicky and spooky at times, bonefish are voracious feeders, and will often eat recklessly. We like to call aggressive bonefish "suicidal." As a beginning bonefisher you will want to see as many suicidal fish as possible. Third, bonefishing is pure fly-fishing, meaning that you stalk the fish, see them, and then sightcast to them. This visual experience is remarkable and extremely rewarding. Fourth, bonefish are fast and powerful. After you hook up, that first run is awesome. All you can do is let them go and hold on in amazement while your backing melts off your reel.

For a first blue-water angling trip, dorado (also called dolphin fish) is your best bet. Dorado are abundant throughout the Bahamas and they eagerly slam subsurface flies and poppers. Catching them on top or just under is an exhilarating visual experience. The way they accelerate to take a fly is breathtaking. When they feel the hook, they go ballistic, often jumping 10 or more times during a fight. The bright yellow, orange, green, and blue colors of dorado often light up the ocean around buoys or flotsam. When dorado school around these sort of surface structures you can sightcast to them the way you would to bonefish. At other times you troll teasers offshore, not knowing if you'll bring up dorado, wahoo, tuna, or billfish.

Tarpon, Andros Island.

Once you decide on the primary species you want to pursue, you need to pick the best location for that species based on what type of trip you want. If this will be a hard-core fishing trip, you'll want the best guides, and you may not care as much about accommodations, meals, or optional activities. If you're a beginner, you'll want to see as many bonefish as possible, with size of fish being less important. If you're a veteran bonefisher, you might be looking for a fish over 10 pounds and you'll be willing to sacrifice numbers in this pursuit.

Maybe you've decided to concentrate on bonefish, but want some variety as well. Most Bahamian flats destinations offer variety, with barracuda and sharks commonly available. In planning any trip, you'll want to know the best times to go. This becomes trickier when you want to pursue multiple species. Pick the time that is best for your primary species, and then try to overlap with good times for your secondary species.

Everyone wants to know the best times to go to a particular destination. This is usually a combination of prime time for a given species, and prime time for weather. In our experience, the weather has become more unpredictable than ever. So-called prime weather periods have changed so much over the years. We still advise playing the odds, yes, but that said you should go when your schedule allows.

Playing the odds means you'll book your vacation in the more traditional good-weather months of March through June and October, November. In December through February, you'll go to the more southerly islands. Still, there are no guarantees that the wind, weather, or fish will go along even during the traditionally best times. By playing the odds, however, and by choosing the best tides and best guides, you'll have a good chance to enjoy some fine fishing.

Decide on the length of your trip. Some anglers can only get away for a few days. Many people book four-night/three-day fishing packages all over the Bahamas. If this is all the time you have, go for it, but remember that shorter trips are more likely to be affected by weather. Generally, on a seven-day trip, you have a better chance of getting some good weather days. This is simply a matter of putting in your time.

Maybe you'll decide that fishing, relaxing, and sightseeing are of equal importance. In that case, you will still want good guides, but you may also want deluxe accommodations, and maybe some optional activities such as diving, snorkeling, sea kayaking, golf, tennis, or shopping.

Now comes the moment of truth, time to realistically assess your angling ability. If this will be your first bonefishing trip, it doesn't matter how good you are in fresh water or offshore. Consider yourself a beginner, and set your expectations at beginner level. You're going to prepare the best you can, then go and fish the best you can. If you knock 'em dead, great, but if you don't, you can still have a blast, learn a lot, and be better next time.

There are a number of things you can do to prepare for your first bonefishing trip. First, practice casting in the wind. Do it on water or on grass, but do it into the wind, across the wind, and down wind. Work on quickness in delivering the fly, and on accuracy. Quickness means you make a minimum number of false casts, and then shoot your line. One false cast is best, two is okay, three is too many. Work on your accuracy out to 50 or 60 feet. If you can make a quick and accurate cast to 50 or 60 feet, you'll catch more fish than you know what to do with. If you can make a quick accurate cast 30 to 40 feet you'll catch enough fish to be delighted. Make sure you practice with a fly on (hook clipped off), and when the wind is ruffling your shirt.

If you think practicing your casting isn't worthwhile, or if you tell yourself you don't have time to practice, think about tennis or golf. Beginners in either sport, regardless of athletic ability, are not very good at first. Extensive practice is required in both sports to become competent. Fly-fishing is no different. If you spend a couple of thousand dollars on a bonefishing trip, and don't practice before you go, what results can you expect?

Take the time to enjoy assembling your gear. For many anglers, preparing for a trip is half the fun. Playing with gear and flies is like playing with toys. Practice your knots too. Know how to tie a perfection loop, blood knot, Albright knot, surgeon's knot, and improved clinch knot. Knowing a nail knot and a Bimini twist will be helpful also.

We recommend the following books: *Practical Fishing Knots* by Mark Sosin and Lefty Kreh; *Bonefishing with a Fly* by Randall Kaufmann; *Fly-Fishing for Bonefish* by

Dick Brown; *Fishing the Flats* by Mark Sosin and Lefty Kreh; *Fly-Fishing in Salt Water* by Lefty Kreh; *The Essence of Fly Casting* by Mel Kreiger (book and video); *Saltwater Fly Patterns* by Lefty Kreh; *Bonefish Flies* by Dick Brown; *Currier's Quick and Easy Guide to Saltwater Fly Fishing* by Jeff Currier and Doug O'Looney; and *A Fly-Fisher's Guide to Saltwater Naturals and Their Imitation* by George V. Roberts and Arolina Kehoe.

Videos/CD/DVD: *The Art of Knot Tying* by Chico Fernandez; *The Art of Advanced Fly Casting* by Chico Fernandez; *Saltwater Fly Tying* by Lefty Kreh.

CDs: *Tying Flies for Saltwater* by Dick Stewart and Farrow Allen (an interactive CD with full motion video); *Florida East Coast and Bahamas* by Saltwater Software (CD will give you tide information throughout most of the Bahamas); the DVD How to Fly Fish series by Jim and Kelly Watt (several DVDs in the series feature saltwater tips, tactics, flies, and specific discussions of the Bahamas.)

■

We can't stress enough the importance of fishing with a top-quality professional guide. This is absolutely the most important element in a successful fishing trip. We recommend booking guides in advance, through a professional travel consultant who has fished with that guide, or on your own based on the recommendations from someone who has fished with that guide.

When choosing a guide look for the following qualities: personality; experience; professionalism; ability to plan a day's fishing strategy; understanding of tides; understanding of different fish species; boat handling to get you into position to cast; ability to instruct casting and line handling; and the quality of his boat and equipment.

Stephen with guide Michael Carroll, Crooked Island.

Remember that even the best guides have off days sometimes. Anglers paying good money and spending precious time on a trip usually have a hard time with this, but it can happen. You need to get past this by talking to your guide about your concerns. Even top guides will have trouble finding fish on occasion, especially if you are looking for big bonefish, permit, or tarpon. If you have special goals or requests, ask your guide if he thinks there is a reasonable chance for success. If you really want to go tarpon fishing, but your guide says the weather is wrong, we suggest you trust your guide's judgment.

In assessing your ability, consider your skills in the following areas:

Vision: How well can you see fish in varying water conditions and depths? If you fish for a week, you'll probably see better each day.

Casting: How far can you cast accurately in the wind? Practice, practice, practice, and then be realistic about your ability. Then practice some more.

Line handling: How well do you control your line? Do you vary your retrieve? Can you see the fish eat your fly? Do you set well with your line hand? You can learn these skills by listening to your guide and by experimenting on your own.

Fish fighting: Do you have trouble clearing line when a fish takes off? Once the fish is on your reel, can you anticipate when he'll stop, or start running again? Do you know how much pressure you can put on a fish without breaking it off? Experience will improve your skills, as will listening to your guide.

Wind and weather: Can you deal with any weather condition? Count on conditions being challenging; then, if it's gorgeous, so much the better. Wind will make casting more difficult and clouds will make it hard to see. Relax and have fun anyway.

Tackle: Do you have reliable tackle? Is your rod fun and easy to cast? Does your reel have enough fresh backing? Are your leaders and tippets fresh? It does not pay to cut corners with saltwater tackle. You can rely on a good fly shop or mail-order house to tie knots, rig tarpon and billfish leaders, and set up reels, but the more you know the better. And it's fun to learn!

Booking Your Trip

Over the past several years, greater numbers of travelers are booking their own trips directly with lodges and guides. This is due mainly to the easy access to information available on the Internet—to lodge sites that include detailed information on facilities and services, photographs, pricing, and contact telephone numbers and e-mail addresses.

We recommend that all travelers use the Internet, travel guides, and other means to gather information about lodges, hotels, guides, tourist bureaus, travel consultants, and tour operators. But when it comes time to book your trip, we suggest using a qualified travel agent. Reputable fly-fishing travel agencies charge the same price you would pay by booking a lodge or guide directly. There is no premium added. We say this to dispel the misperception that booking directly with a lodge or guide will save you money. In most cases, booking directly will cost you time, and maybe money, in terms of aggravation and inconvenience. Also, if something goes wrong with your trip, trying to deal with a lodge or guide in a foreign country can be difficult at best. You will have no recourse against a Bahamian lodge or guide if you do not receive the services you paid for, while a professional U.S. travel agent will be on your side and will aid in solving any problems.

If you have done your homework, you will be able to supply your chosen travel agent with the necessary information to book the trip you want. The more accurate information you supply, the better job the agent can do. This might include the agent suggesting a different destination from the one you chose originally. Good agents make suggestions based on their experience, and their desire to match you with the location that best fits the information you provide.

If you choose to book directly on your own, we recommend that you request written detailed confirmation of all accommodations and services you have booked, along with an official invoice. You should also request that your chosen lodge or guide provide you with written confirmation of the receipt of your deposits and final payments. While this will not happen with some lodges and guides, it is a good practice to at least make the attempt to secure every aspect of your trip in writing.

CHAPTER 4

ANDROS ISLAND: HEARTLAND OF THE BAHAMAS

A nice catch. (Brian O'Keefe)

A ndros Island is our favorite Bahamian destination, and considered by many people to be the "Bonefishing Capital of the World." We would certainly endorse this title.

Located 150 miles southeast of Miami, and 36 miles west of Nassau, Andros is surrounded by some of the best saltwater flats habitat on the planet. The North, Middle, and South Bights are the heart of this famous fishery, but they are only the beginning. Andros sprawls over 100 miles from the Joulter's Cays on the northern end, to the Water Cays and Curly Cut Cays on the southern tip, and spans 40 miles from the east coast to the West Side. Composed of serpentine channels and creeks, fresh and saltwater lakes, verdant mangrove cays, and countless miles of sandy flats, Andros is blessed with more fertile fishing grounds than any other area in the Caribbean.

Roaming these flats are uncountable numbers of bonefish ranging from three to six pounds. There are also abundant fish in the six- to nine-pound class, plus many unforgettable double-digit giants. If you're looking for BIG bonefish, Andros is the place to take your shot. Andros also offers seasonal fishing for tarpon, permit, barracuda, sharks, jacks, snappers, amberjack, grouper, billfish, wahoo, tuna, mackerel, and dolphin.

The local atmosphere on Andros is a blend of casual everyday life, Caribbean charm and friendliness, plus a pinch of superstition. Most people follow a simple routine.

Nothing is hurried. No traffic. People go to work. Children dress in uniforms and go to school. People believe in local witch doctors, and in the spirit of the mythical Chickcharnie, a small birdlike being with huge eyes and a penchant for mischief. Potions are mixed and blended and taken for good health. People possess ambition and pride, but there is no demanding timetable set for progress.

The roughly 8,000 residents of Andros are concentrated on the eastern coast. The western coast is unsettled and relatively unexplored, as are many of the interior lakes. Andros is the Bahamas' most important farming region, and the largest source of fresh water. Farmland, plus pine and hardwood forests, covers the northern part of the island. Hardwoods include mahogany, horseflesh (a variety of mahogany used in ship-building), and lignum vitae, also known as "sailor's cure" because its sap provided the most effective treatment for syphilis until the 1900s.

Bird life is more prolific on Andros than most other islands, and so is insect life. Due to the large amount of fresh water, mosquitoes, sand flies, and green-headed horse flies, known locally as "doctor" flies, are abundant, especially when the wind is down.

Historically, Andros has always been a mysterious island. Spanish sailors visited in the sixteenth century and called the island "La Isla del Espiritu Santo," Island of the Holy Spirit. This name came from the Spanish belief that the Holy Spirit lives over water, and Andros presented itself to them more as water than land.

Andros's dense lush interior—a combination of mangrove swamps, thorny under-brush, and thick forests—was seen as virtually impenetrable, and perhaps haunted. This inaccessibility and mystique was the draw for runaway slaves and Seminole Indians escaping from the Florida Everglades in the mid-nineteenth century. These refugees settled into peaceful obscurity in the community now known as Red Bay.

Logging, farming, fishing, and sponging have dominated the Andros economy over the past hundred years. Conservation efforts have put an end to logging, at least for the time being, while farming, commercial fishing, and sponging are still important revenue sources. Tourism, which focuses on sportfishing, eco-tours, and diving, is the fastest growing sector of the new economy.

The island residents have adapted well to a tourism-based economy. Many new bonefishing lodges, and a couple of eco-lodges, opened between 2000 and 2004, though the number of new qualified guides has lagged. Western Air has dramatically improved air service from Nassau to Andros's four airports—San Andros, Fresh Creek/Andros Town, Mangrove Cay, and Congo Town. Most important, the locals look forward to sharing their island with visitors, to revealing their secret treasures. This type of outgoing sincerity goes well beyond just good service, and leaves many visitors with a desire to return.

In spite of its size and proximity to Nassau, Andros is one of the least visited of the Out Islands. This is partly due to the overall lack of development, and until recently, the lack of promoted adventure activities.

Small Hope Bay Lodge, established in 1960, has made a consistent and successful effort to promote Andros as a diving and snorkeling destination. The island has more

Tiamo Resort.

dive sites than any other Bahamian location. The world's third largest barrier reef is just offshore, and the Tongue of the Ocean creates unparalleled wall diving.

Small Hope is an ideal place for families and couples looking for a relaxing remote location. Swim, windsurf, dive, snorkel, bike, hike, explore blue holes, and eat delicious food on your own schedule. Guided bonefishing, reef, and offshore fishing can be arranged.

Tiamo Resort, in the South Bight, is one of the most highly regarded eco-lodges in the Caribbean. Accessible only by boat, Tiamo's main lodge and eleven guest suites are situated to overlook the golden sand beach and aqua-colored waters of the Bight. Diving, snorkeling, sea kayaking, swimming, hiking, fly-fishing, and bird-watching are primary activities.

There are a number of possible new developments, such as marinas, resorts, and gated residential communities, which could dramatically change the tourism business. For now, however, Andros is still an intriguing remote location best suited to anglers and outdoor enthusiasts looking for a sense of adventure in a magical place.

The easiest way to reach Andros is by air. Several charter carriers, including one operated by Small Hope Bay Lodge, make this convenient with non-stop service from Ft. Lauderdale. American, Delta, U.S. Air, and Continental have scheduled flights to Nassau daily. From Nassau, we usually fly Western Air to Andros. Western Air operates daily scheduled service to all four Andros airports. We also use several air charter companies out of Nassau to reach Andros when we travel with groups of four or more—traveling with a group of this size, or larger, makes booking a charter economical. You need at least an hour and a half in Nassau to clear customs and walk to the domestic terminal to make Out Island connections.

Check the connection time when you make reservations. If it shows less than an hour and a half, make different arrangements. You can either change your schedule to give you more than an hour, schedule a charter flight, or arrive in Nassau the day before your trip to Andros.

Arriving in Nassau the day before your flight to Andros, or to any of the Out Islands, is a good idea. This will give you time to relax, and Nassau can be a lot of fun. Our favorite hotel is the Hilton British Colonial located on Bay Street. The Hilton provides excellent service, first-class rooms, and many amenities, including a private beach, business center, spa and gym, plus convenient access to all the shops and restaurants on Bay Street. The most popular hotel is the spectacular Atlantis Resort on Paradise Island. For couples and families looking for an extended vacation, this is one of the finest large resort facilities in the world. The most elegant and expensive resort is also on Paradise Island, the One and Only Ocean Club Resort and Spa. If you are only going to spend one night in Nassau on your way to the Out Islands, and you have an early flight the next morning, the best place to stay is the Orange Hill Beach Inn, just a five-minute taxi ride from the airport.

Most taxis operating on New Providence charge zone fares. It is a 10-minute, $15 taxi ride from the international airport to the Cable Beach area. It is a 20-minute, $22 taxi ride to the Hilton. It is a 30-minute (at least), $28 taxi ride to Paradise Island. From the Hilton/Bay Street area to Paradise Island is a 10-minute, $10 taxi ride.

If you spend the night in Nassau, Western Air has early morning flights that will get you to Andros Town or Congo Town in time for a full day of fishing.

For the adventurous traveler with more time, Andros can be reached from Nassau via the Bahamas Fast Ferries, and via several mail boats. Sailing or cruising in private vessels is another popular way to reach Andros from anywhere in the Bahamas. Call ahead to any port to confirm what facilities and supplies are available.

We suggest that you take everything you might need for convenience and safety with you, as supplies can be scarce on Andros. This would include a good first aid kit, sewing kit, and prescription medicines.

Around the Island

North Andros includes the area from the Joulter's Cays to Fresh Creek. This is the most populated area of the island, and the center of the island's farming industry. "Most populated" is a relative term, however, since the two largest towns, San Andros and Nicholl's Town, have a combined population of less than two thousand people. Adding in Morgan's Bluff, Lowe Sound, Red Bay, and Mastic Point bumps the population to around three thousand.

The easiest way to access North Andros is to fly into San Andros on Western Air. Charter flights are also available from Florida and Nassau. The best place to stay is the Conch Sound Inn, located on the road between Nicholl's Town and Conch Sound, a 10-minute walk from the beach. The spacious air-conditioned rooms with private

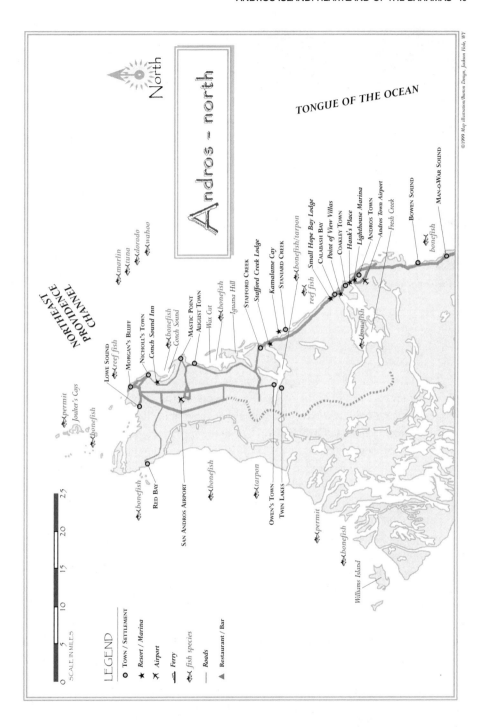

Andros – north

TONGUE OF THE OCEAN

North

NORTHEAST PROVIDENCE CHANNEL

permit
Joulter's Cays
bonefish

bonefish
RED BAY

SAN ANDROS AIRPORT
bonefish

tarpon
OWEN'S TOWN
TWIN LAKES

permit
bonefish

Williams Island

LOWE SOUND
reef fish
MORGAN'S BLUFF
NICHOLL'S TOWN
bonefish
Conch Sound
CONCH SOUND INN
MASTIC POINT
AUGUST TOWN
Wax Cut
bonefish
Iguana Hill

STAFFORD CREEK
Stafford Creek Lodge
Kamalame Cay
STANIARD CREEK
bonefish/tarpon

reef fish
Small Hope Bay Lodge
CALABASH BAY
Point of View Villas
COAKLEY TOWN
Hank's Place
Lighthouse Marina
ANDROS TOWN
Andros Town Airport
Fresh Creek

bonefish

BOWEN SOUND
bonefish
MAN-o-WAR SOUND

marlin
tuna
dorado
wahoo

LEGEND
○ TOWN / SETTLEMENT
★ Resort / Marina
✕ Airport
🚢 Ferry
🐟 fish species
— Roads
▲ Restaurant / Bar

SCALE IN MILES
0   5   10   15   20   25

©1999 Map illustration/Barton Design, Jackson Hole, WY

Stephen with permit, Joulter's Cay, Andros.

baths and mini-refrigerators were renovated in 2002. The bar/restaurant serves hearty Bahamian dishes in a lively atmosphere. Satellite TV is available in the bar. There is a swimming pool in the enclosed patio off the bar.

Morgan's Bluff, named after the infamous pirate, is only 15 miles by boat from Chub Cay in the Berry Islands, and 36 miles from Nassau. For boating anglers, Morgan's Bluff offers easy access and good anchorages in the harbor proper. There is a restaurant and bar that, when open, serves island-style lunches and cold Kalik. Additional anchorages can be found on the tide at nearby Lowe Sound.

Fuel, fresh water, ice, and groceries are usually available in Lowe Sound and Morgan's Bluff, though fruit and staples can run low. If you need a bigger market you'll have to make the trip to Nicholl's Town. We suggest taking a taxi because it is too far to walk when carrying supplies.

The flats habitat from Morgan's Bluff and Lowe Sound to the Joulter's Cays, approximately eight miles as the crow flies, is a vast gourmet feeding area for bonefish and permit. This habitat is part of an extensive ecosystem that extends north across the Great Bahama Bank to Great Stirrup Cay in the Berry Islands, northwest to Bimini and the Gulf Stream, and west to Red Bay. Blue crabs, sea crabs, swimming shrimp, and gobies combine with mussels and clams to create a massive food supply for gamefish. The blue crabs are especially numerous, and their scent in the water is a major draw for numbers of large permit. These crabs are also responsible for the high concentration of big bonefish.

Running from Morgan's Bluff to the Joulter's can be a battering experience when the wind is up, though on a calm day it's exhilarating. Lowe Sound is more protected and provides quicker access to all the cays, including the Joulter's, but navigating is tricky and requires local knowledge. The bonefishing lodge/guide situation is ever evolving in this area. If you want to book a guide here, we suggest that you make inquiries into the current status of operations at the time of planning your trip. As an alternative, several of the best independent guides from Fresh Creek and Cargill Creek (they include Benry Smith and Herman Bain) will trailer their boats up here to guide their clients.

The settlement of Lowe Sound is tranquil and friendly, perched on the water's edge, which is piled high in many areas with conch shells. There is a cement boat ramp for flats skiffs next to a bar and snack stand; that stand serves the some of best fresh conch salad in the islands.

There is good wading for bonefish right in front of the settlement. You can see the Joulter's, along with many other inviting cays in the distance. Miles of flats stretching out from northern Andros become completely dry during low tide, creating wet sandy and grassy hillocks teeming with burrowing shrimp and scampering blue crabs.

There are flats here where you can stand in ankle-deep water and see nothing but ankle-deep water 360 degrees around you. In other areas, deep blue creeks cut through white sand flats that are only a hundred feet wide. Some of the best permit flats lie along the edges of the boating route to the Joulter's Cays anchorage where water depths are 6 to 10 feet. Others lie to the north where white sand turns to dark grass that runs to the horizon.

For boaters, the easiest Joulter's anchorage is at the southwestern tip of the cays, but there is also a good anchorage accessible on the tide at the northeastern tip in a beautiful creek adjacent to a crescent-shaped beach.

The eastern tides, similar to the ones in Fresh Creek and Nassau, influence the fishery most, but tide issues are complicated as you move west. This is the same phenomenon anglers experience farther south when fishing the Bights and moving toward the West Side.

Wind is also a significant factor on the mostly open flats. Lees can be found from the prevailing winds here and there around Pine Cay, Hog Cay and on the western side of Long, Candle and the Joulter's Cays, but the vast area of central flats is completely exposed.

Sand, coral, and mud are the main bottom types. Most are light in color, which makes spotting fish easier. Conversely, the complex bottom structure,

Cargill Creek Lodge.

with countless contours, potholes and troughs, provides great cover for ghostly bonefish. Water depth is especially critical in this region. Bonefish congregate in the deeper channels and troughs waiting for incoming tides to cover the flats so they can begin to forage.

South of Nicholl's Town is Conch Sound, a large protected bay cut into the island. There are several miles of white sand beaches here, plus flats that are wadable at low tide. These flats are the easiest northern ocean-side flats to access because they are not guarded by thick mangroves.

The best reef and offshore fishing begins near Mastic Point. Boaters can travel either inside or outside the reef on the way south. Trolling hookless teasers is a good way to raise a variety of fish. Be prepared with a fly rod, and then have a boat mate yank the teaser away so you can substitute a fly. If you just want some meat for the galley add hooks to the teasers. This is also a good area to fish with conventional gear for grouper.

South of Mastic Point is Mastic Bay, a huge expanse of flats and backcountry shoreline mangroves. The shorelines are rugged and often covered with soft mud, so fishing here is best done from a poled skiff or sea kayak.

Paw Paw Cay and the surrounding cays on the outside of the bay create prime bonefish habitat. The hard sand and coral bottoms are suited to wading. Fishing is best on a low incoming tide. On a high tide, large schools of bonefish lay up on the leeward side of Paw Paw.

Continuing south past Rat Cay, the shoreline cuts back away from the reef toward the Saddle Back Cays. This diverse habitat consists of a series of shallow wadable flats and deeper channels. At low tide you can wade for several miles, but as the tide rises you shouldn't stray too far from your boat. Channels and cuts become waist deep in a hurry and these ocean-side flats are loaded with aggressive blacktip and lemon sharks. If you are looking for big tailing bonefish, this is one of the best rarely fished areas on Andros.

Boaters cruising inside the reef in this area will need to stay on the outside of the Saddle Back Cays. Check your charts and be extremely careful. Accessing the wadable flats in this area is best accomplished by dinghy or flats skiff.

The entrance to London Creek is just south of Saddle Back Cays. Once inside, the creek slices back north then doglegs west for more than eight miles. A shallow draft flats boat or dinghy is the best way to explore this creek, which provides good bonefishing even during stormy weather and winter cold fronts.

The shoreline around Stafford Creek is a series of white sand beaches, coral outcroppings, casuarina trees, and palm trees. Shallow wadable flats are located on either side of the creek mouth. Anglers can walk straight out from the settlement on the north side of the creek to stalk tailing bones on an incoming tide.

For anglers who want to fish this area on their own, comfortable accommodations are available at Love at First Sight. This island-style nine-room motel sits right on Stafford Creek, just north of the highway bridge. The motel has a swimming pool, large restaurant and bar, and a deck on the water for sipping cold Kaliks after fishing. Complete bonefishing packages are also available.

The entrance to Stafford Creek itself flows like a river, especially on the falling tide. The water is up to 15 feet deep here. A jetty whirlpool, which can be extremely dangerous to boaters, is located at the far southern corner of the creek mouth. Just beyond the jetty pool, the creek makes a hard left and passes under the highway bridge.

If you're standing on the bridge the creek looks like a wild Rocky Mountain river. On an incoming tide, the clear green water rips through the narrows before settling into the wider expanse of the inner creek. Rock and coral banks topped with native pines rise to 200 feet as the creek swells and turns west.

Just before the bend, on the southern shore, is the site of Stafford Creek Lodge. The lodge, owned and operated by Prescott and Samantha Smith, opened in October 1998. Catering to just six guest anglers at a time, the focus here is on great fishing and service. Large air-conditioned rooms overlook the water and dock. The landscaping is a pleasing blend of native plants and stone paths leading from the guest rooms to the lodge, the dock, and gazebos.

Stafford Creek Lodge.

Stafford Creek guides fish the Joulter's Cays from Lowe Sound, as well as miles of creeks and outside ocean flats. The drive from the lodge to Lowe Sound takes about 20 minutes on the main highway. If you are interested in booking at Stafford Creek Lodge, you will need to make your reservations at least six months in advance, and a year in advance for April and May.

Stafford Creek sprawls inland for over 10 miles in a series of channels, flats, and connected lakes. When the wind is howling and most flats on the island are unfishable, anglers can still enjoy a good day of bonefishing here or in London Creek. Tarpon, permit, jacks, and snappers can be found in the creek throughout the year.

South of Stafford Creek, anglers can wade the Blanket Sound flats on firm sand and coral bottoms. Boaters need to stay well off the shoreline all the way to Staniard Rock Passage. The golden sand banks that protect the northern entrance to Staniard Creek make it easy for wading anglers to see ocean-dark bonefish cruising out on a falling tide.

The Staniard Creek area is lush, laced with mangroves, casuarinas, and coconut palms that hover over white sand beaches. An offshore breeze helps keep the bugs down almost year round. The peaceful island settlement is accessed by a bridge just off the main highway.

Kamalame Cay Resort, with its adjoining private marina and villas on the south end of Long Bay Cay, is on the northern end of Staniard Creek. Casually elegant accommodations here cater to fly-fishers and their non-angling companions. While there are numerous areas to wade on your own, Kamalame guides fish from here all the way to the Joulter's Cays and Red Bay.

The Staniard Creek Quality Inn is located on one of the three arms of the creek just south of Kamalame. Clean rooms, some with air-conditioning, offer the budget-minded angler access to this area. During lower tidal periods it is possible to wade for bonefish right in front of the hotel. There are other good wading options to the north and south on bottoms that vary from hard sand to mushy grass.

The nine-mile coastline from Staniard Creek to Fresh Creek is a relatively straight southeasterly shot. The highway takes a more circuitous route and is in good condition. Driving time from Fresh Creek to Staniard Creek is about 20 minutes. For boaters, the passage inside the reef is straightforward, though it's better to stay out near the reef as coral heads and sand banks rise near the surface on low tides.

Flats anglers rarely fish this nine-mile stretch. Some guides from Small Hope Bay work this area but they usually go south instead. The best fishing is on the outer flats that are difficult to reach from shore. A flats skiff or a dingy offers the best access.

Stephen teaches casting to some guides-in-training at Stafford Creek Lodge.

Small Hope Bay Lodge is located on a protected beach north of Fresh Creek. Comfortable accommodations are on a serene stretch of white sand. The casual relaxing atmosphere is ideal for families or couples who want to combine superior diving with a variety of water sports and fishing.

The reef fishing along this stretch is outstanding. Jack crevalle, mackerel, amberjack, barracuda, grouper, and a variety of sharks are abundant. Trolling teasers is consistently effective. Fly-fishers will have their best chances for success using chum to concentrate the reef fish into a feeding frenzy. The best offshore outfitter in the area is Tongue of the Ocean Sport Fishing Charters.

Point of View Villas, a 14-suite resort, is a quarter mile north of the Fresh Creek bridge. Their restaurant is one of our favorites in the area.

Hank's Place restaurant and bar in Fresh Creek is our top pick for enjoying the local scene, eating delicious fresh seafood, and sipping sunset cocktails. Anglers who want to fish the Fresh Creek area on their own can stay at nearby George's Point Villas and rent a boat from Hank's to explore the creek and the outside ocean flats.

The next section of the island, central Andros, runs from Fresh Creek/Andros Town to Behring Point. Fresh Creek offers one of the best anchorages on the island. Fresh Creek, also known as Coakley Town, sprawls along the north shore of the creek, while Andros Town occupies the south bank. The Andros Town Airport, a couple minutes drive south of the settlement, is the airport used most often by anglers traveling to fish this area. Western Air operates two scheduled flights from Nassau every day.

A good place to stay in Fresh Creek is the Lighthouse Yacht Club and Marina on the south side of the creek. The spacious villa rooms have air-conditioning, tile floors, private baths, and they overlook the swimming pool and marina. A restaurant and bar are on the premises.

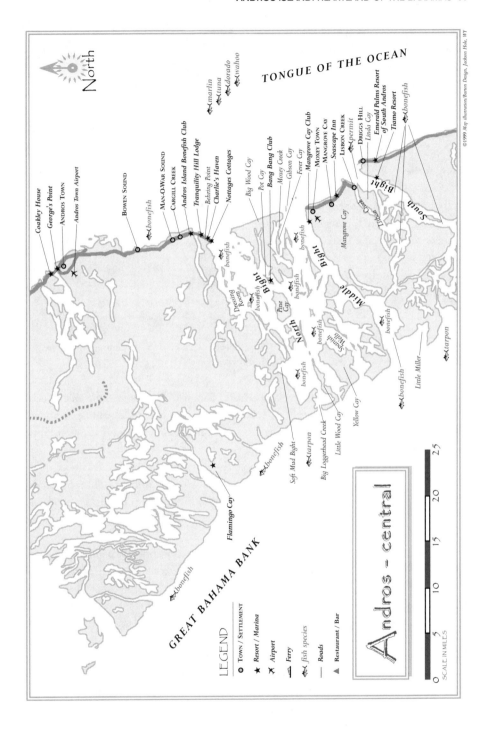

The marina offers boaters 17 slips with water, electricity, and fuel. We have rarely seen a vacant slip here, so we suggest calling ahead for reservations.

Across the road from Lighthouse is the Androsia factory outlet for unique island-style clothing. Kim and many of our women angling friends are frequent shoppers here.

Papa Gay's Chickcharnie Hotel, located across the creek from Lighthouse, is a pastel-colored three-story structure that sits on the water's edge. Rooms are comfortable and priced to meet the demands of budget-conscious anglers. A local store sells groceries, drugs, suntan lotion, insect repellent, and other essentials.

The Coakley House, a private fully furnished three-bedroom, three-bath villa overlooking the ocean flats, is owned by Small Hope Bay Lodge. This is a recom-

Dock at Lighthouse Yacht Club and Marina in Fresh Creek.

mended lodging option for couples, groups, and families. You can rent the villa as is or with maids, cooks, and other services. Independent bonefish guides can be arranged. The guides will pick you up on fishing days. The full diving program at Small Hope Bay is available to guests renting the villa.

A mile and a half south of Andros Town is the main base for the Atlantic Undersea Test and Evaluation Center (AUTEC). This area is off-limits and should be avoided. The U.S. Navy uses this base for submarine warfare testing. Helicopters, destroyers, and support ships are all a common sight along the eastern shoreline of Andros.

Some of the best ocean-side flats in Andros begin about two miles south of AUTEC. The shorelines inside Plum Cays and Mastic Cays are a maze of mangroves that provide food and shelter to thousands of bonefish. Ambushing these fish on the open flats and around the cays as they tail their way in and out is incredible sport.

More outstanding ocean-side flats begin again around Kits Cay and continue to White Bight. Man-O-War Cay, Kiss-it Cay, and Simms Cay are the heart of this wade-fishing paradise. The best times to fish low incoming tides are in the early morning and late afternoon, but the fish will feed here any time the tide is right.

We have often waded for tailing bones for hours at a time in the Simms Cay area. The golden sand bottom is like walking on carpet. The dark ocean bonefish can be spotted a hundred yards away. On calm days you can see tails, dorsals, and wakes in

Tranquility Hill Lodge.

every direction. A five-pound fish is only average here. We've caught fish up to 14 pounds on these flats in ankle-deep water.

Some of these ocean flats can be accessed from shore around White Bight, but most of the shoreline and land area is too dense with vegetation to pass through from the highway. The best flats are outside across channels that are too deep to wade, and caution is necessary due to the high number of aggressive blacktip sharks.

Bruce Farrington's Mount Pleasant Fishing Lodge can be a base for anglers who want to wade on their own around White Bight. The small lodge features several cottages steps away from the beach and bonefishing guides can be arranged.

Another AUTEC base is positioned just north of Salvador Point. Around the point is the entrance to Cargill Creek, a deep channel that cuts through two light-bottomed bonefish flats. The Andros Island Bonefish Club is on the northern shore where the creek widens. Captain Rupert Leadon, the owner of the Bonefish Club, has purchased the neighboring Creekside Lodge, and now operates both lodges as a single facility.

The lodge facilities include spacious air-conditioned guest rooms with two double beds, mini-refrigerators, and private baths, two full-service bars, two restaurants, satellite television, and a freshwater swimming pool. Rupert runs one of the best flats fishing programs in the Bahamas. His top guides are excellent and his staff is friendly and helpful.

The Bonefish Club and Tranquility Hill Fishing Lodge have larger boats for reef and offshore fishing. Crews from both lodges are expert in the use of conventional tackle and adequate with fly-fishing gear. Dolphin is the most abundant offshore species, with wahoo, tuna and billfish available in season. The reef fishing for grouper, amberjack, sharks, and barracuda is consistently good.

Tranquility Hill Lodge owner/partner and fishing guide, Ray Mackey.

South of Cargill Creek is Behring Point and the entrance to the North Bight. Tranquility Hill Fishing Lodge rests on a hillside clearing overlooking the ocean and the Bight. Owned and operated by the Neymour and Mackey families, this is one of our favorite lodges. Service and food are first-rate. All guests are made to feel at home. Legendary guide Ivan Neymour runs a fishing operation that will satisfy the most demanding anglers.

Down the road from Tranquility is Charlie's Haven, the home and lodge of another bonefishing legend, "Crazy" Charlie Smith. Charlie has explored and guided in the Bights for more than 30 years. His enthusiasm for fishing is infectious and he still guides a very loyal clientele.

Charlie is an amazing personality who can keep you entertained for days by passing on the fishing lore of Andros. He started his career as a chef and he still cooks for his guests. Accommodations are in comfortable rooms with private baths, some with air-conditioning.

Another recommended place to stay is Nottages Cottages, located at the end of the Behring Point settlement road, a short walk past Charlie's Haven, on the north shore of the North Bight. An expansive bonefish flat is right out front. Easy wading and good fishing are possible during low incoming tides.

One of our favorite all-time guides, Charlie Neymour, has taken over the operations at Nottages. All the facilities were remodeled and upgraded in 2004. Nottages has eight comfortable motel-style rooms with air-conditioning, private baths, and mini-refrigerators. The large dining room and bar are decorated with Androsia curtains and tablecloths. Home-cooked meals are excellent, and anglers can watch satellite TV in the bar. A wrap-around deck overlooking the water is used for barbecues and après-fishing cocktails. The lush landscaping, including aloe trees, coconut palms, and a variety of orchid plants, is maintained by the remarkable Daisy Nottages, the owner of the property.

Daisy can go out and catch grouper off the reef or mix a potion to cure whatever ails you with equal ease. Her health potions are for sale, including her famous potency formula.

**Andros guide Charlie Neymour.
(Ric Fogel)**

The North Bight fishery is consistently one of the best in the Bahamas for big bones. It is also the home of the original Bang Bang Club on Pot Cay. Charlie Smith has rebuilt much of the club and is booking anglers into this historic site.

There are more top professional independent guides in the Cargill Creek–Behring Point area than anywhere else in the Bahamas. Guides who receive our highest recommendation include Charlie

Guides Frankie Neymour and Dwayne Neymour, Tranquility Hill Lodge.

Neymour, Andy Smith, Barry Neymour, Frankie Neymour, Benry Smith, Herman Bain, Dwain Neymour, Deon Neymour, and Ricardo Mackey. And of course there are many other highly qualified guides who work independently and with the various lodges.

Other top-rated guides are sometimes independent, but they are usually associated with their lodges—Ivan Neymour at Tranquility Hill, Rupert and Nick Leadon at the Bonefish Club, and Prescott Smith at Stafford Creek Lodge are examples. (Please see the Independent Guides section at the end of each chapter for contact information.)

Just across a channel from Pot Cay is Pine Cay, the north shore of which is a series of connected light-bottomed flats, small bays and coral points that draw incredible numbers of big bonefish into skinny water. Over the years we have had some of our best fishing for big tailing bones on these flats.

The entire north shore of the North Bight provides a lee for fishing during cold fronts, or when high winds pick up out of the northeast. Areas like the Dressing Room, Soft Mud Bight, and Yellow Cay can be fished throughout the day on the proper tide. The numbers of fish in these areas can defy imagination, and even better, these fish are usually aggressive to a fly.

On the south side of the North Bight lies uninhabited Big Wood Cay. The hard white sand flats are easy to wade. You can spot bonefish a long way off. Australian pines, casuarinas, coconut palms, and mangroves line the gold sand beaches where big bones cruise in six inches of water to feast on sea crabs. If you're looking for big bones that are a challenge to catch, this is a dream spot. If spooky, finicky fish easily frustrate you, you should avoid this area.

A fun option for catching a variety of fish is the Shark Hole, located in the middle of the North Bight between Nottages Cottages and Big Wood Cay. Blind casting can produce jacks, mackerel, snapper, barracuda, and sharks.

The ocean-side flats off Big Wood Cay between the North Bight and the Middle Bight are fished by only a few guides. Long stretches of white sand are fun to wade on incoming tides in the morning or late afternoon. This is also an excellent area to fish for permit on a high tide when the wind is blowing out of the west.

Cruising outside Big Wood Cay is the easiest and fastest way to reach the Middle Bight from Behring Point if the wind is down. Isolated coral heads and sand bars make it necessary to stay well off the shoreline however. If the wind is up, this is dangerous choppy water for a flats boat, though larger vessels can make the passage outside the reef without problem.

During rough weather flats boats take the inner passage through the North Bight, past Pot Cay, around the western end of Big Wood, past Kim's Cay, then either through Blue Creek or straight out toward High Ridge Cay. Navigating this passage requires extensive local knowledge, as does fishing anywhere in the Bights.

Assuming you can take the outside route, another AUTEC base is located on the southeastern corner of Big Wood Cay at the mouth of the Middle Bight. Deep blue water signals the channel entrance to the Bight with Gibson Cay to the south. The inside flats off Gibson Cay are easy to wade on a low incoming tide, and you can often see waves of bonefish tailing over the light sand bottom, though these have become tough fish to catch in the past few years.

Many people believe the Middle Bight is home to the largest bonefish in the world. We tend to agree. The names of the flats—"the promised land," "land of the giants," "land of a thousand tailing bones"—conjure images that make anglers weak in the knees.

For this reason, guides from Cargill Creek and Behring Point make the 30- to 50-minute run down here whenever the weather is good. Moxey Creek, Fever Creek, Fever Cay, and Blue Creek are fished on a regular basis. While these flats are still among our favorites, the bonefish here are educated. Longer casts and excellent line control are required to catch fish, especially the big boys. We recommend using fluoro-carbon leaders at least 10 feet in length.

Beginners fishing this area will do best by wading. Wading Fever Creek on the last half of the falling tide can produce multiple shots at fish in the five- to seven-pound range, and that magical ten-pounder could turn up any time.

Generally, we prefer to fish the beginning of the incoming tide here, and then the last half of the falling tide. Mangrove shorelines and back bays draw high numbers of bonefish to feed on sea crabs. If your timing is just a touch off you won't catch these fish going in. Waiting for them to come out is more effective. There are a number of good ambush points to intercept fish returning to the deeper channels. On bad weather days, days that are dark and windy, we often fish ambush points because the fish are easy to spot as they work their way out of the mangroves.

Many anglers fish Andros specifically for big bonefish. Of course everyone would like to catch a big fish, a fish 10 pounds or better. But pursuing big bonefish is different from just going bonefishing; it requires patience and selectivity. Usually, you fish different types of flats and deeper water when you pursue big bones. It's harder to spot fish in deeper water, and you need to fish a fly that will sink fast; like a Clouser's Minnow. You probably won't see as many fish as you would on a "regular" bonefish flat: you are sacrificing numbers for size.

We often hear anglers at the lodges lamenting the fact that they aren't catching any "big" fish. While it is possible to catch big bones fishing the regular flats, you usually need to make a special effort. When you see a group of fish, don't make an indiscriminate cast. Take a few seconds to scan the group. Make your cast specifically to the biggest fish, and away from the smaller fish. Smaller fish are faster, and often more aggressive, so if you cast near them, they will get your fly first.

A good-sized bonefish.

Sometimes this strategy means not casting at all. If you see smaller fish on a big bonefish flat, don't cast! If you hook one, you can be sure of seeing a 10-pounder a minute or two later while you're playing that smaller fish. We sometimes pass up shots at bonefish in the eight- and nine-pound class while stalking the really big boys.

Keep in mind that big bones are a challenge to catch. We define big bones as 10 to 11 pounds. Giant bones are 12 pounds and up. These fish are their own separate breed. Think of giant bones being as tough to catch as permit and you'll have a true idea of the challenge.

Continuing on, Mangrove Cay forms the southern shoreline of the Middle Bight. The cay is marked by tall green hills that are set back from white sand beaches and jagged black stone and coral outcroppings. Moxey Town is on the northeastern corner of the cay. Known locally as Little Harbour, the town is nestled in groves of coconut palms and rimmed with sandy beaches. Anchorages are available in the cove off Moxey Town and around the government dock, though this area is rough during high north-eastern winds.

Fuel, water, groceries, liquor, and hardware are available in Moxey Town. The Mangrove Cay airport is a two-minute car ride from town. Western Air flies in twice daily from Nassau. Charter air service is available through a number of carriers.

Moxey's Guest House & Bonefishing Lodge is in the center of town, directly across from the harbor. Accommodations are rustic but comfortable. The bar, with its shaded deck, is a relaxing place to enjoy a cold Kalik after fishing.

Set on the waterfront just west of town is the area's premiere bonefishing operation, the Shackleton–owned Mangrove Cay Club. The club can accommodate 16 anglers in spacious air-conditioned suites with porches just steps away from the sea-green water. The large clubhouse includes a dining room, bar, satellite TV, and screened-in deck at water's edge. Manager Liz Bain and chef Iyke Moore are two of the best in the business at keeping guests happy and well fed. Quality flats boats and a reliable professional guide staff round out the package.

The Mangrove Cay location is unequaled for timing any of the Middle Bight tides, or fishing deeper into the Middle Bight, and all the way to the West Side. In addition, the South Bight and Lisbon Creek are only 20 minutes away.

Reef fishing off Moxey Town and Middle Bight Cay is excellent. Local commercial fishermen often supply their northern neighbors with grouper, snapper, barracuda, conch, and lobster. An AUTEC buoy straight out from Gibson Cay is the best dolphin magnet we've ever seen. When the seas are relatively calm, it is common to hook lots of dolphin using mullet patterns, offshore deceivers, or saltwater poppers, and a 10-weight fly rod.

Continuing south of Moxey Town inside the reef is easy for boaters. There are a few coral heads and sand bars but nothing like up north. A good road connects Moxey Town to the southern end of Mangrove Cay at Lisbon Creek. There are several lodging options along this pleasant stretch of coconut palm shaded beaches. The Mangrove Cay Inn is a good spot for anglers looking to fish on their own. The Seascape Inn, offering five cottages with private decks, is a favorite for anglers and non-anglers alike. Owners Mickey and Joan McGowan run a first-class operation. Their restaurant serves delicious fresh seafood and Joan bakes fresh banana bread and muffins for breakfast. Mickey runs a dive program and can book you with top independent guides.

South Andros runs from the South Bight, which includes Lisbon Creek, past the end of the island proper, to the Grassy Cays and Water Cays.

Victoria Point, White Bay Rock, and Flat Rock signal the entrance to the South Bight from the north. The entrance to Lisbon Creek is just inside the South Bight on the northern shore. Dredging has created a deeper channel into Lisbon Creek, where the mail boat and commercial fishermen use the concrete government dock.

The settlement is quiet and charming, shaded by pine and palm trees. The bonefishing in Lisbon Creek is temperamental. When it's on, it's awesome, with lots of fish and big fish. When it's off, you'll catch some smaller fish while trying to figure out what's happening. Either way, spending part of a day in the creek is enjoyable. Miles of mangrove-lined flats and protected bays produce abundant food and shelter for gamefish. Parts of Lisbon Creek are much like Stafford Creek, with high pine-covered hills that provide protection even on gale-force days.

You could spend weeks exploring the back marls that penetrate deep into Mangrove Cay in a maze of small creeks, channels, flats, and lakes. Several channels connect to a main channel leading back to the Middle Bight. These areas hold good numbers of permit at times, though we haven't figured out any pattern for predicting their movements. We have spent some time hiking through mucky mangroves to reach tailing fish in shallow lakes that fill only on the highest tides. These areas are so dense with crabs that you can't help stepping on them as they try to scamper out of your way.

Fishing with a guide is essential in this area, as it is easy to become stranded when the tide is falling. A low incoming tide and the last half of a falling tide will produce the best bonefishing. During higher tidal periods the fish push as far back into the mangroves as they can, which often makes them unreachable.

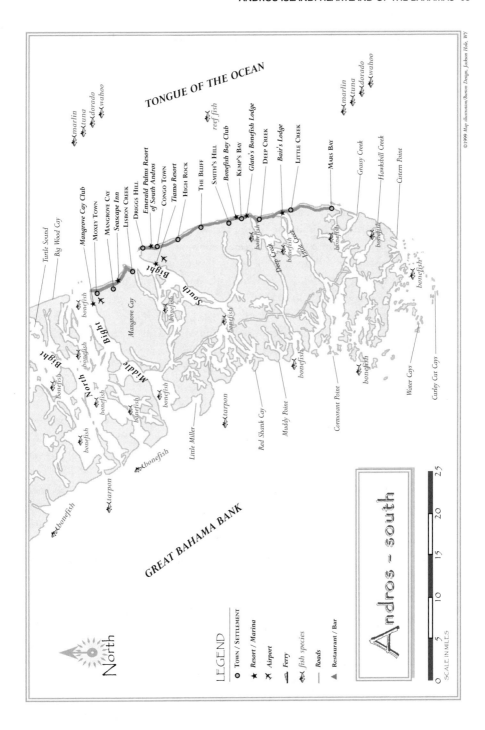

©1999 Map illustration/Barton Design, Jackson Hole, WY

TONGUE OF THE OCEAN

GREAT BAHAMA BANK

North

LEGEND
○ TOWN / SETTLEMENT
★ Resort / Marina
✕ Airport
⤧ Ferry
🐟 fish species
— Roads
▲ Restaurant / Bar

Andros – south

SCALE IN MILES
0   5   10   15   20   25

We haven't spent much time fishing for tarpon in Lisbon Creek, but our moderate success leads us to believe that tarpon migrate through this area on an annual basis, and that smaller resident tarpon are in the creek year round. This is definitely true of the South Bight, especially toward the West Side, where tarpon fishing can be spectacular.

The South Bight doesn't have the reputation of the North and Middle Bights, but don't tell that to the bonefish. Good numbers of fish, plus giant fish roam these coral and sand flats. Many shoreline areas offer excellent wading for tailing fish, though these fish can be extremely spooky. And if you're looking for permit, you'll have a better than average chance of seeing one here.

The South Bight cuts all the way through to the West Side like its northern cousins, exiting at Miller Creek and Red Shank Point. The boat ride to the West Side feels like an adventure into primordial times. The water blends intense shades of blue and green over lush bottom structure. Green, yellow, and gold shorelines narrow as you head west past 30 or so blue holes that can boil with jacks, snappers, and barracuda. If you're looking to catch a variety of fish, you can work the blue holes with deceivers, glass minnows, and Clouser's.

Back on the eastern side of the island, Driggs Hill is situated on the southern point entrance to the South Bight directly below the AUTEC base on Golding Cay.

Recreational boaters would be better served by anchoring around the corner in the South Bight. A five-minute boat ride into the Bight will deliver you to the private dock of Tiamo Resort, an eco-lodge that was carefully placed into the lush landscape and coconut groves and fronted by a stunning white sand beach. Eleven guest cottages with wrap-around porches are built on stilts to take advantage of the cooling breezes. The main lodge—living room, library, bar, dining room—is the gathering place for guests in the mornings and evenings. Delicious fresh cuisine is prepared daily to suit the most discriminating palate.

While Tiamo focuses more on eco-adventures like sea kayaking, snorkeling, diving, hiking, and nature walks, they also arrange guided bonefishing with independent guides.

Boaters can continue on south from Driggs Hill inside the reef using normal precautions. Coconut palms and curvy beaches make up the shoreline. A couple of miles south is the Emerald Palms Resort of South Andros (previously called Emerald Palms By-the-Sea, and the Ritz Beach Resort). Emerald Palms was completely renovated in the fall of 2003. The work included adding 20 luxurious one- and two-bedroom cottages with individual gardens and private decks. The cottages have marble floors, mahogany furniture, and king-size beds. The clubhouse guest rooms run along the blue-tiled pool and out to the beach. A cabana bar overlooks the gin-clear sea. The restaurant serves Bahamian-style breakfasts and lunches and theme-night four-course dinners. Grilled seafood, steaks, and whole lobsters are specialties.

Emerald Palms is suited for anglers who want to fish on their own, or for anglers who will be traveling with non-fishing family and friends. The hotel can book local guides like Stanley Forbes. Congo Town is just another mile down the highway, which was repaved all the way to Mars Bay in 2004. The Long Bay/Congo Town airport is a couple of minutes away by taxi. The airport was renovated and the runway extended in fall 2003. Western Air flies here twice daily from Nassau. The 6,000-foot runway and customs services make this airport convenient for travelers using their own private aircraft and for charter flights.

South of Congo Town, the Long Bay Cays create a comfortable lee anchorage for boaters. Directly inland is the settlement of The Bluff, a fishing community that sits on a stone upthrust overlooking several miles of broad beaches. If you need a post office, clinic, telephone/fax office, or library, The Bluff is home to the South Andros government complex.

Another short run south brings you to Kemp's Bay. An abandoned AUTEC base was the reason for a dredged channel leading into the concrete dock used by the mail boat and a variety of local fishing vessels. Diesel fuel, gas, water, and ice are available, though you should arrange for supplies ahead of time or be prepared to hang out and be patient.

Supplies are best arranged for with Rahming Marine. The Rahming family runs a hardware store, grocery, laundry service, and you might even be able to rent a car from them. Make sure to confirm this in advance.

The Bonefish Bay Club is a short walk from the concrete dock, though most anglers arrive by taxi from the airport. This is a good spot for anglers looking to fish the remote areas of South Andros. The lodge, as of 2004, was under new American management. Rooms, food, and boats were all upgraded at this time. The lodge can accommodate up to 20 anglers.

South of Kemp's Bay is the settlement of Deep Creek and the entrance to the creek itself. Both Deep Creek and Little Creek, about a 10-minute run to the south, offer protected fishing in bad weather.

Bair's Lodge (formerly Bair Bahamas Guest House) is on a private stretch of sand between Little Creek and Deep Creek. The lodge was purchased by Nervous Waters in 2003 and completely renovated for the 2003/2004 season. This is our pick as the best bonefishing operation in South Andros. New boats will be in use for the 2004/2005 season. Eight guests at a time stay in four spacious, delightfully appointed bedrooms. The air-conditioned lodge includes a bar, living room/dining room, satellite TV, Internet access, and a private terrace and beach fronted by a productive bonefish flat. The food and service are outstanding. Bair's well-trained guides meet anglers on the beach each morning. The wade fishing throughout South Andros is some of the best on the planet.

South of Little Creek the barrier reef turns out away from land around High Point Cay. Numerous sand bars dot the green water. On land, the road ends in the serene settlement of Mars Bay. The bay is really a blue hole encircled by shallow light-colored flats and bars. At times, permit feed around the bars on a high tide.

Grassy Creek is a short run south of Mars Bay. The creek, which connects to Little Creek, is a beautiful wilderness bonefish area. Schools of fish numbering in the thousands move in and out of this area throughout the year.

Bair's Lodge.

Grassy Creek Cays is just offshore. Good anchorages are available for boaters and the snorkeling is sensational, though you have to pay attention for sharks. The cays are surrounded by flats that are easy to wade and covered with aggressive bonefish that have rarely seen a fly. The reef fishing is world-class. Once you have a chum line going you will be amazed at the numbers and variety of fish you can catch with flies or conventional gear.

Hawksbill Creek lies farther south along the coast and is another bonefish haven. Flats boats can maneuver in over the shallow sand bar at the entrance on the right tides but careful planning is necessary to avoid becoming stranded.

Jack Fish Channel is at the very southern tip of the island. Miles of wadable sand flats, little creeks, channels, and islets create a home for schools of bonefish that can color acres of flats a fine shimmering silver. These masses of fish swim in waves that ripple the water across a hundred square yards. The fish in these schools average one to three pounds.

For bigger fish we work the deeper channel edges and the many sand bars that drop off into turquoise cuts. On occasion we have seen permit when pursuing the bigger bones.

This habitat continues around the tip of the island, then up along the West Side to the Water Cays. This is the area where Stanley Bain located his Grassy Cays Bonefish Camp, which has now been closed for years.

Shallow water, sand bars, and tricky varying tides are a hazard to boaters in this area. We have found that published tide charts are not reliable for navigating here, and even less reliable for predicting fish behavior. Stanley Bain and his guides spent years exploring and fishing this area before they became comfortable with the unique tides and currents on the southwest side of the island. Consider this region to be unexplored territory and use the appropriate precautions.

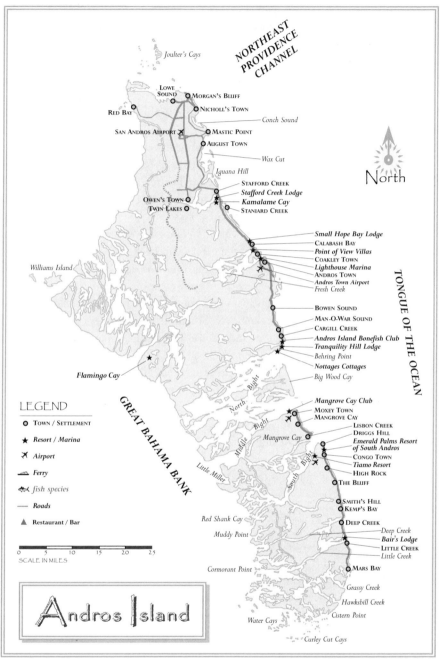

Joulter's Cays

NORTHEAST PROVIDENCE CHANNEL

LOWE SOUND
MORGAN'S BLUFF
RED BAY
NICHOLL'S TOWN
Conch Sound
SAN ANDROS AIRPORT
MASTIC POINT
AUGUST TOWN
Wax Cut
Iguana Hill
STAFFORD CREEK
Stafford Creek Lodge
Kamalame Cay
OWEN'S TOWN
TWIN LAKES
STANIARD CREEK

North

Williams Island

Small Hope Bay Lodge
CALABASH BAY
Point of View Villas
COAKLEY TOWN
Lighthouse Marina
ANDROS TOWN
Andros Town Airport
Fresh Creek

TONGUE OF THE OCEAN

BOWEN SOUND
MAN-O-WAR SOUND
CARGILL CREEK
Andros Island Bonefish Club
Tranquility Hill Lodge
Behring Point
Nottages Cottages
Big Wood Cay

Flamingo Cay

North Bight

GREAT BAHAMA BANK

LEGEND

◎ TOWN / SETTLEMENT
★ Resort / Marina
✈ Airport
🚢 Ferry
🐟 fish species
— Roads
▲ Restaurant / Bar

0   5   10   15   20   25
SCALE IN MILES

Mangrove Cay Club
MOXEY TOWN
MANGROVE CAY
LISBON CREEK
DRIGGS HILL
Mangrove Cay
Emerald Palms Resort of South Andros
CONGO TOWN
Tiamo Resort
HIGH ROCK
THE BLUFF

Middle Bight

Little Miller

South Bight

Red Shank Cay
Muddy Point

SMITH'S HILL
KEMP'S BAY
DEEP CREEK
Deep Creek
Bair's Lodge
LITTLE CREEK
Little Creek
MARS BAY

Cormorant Point

Andros Island

Grassy Creek
Hawksbill Creek
Cistern Point
Water Cays
Curley Cut Cays

©1999 Map illustration/Burton Design, Jackson Hole, WY

The West Side of Andros is uninhabited. Special attention must be given to the tides when fishing or navigating this massive area. This attention must include the understanding that tides here can vary with weather conditions more than other areas due to the vast stretches of shallow water. An uncountable number of creeks, sand bars, and back bays compose the region along the coast from the Water Cays north to Miller Creek.

During windy conditions, especially when winds blow from the west, the water along the coast turns milky white. Sight fishing during these conditions is impossible and boating is dangerous.

The only way to fish this region is by enduring long boat rides from South Andros lodges or longer runs from the Bights lodges. What about a motherboat? The Bahamian government has set specific rules for floatplane and motherboat fishing throughout the Bahamas. It is strictly illegal to fish with a commercial floatplane or motherboat outfitter without using Bahamian guides.

There are only a handful of guides who are qualified to take anglers into this area. The fishing for bonefish and tarpon in the creeks and back bays is excellent but it is easy to become lost or stranded by an outgoing tide. For do-it-yourself experienced boaters and anglers, the use of sea kayaks deployed from a motherboat is a good method for fishing this region. Sea kayaks give you mobility in any tidal situation and flexibility if you make a navigational mistake. Sea kayakers and others traveling inland should be aware that the doctor flies and no-see-ums can be fierce when the wind is down, or any time in the spring and summer.

The Miller Creek and Little Miller Creek bays can produce good tarpon fishing on the proper tides. Miles of white sand flats that average four to six feet in depth are home to tarpon that run between 50 and 120 pounds. These are resident fish that swim between the creeks and the outer banks on a regular basis. Whenever water temperatures reach 75°F (24°C) or higher, these tarpon roam the flats. Larger migratory tarpon running up to 200 pounds are present from May through October.

Miller Creek pours out onto the West Side flats in the center of a huge bay with Red Shank Point an obvious landmark to the south. Several other smaller creeks enter the bay and all are tarpon magnets. Sea turtles are abundant in this area. They commonly roll on the surface, which can trick you into thinking they're tarpon if you don't get a good look. Remember that tarpon like to follow land and bottom contours. They are also creatures of habit and these habits are influenced by wind direction. We prefer to fish lee shorelines, poling into the incoming tide.

Another large bay is north of Miller Creek. Several other creeks feed this area as well. We have only fished here a few times but have caught tarpon on each occasion. The long mud bank and mangrove shoreline continuing north is home to a parade of bonefish and an occasional permit.

At the end of this shoreline is a wide mangrove-covered point, which signals another massive white-bottomed bay. Little Miller Creek is at the back of the bay. Four other significant creeks feed these flats also. Fishing either the north or south shoreline is the best way to play the odds on an incoming tide.

Kim on a flat on West Side of Andros.

North of Little Miller is the expansive opening to the Middle Bight. Deep blue channels cut into white sand flats that are some of the most arresting in the Bahamas. Running out here in a flats boat on a calm day is an ultimate thrill. The vast serene ocean melts into the sky. You could be the only people in the world. Imagine complete peace. Daydreams blossom. Thousands of bonefish and tarpon roam on every tide.

Miles of white sand flats, hard enough to wade in some places, run along the low limestone, coral, and mangrove shorelines on the way north to Spanish Wells and Yellow Cay.

Spanish Wells and Yellow Cay form their own complex mini-ecosystem. This area is easily reached for day fishing from Behring Point or Cargill Creek. Hundreds of cays and many creeks throughout Spanish Wells connect to sand and grass flats, many of which are protected on windy days. On calm days, tarpon roll in the deeper bays and cuts.

Yellow Cay draws high numbers of bonefish, but the real fun here is hunting big bones. Fish in the 7- to 10-pound range feed along the shorelines year round. When the wind blows hard the water on some of these flats turns a milky yellow color that can make seeing fish difficult.

Little and Big Loggerhead Creeks lie to the north. Both creeks connect the North Bight to the West Side. Little Loggerhead is a straight shot between high mangrove banks. When the tide is moving this creek is like a ripping river. On bad weather days, this is a pleasant place to anchor up and blind cast for a variety of species. Jacks, mackerel, sharks, tarpon, and barracuda are usually in the creek. We like to blind cast surface poppers for jacks, sharks, and barracuda. For mackerel, we usually go with sardina or glass minnow patterns.

Outside Big Loggerhead is a massive sand flat that curves to the north away from the shoreline. Water depths average 8 feet and dip to 12 feet in places. We've fished

Flamingo Cay floatplane.

this outside flat on numerous occasions when hundreds of rolling tarpon turn the water surface silver.

A quarter of a mile north is a sand and coral point where giant tarpon congregate between May and October. In spite of how good the tarpon fishing can be in this area, it is not one of our favorite places because of the boat traffic. This section of the West Side is the most heavily fished, though "heavily fished" is certainly a relative term in this case.

The Andros Island Bonefish Club and the Mangrove Cay Club send guides out this way almost every day. We can't blame them because the bonefishing along the shorelines all the way to Cabbage Creek is sensational. Fish swim in waves along the sand and coral banks. Double hook-ups are common. When the wind is from the northeast, and you're fishing an incoming tide, you can count on high numbers of bones with fish averaging close to five pounds.

We consider Cabbage Creek the practical cut-off point for day trips from Behring Point, Cargill Creek, and Mangrove Cay lodges. Even in a fast boat, this is at least an hour-and-a-half run one way.

The territory from Cabbage Creek to Williams Island is wild and pristine. Boaters must use extreme caution, including flats boaters, as shallow sand banks extend out from the island for miles. The water here is so clear and mesmerizing that you can see virtually every scale on every fish. When you catch a bonefish, it is striking how its blue fins contrast with the silky white bottom. The outer sand banks along this coast hold some of the largest bonefish we have ever seen, including some fish pushing 20 pounds.

This area is also the home of Flamingo Cay, a unique fishing and hunting lodge owned by Charlie Bethel. Tucked into a small creek at the back of a sprawling bay called Wide Open, Flamingo Cay accommodates six guests per week. Guests fly into the lodge from Nassau via private floatplane. You can choose a fishing package only, or a hunting and fishing combo. Along with sensational bonefishing, tarpon fishing can also be outstanding. Bird shooting is available inland with access via the lodge's airboats.

Food, service, and the Bethel hospitality are memorable. Many guests book the same week year after year. We recommend that you book this location a year in advance.

Continuing north, Williams Island is often used as an anchorage for private yachts. The owners of these yachts hire Bahamian guides to explore this incomparable fishery. Charlie Neymour, Frankie Neymour, and Barry Neymour are guides who have fished here extensively with yacht owners. The numbers of bonefish around Williams Island and in the nearby creeks can be overwhelming and, surprisingly, there is a high percentage of fish over eight pounds. Permit also inhabit the deeper flats around the island in good numbers.

The area between Williams Island and Red Bay is the substance of a saltwater angler's dreams. High concentrations of bonefish, permit, and tarpon make this grand slam territory. Countless creeks and back bays cut into the shoreline for miles.

Guides from Stafford Creek Lodge and Kamalame Cay trailer their boats to Red Bay then fish south toward Williams Island. Independent guides Benry Smith and Herman Bain (Bain was the head guide at Kamalame for years) also fish out of Red Bay, with their clients staying in Morgan's Bluff, Nicholl's Town, or Conch Sound.

Fishing Highlights

Traditionally, the best times to fish Andros are March through late June, then again in October and November. You can have quality fishing in December, January, and February, but these months have a greater chance of suffering through cold fronts that can bring high winds, cloud cover, and chilly temperatures. July, August, and September are the main tropical storm and hurricane months.

With due consideration given to the so-called best times for good fishing and good weather, we'd like to say that all saltwater flats fishing is at the whim of Mother Nature. The past few years have seen crazy weather patterns as the rule, with January calm and beautiful and April super windy. The weather can be good or bad any time. We have given up any attempts at predictions. The weather is the weather. Learn to deal with it. If you are prepared for any condition, you will feel particularly blessed and appreciative on those gorgeous calm days.

So back to January and February. If these are the only two months you can go flats fishing, Andros is a great place to take your shot if you're hunting big fish. More double-digit bonefish are landed in February than any other month. Also keep in mind that Andros covers a vast fishing area. There are miles of creeks, especially on the northeast coast, where anglers can fish in relative calm even on the windiest of days.

Remember too that the term "cold front" is a relative term. While a cold front can plunge air temperatures into the high 40s for a day or so, a tropical climate sets the tone. Andros temperatures average 78°F (26°C), with daytime temperatures usually in the 80s. Average water temperature ranges from 70°F (21°C) in January to 90°F (32°C) in August.

The Andros fishery is one of the most varied on earth, yet it can be analyzed with some general rules in mind, as can most other Bahamian fisheries. Flats that drop off into ocean-side areas or deeper creeks and channels tend to fish better on the incoming tide. These flats are also better in poor weather conditions, especially when air temperatures drop or rise dramatically. Interior flats and creeks lined with mangroves are usually better on falling tides and in more stable weather conditions.

Kim, West Side, Andros.

We prefer to fish spring tides in Andros during April, May, and June. This is a low tidal time of the year. The spring tides produce stronger currents and greater changes in water depths. This allows more bonefish to move onto the flats and to penetrate deeper into remote areas in search of sea crabs. We prefer to fish neap tides in October and November because these are the highest tidal periods. Spring tides during the fall can be so high that there is virtually no low tide during the day. This means bonefish can hide miles back into the mangroves where they become inaccessible. These tidal times and preferences apply to most other islands throughout the Bahamas.

Fish are creatures of habit. You need to be observant and patient for maximum success. Make notes in a journal, then try to make predictions about a particular area and a particular tide. This kind of game is lots of fun, and extremely satisfying when your predictions turn into fishing success.

If you spend some time on Andros, or any other Bahamian island, you will discover a variety of flats, and each must be viewed as distinct when piecing together your angling strategy. If you are a freshwater angler, think of the flats as being like big rivers, small rivers, streams, spring creeks, or lakes, each with its own characteristics and tactical demands.

Different types of flats include ocean flats; reef flats or transition flats between reefs; interior flats; mangrove flats that extend from land or cays; and island or cay flats surrounded by deep water. Each type of flat can have different types of bottoms.

Ocean flats tend to have hard sand or coral bottoms that can be waded. The White Bight area, for example, has a mixture of hard sand and pulverized coral sprinkled with brittle crunchy coral. This habitat is loaded with shrimp and crabs. On an incoming tide, this area offers some of the best wade fishing for tailing bonefish you can imagine.

Reef or transitional flats are usually hard-bottomed also, but they can be very difficult to wade due to uneven contours and sharp protruding coral. Contours, troughs, holes, and little caves are safe havens for baitfish and crustaceans. Larger gamefish like jacks, snappers, and mackerel are lured to these areas on a regular basis.

Interior flats tend to have soft mud or ooze bottoms, and can be impossible to wade without sinking up to your hips in goo. These flats are best fished from a poled skiff. Interior flats in the Middle Bight area are home to good numbers of double-digit bonefish that punch fist-sized holes in the bottom while routing for shrimp and crabs.

Mangrove flats are usually fed by creeks and can be soft or hard-bottomed. The key to fishing these flats is to figure out the path bonefish will take in and out. This can be difficult on an incoming tide. On a falling tide, however, you can set up ambush points that can yield amazing results.

The importance of water temperature can't be emphasized enough. It is the key to finding fish. It is also the ticket to determining when to pursue larger bonefish. Larger bonefish either like, or can tolerate, colder water than smaller fish. This is a primary reason why the largest bonefish in Andros are consistently caught in February and March.

Water depth is another important factor. Bonefish like to move and feed at a constant water depth. They will congregate in pockets, channels, and creeks waiting for the incoming tide to reach the proper depth before they move onto a flat. Conversely, bonefish will wait for a falling tide to reach a specific depth before moving out of the mangroves. We have seen large bones wait until the water barely covers their shoulders before making a dash for deeper channels.

Like trout in streams, bonefish are drawn to structure. Andros possesses thousands of mangrove-lined or coral-lined white-bottomed bays. These bays are usually linked by coral-covered points. Count on finding bonefish near each point and at the beginning and end of each bay. The bones will be hunting large shrimp and a variety of crabs so consider matching your fly to these food sources.

Tides influence flats fishing more than any other type of fishing. Tides dictate where and when fish will be and vary greatly from area to area. It is vital to be observant. You cannot rely on fish to be on the same flat at the same time each day because tides move forward approximately 50 minutes every day. Also, wind and current conditions vary as does water depth and volume. Remember this when you want to return to a place where you experienced good fishing, but your guide decides to take you somewhere else. There is a reason for this. The guide understands the tides and water temperatures.

Most areas of the Bahamas, including Andros, have two high tides and two low tides, semidiurnal tides, during a day. The moon is the biggest influence on tides and its relationship to the sun is also significant. This relationship produces higher highs and lower lows at specific times of year. As mentioned before the highest highs of the year in Andros are in October.

Spring tides occur with the full moon and new moon, when the sun and moon are in direct alignment with the earth. This alignment causes higher tides than neap tides, which are first- and third-quarter periods, with the moon positioned at right angles to the alignment of the earth and sun.

Tides rotate on a two-week cycle. This means fishing conditions on a given flat will be approximately the same every two weeks. Opposite fishing conditions will exist on a given flat in one week. Every day one high tide is higher than the other high and one low tide lower than the other. If you can make these distinctions, and note game-fish behavioral differences, you can increase your fishing success.

Barometric pressure and wind are other significant influences on the tides. High pressure inhibits tidal flow onto the flats. Wind direction, speed, duration, and fetch (the distance over which the wind blows) all affect the tidal ranges. Charlie Smith believes that barometric pressure is more influential on bonefish behavior than water temperature. Smith is convinced that low summertime pressure is a bigger factor in driving fish off the flats than high water temperatures. Smith has proven his theory for more than 30 years by consistently catching fish throughout the summer season, even in the middle of the day, when no other guides will venture onto the flats.

Remember, too, that tides do not rise and fall at a uniform rate. There is usually a slack period at both the top and bottom of a tidal change. It is common for a two- to three-hour period of either a rising or falling tide to produce the best fishing, while the other hours are slower. In Andros this slower fishing scenario can often be avoided by running east or west through the Bights.

Wind and weather are part of the habitat and creators of the fishing conditions. Bonefish are schizophrenic when it comes to the weather. They "smell" weather coming according to the Andros guides and we have come to believe this over the years. It might be a calm sunny day but the bonefish won't touch a perfectly presented fly. They spook two hundred feet out. When bonefish smell bad weather they move from the interior flats to the outside ocean flats and then to deeper water. Conversely, when you see bonefish streaming into the Bights you can bet good weather is coming and will stay for a while. When you catch bonefish moving in expectation of good weather, you can experience fishing beyond compare.

We prefer at least a little airflow. The fish tend to be less spooky and a breeze can keep the bugs down. Bonefish tend to swim into the wind. A good guide takes advantage of this phenomenon and sets up anglers to cast downwind. On larger wadable flats, however, bonefish will disperse in ways that make casting into the wind the best option. Understanding changing conditions and remaining flexible in your strategy is a key to success.

Baitfish and other food sources don't fight the tides, they go with the flow. All predatory fish know this. Barracuda, for example, are great ambush artists. The strength of a tidal current is important in analyzing how gamefish will pursue their food. Stronger currents carry food scents farther and faster and bring in more and larger bonefish and permit. Strong tidal currents correspond to spring tides while lesser currents are present with neap tides.

The most common flats foods include mantis shrimp, snapping shrimp, swimming shrimp, grass shrimp, swimming crabs, sea crabs, mud and stone crabs, clams, mussels, and gobies. Snapping shrimp are more common in Florida and the northern Bahamas, but these burrowing miniature lobster look-alikes are also found throughout Andros. Clouser's Minnows and Borski's Swimming Shrimp are effective in imitating these food sources in deeper water. For skinny water, we prefer a Blind Gotcha, Bonefish Special, Greg's Flats Fly, or Spawning Shrimp.

Grass shrimp are inclined toward areas of turtle grass and higher than normal salinity common to Grand Bahama and Abaco. There are few areas like this in Andros, though these shrimp do like to hang around mangrove roots where larger bonefish actively seek them out. Remember this when fishing for the monster bones in the Middle Bight.

There are more than 60 species of mantis shrimp in the Caribbean. They prefer to burrow in mud and sand bottoms. In Andros, mantis shrimp grow to three inches in length and look like small lobsters with their sharp claws and fantails. Large bonefish often cruise in deeper water, three to six feet, over these types of flats. We like to fish heavy lead-eyed Gotcha Clouser's Minnows or Bunny Gotchas because they sink quickly and kick up mud when bounced off the bottom.

Crabs live primarily in shallow water habitat and are a key reason bonefish risk moving into skinny water. Fly imitations need to be the right size and color. We prefer small Tan Yarn Crabs for fishing tailing fish on the ocean flats. It's an exhilarating sight to see a huge bonefish attack a Yarn Crab with reckless abandon in ankle-deep water.

Swimming crabs and sea crabs are the most common varieties on Andros, with the blue crab the most common of these. Blues are very aggressive and will defend themselves against attack. Bonefish are used to being pricked by crab claws as they subdue this food source. This explains why a missed hook set that sticks the bonefish will usually not scare the bonefish away. The fish will actually become more eager to eat the fly a second or third time.

Mud and stone crabs are also prolific in Andros and throughout the Bahamas. They live in the intertidal coral areas that are mixed with mud and sand. Bonefish crave these crabs, and will eat all they can in a given area. You should never underestimate a bonefish's ability to reach a crab on dry land either, something we've seen on several occasions.

Gobies are the most common flats baitfish in the Bahamas. They prefer intertidal waters with sand, mud, or coral bottoms. Their ventral fins form a suction-like disc that allows them to hold to any stationary bottom, which comes in handy during strong tidal fluctuations. Gobies can also live out of the water for several hours. It is common to see them lying on wet sand flats at low tide.

Needlefish are ubiquitous on Andros, and a favorite food for big bonefish. Pipefish and sea horses are found in the few areas of grassy bottoms. A sea horse is really a curled pipefish with a slanted head. Pipefish and sea horses move slowly and are easy prey when their chameleon-like attempts at camouflage fail.

Mollusks include snails, clams, mussels, squid, and octopus. Andros has plenty of each. When bonefish or permit feed on mussels and clams they can become very finicky. Squid and octopus are also favorite foods for offshore gamefish including dorado, wahoo, and billfish.

White worms are another key part of Andros bonefish diets. Bonefish really focus on this food source in May, October, and November. Why? We have no idea. This is just a behavior we have observed over the years, and our fishing success improved dramatically because of the observation. Successful flats guides and anglers are good students of gamefish behavior, and are always ready to adapt to a given situation.

A unique feature about Andros is the character of the Bights. There is always a high and low tide phase somewhere, and most tidal stages in between. For example, when the tide is at its highest on the east coast, it is at its lowest on the West Side. As a boat progresses from east to west, the tide is at varying stages of rising and falling.

For anglers looking for specific tidal conditions this is an exciting situation. With the aid of a fast boat, anglers can fish an incoming tide most of the day, or a falling tide, or any stage of the tide that seems desirable.

One of our favorite fishing day options is to stalk tarpon on the last half of the incoming tide on the West Side in the morning, then dash to the east coast to fish the incoming tide on the ocean flats for big bonefish. In this scenario, we have experienced days in which we battled tarpon over 100 pounds, then bonefish over 10 pounds. This strategy has also put us in position to finish the day going for permit on a high ocean-side tide. Unfortunately for us, the huge Andros permit have never been hungry for our flies on a day we had success with tarpon and bonefish. So . . . we're still pursuing that elusive Andros grand slam.

The scenario above is just one of a countless number of daily strategies that can be pursued in Andros for a variety of species. In choosing a strategy, remember that the time of day a tide occurs is more important than the strength of the tidal flow. In Andros it is easy to make the time of day factor work, but at most saltwater flats destinations this is not the case. Don't just plan a trip based on a spring tide or neap tide. Consider the time of day the tides occur, too.

Another feature unique to Andros is the amount of fresh water that influences food sources, water salinity, and the migratory patterns of the gamefish. Countless miles of creeks penetrate the landmass of Andros from every point of the compass. These creeks sometimes turn yellow with fresh water after a heavy rain, which creates additional habitat for crabs and shrimp. After several days of tidal changes the scent of these crabs lures bonefish and other gamefish deep into the backcountry. These areas also become the breeding grounds for baitfish and bonefish.

The relationship of the nursery areas in Andros to other islands, and the overall Andros fishery, is not well understood. Through continued observation, however, we have been able to predict some migratory patterns and spawning behaviors for tarpon and bonefish. These predictions are based on specific areas at specific times of year. The West Side of the island has been the focus of much of our attention, especially in the vast areas south of the Middle Bight. Over the years we have observed a "bonefish highway" that can literally be a traffic jam of fish. When you reach this highway at the right tide at the right time of year, it can be a fishing experience you will never forget.

A final note on the unique features of Andros deals with the myriad of land-locked lakes. Many of these lakes—more than 30 are at least three miles long—have

Guide Andy Smith with a barracuda caught in one of the creeks on the West Side.

never been fished or explored. Others were fished 30 or 40 years ago but not since. Duck hunters have enjoyed great sport on these lakes over the years without ever wetting line.

Some of the lakes have a high salinity level while others are brackish or completely fresh. Rain changes the salinity on a regular basis. Access to most of these waters is difficult, though old logging roads come to within several hundred yards of several of the northern bodies of water.

Our explorations have been mostly on foot, hiking 30 minutes to 2 hours through mangroves, broken coral, and muck to reach a given lake. At times the rewards have been spectacular. Can you imagine wade fishing for 100-pound tarpon, for cubera snappers that go 30 to 100 pounds, for voracious jacks, and for permit?

File this away in the back of your mind as one of the last frontiers of saltwater fly-fishing. And keep in touch with us for continued updates. Charlie Neymour—the friend and guide who has led us on most of our lake adventures—has plans to offer anglers and hunters exclusive packages into this unique wilderness.

It is no surprise that bonefish are the number one flats gamefish in Andros and throughout the Bahamas. The overall coral, mud, and sand composition of the flats in Andros inspire bonefish to forage for food. As bonefish move over these flats they exhibit a rooting behavior, and they are often seeking out specific foods such as crabs, clams, and mussels. Bonefish prefer these bottom dwelling mollusks and crustaceans but will pounce on flies that look nothing like their preferred foods. Still, matching flies to food sources is important in terms of size, silhouette, and color, just as it is in trout fishing.

The Middle Bight is a classic area where dense crab populations live in shallow water along the banks and mangroves. When you roam the wadable flats around Fever Cay on a low tide you'll see hundreds of crabs scampering through puddles between glistening humps of coral and sand. A small Tan Yarn Crab is our fly of choice in this area.

At the southern tip of the island there are many square miles of wadable flats that are home to mantis shrimp. These creatures are not easy to spot but you can find them if you do some digging on flats that have gone dry at low tide. If you only fish one fly here it should be a translucent-colored shrimp pattern with rubber legs.

While we've seen bonefish on the flats in 66°F (19°C), water, 70°F (21°C), is the minimum we prefer. We fish the outside ocean flats when the water is in the cooler ranges. As water warms, between 75°F (24°C) and 85°F (29°C), the interior flats really turn on. Fish pour into the Bights from the east and west and appear out of the deeper creeks and channels. Above 86°F (30°C) fish usually move back to deeper water or to the

Stephen with bonefish, while Charlie Neymour looks on.

ocean-side flats. In May and June it is common to see huge areas of mud in the deeper channels inside the bights. These muds are made by huge schools of bonefish tearing up the bottom in search of food.

Oxygen levels are also an integral part of this temperature factor. The greater the tidal flow that exists, the more oxygen the water carries. This is another reason we prefer spring tides from April through June, and that we focus on ocean flats in hot weather.

The color of a bonefish varies depending on location. Outside ocean fish have dark-green backs that sometimes appear black in the water. These fish usually swim over darker coral bottoms and they are super-strong. These dark-green fish will often rip off 200-plus yards of backing on their first run. Concentrations of these fish live along the eastern coast. Some of our favorite areas include Long Bay Cay, White Bight, Big Wood Cay, the mouths of the Middle and South Bights, and the flats between Grassy Creek and Cistern Point.

Inside fish, fish that spend most of their time in the Bights and creeks, are light in color, ranging from tan to a silvery white. These fish are much more difficult to see than their ocean cousins. Fish on the West Side have this color scheme also. The West Side is similar to an endless inside flat—and just a small part of the Great Bahama Bank—because of its shallow depth and bottom character which is a mixture of white gooey mud and hard coral sand.

Spotting bonefish is a developed skill, just like casting and line control. Total concentration is required. If you are observant, you can learn to spot slight changes in color or hints of movement that are the keys to developing your "bonefish vision."

Spotting bonefish over light-colored bottoms is much easier than seeing them over dark turtle grass. Since most bottoms in Andros are light in color it is an ideal place for beginning saltwater anglers. When you focus on the bottom you should look for signs of feeding. A puff of mud will indicate that a bonefish is nearby. Look for a flash, a change of color, a sign of movement. In shallow water, especially on calm days, you can see surface signs like nervous water, wakes, or actual bonefish tails and fins.

Tune yourself in to the world of flats gamefish. Allow yourself to be absorbed by it and your fishing success will improve dramatically.

Resident tarpon are plentiful year-round. The best fishing is weather dependent with calmer weather providing ideal conditions. Tarpon will first appear on the flats when the water temperature reaches 75°F (24°C). A degree or two colder and the fish will stay in the creeks or on the outside banks. This minimum temperature is usually reached at some point most months of the year. A couple of warm, calm days in a row is all it takes.

A common misconception about the Andros tarpon fishery is that the fish are just in the creeks. Well, it's true—there are tarpon in the creeks. Anglers can blind fish for them any time. You can also sight fish to rolling fish, but Andros tarpon also move across vast stretches of white sand flats on most tides. You can see them swimming hundreds of yards away as you would in the Florida Keys. If you want to experience some of the best tarpon fly-fishing anywhere, you should consider booking a top independent guide in May, June, or July.

Remember that good fishing is based on the number of opportunities that are available. Good catching depends on an angler's ability and some luck. Many anglers are not yet prepared to hook and then land a tarpon on a fly. Beginning tarpon anglers need to work their way up the skill ladder. Be happy when a fish explodes on your fly. Be ecstatic when you first feel your hook tight against the tarpon's mouth. Go nuts when the fish jumps. Don't despair when the hook flies free and your line goes slack. If anything, jumping and losing a tarpon should make you more determined when the next opportunity strikes.

Our perception of the permit fishery continues to evolve. While fishing central Andros, the outside flats along the east coast, or the Bights, you might see an occasional permit. These areas would not be high on anyone's list of hot permit spots, however.

Sure, there are places like Black Rock and Sunken Rock where you can count on seeing a few permit on the high

A twin catch—enough to put a smile on any face! (Brian O'Keefe)

tide in calm conditions. There are some spots on the West Side and in the South Bight where you should have your permit rod rigged. But if permit are your main quarry, you'll be better off fishing somewhere else.

The best areas for permit are from the Joulter's Cays to Red Bay and on down to Williams Island. At times you can find good concentrations of this most elusive and prized gamefish. An average fish is 20 pounds, with 35- to 40-pound monsters not uncommon. The prime months are May through August.

Snapper fishing is a lot of fun, something we enjoy on most trips. Mutton snapper is the real prize here. March and April are the only months you can count on for concentrations of fish in shallow water. Bonefish tackle and flies work well, with our favorite fly being a Pink Clouser's Minnow. Mangrove snappers are ubiquitous year round, and as their name implies, they concentrate around mangroves, especially in the deeper pockets around the root systems. They also like to hang out in the coral pockets off the points of connecting bays, and in the many creeks with their yellowtail cousins. If the weather is tough, and bonefish are scarce, you can still have a blast catching mangrove snappers that run up to five pounds.

Barracuda can turn a slow day of fishing into a fast-paced one. These sleek lightning-fast fish deal with cold weather better than most other gamefish. The winter months are especially good. We often carry a rod rigged just for 'cuda. Four to six inches of wire tippet is all you need to add to a seven-foot leader. While sight-fishing is what we enjoy most, blind fishing the many creeks throughout the island can produce large barracuda as well as blacktip and lemon sharks.

Sharks are exciting gamefish, and are often overlooked by fly anglers. These predatory fish prefer warm weather and warm water. When water temperatures are below 70°F (21°C) sharks will stay in deeper areas. When temperatures warm to over 75°F (24°C) on the flats you'll see lots of lemon and blacktip sharks cruising the shallows. When it comes to a wild, acrobatic fish, a blacktip shark rates with the best of them.

The Tongue of the Ocean pushes in along the eastern shore, dropping to depths of six thousand feet along the world's third largest barrier reef. The reef extends for over 140 miles and has only a few openings for boats that are not blocked by the inner reef. Just off the outer reef are fertile fishing grounds for marlin, sailfish, dolphin, tuna, and wahoo.

A huge barracuda; when the bonefishing is slow, 'cudas will often take up the slack. (Brian O'Keefe)

Minutes away over the inner reef, sharks, barracuda, amberjack, mackerel, grouper, snapper, and rockfish can be found in abundance.

Grouper fishing peaks in January. Conventional angling gear works best in deeper water around the reefs and drop-offs. Prime time for wahoo is January through March. These greyhounds of the sea are best pursued by trolling with conventional gear along the outside edges of the Tongue of the Ocean reefs. By using chum, it is possible to take a wahoo on a fly during this period. Wahoo run between 30 and 80 pounds here. Tackle should include a 12-weight fly rod and single-strand wire shock tippet.

Fishing for sails and marlin begins in March, with May through July being the prime months. There are few fly-fishing savvy crews so most billfishing is accomplished by trolling with conventional gear. If you have experience fly-fishing for billfish, you might be able to get in some shots during June and July with traditional teasing methods.

April through July is the prime period for dorado (dolphin). Fly anglers can experience sensational action around the naval buoys off the eastern coast. It is not uncommon to hook-up 10 to 20 dorado in a day on a variety of surface poppers and mullet patterns fished on 10- to 12-weight fly rods. When fish are around the buoys you can either blind cast or pick out specific fish and sight cast. Traditional trolling methods are also effective along the reef.

Mackerel fishing with an 8-weight fly rod is good throughout the spring over the reefs. Using chum to get these voracious feeders into a boiling frenzy is the best method. Remember to use wire tippet against their razor-sharp teeth. Best flies include glass minnow patterns, Abel anchovies, and Carter Andrews' "Snak Pak" series.

Amberjack are one of our favorite reef fish. These ferocious fighters are best pursued with a 12-weight rod and at least 60-pound shock tippet. Using chum is the best method for luring amberjack into casting range. A few fish show up in February, but March is when the fishing turns on; prime conditions usually last through the summer.

Allison tuna also show up in February, with better numbers beginning in March and running through June. Blackfin numbers increase in May and reach their peak in June and July. Bluefin numbers are fair in April and good in May. Bonito start running in May, with peak numbers in June and July.

Optional Activities

Small Hope Bay Lodge, Tiamo Resort, Kamalame Cay, and Emerald Palms of South Andros are the best lodging options for visitors looking for non-fishing adventure activities. Small Hope is Andros' diving and snorkeling headquarters. Experienced divers from around the world travel here for the "Over the Wall" and blue-hole dives featured at this resort. Small Hope is also an excellent choice for beginning divers, for people looking for certification, and for snorkelers.

Activities programs at Small Hope, Tiamo, and Kamalame include sailing, windsurfing, sea kayaking, diving, snorkeling, swimming, eco-tours, biking, hiking, and wilderness camping. Andros should be considered a remote location with an inspiring expanse of pristine, unexplored territory. If you're looking for any kind of shopping, nightlife, golf, or other related activities, this is not the place for you.

Lodging, Guides, and Services

Featured Lodges

Tranquility Hill Fishing Lodge

Behring Point Owned and operated by the Neymours and Mackeys, this comfortable lodge has air-conditioned rooms with private baths, a relaxed dining room, separate bar with satellite TV, and an outdoor deck overlooking the North Bight. Wadable flats are right out front. Ivan Neymour runs the fishing program, which is one of the best in the Bahamas. Guides are flexible in their fishing hours, meaning you will fish the best tides at the appropriate times. Fishing areas include the North, Middle, and South Bights, outside ocean flats from Bowen Sound to Moxey Town, and the vast West Side region. Bahamian charm and hospitality are in abundant supply here. Guests are made to feel like part of the family and the food is exceptionally good.

Season: October through June.

Suitable For: Anglers only.

What's Included: Air-conditioned room with private bath, three meals daily, guided fishing, taxes. Trips of any length are available.

Not Included: Airfare to/from Andros Town, taxi transfers, alcoholic beverages, gratuities, fishing tackle.

Pricing: $$

Contact: Reservations and information, telephone/fax, 242-368-4132 or 866-963-7870.

Internet: www.tranquilityhill.com

E-mail: info@oregonrivers.com

Nottages Cottages

Behring Point Operated and managed by Charlie Neymour and Fatiha Lamghari, this waterside lodge was remodeled and upgraded in 2004. Eight comfortable air-conditioned guest rooms have mini-refrigerators and private baths. Androsia batik curtains and linens adorn the rooms and the main lodge area that includes a spacious dining room and bar with satellite TV. A large shaded deck overlooks the water. Prime wadable flats are right out front. Charlie and Fatiha have a number of plans in the works for more upgrades and additions in 2005. Charlie also plans to offer boar-hunting and wing-shooting programs in addition to his outstanding fishing program. Campout trips can be arranged to fish remote areas of the West Side. Fishing areas include the North, Middle, and South Bights, outside ocean flats from Bowen Sound to Moxey Town, and the vast West Side region. If you want to fish with Charlie, you need to book months in advance. Charlie works with all the top independent guides.

Season: October through June.

Suitable For: Anglers only.

What's Included: Air-conditioned room with private bath, three meals daily, guided fishing, taxes. Trips of any length are available.

Not Included: Airfare to/from Andros Town, taxi transfers, alcoholic beverages, gratuities, fishing tackle.

Pricing: $$-$$$

Contact: Reservations and information, 242-368-4297 or 866-963-7870.

Internet: www.bigcharlieandros.com

E-mail: bigcharlieandros@yahoo.com

Andros Island Bonefish Club

Cargill Creek Owned and operated by the famous Captain Rupert Leadon, the Bonefish Club has a long tradition of serving anglers. The Bonefish Club now includes the contiguous property of Creek-side Lodge. The joint facility, perfectly located on Cargill Creek, has more than 20 air-conditioned rooms with private baths, two restaurants, two bars with satellite TV, two docks, a swimming pool, waterside gardens, and wadable flats in front of the property. Fishing areas include the North and Middle Bights, outside ocean flats from Bowen Sound to Moxey Town, and the vast West Side region. Some of the best guides on the island work here. The atmosphere at this lodge is fun and festive, with live bands often playing on the weekends.

Season: October through June.

Suitable For: Anglers only.

What's Included: Air-conditioned rooms, all meals and snacks, airport transfers, guided fishing, and taxes. Trips of any length are available.

Not Included: Airfare to/from Andros Town, alcoholic beverages, gratuities, fishing tackle.

Pricing: $$-$$$

Contact: Reservations and information, 242-368-5167; fax 242-368-5235.

Internet: www.androsbonefishing.com

E-mail: androsbonefish@batelnet.bs

Small Hope Bay Lodge

Fresh Creek A special diving and beach retreat for couples, families, and small groups. Twenty cottages are situated on the beach, each with private bath, double beds and ceiling fans. The magnificent Andros Barrier Reef is one mile offshore, about a 10-minute boat ride. For the ultimate in diving, try the "Over the Wall" dive. Descend down to 185 feet along the 6,000-foot vertical drop of the Tongue of the Ocean. Excellent bonefishing options with independent guides are available in the Fresh Creek, White Bight, Staniard, and Stafford Creek areas. Full- and half-day reef or offshore fishing trips are available. Small Hope provides air charter service from Ft. Lauderdale to Andros Town. This is a reliable economical way to travel to and from Andros.

Season: October through June.

Suitable For: Anglers and non-anglers. SHB receives our highest recommendation for combining fishing with water sport activities.

What's Included: Round-trip airport transfers, beachfront accommodations, three meals daily, afternoon snacks, all bar drinks and beverages, service charges, Bahamian taxes, introductory scuba lessons, and free use of snorkeling equipment, bicycles, sailboats, and windsurfers. Trips of any length are available.

Not Included: Airfare to/from Andros Town airport, gratuities, guided fishing (optional/additional).

Pricing: $$-$$$

Contact: Reservations and information, 800-223-6961 or 242-368-2014; fax 242-368-2015.
Internet: www.smallhope.com
E-mail: SHBinfo@SmallHope.com

Mangrove Cay Club

Mangrove Cay   A casually elegant lodge with eight guest cottages (accommodating 16 anglers) set on the water's edge of the Middle Bight. Each cottage is air-conditioned and includes a bedroom, sitting room, terrace, and private bath. The airy main lodge has a bar, lounging area, dining room, satellite TV, and a screened-in deck adjacent to the dock. Chef Iyke Moore, one of our favorites in the Bahamas, prepares delicious meals along with his famous Key lime pie. Well-trained guides work out of comfortable Dolphin superskiffs. The fishing grounds cover the Middle and South Bights and more than 60 miles of the West Side.
Season: October through June.
Suitable For: Anglers and non-anglers.
What's Included: Round-trip airport transfers, accommodations, all meals and snacks, guided fishing, and taxes.
Not Included: Airfare to/from Mangrove Cay airport, alcoholic beverages, gratuities.
Pricing: $$$-$$$$
Contact: Reservations and information, 800-245-1950.
Internet: www.mangrovecayclub.com, www.frontierstravel.com
E-mail: mangrovecayclub@shackletonint.com or info@frontierstravel.com

Tiamo Resorts

South Bight   There are no phones or TVs at this gem of resort that is accessible only by boat. The main lodge is an expansive gathering place with wood-beamed ceilings that naturally combine bar, lounge, library, and dining room. Eleven bungalows with wraparound porches are strung out along the powdery beach shaded by coconut palms. Bedrooms with soft linens are positioned to receive the cooling ocean breeze. Leisurely meals include seafood delights, homemade breads, and luscious desserts. Guided snorkeling, sea kayaking, nature hikes, and fly-fishing excursions can be arranged at your whim.
Season: October through June.
Suitable For: Anglers and non-anglers. Our top recommendation for eco-travelers who also want to work some bonefishing into an overall relaxing vacation.
What's Included: Round-trip airport taxi/boat transfers, accommodations, all meals and snacks, resort eco-activities, use of resort equipment, and taxes.
Not Included: Airfare to/from Congo Town airport, alcoholic beverages, gratuities, guided fishing (optional/additional).
Pricing: $$-$$$
Contact: Reservations and information, 242-357-2489; fax 305-768-7707.
Internet: www.tiamoresorts.com

Bair's Lodge

Little Creek   Purchased in 2003 by Nervous Waters, a premiere Argentinean fly-fishing lodging company, the lodge was remodeled in the summer of 2003, and then expanded in 2004. Eight anglers are accommodated in four spacious air-conditioned guest suites. Excellent meals are served in the dining room overlooking the beach, with specialties such as fresh seafood, fried chicken, steaks, and other delicious treats, including scrumptious Key lime pie. The fishing program covers miles of flats and creeks around South Andros. Deep Creek, Little Creek, and Grassy Creek offer protected fishing in rough weather. If you like to wade fish, this is one of the best locations in the Caribbean. The well-trained guides are friendly and knowledgeable. They work out of new (2004) Dolphin superskiffs. A tackle shop has all the necessities, including rental fly-fishing gear. You can stay connected to the outside world with phone and Internet access.

Season: October through June.

Suitable For: Anglers only.

What's Included: Accommodations, all meals with wine, open bar, guided fishing, airport transfers to/from Congo Town, and taxes.

Not Included: Airfare to/from Congo Town, gratuities.

Pricing: $$$$

Contact: Reservations and information, 866-963-7870 or in Argentina +54 (11) 4331-0444.

Internet: www.bairslodge.com

E-mail: info@nervouswaters.com

Flamingo Cay

Wide Open, West Side The only lodge located on the remote West Side of Andros. Lodge guests arrive via floatplane at this small resort nestled along the banks of a mangrove-lined creek in absolute solitude. The property was acquired by the Bethell family in the 1920s. Charles W. F. Bethell maintained the property for waterfowl shooting in the 1950s. His grandson, Charlie Bethell III has restored the existing camp, added additional accommodations and amenities, and opened the lodge as a unique venue for waterfowl and flats anglers to enjoy. Guests are accommodated in spacious air-conditioned cottages with private baths, comfortable sitting areas, and large decks overlooking the creek. Meals are hearty and festive with fresh seafood a specialty. Flamingo Cay takes only six anglers/shooters at a time (eight on special request). Guests can book fishing only, hunting only, or combination packages. Most fishing is done from Hells Bay flats skiffs, while other hunting and fishing areas are accessed by canoe or Air Gator Airboat. Space is at a premium and should be booked well in advance.

Season: Fishing is October 1 through June 15; shooting is October 15 through March 31.

Suitable For: Anglers only.

What's Included: Accommodations, all meals with wine, open bar, guided fishing, guided shooting, floatplane transfers to/from Nassau, and taxes.

Not Included: Airfare to/from Nassau, gratuities to guides and staff.

Pricing: $$$$

Contact: Reservations and information, 242-357-3894 or 242-357-4514.

Internet: www.flamingocay.com

E-mail: flamingocay@earthlink.net

Kamalame Cay

Staniard Creek One of the most luxurious resorts in the Out Islands, on a 96-acre private cay lined with white sand beaches and coconut palms. Air-conditioned marina rooms with private baths are booked with most fishing packages. You can upgrade to cottages and villas on the beach with sitting areas, soaking tubs, and French doors that open onto private terraces and gardens. Meals and cocktails are served in the verandah-wrapped, plantation-style Great House adorned with cushy, oversized furniture and antiques. Dining is an experience—fresh fruits, beef tenderloin sandwiches, homemade breads and soups, and innovative seafood dishes. Amenities include a full marina, dive shop, swimming pool, tennis court, in-room massages, and Internet access. This is a premiere location for non-anglers to enjoy themselves while friends or family members go fishing.

Season: October through June.

Suitable For: Anglers and non-anglers.

What's Included: Accommodations, all meals with wine, open bar, guided fishing, airport transfers to/from Andros Town, and taxes.

Not Included: Airfare to/from Andros Town, gratuities to guides and staff.

Pricing: $$$$

Contact: Reservations and information, 242-368-6281 or 800-688-7678; or for fly-fishing packages, 800-245-1950.

Internet: www.kamalame.com, www.frontierstravel.com

E-mail: Kamalame@batelnet.bs, info@frontierstravel.com

Stafford Creek Lodge

Stafford Creek Prescott and Samantha Smith's lodge is situated on a bend in Stafford Creek overlooking the water and the surrounding pine forests. The lodge accommodates only six anglers in private guest rooms with ceiling fans and air-conditioning. Personal service and premiere fishing are the focus here. Fish outside ocean flats, various creeks that offer good fishing even in bad weather, landlocked lakes, Red Bay, and the Joulter's Cays. This lodge books up months in advance, so plan ahead. Minimum stay is three nights/two days fishing.

Season: October through July.

Suitable For: Anglers only.

What's Included: Accommodations in air-conditioned rooms with private baths, three meals daily, guided fishing, taxes. Single rates are available.

Not Included: Airfare to/from Andros Town or San Andros, taxi transfers, alcoholic beverages, gratuities, fishing tackle.

Pricing: $$$

Contact: Reservations and information, telephone/fax, 242-368-6050.

Internet: www.staffordcreeklodge.com

E-mail: sclodge@hotmail.com

Additional Accommodations

Seascape Inn

Mangrove Cay Five individual cottages with private decks overlook the ocean. The elevated bar/restaurant is the place to relax. Grilled steaks, coconut grouper, and chicken in white wine sauce are dinner highlights. The hearty breakfasts are delicious and include fresh-baked banana bread and an assortment of muffins. Owner Mickey McGowen heads the diving program and can arrange for a fishing guide. There are good wading flats in front of the lodge.

Pricing: $$

Contact: Reservations and information, 242-369-0342.

Internet: www.seascapeinn.com
E-mail: relax@seascapeinn.com

Point of View Villas

Fresh Creek The property has 14 two-bedroom villas with central air-conditioning, spacious living rooms, private baths, and kitchenettes, a swimming pool, restaurant, and bar on the waterfront overlooking the Tongue of the Ocean. Fishing guides can be arranged or you can fish on your own. It's about a five-minute drive to Fresh Creek, and about five minutes from Small Hope Bay. This is a pretty spot and suitable for non-anglers.
Pricing: $$$
Contact: Reservations and information, 242-368-2750.
Internet: www.pointofviewbahamas
E-mail: capt_cornelius@hotmail.com

Bang Bang Club

Pot Cay This private island club on Pot Cay in the North Bight is the realized dream of legendary guide Charlie Smith. Ideally situated across from Pine Cay, the club has comfortable air-conditioned rooms with tile floors and private baths, a dining room and bar, and waterfront dock. There is no better access to some of the best "big fish" flats in Andros. Charlie works with most independent guides.
Pricing: $$-$$$
Contact: Reservations and information, 866-712-7303.
Internet: www.bangbangclub.com
E-mail: info@bahamasfish.com

Lighthouse Yacht Club & Marina

Fresh Creek Eight villa suites and 12 standard rooms, all air-conditioned with telephone, cable TV, and private baths. Restaurant, bar, and swimming pool. A meal plan is available. Fishing and diving can be arranged. The 18-slip marina offers full service to boaters. This is a popular marina, so slip reservations are necessary.
Pricing: $$-$$$
Contact: Reservations and information, 242-368-2305; fax 242-368-2300.
Internet: www.androslighthouse.com

Bonefish Bay Club of South Andros

Kemp's Bay Under new American management as of 2004, the Club has 10 comfortable air-conditioned rooms, a good restaurant, and a well-organized fishing program. A good choice for fishing Little Creek, Deep Creek, and the southern flats between Grassy Cay and the Water Cays.
Pricing: $$-$$$
Contact: Reservations and information, 800-766-9137.
Internet: www.bonefishbayclub.com

Emerald Palms Resort of South Andros

Driggs Hill Completely renovated in November 2003, this upscale property added 20 luxurious one- and two-bedroom cottages with individual gardens and private decks surrounded by palm trees. The clubhouse rooms run along the blue-tiled pool and out to the beach. A cabana bar overlooks the gin-clear sea. Grilled seafood, steaks, and whole lobsters are specialties, served in the casually elegant poolside restaurant. Fishing, diving, snorkeling, and other activities can be arranged.

Pricing: $$$-$$$$

Contact: Reservations and information, 800-824-6623 or 242-369-2713.

Internet: www.emerald-palms.com

E-mail: info@emerald-palms.com

Glato's Bonefish Lodge

Deep Creek   Waterfront at the entrance to Deep Creek, this is a rustic two-story lodge with 12 motel-style rooms. The people here are friendly and the food is good. The least expensive option for fishing South Andros.

Pricing: $$

Contact: Reservations and information, 242-369-4669.

Internet: www.islandeaze.com/glatos

E-mail: glatfish@batelnet.bs

Conch Sound Inn

Conch Sound   Four two-bedroom suites with kitchenettes, plus six hotel rooms, all air-conditioned with private baths. Restaurant, bar, satellite TV, and swimming pool, located 5 minutes from the ocean and a 10-minute drive to the boat launch at Lowe Sound. Bonefishing and diving can be arranged.

Pricing: $$-$$$

Contact: Reservations and information, 242-329-2060; fax 242-329-2338.

Chickcharnie Hotel

Fresh Creek   Ten of the small rooms are air-conditioned and have private baths. This is a good location right on Fresh Creek for anglers on a budget. The restaurant serves excellent spicy seafood. Fishing guides can be arranged.

Pricing: $-$$

Contact: Reservations and information, 242-368-2025; fax 242-368-2492.

Love at First Sight

Stafford Creek   An alternative option for fishing on your own or booking a complete bonefishing package to explore North Andros. Nine air-conditioned double rooms, restaurant, bar, swimming pool, sun deck, all on scenic Stafford Creek.

Pricing: $$-$$$

Contact: Reservations and information, 242-368-6082.

Internet: www.bonefishandros.com

Do-It-Yourself Options

Coakley House, Private Rental Villa

Fresh Creek   A three-bedroom villa with creekside decks and a private dock at the entrance to Fresh Creek. Each bedroom has air-conditioning and a private bath. There are views of both the ocean and the creek from picture windows in the large living room and dining room. The house has everything you need for a self-sufficient vacation: a fully equipped kitchen, washer/dryer, TV/VCR, tape/CD player, linens, and towels. Car and boat rentals or maid and cook services can be arranged at an additional cost. Fishing guides can be arranged and they will pick you up at your private dock. The walk into Fresh Creek takes five minutes. Small Hope Bay Lodge owns the villa so all of the resort's activities and facilities are available to villa guests.

Season: October through June.

Suitable For: Anglers and non-anglers.

What's Included: Accommodations only, though all other services including maids and meals can be arranged.

Not Included: Airfare to/from Andros Town airport, ground transfers, gratuities, and all optional fishing and activities.

Pricing: $$-$$$

Contact: Reservations and information, 800-223-6961 or 242-368-2014; fax 242-368-2015.

Internet: www.smallhope.com

E-mail: SHBinfo@SmallHope.com

George's Point

Fresh Creek A popular choice for do-it-yourselfers looking for easy access to bonefishing and reef fishing. These two oceanfront villas are located near the mouth of Fresh Creek. Each villa is air-conditioned and includes private bath, hair dryers, ice, kitchenettes, and Internet access. It is just a short walk to town and the beaches. Hank's Place Restaurant and Bar, our favorite in the area, is just four blocks away. Hank's Place rents boats. Diving and snorkeling can be arranged with Small Hope Bay. Independent fishing guides can be arranged, or you can book your own guide. Tide tables for Andros are available on their Web site.

Season: October through June.

Suitable For: Anglers and non-anglers.

What's Included: Accommodations only.

Not Included: Airfare to/from Andros Town airport, ground transfers, gratuities, and all optional guided fishing, boat rental, and other activities. You can stock up on food in town for your kitchenette, but some supplies may or may not be available.

Pricing: $-$$

Contact: Reservations and information, 242-368-2238.

Internet: www.georgespoint.com

E-mail: info@georgespoint.com

Independent Guides

The following are Andros Island independent guides we have fished with and recommend, though there are many other good ones, and many more who work exclusively for particular lodges. It is not always easy to reach these guys so you just have to keep trying, or work through a booking agent who has a relationship with them.

Charlie Neymour: 242-368-4297; fax 242-368-4296

Andy Smith: 242-368-4044 or 242-368-4261

Barry Neymour: 242-368-4485

Frankie Neymour: 242-368-4067

Benry Smith: 242-368-2204

Herman Bain: 242-368-4367; cell 242-357-2375

Dwain Neymour: 242-368-4132

Deon Neymour: 242-368-4132

Ricardo Mackey: 242-368-4132

For up-to-date information, see our Web site at www.bahamasflyfishingguide.com, or cruise the net.

Services

Diving and Snorkeling: *Small Hope Bay* offers one of the best dive programs in the Bahamas. Contact them directly at 242-368-2014. Most lodges in central Andros can make these reservations for you, but it will usually be through Small Hope. If you are staying on Mangrove Cay, Seascape Inn has the best diving program, but this is mainly for their guests. They will take people not staying with them with advance notice and a party of four or more. Contact Seascape at 242-369-0342.

Restaurants: Most lodges offer meal plans. When we are not on a meal plan, and staying in central Andros, our favorite place to eat is *Hank's Place Restaurant and Bar* on the water in Fresh Creek. Bahamian specialties—pan-fried grouper, baked hog snapper, and fresh conch salad—make it a favorite gathering place for locals and visitors. Fresh lobster, prepared to your liking, is available in season (August–March). Hank's signature cocktail, aptly named "Hanky Panky," is a dynamite frozen rum and fruit concoction. Contact: 242-368-2447.

Car Rentals: This is not easy. Your best bet is to arrange a rental through your hotel or lodge.

Taxi Service: Most lodges will arrange to have a taxi meet you at the airport as part of your trip. Once at a lodge, they can arrange for a taxi to take you most places on the island. Be sure to ask about the cost up front. The taxi driver we use most often in north and central Andros (Andros Town and San Andros airports) is "Doy" Leadon. He can be contacted directly at his airport telephone 242-368-4009, or at his home number 242-368-5047. Doy has two taxis including a 12-passenger air-conditioned van. Another reliable driver is Johnny Sanders. Johnny is also the manager for Western Air at the Andros Town airport. Johnny has three taxis including a 12-passenger air-conditioned van. Contact Johnny at 242-368-2759, 242-368-2766, or 242-329-7137.

On South Andros (Congo Town airport), Kim Johnson is our favorite taxi driver. Kim has a comfortable air-conditioned van that can take up to eight passengers. Contact her at 242-369-5024.

Grocery and Liquor Stores: Available in most of the major settlements. The ones that are best stocked are in Nicholl's Town, Fresh Creek, Bowen Sound, Cargill Creek, Driggs Hill, The Bluff, and Kemp's Bay. If you need groceries be sure to check the mail boat schedule and do your shopping right after it arrives.

Banks: There is a bank in San Andros, one in Fresh Creek, one on Mangrove Cay, and one in Kemp's Bay. These banks are usually open three days a week, though this is not guaranteed. If you need cash, take it with you.

Government Clinics: Clinics are located in Lowe Sound, Nicholl's Town, Mastic Point, Fresh Creek, Mangrove Cay, and The Bluff. All are nurse-staffed except there is a doctor usually available in Fresh Creek, and sometimes in The Bluff.

New Developments

Charlie Neymour has plans to continue his Nottages Cottages lodge expansion at Behring Point. This includes building one- and two-bedroom guest cottages and a small boating facility. Charlie is also preparing to launch his boar and wing-shooting programs in 2005. This plan includes a possible lodge to be built in the remote outback land-locked lakes region, which would also open up the sensational fishing in these lakes.

The Bahamian government has had the Lighthouse Yacht Club and Marina up for sale for years. In 2004 there were several serious interested parties. We've heard that a deal is pending. If so, upgrades and new development would begin in 2005.

The most development activity in recent years has been on South Andros, which ironically was the least developed area for the past 20 years. With the passing away of the owner of Emerald Palms, the resort was up for sale in 2004. We've heard a developer—who wants to add a marina and casino—is negotiating for this property. If successful, that sort of development would dramatically change the sleepy character of this part of the island.

The 61-foot shallow-draft Hatteras *Outpost* is being operated by Angling Destinations (800-211-8530, www.anglingdestinations.com) on the West Side from Little Loggerhead Creek to Williams Island. While it is possible to fish part of this area as a long day trip from Behring Point, if you really want to spend time in this unique area, fishing from a motherboat is the best way to do it. Trips for four anglers per week are operated during six weeks in the spring. You need to call well in advance for reservations.

For on-going updates on the happenings on Andros Island, please log on to our Web site at www.bahamasflyfishingguide.com.

CHAPTER 5

GRAND BAHAMA ISLAND

Aerial view of Freeport and the flats fished at Pelican Bay.

rand Bahama Island is a 90-mile-long strip of low-lying land 56 miles east of Palm Beach, Florida and 85 miles northeast of Miami. When we first mention Grand Bahama to people, they often look puzzled; then we say "Freeport" and instant recognition blossoms.

Freeport/Lucaya, with a population of more than 40,000, is the Bahamas' second largest city. Compared to Nassau, the atmosphere is more casual and cosmopolitan, less jammed up and frenetic. The feel of the city is breezy and welcoming. The streets are wide, with numerous roundabouts, and are often bordered by well-manicured Bermuda grass, casuarina trees, and Australian pines. Downtown, traffic tangles for 15 to 20 minutes in the morning and late afternoon. Nothing to sweat, mon. You can drive the length of the island in an hour and a half.

None of this is an accident. Freeport/Lucaya was created from scratch, thanks to Wallace Groves' idea for a free-trade center, and the subsequent passage of the Hawksbill Creek Agreement in 1955. Since the city was also built to attract tourism, it's no wonder it has done just that, becoming an outdoor enthusiast's playground with championship golf courses, tennis, scuba diving, attractive resorts, and some of the best fishing in the islands. Toss in casino gambling, duty-free shopping, a variety of quality restaurants, and lively nightlife and you have a winning combination for a wide range of vacationers.

The city's goal of becoming a major international seaport and free-trade center was accomplished in 1997 when Hutchison Port Holdings officially opened the 78-million-dollar Freeport Container Port. This facility has become one of the Western Hemisphere's most important trans-shipment centers. Hutchison has plans for further expansion that will include a liquid natural gas storage facility with a direct pipeline to Florida.

Hutchison Ports Properties, in partnership with Grand Bahama Development Corporation, has completed several phases in the redevelopment of beachfront property adjacent to the Bell Harbour Channel. The mega-resort, Our Lucaya, was completed in 2000. Starwood Hotels and Resorts took over management of the resort in 2003 and divided the facility between their Westin and Sheraton brands. The resort includes 1,300 rooms, state-of-the-art international convention facilities, the Isle of Capri casino, numerous restaurants and bars, sprawling outdoor pools, acres of white sand beaches, tennis courts, and the Bahama Reef golf course.

The Crowne Plaza Golf Resort & Casino, also known as the Royal Oasis, and formerly known as the Bahamas Princess Country Club, is another premier resort development that has sparked tourism on Grand Bahama. Located in the center of Freeport, the resort includes a thousand acres of tropical gardens, sprawling pool areas, a beach lagoon and water park, and two lush championship golf courses.

On the West End of the island, the Old Bahama Bay resort and marina development was completed in 2001. Continued expansion is planned and it includes exclusive beachfront home sites and condominiums. As opposed to the development going on in Freeport/Lucaya, this location offers the quiet ambiance of the family islands.

All this development has kicked up the energy level around Freeport. Taxi drivers are quick to engage you with their opinions, yea or nay, about what's going on. If you need information, definitely ask a cabby, or a waiter in one of the better restaurants.

Other service personnel working in a variety of tourist-related businesses exude a similar enthusiasm. Entrepreneurs are everywhere, and notably so in the fishing business. There are a number of new small bonefish lodges and accommodation options for do-it-yourself anglers and vacationers. An increasing number of independent bone-fishing guides have also emerged to service the growing demand for guided fishing day trips. Several of these guides include fly-fishing equipment and flies in their daily service along with pick-up and drop off at the various Freeport hotels and resorts.

While Freeport is the center of activity on Grand Bahama, it's hardly all there is to the island. To the east of Freeport, vacationers can enjoy a true Out Island experience. Once you drive past the roundabout leading to Port Lucaya, you are in the country. You'll cross several causeways spanning miles of man-made channels, including the Grand Lucayan Waterway, before you reach the Lucayan National Park.

The park is composed of pine forests with nature trails, deserted beaches, and observation decks to view the world's longest charted cavern system. North Riding Point Bonefishing Lodge is here also, at Burnside Cove. Then you have a straight shot along miles of seaweed-strewn beaches until you reach McLean's Town. There are several comfortable lodging operations associated with bonefishing guides on this stretch of beach including the Ocean Pearl Resort and Club at High Rock. In McLean's Town you will find the dock used by Deepwater Cay Club to pick up guests for the short boat ride to their private island resort.

Scattered across the east end you can find remnants of the earliest Arawak civilizations along with artifacts from the infamous pirate days. The ocean out here is remarkable. Vivid shades of blues and greens wash across black coral reefs and sparkle in the shallows over turtle grass and bleach-white sand.

Talking to the people in McLean's Town is like talking to the people on Long Island or Cat Island. Friendliness runs in their blood, as does fostering a relaxed attitude. These are the qualities of Grand Bahama that combine with the growth of Freeport to make this island the perfect vacation choice for anglers and their non-fishing companions.

The Freeport International Airport has direct flight service from Miami, Ft. Lauderdale, and West Palm Beach on American Eagle, Bahamasair, Comair, and Continental/Gulfstream. ATA has direct service from Atlanta. We also use several air charter companies out of West Palm and Ft. Lauderdale. This becomes more economical if you have a group of four or more.

Western Air has the most reliable service from Nassau, though Bahamasair offers more flights as of late 2004.

Around the Island

The West End of Grand Bahama is perched on the edge of the Little Bahama Bank where the Straits of Florida meets the Northwest Providence Channel. The confluence of currents that sweep in over the shallows aid in creating prime habitat for bonefish, permit, tarpon, and other gamefish.

The Old Bahama Bay Marina, completed in 2001, is a modern facility with 72 slips that can accommodate boats up to 120 feet. Boaters should use VHS Channel 16 to communicate with the marina. The Dockside Grille restaurant, overlooking the marina, is open daily for breakfast, lunch, and dinner.

Along with the marina, the Inn at Old Bahama Bay creates one of the most appealing small luxury resorts in the islands. Forty-seven suites are arranged in nine two-story villa-style buildings on the beach. Amenities include a swimming pool, tennis courts, water sports center, guided diving and snorkeling excursions, spa services, and fine dining in the elegant Aqua restaurant.

The strong tidal currents that run between West End and Indian Cay sweep baitfish in and out of this channel. Tarpon, barracuda, blacktip, and lemon sharks use the channel for daily feeding. The tarpon cruise the bank north up to Wood Cay and Sandy Cay, then enter the flats in that area through the cuts and creeks.

Permit follow similar patterns, penetrating farther into the flats and working along the banks where deeper water pushes up against mangrove-lined cays.

Rich flats spread out from the mainland all along the indented shore.

There are countless cays, rocks, creeks, flats, and shallow bays in the area that contain habitat loaded with bonefish averaging five to six pounds. Bottom structure varies from hard white sand to irregular corral and turtle grass. Grass, mantis, and snapping shrimp provide a rich food source for bonefish all along the northwestern shoreline.

The West End settlement itself is one of our favorites in the islands. Sprawled along the sea just east of Old Bahama Bay, this fishing village is the self-proclaimed "Home of Hospitality," and also the home of Israel Rolle, otherwise known as the famous "Bonefish Foley."

West End enjoyed its heyday during Prohibition when liquor and gunrunning turned it into a boomtown. Later, the Star Hotel, the oldest hotel on Grand Bahama, became the center of tourism in the 1940s and 1950s. Today the settlement is laid back and charming, with several small bars and restaurants where visitors can sample homemade conch ceviche and warm johnnycake, all washed down with a cold Kalik. The best of these little joints is Rosie's Chicken Nest. We never go to West End without stopping in at Rosie's. The Star Hotel no longer takes guests, but its lively bar is a fun stop, especially during the annual homecoming in June.

For anglers looking to fish on their own, the flats off West End are easily accessed from the highway that runs back to Eight Mile and Freeport. This fertile habitat continues on through more creeks and mangrove-rimmed cays that create a maze that can only be navigated in flats boats with local knowledge. Cruising boaters need to take a wide loop north past the government wharf before attempting to turn back in to Hawksbill Creek.

There is a huge area of rich bonefish flats that spread out from the mainland all along the indented shoreline. The professional guides from Pelican Bay, along with some of the independent guides, fish this area on a regular basis.

The highway from West End to Freeport is in good shape, though it provides little access to the water, as the shoreline is dense with mangroves and other vegetation on the lee side of the island. There are a couple hidden bays we fish from this area that reach within 50 feet of the road, but unless you stopped and looked hard, you wouldn't see the water from the highway.

The highway passes through the settlement of Eight Mile, the largest settlement on the island. The town is really a string of villages built on eight miles of solid rock.

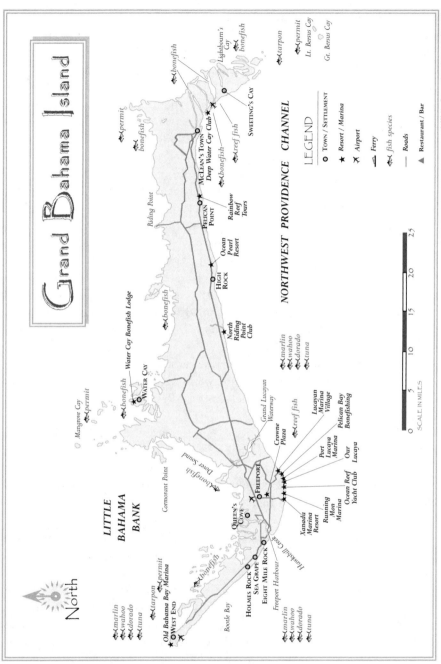

Grand Bahama Island

North

LITTLE BAHAMA BANK

NORTHWEST PROVIDENCE CHANNEL

LEGEND

○ TOWN / SETTLEMENT
★ Resort / Marina
✈ Airport
⟷ Ferry
🐟 fish species
— Roads
▲ Restaurant / Bar

SCALE IN MILES

0   5   10   15   20   25

marlin
wahoo
dorado
tuna

Old Bahama Bay Marina
WEST END

Bootle Bay

bonefish

tarpon
permit

Cormorant Point

Mangrove Cay

permit

bonefish
permit

Water Cay Bonefish Lodge

bonefish
WATER CAY

Dover Sound

bonefish

Bonefish

QUEEN'S COVE

FREEPORT

Grand Lucayan Waterway

Crowne Plaza

reef fish

Lucayan Marina Village
Pelican Bay Bonefishing
Port Lucaya Marina
Our Lucaya
Ocean Reef Yacht Club
Running Mon Marina
Xanadu Marina Resort

Hawksbill Creek

Freeport Harbour

HOLMES ROCK
SEA GRAPE
EIGHT MILE ROCK

marlin
wahoo
dorado
tuna

North Riding Point Club

bonefish

HIGH ROCK

Ocean Pearl Resort

PELICAN POINT

Rainbow Reef Tours

Riding Point

McLEAN'S TOWN
Deep Water Cay Club

bonefish

reef fish

SWEETING'S CAY

bonefish

Lighthouse's Cay

bonefish

tarpon

permit

Lt. Berus Cay

Gt. Berus Cay

marlin
wahoo
dorado
tuna

reef fish

©1999 Map Illustration/Burton Design, Jackson Hole, WY

There are inviting beaches on the south ocean side off Eight Mile, plus some wadable flats. A few big bonefish and permit cruise these flats, though conditions are usually windy and challenging. If you are a skilled angler who likes to hunt big fish, and you don't mind going fishless, you might try these flats on an incoming tide.

Back on the northern lee side of the island, most of the bottom structure is grass and coral until you near boating markers that indicate the entrance to Hawksbill Creek. Here, a number of gold and white sand flats blossom from the mainland. The northern end of the creek, which provides access to the Little Bahama Bank, is only accessible to smaller boats on the proper tide. A number of guides launch and retrieve their flats boats inside the creek at Queen's Cove.

Hopping back to the south side again, most boaters cruise offshore from West End, past Settlement Point, then on to the series of marinas servicing Freeport and Port Lucaya. Deep water surges to within a few hundred yards of Settlement Point—a prime spot for blue-water anglers to fish for skip jacks, tuna, dorado, and other species in season.

Boaters eventually reach an elbow joint of land that is the entrance to Freeport Harbour. The harbor was originally formed by the southern section of Hawksbill Creek. This is a massive commercial harbor, jointly owned by the Grand Bahama Port Authority and Hutchison, and is used primarily by ocean-going container ships and commercial cruise ships.

While eating at a popular restaurant on the harbor, Pier 1, it is a stunning sight to look out into the night and see one of the world's largest cargo ships rumbling by, escorted by half a dozen tugboats lit like Christmas trees. The ships pass so close you can almost touch them.

The main highlight of eating at Pier 1, however, is the shark feeding. Every hour on the hour, a ship's bell clangs as pounds of chum and bread are tossed out into the clear floodlit water. The resulting feeding frenzy is an awe-inspiring sight, though not because of any sharks. Huge jacks slam the surface with ferocious intensity, along with their cousins, the ever-elusive permit. If only permit would feed so aggressively when fly-fishers made their offerings; wouldn't that be something to see?

The towering orange cranes used to move tons of cargo can be seen for miles from both sides of the island. Boaters can stop in Freeport Harbour to clear customs but it is recommended that recreational boaters use Xanadu Marina, Running Mon Marina, Ocean Reef Marina, Port Lucaya Marina, or Lucayan Marina Village to engage services.

Private homes, condominiums, and resort developments flank the white sand beachfronts between the channels leading to these marinas. Bell Channel is the entrance to the Port Lucaya Marina and the Lucayan Marina Village. Boaters turning left once inside the bay will cruise past Pelican Bay Hotel and the UNEXSO Dive Center before reaching Port Lucaya Marina. The marina has more than 100 slips with full services for boats up to 175 feet.

The marina adjoins the Port Lucaya Resort Hotel, the Port Lucaya Marketplace, and Count Basie Square. The casual hotel offers comfortable air-conditioned rooms, a

Shops at Lucaya Marina, Count Basie Square.

swimming pool, restaurant and bar, with boat slips around three sides. The Marketplace is a pleasing maze of 80-odd stores, shops, and boutiques, plus a colorful straw market, and at least 20 cafes and restaurants. For our money, this is the best shopping area in Freeport/Lucaya, far surpassing the more publicized International Bazaar.

Count Basie Square, ringed with bars and restaurants, is our favorite spot for nightlife. You can walk here in less than five minutes from Pelican Bay, or from the Westin and Sheraton Our Lucaya resorts. The Square features live music every night and some of the most mind-boggling limbo dancers you can imagine. Would you believe limboing under a cane bar set on top of two Kalik bottles? You can join in the dancing or just hang out in the festive atmosphere while sipping a cool drink and smoking a Cuban cigar.

One of our favorite restaurants on Grand Bahama, Luciano's, is on the corner of the Square overlooking the marina. La Dolce Vita, The Pub at Lucaya, Zorba's, and Pisces are other Marketplace restaurants we have enjoyed on a regular basis.

All this activity is just down the way from our favorite place to stay in the area— Pelican Bay at Lucaya, a charming boutique hotel that combines Caribbean style with European service. This is also the home of Pelican Bay Bonefishing. There is no better place in the Bahamas to combine the highest-quality bonefishing with an ideal resort vacation.

The hotel has 48 over-sized, air-conditioned rooms with private baths, refrigerators, coffeemakers, satellite TV, and private balconies overlooking the pool, Jacuzzi, and marina. Or guests can choose from an equal number of 750-square-foot suites with separate bedrooms and living areas. A poolside bar whips up tasty rum drinks and snack foods, and is an ideal place to relax after fishing. The Ferry House restaurant, one of the best on the island, serves delicious fresh

Entrance to the Pelican Bay Hotel.

Ferry House Restaurant at Pelican Bay.

pastries at breakfast and features an appetizing dinner menu with fresh fish specialties nightly.

A complimentary ferry service runs from the hotel to the Lucayan Village Marina, which is flanked by some of the most luxurious condominiums anywhere. Full service for boaters is available here. Amenities include a swimming pool and bar, and golf can be arranged at the Lucayan Country Club.

Up the street and across the road from Pelican Bay and the Port Lucaya Marketplace are the Our Lucaya Westin and Sheraton resorts. This is really just one giant resort complex. The Westin side is quieter and more luxurious with the Bell Harbour channel bordering it on the west. The Senses Spa and Fitness Center is located here, and is available for Sheraton and Pelican Bay guests as well. The main lobby building for the Westin is styled after a grand colonial mansion. It houses a lively mahogany-paneled cigar bar and Churchill's Chop House, one of the best fine-dining restaurants on the island.

The Sheraton section is often filled with families with young children and package-plan vacationers intent on having a wild time. This includes the infamous Spring Break crowd. If you want action, this is the place for you. If you want peace and quiet, you will rarely find it here.

Iries restaurant and bar is part of the Sheraton complex. They serve delicious Caribbean dishes at dinner, and their bar is renowned for making the best mojitos outside Havana. Actually, we like the mojitos at Iries better than those served anywhere in Cuba.

A 10-minute taxi ride inland from Our Lucaya will take you to the International Bazaar and the Crowne Plaza Royal Oasis Golf Resort & Casino complexes. The massive Royal Oasis encompasses more than a thousand acres with the main Tower Hotel and casino complex across the street from the Country Club wing and golf courses. Deluxe air-conditioned rooms and suites are available at both locations. The complex has numerous restaurants and bars, including fine dining at the Rib Room for steaks and prime rib, and at Paradiso for Italian cuisine. Additional amenities include a fitness center, spa, jogging trails, and water park.

The striking red Torii Gate outside the entrance to the International Bazaar, on West Sunrise Highway and East Mall drive, has been a landmark since the 1960s when this shopping center was built. The Bazaar features different themed sections to reflect its international atmosphere—Africa, the Middle East, the Caribbean, France, Italy, and others. Name-brand shops such as Cartier and Gucci blend with unique stores that sell regional crafts. There are plenty of places to grab a snack, a drink, or a full meal.

Now back to the ocean. The run for boaters on the southern side of the island from Bell Channel to McLean's Town offers splendid views of powdery white beaches shaded by palms and Australian pines, but there are no good harbors. Trolling lures outside the reef can produce quality fishing for skipjacks, blackfin and yellowfin tuna, wahoo, mackerel, and other species in season. When the weather is calm, there are several reefs that can be fished with fly rods using poppers and Clouser's minnows.

McLean's Town is the jumping off point for the Deep Water Cay Club, one of the most venerable bonefishing destinations in the Bahamas. Deep Water Cay is located on a private island across from the settlement. Anglers can drive from Freeport to the McLean's Town dock, then take a ferry ride across, or take a charter aircraft from the States directly to the resort's private airstrip.

Deep Water Cay Club.

In 2000, Deep Water Cay was purchased by a private group of investors who have turned it into a private club managed by the Greenbrier Sporting Club. The Greenbrier has a fine reputation for managing five-star properties, which is the level of service they have brought to Deep Water Cay.

The Cay's private runway has been extended to 4,200 feet. A swimming pool and tennis courts were added, along with other amenities to not only serve bonefishing guests, but to also accommodate club members who can build private homes on the island. More than 70 home sites have been platted.

Productive white sand and turtle grass flats are sprinkled throughout this area. While bonefish are plentiful, so are many other gamefish species. The deeper creeks, cuts, and bights between the sizable cays stretching to the south are loaded with jacks, cubera snapper, barracuda, sharks, tarpon, and the occasional permit.

To the north of Deep Water Cay the island forms a point ending with Grassy Cay, which leads into another string of cays running across to Little Abaco. This is the boaters' northern entrance to the Bight of Abaco, and one of the best flats areas on the Little Bahama Bank. Guides from Deepwater fish here in good weather. They also run south to Sweeting's Cay, East End Bush, and Red Shank Cay in search of permit and big bonefish.

Heading back west, the northern coast of Grand Bahama is a flats fisherman's dream. This remote area is one of the main reasons the North Riding Point bonefishing operation began. North Riding Point guides trailer their boats to four different launch sites to access the north coast, including areas of the Water Cays, and all the way out to Mangrove Cay during calm weather.

Turtle grass and dark coral make up most of the bottom structure, though there are areas of white sand, including a sparkling white sand bank at Mangrove Cay that is home to huge bonefish and permit.

We have had a number of thrilling experiences fishing to double-digit bones around the Water Cays. A bonefishing operation is now in business here. The Water Cay Lodge can accommodate four hard-

North Riding Point Club.

core anglers in comfortable air-conditioned rooms. Nothing fancy, but the location is dynamite for fishing these remote flats that are often hard to reach any other way due to weather and tidal conditions.

Bonefish flats continue west toward Cormorant Point, where the fishing grounds for Pelican Bay and North Riding Point intersect, though Pelican Bay guides also fish the Water Cays when the weather cooperates. There are more sandy-bottomed flats in this area all the way to Dover Sound, which is the entrance to the Grand Lucayan waterway. The waterway is a seven-and-a-half mile-long canal that bisects Grand Bahama. It offers good anchorages and wind protection for boaters, plus it forms a miles-long maze of back channels with hundreds of waterfront lots for sale.

Around the point from Dover Sound are several miles of mangrove-lined shorelines, Crab Cay, and Little Crab Cay. It's hard to keep track of all the Crab Cays in the Bahamas, isn't it? Though this area produces excellent bonefishing, including some big fish, it is not visually appealing. There are huge sand piles with accompanying gravel pits, cranes, and other heavy machinery at work here. Planes are constantly taking off and landing at nearby Freeport International Airport. In bad weather, however, this is a protected area, and it's a short run from Queen's Cove and Hawksbill Creek.

Fishing Highlights

Grand Bahama's relatively northern location puts it in the path of strong winter winds and cold fronts moving across from Florida. These cold fronts are common from mid-November to the middle of March, though they can occur from October into May.

A major cold front can last four to five days, while weaker fronts can be through in a couple of days. Anglers fishing from the West End out to Cormorant Point will have little protection from these winds. Pelican Bay guides and independent guides working out of Freeport usually fish west of Hawksbill Creek during bad weather to gain some lees in the series of mangrove cays running parallel to the shoreline. It is possible to run east, though the pounding you take from the prevailing northern winds may be worth it, may be not. On the plus side, this area has more than its share of bonefish in the 8- to 12-pound range, and these fish have a high tolerance for cold weather and water. If you've worked on your casting in the wind, you can turn a rough day into a big success by catching a couple of hefty bonefish.

Pelican Bay guides also have some reliable spots around West End that work well in bad weather, and they will trailer their boats to launch at West End as well.

North Riding Point guides and anglers are also hampered by cold fronts, though one of their launching sites are in a more protected area on the north coast. A couple of these sites are dependent on the tides, but they can be made to work for at least part of the day.

A nice Grand Bahama bonefish.

Deep Water Cay Club has the most options for protected areas in bad weather. Rummer Creek, Big Harbour Creek, and other similar areas are easily accessible from the club dock, plus there are wadable flats nearby.

The shoreline flats around Grand Bahama are mostly lined with mangroves. Bottom structure is predominantly irregular coral of varying dark colors and turtle grass. Due to this structure, anglers more often fish from flats boats than by wading, though there are good flats to wade in places along the southern shoreline.

The grassy bottoms interspersed with massive mangrove root systems create a rich diversity of food, including a variety of shrimp. Because of this, bonefish can be extremely selective in what they eat. Look more for grass shrimp around the mangroves, and snapping shrimp in the turtle grass. A Borski's Fur Shrimp or Bonefish Critter is a good fly pattern in both areas.

Crabs tend to be more prevalent on the coral flats, with clams and mussels abundant on the many gold-colored sandy flats. Bonefish are opportunistic feeders in these areas. Fly choice is a matter of picking a pattern that will get down fast into the feeding zone, which makes lead-eyed flies the way to go.

If you're planning a visit to Grand Bahama, remember that the best months for bonefishing are April through July, and October and November. While some islands farther south tend to close up in July, this is a great time to fish Grand Bahama, especially the West End area.

March is also a prime month, but those cold fronts can get you. If this is the only time you can go, pack your bags and give it a shot. August and September can be

Loading up for a morning of fishing out of Pelican Bay Hotel.

good, though this is hurricane season. The period from December through February is a crapshoot with the weather, though non-anglers can enjoy themselves with a variety of activities. During these months it makes sense to plan a general vacation, with fishing just one of your activities. When you hit nice weather, get out on the flats in a hurry because the bones will be feeding with a vengeance.

Our favorite flies for bonefish vary depending on specific areas. We recommend a selection of flies that should include: #4-6 Gotchas and Bunny Gotchas; #4 Skinny Water Clouser's in tan and orange; #4-6 Crazy Charlies in gold, pink, and pearl; #4 Simram with small eyes; #4 Puffs in pink and tan; #4-6 Greg's Flats Fly; #4-6 Tan Mantis Shrimp; #4 Snapping Shrimp; #4-6 Hoovers in pink and gold; #4-6 Horrors in pink and yellow; #4 Bonefish Special; #6 Yarn Crabs; #4 Del's Merkin.

Greg Vincent, director of bonefishing at Pelican Bay, has developed a series of bunny flies that are extremely effective in the many different flats situations around the island. The flies rely on the natural action of the rabbit fur, are sized to fish varying depths of water, and color schemes are matched to specific bottom structure. If you are fishing out of Pelican Bay, be sure to ask Greg for an assortment.

Leaders should be at least nine feet, and in some areas, like the heavily fished flats around Deep Water Cay, you'll need up to 12-foot leaders. The best material to use is fluorocarbon, though we also like regular mono produced by Ande, Mason, and Maxima.

We prefer to fish incoming tides throughout Grand Bahama, though many areas never have a full incoming or outgoing tide. This often happens in April and May when you have the lowest tidal movements of the year.

We also prefer a neap tide to a spring tide in the fall due to the generally lower water levels. Because both ends of the island are near edges of the Little Bahama Bank, lower water doesn't hurt gamefish or baitfish movement.

Spring tides are still good, but they force more bonefish into the mangroves along the shorelines. You can go in and get them, but you'll break off more than you will land. A spring tide presents a prime opportunity to fish some of the cays farther off the mainland, especially the Water Cays and the cays north of West End.

Spring tides are the best times to fish for permit, with April through July the best months. While we have seen permit on many flats across the north shore of the island, fishing the far ends will usually give you the most shots. The guides out of Pelican Bay have begun to dial in the permit fishing, finding these elusive creatures on a fairly consistent basis near West End. What fly to use? When in doubt, go with a Del's Merkin or a Captain Crabby.

Anglers staying at Deep Water Cay will also have shots at permit during these months, especially during calm weather when the guides can run down to the Red Shank banks. Permit laze along here on the high tide, feasting on blue crabs. This area, which runs along the edge of the Little Bahama Bank all the way to Moore's Island, holds permit that average 30 to 40 pounds.

Tarpon can be caught on both ends of the island, but we'll vote for West End as the best area for the silver king. May through July are the best months, with October and November decent. On occasion, the guides here will make an effort to look for tarpon, but tarpon are usually incidental around Grand Bahama. Carry a 10-weight in the boat rigged with a Shallow Water Cockroach or a Black Death, just in case.

The 10-weight tarpon rig will also serve as a good all-around utility rod for sharks, barracuda, jacks, and cubera snapper. You can use the 80- to 100-pound shock tippet you use for tarpon on these fish, though you will need wire shock tippet for sharks and barracuda if these species are your primary targets.

Sharks are often overlooked as a fly rod gamefish, but they provide exciting sport. Sharks prefer warm weather and warm water on the flats. Though they are available year-round, April through June are the best months. Lemon and blacktip sharks inhabit most bonefish flats and ambush points around those flats. When you see these sharks on a flat, you can take this as a sure sign bonefish are in the vicinity.

When it comes to a wild, jumping, fighting fish, a blacktip shark rates with the best of them. If you prefer to settle in for a long bulldog battle, hook up a lemon. Our favorite way to catch sharks is with a surface popper. Watching a shark slash at a surface popper is a thrill, even though they often miss the target. Large streamers like Deceivers, especially in orange or red, will get you more hook-ups.

Barracuda are fun to catch on fly or spin tackle. (Brian O'Keefe)

Kim with West End guide Bonefish Foley.

A Popovic's Banger and a Foam Boilermaker are our favorite flies for catching barracuda too. Barracuda hit their prey with ferocious intensity and are equally fun to catch on fly or spinning tackle. If fishing is slow and you need to connect with something, tossing a green tube lure to a barracuda is like money in the bank. Barracuda don't mind cold water, which means you can find them on the flats throughout the winter. They cruise the flats in warmer months at times, though they usually prefer to congregate around reef structure during the summer.

The best fishing for gray, mutton, and cubera snappers is out of Deep Water Cay, and is equally fun with fly or spinning gear. Cubera snapper are the trophies here. These fish run 30 to 80 pounds. You'll need your 10-weight if you want to land one.

Cuberas have huge canine teeth and they strike with the killer instinct of a barracuda. We recommend at least 30-pound wire tippet, though 100-pound mono shock will usually hold. You'll find cuberas in many of the creeks and deeper cuts around Deep Water Cay year round, with April through June being the best months. #2/0 Clouser's Minnows in a variety of colors are our favorite flies for these voracious fish, but any well-presented fly will usually provoke them.

You'll find a variety of jacks living in the same areas as the cuberas. Deep Water Cay is famous for large aggressive bar jacks and horse-eyed jacks. While we recommend 30- to 40-pound shock tippet when going after these bullies, you can catch the smaller ones on the flats with your bonefish outfit.

The West End of Grand Bahama enjoys premiere offshore fishing due to its proximity to the Northwest Providence Channel and the Straits of Florida. April through July is the best period for most species, including blue and white marlin, sailfish, dorado, skipjacks, blackfin, yellowfin, and Allison tuna.

Greg Vincent and his guides at Pelican Bay are the only fly-fishing savvy crews on Grand Bahama, though there are a number of fine crews skilled in the various conventional gear tactics. Old Bahama Bay Marina has boats for hire with all tackle and bait provided. Xanadu, Running Mon, and Port Lucaya marinas also have boats available for fishing charter. From these marinas you might also want to try reef fishing for grouper, amberjack, and kingfish. Use chum over the reefs if you want to give fly-fishing a shot.

Dorado and wahoo are two of the most popular blue-water fish to pursue from Grand Bahama. January and February are the prime months for wahoo off West End, though the weather can be tough. Anglers with conventional gear can hook up more than 20 wahoo some days. Dorado start to show up in January, but April and May are the best months.

When we think of Grand Bahama, we see quality bonefishing operations evenly spaced across the island. Pelican Bay, North Riding Point, and Deep Water Cay each have unique qualities, offering anglers of all ability levels the opportunity to fish with high-caliber guides.

With easy access from the States, a blend of city life and Out Island charm, first-class accommodations, and a variety of activities for non-anglers, Grand Bahama makes its case for being one of the top fishing and vacations destinations in the Bahamas.

Optional Activities

Diving and snorkeling top the list of non-angling water sport activities. Grand Bahama is the best location in the islands to dive with dolphins in the wild. This can be arranged through UNEXSO's Dolphin Dive program. Resident dolphins from the Dolphin Experience Center rendezvous with divers at a reef about a mile offshore. If you want a less adventuresome dolphin experience, you can visit the UNEXSO dolphin center for two hours, or make a day of it. The center is a well-organized series of pens with interspersed floating docks inside Fortune Bay.

The UNEXSO headquarters in Port Lucaya, next door to Pelican Bay, was renovated in 2003. Now called Sun & Sea Outfitters, the 4,500-square-foot retail store stocks everything from tropical clothing to snorkeling and diving equipment to sunglasses, T-shirts, and film. Also on-site are the Dive-in Bar & Grill and a large swimming pool where beginning dive classes are taught.

If you want to dive with sharks (we don't), there are two feeding programs, one with UNEXSO and the other with Xanadu Undersea Adventures. In both programs,

The Dolphin Experience at UNEXSO in Freeport.

you can watch an experienced diver hand-feeding baitfish to a swarming school of reef sharks.

Grand Bahama is home to a number of blue holes inside reefs where experienced divers can descend along the rich coral walls. Cave diving is also spectacular here because the reef structure sits atop a massive limestone base that is carved into the second largest underwater cave system in the world. Located in Lucayan National Park, the caves are still being explored, and there are special dive programs hosted by UNEXSO that can take certified divers inside.

Additional water sports include sailing, boating, jet skiing, windsurfing, parasailing, and swimming, with the epicenter for these activities being the Our Lucaya resorts. The various marinas and some of the other resorts have rental equipment available as well.

Golf is a highlight for many visitors to Grand Bahama. The five courses are the Royal Oasis Emerald and Ruby courses, the Lucayan Country Club course, the semiprivate Fortuna Hills course, and the Bahama Reef course at Our Lucayan Resort.

Tennis courts are available at the Lucayan Country Club, the Royal Oasis, and at Our Lucaya.

Any exploration of Grand Bahama usually begins at Lucayan National Park. Pine forests laced with nature trails and limestone caves are two of the highlights. The small park also provides a sampling of 250 species of plants, making it an ideal outdoor classroom for visitors interested in learning more about the flora of the Bahamas.

Legend says the Park contains an ancient cemetery of the Lukka-Cairi, the Arawak Indian tribespeople who lived on the island long ago. Remnants of their civilization have been found in Ben's Cavern, the most famous of the Park's caves. Sea kayaking excursions can be arranged in and around the park, and on the north side of the island around the Water Cays.

The Rand Nature Center is another favorite site for visitors. Nature trails wind through 100 acres of Bahamian forest that is home to pink flamingos and more than 20 species of native orchids.

Shopping is a favorite pastime for many visitors. The Port Lucaya Marketplace is Kim's favorite place to shop, maybe because it's convenient to hit after a day on the flats, and definitely because of all the jewelry stores. Some stores and all of the restaurants stay open most evenings until 10:00 P.M. The atmosphere is lively and fun, and is enhanced further by the marina location. Several stores carry a good selection of Cuban cigars. If you're looking for a gift to take home to your family, you'll be able to find something here or across the street in half a dozen gift shops spread out through the Our Lucaya resort.

The International Bazaar, adjacent to the Royal Oasis resort near downtown, was designed and decorated by a Hollywood set director to be a world village depicting the cultures and architecture of different countries. Narrow streets wander in every direction, lined with shops, restaurants, and cafes. Mall hours are 10:00 A.M. to 6:00 P.M.

Lodging, Guides, and Services

Featured Lodges

Pelican Bay Bonefishing

Lucayan Marina   Our top choice for quality bonefishing combined with a variety of vacation services, Pelican Bay is an ideal location for an overall couples or family vacation. Bonefish average five pounds, with many fish eight pounds and up. Guided fishing is done from Maverick Mirage flats boats. Anglers are picked up at the hotel each morning and driven 15 minutes to the Queen's Cove launch site. Other launch sites, including the West End, are used as well. Pelican Bay Resort has 69 deluxe rooms and 48 luxury suites located on the marina with two freshwater swimming pools, two Jacuzzis, pool snack bar, and Ferry House restaurant. Rooms and suites include air-conditioning, private baths, balconies, minibars, and satellite TV. Twenty restaurants and 80 shops are located around Count Basie Square at the Port Lucaya Marketplace, a five-minute walk from the hotel, and across the way at the Our Lucaya Resort. Pelican Bay guests have reciprocal privileges to use all facilities, including the spa and health club, at Our Lucaya.

Season: October through July.

Suitable For: Anglers and non-anglers.

Optional Activities: Five championship golf courses, tennis, casinos, swimming, hiking and exploring, sailing, beach sports, dolphin experience, snorkeling, diving, fine restaurants, nightlife, and shopping.

What's Included: Accommodations, guided fishing, breakfast and lunch, and Bahamian taxes.

Not Included: Dinner, alcoholic beverages, optional gratuities to guides, optional activities.

Pricing: $$$

Contact: Reservations and information, 242-373-9550; fax 242-373-9551.

Internet: www.pelicanbaybonefishing.com

E-mail: gregfish@coralwave.com

North Riding Point Club

Burnside Cove   The serene beachfront location will put a smile on anyone's face, as will the elegant air-conditioned rooms and main lodge. The fishing program focuses on the central portion of the northern coast, with five access sites for fishing the best tides. Dover Sound, the Water Cays, and the North Riding Point areas are highlights. There are also some excellent wade fishing flats in this area. The guides (7 guides with a maximum of 14 guest anglers) drive the guests from the lodge each day, 15 to 30 minutes, to the launch sites. Bonefish average 5 to 6 pounds, with fish over 10 pounds possible. Dining is a highlight with special pride taken in presenting a variety of excellent food. A freshwater swimming pool overlooks the white sand beach, and all the amenities of Freeport are only a 20-minute drive away.

Season: Mid-September to mid-July.

Suitable For: Anglers and non-anglers.

Optional Activities: Diving, snorkeling, hiking through nearby Lucayan National Park, swimming, relaxing in beautiful surroundings, or taking short trips to Freeport for anything from golf and tennis to shopping and nightlife. Space is at a premium here since repeat clientele books well in advance. A year ahead for prime dates is recommended.

What's Included: Freeport International Airport transfers, deluxe accommodations, all meals including wine and liquor, guided fishing, and Bahamian taxes.
Not Included: Optional gratuities to guides and staff.
Pricing: $$$$
Contact: Reservations and information, 912-756-4890 or 242-353-4250 or call Frontiers Travel, 800-245-1950.
Internet: www.northridingpointclub.com
E-mail: northrpc@aol.com, bonefish@broadband.bs

Old Bahama Bay

West End   One of our favorite spots to relax, hang out in barefoot luxury, and, of course, catch some big bonefish. The resort accommodations include hotel rooms, 43 junior suites, and 6 one- and two-bedroom suites. Each spacious air-conditioned suite is steps away from the beach, and is furnished with custom Island-Plantation–style décor. Bathrooms feature fluffy towels and robes, soaking tubs, and granite-top double sink vanities. A 4,000-square-foot swimming pool with infinity edge overlooks the sea-green bay. The fitness center can arrange for spa and massage treatments. Casual dining is available in the Dockside Grille. For fine dining, the Aqua Restaurant is one of the best on the island. The 72-slip marina offers full services to boaters. The resort can arrange independent fishing guides or you can book them on your own. Flats fishing in the area is excellent, as is the offshore fishing in season.
Season: October through July.
Suitable For: Anglers and non-anglers.
Optional Activities: Diving, snorkeling, sailing, water sports, beachcombing, or taking short trips to Freeport for anything from golf and tennis to shopping and nightlife.
What's Included: Accommodations. Packages are available, but this is a do-it-yourself location in terms of setting up fishing and other vacation activities.
Not Included: You choose what to include or not.
Pricing: $$$
Contact: Reservations and information, 800-572-5711 or 242-350-6500.
Internet: www.oldbahamabay.com
E-mail: info@oldbahamabay.com

Deep Water Cay Club

McClean's Town   Tucked away on a remote cay off the east end of Grand Bahama, this renowned bonefishing destination is now a private equity club. Fertile habitat from flats to creeks to reefs and blue holes stretches over 250 square miles, creating a fishery for permit, sharks, barracuda, snappers, and jacks in addition to all the bonefish. Guides from McLean's Town have fishing in their blood, and they present themselves in a professional manner. The lodge facilities can accommodate up to 22 guests in air-conditioned private cottages, including 2 two-bedroom cottages. The clubhouse is casually elegant and spacious, with bar, dining room, game room, and unrestrained views out over the swimming pool and turquoise bay. Tennis courts are just a short walk from the clubhouse. We recommend booking well in advance since repeat clientele keeps the lodge busy.

The club is open to the public but, as a private club, members have the first shot at reservations. Prime dates are often taken by members and are not available to the public. Oceanfront home sites that include memberships are for sale. A private airstrip is available for guests to arrange charters or to fly in on their own aircraft.

Season: Mid-September through July.

Suitable For: Anglers and non-anglers.

Optional Activities: Sea kayaking and snorkeling excursions, swimming, blue-water fishing, sporting clays, beach and eco-explorations, tennis. A spa and fitness center with private massage rooms is planned for completion in 2005.

What's Included: Oceanfront air-conditioned rooms, all meals, guided fishing, staff gratuities, and Bahamian taxes.

Not Included: Air or ground transfers to the lodge. (We recommend the charter flight from Ft. Lauderdale or West Palm Beach directly to Deep Water Cay, though a taxi transfer from Freeport is available.) Alcoholic beverages, gratuities for fishing guides.

Pricing: $$$-$$$$

Contact: Reservations and information, 912-756-7071.

Internet: www.deepwatercay.com

E-mail: info@deepwatercay.com

Additional Accommodations

Water Cay Bonefishing and Eco Lodge

Water Cay   A relaxed remote location to access some of the best fishing on the island. The comfortable laid-back lodge can accommodate four anglers in clean air-conditioned motel-style rooms. The lodge provides airport pick-up and boat transfer to the island.

Pricing: $$

Contact: Reservations and information, 800-211-8530.

Internet: www.anglingdestinations.com

Port Lucaya Resort and Yacht Club

One hundred fifty air-conditioned motel-style rooms on the marina. Large swimming pool, Jacuzzi, restaurant, and bar. Great location on the marina, adjacent to the Port Lucaya Marketplace and Count Basie Square. Five-minute walk to the UNEXSO Dive Center. Across the street from the Lucayan, the new mega-resort, casino, and golf complex.

Pricing: $$-$$$

Contact: Reservations and information, 242-373-6618 or 800-582-2921; fax 242-373-6652.

Crowne Plaza Royal Oasis Golf Resort and Casino

This is a major resort complex with 845 air-conditioned rooms and suites. The casino is located in the Tower; the country club is across the street. Nine restaurants are available, including the Crowne Room. Amenities include a million-gallon beach pool with water slides and waterfalls, two 18-hole championship golf courses, tennis courts, fitness center, Serenity European-style spa, jogging trails, and nightclub. Independent fly-fishing guides can be arranged.

Pricing: $$-$$$$

Contact: Reservations and information, 242-350-7000 or 800-2Crowne; fax 242-350-7002.

Internet: www.theroyaloasis.com, www.crowneplaza.com

E-mail: reservations@crowneplazagrandbahama.com

Our Lucaya Beach and Golf Resort

Westin and Sheraton Resorts This mega-resort opened in April 1999. It is our top choice as an all-around vacation location on Grand Bahama. The lodge is divided into two sections—the Westin at Our Lucaya, and the Sheraton at Our Lucaya. The Westin offers luxury accommodations in 222 Lighthouse Pointe rooms and suites, and in 527 Breakers Cay high-rise rooms and suites. The resort's spa and fitness center is located in the Westin wing, along with the convention facilities, and a large free-form pool and lap pool. The Sheraton has 511 rooms in the Reef Village, a family-style resort with large pools, water slides, and a kid's camp. Both resorts share a gorgeous oceanfront of white sand beaches, a modern casino, nine restaurants, including fine dining at Churchill's, and casual Caribbean dining at Iries, tennis courts, and golf course. The resort is directly across the street from the Port Lucaya Marketplace and Marina.

Pricing: $$-$$$$

Contact: Reservations and information, 242-373-1333 Westin; 242-373-1444 Sheraton.

Internet: www.starwood.com

Grand Bahama Bonefishing

Our Lucaya Beach and Golf Resort Here you can enjoy the luxury of the Our Lucaya resort, and fish with some of the best guides in the Bahamas. The well-known Pinder brothers are the heart of this program that puts anglers on fishing grounds from the Water Cays to the West End. Dolphin Superskiffs powered by 90-hp Yamaha motors are outfitted with leaning bars on the casting deck and poling platforms on the rear. Each boat is equipped with a radio, life preservers, and all safety equipment. Non-anglers will be happy at the resort or tooling around Freeport while anglers hit the flats.

Pricing: $$$

Contact: Reservations and information, 800-211-8530.

Internet: www.anglingdestinations.com

Do-It-Yourself Options

Rainbow Reef Tours

Pelican Point This company can help the adventure traveler and angler with accommodations, snorkeling trips, bonefishing trips, and eco-tours. Miles of white sand beaches in this area are perfect for catching rays and relaxing. The Pelican Point Beach Lodge has one- and two-bedroom cottages with full kitchens on the beach. Recommended fly-fishing guide Bill Humes is part of the Rainbow Reef's team. This is a good option for combining guide fishing with fishing on your own.

Pricing: $-$$

Contact: Reservations and information, 242-353-6013.

Internet: www.rainbowreeftours.com

Ocean Pearl Resort

High Rock We wouldn't call Ocean Pearl a resort, but that's the way these small places describe themselves. Instead, this is a comfortable motel/hotel on the beach, a relaxing out of the way place to hang out, fish, sea kayak, snorkel, or do nothing. And it's just a 30-minute drive to Freeport if you get an itch for a faster pace. Fly-fishing guides can be arranged.

Pricing: $-$$

Contact: Reservations and information, ask for Doris at 242-353-4224.

Internet: www.oceanpearlresort.com

Marinas

Grand Bahama Island has a number of marinas. Four are official ports of entry: Old Bahama Bay Marina, Xanadu Marina, the Lucayan Village Marina, and Port Lucaya Marina. Freeport Harbour, even though not a marina, is also an official port of entry.

All visiting boaters should call on a recognized port of entry upon arrival in the Bahamas. If you arrive at a marina that is not a port of entry, you can clear your boat by contacting Bahamas Customs and Immigration and arranging to have officers visit your vessel.

Boaters should contact harbor control or marina offices en route on VHF Channel 16 to provide pre-arrival information of your vessel's name, registration number, and last port of call. Similarly, providing pre-departure information to the marina officials is your responsibility.

Ocean Reef Yacht Club

Fifty-two slips, with vessels up to 180 feet. Depth dockside is six feet. Electricity, water, ice, showers, cable, and satellite TV. Charters arranged; boat rentals, tackle, and bait are available. VHF Channel 16. One-, two-, and three-bedroom air-conditioned suites and villas are available with amenities that include a swimming pool, Jacuzzi, and tennis courts.
Contact: Reservations and information, 242-373-4661/2; fax 242-373-8621.
Internet: www.oryc.com
E-mail: oceanreef@coralwave.com

Port Lucaya Resort & Yacht Club

One hundred slips, with vessels up to 175 feet. Water, ice, showers, laundry, marina supplies, and groceries. Charters arranged and boat rentals are available. Telephone and cable TV hook-ups. Adjoins Port Lucaya Marketplace, with shops, restaurants, bars, and entertainment. Next door to Underwater Explorer's Society (UNEXSO). VHF Channels 16 and 72. Port of Entry.
Contact: Reservations and information, 242-373-9090; fax 242-373-5884.
Internet: www.portlucaya.com
E-mail: info@portlucayamarina.com

Running Mon Marina & Resort

Sixty-six slips. Electricity, water, ice, showers, laundry, satellite TV. Tami-lift to 40 tons. Tackle shop with bait. Charter fleet on site. Thirty-two comfortable air-conditioned guest rooms and swimming pool. Grand Bahama Scuba Dive Center is five minutes away.
Contact: Reservations and information, 242-352-6834 or 800-932-4959.
Internet: www.running-mon-bahamas.com

Xanadu Beach Marina & Resort

Seventy-seven slips, with vessels up to 200 feet. Depth dockside is eight feet. Fuel, water, ice, laundry, showers, telephone, satellite TV. Restaurant and bar. Marine and tackle shop, gift shop, pharmacy. Sportfishing charter boats available. Diving and snorkeling trips arranged. VHF Channel 26. The accompanying hotel tower has 137 air-conditioned rooms, plus 47 suites in two-story structures around the marina, restaurant, three bars, swimming pool, tennis courts, and beach access.
Contact: Reservations and information, 242-352-6782; fax 242-352-5799.
Internet: www.xanadubeachhotel.com

Lucayan Village Marina

One hundred fifty slips, with vessels up to 150 feet. Full services for boaters include fuel, water, ice, bathhouse, electricity, phone and satellite TV hook-ups, swimming pool, bar, restaurant, luxury townhouse suites, all facilities at Pelican Bay Resort. Open 24 hours. Port of Entry and immigration services. VHF Channel 16. This is one of the most deluxe service-oriented marinas anywhere.
Contact: Reservations and information, 242-373-8888; fax 242-373-3616
Internet: www.lucayanmarinavillage.com

Independent Guides

There are a number of Grand Bahama independent guides. Here are a few we have used, or have been recommended by readers.

Israel Rolle, better known as the famous Bonefish Foley, works out of West End. Tommy and Carl Rolle, sons of Bonefish Foley, work for Pelican Bay, but also take some independent trips in the off-season. Contact them at 242-346-6060.

Samuel Taylor works out of Freeport and will pick you up at your hotel. He has fly-fishing and spinning gear available for client use. You can contact him at 242-352-8679 or 242-557-6284 or e-mail bonefishsam@hotmail.com.

Omeko Glinton works out of Freeport and will pick you up at your hotel. Contact him at 242-353-3047.

Bill Humes can be contacted at www.rainbowreeftours.com or by phone at 242-353-6013. Bill will pick you up at your hotel, or you can meet him at East End.

Captain Perry Demeritte, out of McLean's Town. Captain Perry will pick you up at your hotel for a full or half day of fishing. He has fly rods and spinning rods for rent. You can contact Captain Perry at 242-353-3301. You can also visit his Web site at www.captainperry.com or e-mail him at perrybonefish@batel.net.

Captain Henry Roberts works out of Freeport and will pick you up at your hotel. You can call him at 242-353-2018.

Services

Diving, Snorkeling, and Water Sports: *Underwater Explorers Society (UNEXSO)* is located between the Pelican Bay Hotel and the Port Lucaya Marina inside Bell Harbour. The new facility (completed in 2003) includes a 4,500-square-foot retail center, dive shop, restaurant and bar, and a pool for beginning dive instructions. Adventure diving excursions with a qualified professional staff. Dolphin encounters and shark feeding dives. Instruction for all levels. Photo lab. Snorkelers and beginner divers welcome. Reservations and information: 800-922-3483 or 242-373-1244; Internet: www.unexso.com; e-mail: info@unexso.com.

Xanadu Undersea Adventures is a complete dive center for beginning and experienced divers, located at the Xanadu Beach Hotel. World famous shark dives. Nitrox available. Reservations and information, 242-352-3811 or 242-352-5856; fax 242-352-4731; Internet: www.xanadudive.com;

e-mail: divexua@batelnet.bs.

Restaurants: Our favorite restaurants in the Port Lucaya Marketplace include *Luciano's*, the *Ferry House at Pelican Bay*, *La Dolce Vita*, *Zorba's*, *Pisces*, and *The Pub*. At Our Lucaya Resort we like *Churchill's Chop House* for fine dining, *Iries* for casual Caribbean food and awesome mojitos. The *Arawak Dining Room* at the *Lucayan Country Club* is excellent for lunch and dinner. *The Stoned Crab* on Taino Beach serves good seafood in a beachside setting. *Pier 1* at Freeport Harbor is a fun experience. You should eat here just to see the shark feedings. Things are always changing, so we recommend talking with the staff at your hotel to get their suggestions.

Car Rentals: The big agencies like *Avis*, *Dollar*, and *Thrifty* have offices at the airport. A local agency is *Bahama Buggies* near the International Bazaar, 242-352-8750. We recommend booking your rental car in advance, or through your hotel after you arrive.

Taxi Service: Very good on the island, with zone fares regulated by the government. We still advise asking about fares up front.

Shopping: Grocery stores, liquor stores, pharmacies, cigar shops, and just about every other kind of shop you would need are available in Freeport and Port Lucaya. Once you drive east, services and stores will be limited, as they are on the Out Islands.

Medical Facilities: The government-run *Rand Memorial Hospital* is a good medical facility with 74 beds. Ambulance, police, and fire department services are available in Freeport and Port Lucaya.

Banks: A number of banks are open 9:30 A.M. to 3:00 P.M. Monday through Thursday, and 9:30 A.M. to 5:00 P.M. on Friday. Several ATMs are available, but don't count on them.

New Developments

Increasing numbers of fly-fishing guides are tossing their rods into the independent guiding ring. Check with your hotel for their recommendations. There are a number of smaller motels and lodges springing up, especially to the east, around McLean's Town. Some are comfortable and appealing while others will be a disappointment. Check these places out carefully before making a reservation.

The ongoing luxury home and condominium development at Old Bahama Bay continues to expand. Similar developments for private homes, townhouses, and condos are in the works all across the island. Several new large-scale resorts are in the planning process, but may or may not ever happen. One grand resort idea is the creation of five islands off Port Lucaya. The islands would be home to a resort and casino that would dwarf the Atlantis complex on Paradise Island. This idea is from a company that has already accomplished something similar near Dubai, so they might be serious. We'll see.

Log on to our Web site, www.bahamasflyfishingguide.com, for the most up-to-date information.

CHAPTER 6

THE ABACOS

North Abaco.

Abaco is a mini-archipelago that stretches in a languid crescent for more than 120 miles, beginning with Walker's Cay in the north, and running to the end of the Little Bahama Bank in the south at Sandy Point and Hole in the Wall.

Palm Beach, Florida, lies 200 miles to the west, while Abaco's sister island, Grand Bahama, is a short boat ride away from Coopers Town and Little Abaco.

The three distinct regions that comprise Abaco are Little Abaco, Great Abaco, and the offshore cays. Including these cays, Abaco encompasses roughly 650 square miles, with a population of about 10,000 full-time residents.

The dazzling offshore cays bob in the Atlantic mostly east, and some north, of Great Abaco. The larger populated cays include Walker's, Green Turtle, Great Guana, Man-O-War, and Elbow. The majority of the cays are uninhabited and, together, these cays provide a 100-mile-long sheltered cruising area for boating and fishing enthusiasts. This is one reason why Abaco is dubbed the "Sailing Capital of the World," though the people of Great Exuma would argue that point. There is no arguing, however, that Abaco's protected waters, safe harbors, deluxe marinas, charming settlements, secluded coves, and sparkling sand beaches make this little archipelago a dream destination.

A warm and welcoming people, Abaconians are resourceful by nature, necessity having dictated their vocations toward boatbuilding, farming, sailmaking, and crawfishing.

We may start to sound like a frozen CD, but meeting the people of Abaco is one of the highlights. Their forebears date back to 1783 when Loyalists and slaves arrived after being forced out of the Carolinas and other colonies at the conclusion of the American Revolution.

Abaconians are industrious, church-going people with a strong sense of loyalty and a belief in self-reliance. Looking around the island, it is easy to see that a pride in craftsmanship, in everything from home construction to crafts to shipbuilding, is central in their daily lives.

The tranquil local atmosphere is a great tonic for any business or other problems you may have left back home. This sense of well-being often seeps into visitors a day or two after arrival without any awareness. All of a sudden you just feel more relaxed, more at peace. Eating the local food helps, as it focuses on fare from the sea, and is prepared in a variety of spicy recipes.

When you look around you see people going about their daily lives with a simple sense of purpose. There is little unemployment on Abaco. This admirable work ethic has brought considerable prosperity to the island, most notably due to commercial fishing and tourism. If you have questions, it's easy to find someone with the answers. It's also nice to realize that people here haven't yet become jaded by tourism, as locals have in other countries with tourist economies. This is a place where you can feel content in an uncrowded environment, yet still have access to whatever level of accommodations and services you desire.

While there are good qualities about Abaco from head to toe, we have to confess to a special feeling for Treasure Cay, and its offshore neighbors, Green Turtle, Great Guana, Man-O-War, and Elbow Cays. Great fishing opportunities combined with wonderful accommodations, an abundance of activities, and mind-melting serenity make this area unique in all the Bahamas.

Sailing, boating, diving, snorkeling, beachcombing, fishing, and other water-related activities are undoubtedly the focus of most visitors. An activity we highly recommend is exploring the offshore cays, finding your own deserted beach, and spreading out a great picnic on the pristine sand. Then, if you have a fly rod, wander over to a secluded cove and catch a few tailing bonefish.

Eco-tourism has become the "in" thing throughout the islands. Hiking and biking are popular through natural areas ripe with bird and plant life. Sea kayaking in pristine protected areas provides a rewarding sense of adventure. More conventional activities include golf, tennis, and beach volleyball. And if you don't feel like doing anything, that's a highly rated activity, too.

The commercial hub of Abaco, and third largest town in the Bahamas, is Marsh Harbour. The town supports a full array of services to visitors, including one of the best medical clinics in the islands.

Convenient commercial air service to Marsh Harbour and Treasure Cay airports, from Florida or from Nassau, make Abaco an easy destination to reach. American Eagle flies daily to Marsh Harbour from Miami. Bahamasair flies daily from Nassau to both airports. Air Sunshine and Island Express serve both airports from Ft. Lauderdale. Continental/Gulfstream flies to both airports from various Florida airports.

Air charter services from Florida and Nassau have economical service for families or fishing parties who prefer this extra convenience. If you want to take the casual approach, scheduled mail boats from Nassau visit ports up and down the island on a weekly basis. Scheduled ferry service from Marsh Harbour and Treasure Cay to the offshore cays is convenient and reliable, though you can choose to rent your own boat.

Most ferryboats are covered, so you stay dry even in rough weather crossings, but you should be prepared for bad weather. We always take rain jackets with hoods on the ferryboats just in case, and we wear either sandals with good support, or tennis shoes because the gunwales of the ferries and the docks are usually slippery. High-traction soles are a must.

Around the Island

Walker's Cay is the northernmost inhabited cay in the Abacos and the Bahamas. It lies on the northeastern edge of the Little Bahama Bank, a short distance from some of the best blue water fishing in the Atlantic Ocean.

The resort cay has long been famous as a boaters' haven and for its billfish tournaments. More recent notoriety has been achieved from Flip Pallot's ESPN television series, The Walker's Cay Chronicles.

The Walker's Cay Hotel and Marina dominates the island, with the hotel itself perched on the highest ground overlooking the aqua-colored water covering the shallow banks to the west. The hotel and marina serve a variety of boaters interested in cruising, diving, and fishing. The marina has space for 75 boats. Hotel amenities

Heading out for a day of sun, relaxation, and hopefully a few 10-pound bones. (Brian O'Keefe)

include a restaurant, bar, two swimming pools, and a tennis court. Accommodations are in deluxe rooms and larger villas.

The airstrip is used by the resort's aircraft, bringing in vacationers from Florida, though it is available to commercial charters and private pilots. The customs office is located nearby.

Complete diving and fishing packages are available through the Walker's Cay Hotel. It is possible to combine blue-water fishing for billfish, wahoo, tuna, and dorado, with flats fishing for bonefish, permit, barracuda, and sharks. Reef fishing throughout the area is sensational.

Flats fly-fishers should be aware that bonefishing immediately around Walker's is not very good. Runs of 20 minutes to an hour to Tom Brown's Cay, Grand Cays, and even Double Breasted Cays, produce the best bonefishing. If the weather is rough, these runs can be uncomfortable, or even impossible.

Grand Cays are southeast of Walker's and the grouping of small islands covers a considerable area. The shallow water within the islands is ideal habitat for bonefish and a variety of snappers. Pretty beaches face the ocean side of the cays, while mangrove-lined creeks snake in every direction. The wider lagoons and broader sounds have skinny water flats that are bonefish magnets. Navigating these areas is tricky at best, and we recommend using a local guide. If boaters wish to try it on their own, take a little Avon dinghy and your GPS, and be careful.

There is a protected harbor for boaters next to the Grand Cays settlement. Space for about a dozen boats is available at the dock facilities of the Island Bay Front Hotel. The hotel has basic air-conditioned rooms, plus fuel, water, and ice for boaters. Rosie's Place serves good local dishes including some of the best grouper and snapper we've tasted. Two smaller grocery stores have a decent selection of the necessary foods, plus some over-the-counter drugs and medicines. There is also a tempting bakery. A freighter from Nassau arrives at the cay about every 10 days, so the stores are stocked when the boat arrives, and then become sparse as the days pass before the next boat.

The settlement population is around 400 people who make their living fishing or as resort employees at Walker's Cay. These are exceptionally friendly people, who can tell you stories for hours, while never missing a beat in a domino game. Bring up the subject of fishing and you'll hear incredible tales of giant bonefish, permit, jacks, and cubera snapper.

Grand Cays creates a convenient base for adventurous fly-fishers cruising the cays of the Little Bahama Bank during April, May, and June. While offshore fishers would be better served at Walker's Cay, flats fly-fishers will do better stationed here. There are miles of soft grassy flats and harder wadable sand and coral flats that are home to countless bonefish that rarely, if ever, see a fly. Shrimp and crab populations are amazing, as you can see in many areas at low tide. Creek, cut, and reef fishing is outstanding. Grey snappers line the mangroves, while jacks, cuberas, and barracudas fill ambush points during the last half of falling tides.

Walker's Cay ★ Walker's Cay Hotel & Marina
Walker's Cay

Grand Cay

Double Breasted Cay

Abacos

North

Stranger's Cay

LITTLE BAHAMA BANK

Carter's Cay

Great Sale Cay

Paw Paw Cay

Fish Cays

Moraine Cay

Pensacola Cays

LITTLE ABACO

Lt. Cave Cay

○ FOX TOWN
○ CROWN HAVEN
○ WOOD CAY

Big Hog Cay

Spanish Cay Resort & Marina ★
Spanish Cay

Cross Cay

Mangrove Cay

○ CEDAR HARBOUR

Big Jerry Cay

Randall's Cay

Powell Cay

○ COOPER'S TOWN

NORTH ATLANTIC
OCEAN

Bamboo Cay

○ BLACKWOOD VILLAGE

Nun Jack Cay
Crab Cay
Green Turtle Cay

BIGHT OF ABACO

Treasure Cay Airport ✈

Green Turtle Cay Club & Marina ★
Bluff House Beach Hotel ★

Snapper Cay

Green Turtle Cay Ferry

Whale Cay

Big Joe Downer Cay

★ Banyon Beach Club
★ Treasure Cay Resort & Marina

Dolphin Beach Resort ★
Guana Seaside Village ★
Great Guana Cay

Woolen Dean Cay

THE MARLS

Schooner's Landing Resort ★
Man of War Cay

Marsh Harbour Airport ✈

Abaco Beach Resort & Marina

○◉ MARSH HARBOUR
Albury's Ferry

SPRING CITY ○

Snake Cay

○ HOPE TOWN
Elbow Cay

HARD BARGAIN ○

Moore's Island

Tilloo Cay

Shallow Water Point

Lynard Cay

Cornwall Ft.

CHEROKEE ○
Ocean Point

Nettie's Different of Abaco

Eight Mile Bay

Disney Cruise Ship Dock
Castaway Cay ★
Gorda Cay

○ CROSSING ROCK

Rickmon Bonefishing Lodge ★
SANDY POINT ○
Rocky Point

Grape Tree

Cross Harbour

Hole in the Wall

NORTHEAST PROVIDENCE CHANNEL

LEGEND
○ TOWN / SETTLEMENT
★ Resort / Marina
✈ Airport
⚓ Ferry
🐟 fish species
— Roads
▲ Restaurant / Bar

0 5 10 15 20 25
SCALE IN MILES

©1999 Map Illustration/Burton Design, Jackson Hole, WY

Local guides are available in Grand Cay and can be contacted through the hotel or through Rosie's. The best means of communication throughout the cays of Abaco is by VHS radio. Channel 68 is the general hailing and emergency channel in this area, so it should be used only when necessary. Rosie's can usually be reached on Channel 16.

Continuing southeast, Double Breasted Cays are composed of countless rocks, sandbars, channels, cays, and cuts. White sand beaches dot many of the cays. Navigating larger boats is tricky in this area. It makes sense to find a safe anchorage, and then explore the flats and creeks in a dinghy or smaller launch. Bonefishing here is excellent, especially during neap tides, when the incoming tide is in the morning or late afternoon.

A long series of cays and rocks continues in a southeasterly direction toward Great Abaco. Stranger's Cay, Joe Cays, Carter Cays, Fish Cays, and Moraine Cay are some of the more notable. We fished the flats south of Little Carter Cay in spring 2004 with great success. The fishing was so good here we had to pass up many other flats that looked as good or better before heading back to Crown Haven.

While this type of fishing is hit or miss without specific local knowledge, boating anglers can find these opportunities throughout this region. You just have to have your mind in tune with the habitat. Pay specific attention to the bottom structure. A common denominator we look for is a combination of deeper water feeding shallower flats. Check out the tidal flow direction and this will tell you where to look for approaching bonefish.

The largest cay in the area, lying southwest of the Carter Cays, is Great Sale Cay. This low-lying cay is about five and a half miles long with huge marshy areas that are prime spawning grounds for a variety of crabs, shrimp, and baitfish. Many of the marshes are lined with thick mangroves, and off the mangroves are wide areas of grassy flats. Essentially, this is a food factory for bonefish, snappers, barracudas, sharks, and rays.

The dark grass flats make it hard to spot bonefish without good sunlight, though during calm conditions you can see tails and wakes in every direction. If you just want to catch a lot of bonefish, with fly or conventional gear, wait for high tide, especially during spring tides, and you'll see bonefish muds the size of large sandbars.

Great Sale Cay is often used as a stopover point for boaters traversing the Little Bahama Bank from West End, Grand Bahama to the northern Abaco cays and Little Abaco. The West End Bars of Little Abaco are a short boat trip southeast of Great Sale Cay.

Boaters can cruise along the eastern length of the bars to Hawksbill Cays or to Fox Town in water that averages 10 feet deep. This direction is traveled more by boaters because it feeds the protected waterway between the offshore cays and Great Abaco.

Boaters can also take the route along the leeward side of the West End Bars into the Bight of Abaco. Water depths are skinnier on this side, and navigation requires constant attention over various shallow bars. Taking a path on either side of Cave Cays is the way to go. Fly-fishers will want to proceed between Cave Cays and Cashe's Cay as the bonefishing in this area is consistently good. Permit are available here as well. Boaters should find a safe anchorage around Cave Cays, and then use dinghies or launches to explore the series of cays running in toward Crown Haven.

There are wadable flats throughout the area with bottom structures ranging from hard white sand to uneven coral and soft turtle grass. Wading is especially good around Brush Cay. The turtle grass flats are usually too mucky to wade, but bones love to tail in the dark fertile grass during the low incoming tide. Using a sea kayak here is a good option.

Land-based anglers can reach Crown Haven and Fox Town via the main highway from Coopers Town and Treasure Cay. Several independent guides operate in this area by trailering their boats to the Crown Haven boat ramp.

Fox Town is the main settlement at the north end of Little Abaco. The settlement faces east, overlooking several bays and clusters of black and green outcroppings of rocks that punctuate the aqua-blue sea. Services for boaters are available at the government pier and at the Shell station dock. As it is throughout the Abaco Cays, VHS radios are used more frequently than telephones. Channel 16 will reach the Shell Station, and the manager can help you with most anything you need.

There are a couple of restaurants near the harbor, a general store, and telephone services at the BaTelCo office.

Boaters heading south from Fox Town navigate northeast around Hawksbill Cay before making the turn toward Crab Cay. The grouping of rocks and small cays on the north end of Hawksbill Cay create a number of irregular flats, some no wider than a medium-range cast. These flats, all fed by deeper water, draw decent numbers of bonefish, but more important, they draw huge bonefish. This type of flat is generally overlooked throughout the Bahamas because it requires a lot of hopping around, with only a little fishing, but for anglers looking to hook up some huge bones, it's worth the time.

Little Abaco fattens out before it joins Great Abaco via a narrow causeway that is part of the Great Abaco Highway leading south to Coopers Town. A small series of cays strung along the road, including Wood Cay, are connected by glistening white bonefish flats that are easy to wade.

On the windward side, Cedar Harbour, the Riding Rocks, Crab Cay, and Angel Fish Point create a small bay that is laced with creeks, cuts, and flats. When the wind is down, this is a good option for fishing on your own, and can be productive for bonefish, jacks, snappers, sharks, and barracuda.

Do-it-yourself anglers can set up headquarters at the Tangelo Hotel at Wood Cay. A comfortable windward lodge, Tangelo has a good restaurant, and can arrange for guides, or book you for a complete bonefish package.

Boaters cruising south past Angel Fish Point can choose to veer eastward to Spanish Cay. Once private, the cay is now open to the public. A 5,000-foot runway can accommodate private jets. The marina was remodeled in 2002 along with the restaurant and a number of other resort amenities. The cay is a self-contained vacation destination that includes deserted white sand beaches, rental condos and houses, tennis courts, a dive center, and boat and bike rentals.

A potential danger to boaters, but a bonanza for fly-fishers, is a large shallow bank with accompanying flats stretching southwest from Spanish Cay. We have caught several permit here in the past few years and see them here on a regular basis along with big bones. If you are just cruising through the area, this can be hit or miss, but if you're staying on Spanish Cay, and you put in some time here, the results can be worthwhile. These flats can also be accessed from Coopers Town, though the fishing on the leeward side is so good that anglers rarely head in this direction.

Coopers Town is a well-established community based around a fishing economy. While conch, grouper, snapper, and a variety of other fish produce food and income, lobster, or crawfish as it's called locally, is the high-dollar ticket. The commercial crawfish season runs from August 1 to March 31, and it is not uncommon for entire families to stop everything else and go harvesting during August.

Arriving boaters can find all services at either Murray's dock or the Shell station pier. VHS Channel 16 is the best way to contact both facilities. Grocery stores, restaurants, bakeries, a laundromat, and telephone services are all within walking distance of the docks.

For fly- and conventional fishers, the action here is on the leeward side of Coopers Town. O'Donald Macintosh is the best guide in the area, and one of the most interesting guides to fish with anywhere in the Bahamas. He is also an elected member of the local government, and one of the community leaders. Two of O'Donald's sons, Kirkland and Drexel, have joined him in the guiding business.

A number of rutted dirt tracks lead out to the leeward side of the island. The fishing grounds run from the curvy shorelines of the main island to the outer mangrove-topped cays miles offshore. We often see tailing bonefish at the small dock where O'Donald keeps a boat. A five-minute run to a crescent-shaped group of cays split by a deep creek puts anglers onto large numbers of aggressive bones in the three- to six-pound range.

Mangrove-covered cays, some with blue holes, stretch for miles in every direction, the largest being Randall's Cay to the south. Flats, creeks, and deeper channels fill in the space between the cays with shades of blues and greens that are ever changing.

We fish the turtle grass flats from boats, but much of our fishing time here is spent wading. Hard white sand flats interspersed with crunchy coral and grass provide miles of ankle-deep water for tailing bonefish on the appropriate tides.

This is not an area we recommend fishing on your own unless you have a boat. Even then, good local knowledge is critical, so we suggest fishing with a professional guide. For anglers staying in Treasure Cay, or on the nearby offshore cays, fishing this area with O'Donald can be a highlight of your trip.

Boaters heading south from Coopers Town will find small bonefish flats and good reef fishing around Powell Cay, which is a private island, and then at Manjack, Crab Cay (yes, another Crab Cay), and Fiddle Cay, on the way to Green Turtle Cay.

On land, the Great Abaco Highway takes you south to the Treasure Cay Airport, the Green Turtle Cay Ferry, and then to the resort of Treasure Cay.

Treasure Cay is one of our favorite places in the Bahamas, both as a base for fishing, and for just chillin', mon. The large marina offers full services to boats of all sizes, and you can be sure to see some eye-popping yachts here any time of the year. Boaters have

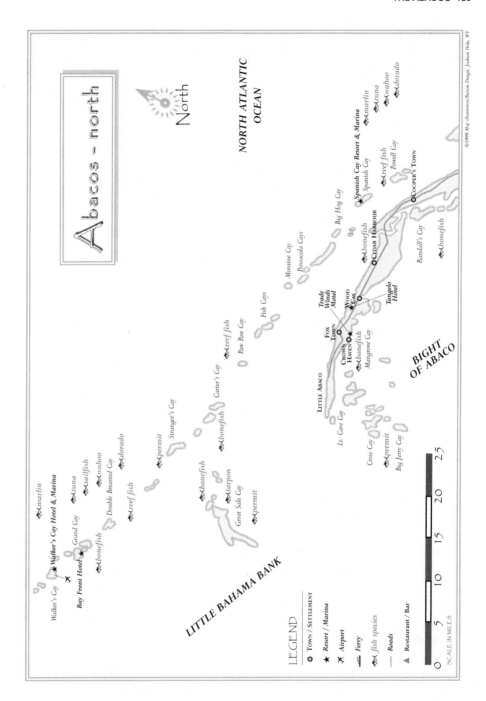

Abacos – north

North

NORTH ATLANTIC
OCEAN

LITTLE BAHAMA BANK

BIGHT
OF ABACO

LITTLE ABACO

Walker's Cay
Walker's Cay Hotel & Marina ★marlin
★tuna
★sailfish
Bay Front Hotel ★ Grand Cay
bonefish ✈wahoo
Double Breasted Cay
✈dorado
✈reef fish
✈permit

✈bonefish
✈tarpon
Great Sale Cay
✈permit
Stranger's Cay

✈bonefish
Carter's Cay
✈reef fish
Paw Paw Cay
Fish Cays

Cross Cay
✈permit
Big Jerry Cay

Lt. Cave Cay

Fox
Town Crown
Haven
✈bonefish
Mangrove Cay

Wood
Cay
Trade
Winds
Motel
Tangelo
Hotel

Moraine Cay
Pensacola Cays
Big Hog Cay

✈bonefish Cedar Harbour

Spanish Cay Resort & Marina ✈marlin
Spanish Cay ✈tuna
✈wahoo
✈reef fish ✈dorado
Powell Cay
Cooper's Town

Randall's Cay
✈bonefish

LEGEND
○ Town / Settlement
★ Resort / Marina
✈ Airport
⌁ Ferry
✈ fish species
— Roads
▲ Restaurant / Bar

0   5   10   15   20   25
SCALE IN MILES

©1999 Map illustration/Burton Design, Jackson Hole, WY

access to all the marina facilities including the swimming pool, bar, Spinnaker's restaurant, and a dive shop.

Condos and villas ring the marina and spread into the gardens that include clay and hard-surface tennis courts. A sprawling grass park in the center of the resort is ringed by a Little Switzerland gift shop, Florence's Café, a laundromat, golf cart and bike rental shops, a small market, and a larger grocery and liquor store.

The pool at Treasure Cay Hotel.

Just across the settlement road is the dazzling Treasure Cay Beach, often rated among the top 10 beaches in the world. The Banyon Beach Club, a relaxing condo complex, is located here, along with a number of houses available for rental. Banyon Beach offers bonefishing packages and is ideally suited to accommodate anglers traveling with non-angling companions. More rental houses are available farther along the road, including the Treasure Houses, and all the way out to Windward Road, which faces Green Turtle, Whale, and Great Guana Cays.

On the way out to Windward Road is the Bahama Beach Club, a luxury condo complex with two- to four-bedroom units for sale or rent. This is a good vacationing option for families and larger groups. Bonefishing guides can be arranged, or you can book your own independent guide who will pick you up at your condo.

An 18-hole Dick Wilson golf course rounds out the resort's amenities. At the far southeastern end of the golf course are bonefish flats that beckon at low tide. These flats are far from being secret, and in fact, they are fished regularly by local ex-pat residents.

Treasure Cay Resort & Marina can arrange bonefish guides and offshore boats. The offshore boats fish the reefs for jacks, barracuda, cubera snapper, and mackerel, and fish the blue water for marlin, sailfish, tuna, and dorado. Most of this fishing is with conventional gear, slinging plugs and spoons over the reefs and using trolling lures.

The people who cruise in this area regularly drag some kind of lure or bait behind their boats to catch a variety of fish for the dinner table.

While Treasure Cay is a convenient vacation base, Green Turtle and Great Guana Cays are more idyllic if you want a more secluded location. Green Turtle Cay is three miles long and about a mile-and-a-half wide. The irregular coastline consists of wavy beaches, grassy dunes, shallow bays, and larger sounds. Growing pineapples, salvaging wrecked ships, and fishing have supported the locals over the years, but tourism leads the economy today.

New Plymouth, located near the southern end of the cay, is a picture postcard New England–style settlement with a main cement dock that is used by the weekly mail boat and the commercial water taxis. Lowe's water taxi service makes the two-mile run from Abaco on a continual basis throughout the day. People coming from Treasure Cay can be dropped off for a couple of hours to look around New Plymouth, take the next ferry over to the Green Turtle Cay Club for lunch or a walk, then take another ferry back to Abaco later in the day.

New Plymouth is a port of entry with full services for boaters, vacationers, and day visitors. The town has a marine hardware store, grocery and liquor stores, a post office, a bank open two days a week, and BaTelCo telephone and fax services. A two-hour stroll through the narrow maze of clean streets will take you to many interesting shops and the Albert Lowe Museum, located in a 150-year-old house. The restored museum displays Alton Lowe's paintings, plus model ships and an inspiring collection of photographs depicting the history of Abaco. At the end of your walk, there are several restaurants and bars where you can enjoy a snack, a rum drink, or an icy Kalik. Not to be missed is Miss Emily's Blue Bee Bar, home of the original Goombay Smash. This funky little place is one of our favorite bars in the Bahamas.

Another cool stop-off is Pineapples, a new (2004) bar with a swimming pool perched on the water's edge looking back across the inlet at New Plymouth. Look for all the golf carts out front and you'll know you're there.

Captain Rick Sawyer lives in New Plymouth and can be booked for full-day guided trips. While there are a number of flats anglers can fish on their own around Green Turtle Cay, we recommend booking at least one day with Rick, especially if you are interested in hunting some double-digit monster bones.

We often reboard the ferry in New Plymouth and head over to the Green Turtle Cay Club or to the Bluff House. You can also rent a golf cart and zip along the beach road to either resort, about a 20-minute ride. Assuming you take the ferry, Black Sound is on your right as you cruise north. Two marinas and additional services for boaters are located here, including boat storage facilities.

Green Turtle Cay Club is at the northern end of White Sound, which is cut in two by a strip of land that separates the deeper water from a large shallow

Miss Emily's Blue Bee Bar, New Plymouth on Green Turtle Cay.

Green Turtle Cay Club.

back bay lined with mangroves. The Club has an atmosphere of casual old-style elegance; with dock space for 35 boats, villa and suite accommodations, a swimming pool, beach, two bars, and a fashionable restaurant.

While any beach-loving vacationer would be happy here, so would an angler. A short walk up over a moderate hill will bring you to Coco Bay. You can have at least two good hours of bonefishing here most days. The bottom structure is a combination of sand and grass, and wading is easy in most parts of the bay. It is a little more difficult, but anglers can also walk to Bluff Harbour Bay and catch bonefish cruising the shorelines on the incoming tide. Bonefish will also lay up in certain areas here during the high tide.

Across the Sound, perched on top of an 80-foot high hill is the Bluff House, a classy hotel with villa and deluxe room accommodations. The bar and restaurant offer sweeping views over the Sea of Abaco, and the food and service are first-rate. You need reservations for dinner during the season.

South of Green Turtle are several private cays, Whale Cay and then Great Guana Cay. In good weather, this is a fun area for recreational boating and reef fishing, though the Whale Cay Passage can be dangerous due to strong crosscurrents that can create unpredictable waves.

Great Guana Cay is one of the most beautiful little islands

Bluff House.

anywhere. The small settlement is like something you would imagine in a South Seas dream: coconut palms, casuarinas, turquoise water, a crescent beach, and welcoming locals. The Great Guana Marina has its dock adjacent to the government dock. There are about 20 boat slips and a dinghy tie-up area for visitors. This is another of our favorite lunch spots on days we go cay hopping. Daily ferry service is available from Marsh Harbor, and the mail boat calls weekly.

Guana Seaside Village is a small and intimate resort that is ideal for a quiet romantic get-away. The next bay south is home to Orchid Bay Marina, and several of the large docks for visiting day boaters to tie up. These docks are jammed on Sundays when it seems like everyone in Abaco arrives for the famous pig roast at Nipper's Bar and Grill. This is a rocking fun party with renowned local bands playing for hours.

Nipper's Sunday barbeque, Great Guana Cay.

Nipper's is on the windward side of the island, roughly in the middle of seven miles of white sand beaches edged by the turquoise sea. If you are looking for a secluded spot to yourself, you can walk the powdery white sands until you find one. Take your mask and fins as the inner and offshore reefs create wonderful snorkeling areas. In places rocky sections of the reef run in to the beach, forming pools and drop-offs. On calm days you can fly-fish these areas for small jacks, snappers, and grouper.

There are also a couple of small leeward bays that offer good fishing for tailing bonefish on the appropriate tides. Bonefish and reef guides can be booked at Orchid Bay Marina, or you can take the ferry across to Abaco and meet O'Donald Macintosh or another independent guide for a day of guided fishing in the Marls.

Man-O-War Cay is the next significant island on the way to Marsh Harbour and Elbow Cay. Two and a half miles long, the enchanting cay is famous for its shipbuilding tradition. The hardy locals can trace every one of their ancestors back to their initial arrival. They credit their strong religious beliefs for their survival through long periods of hard times, which is the main reason the sale of liquor and tobacco is not permitted on the cay.

Man-O-War Cay has two of the best safe harbors in the Bahamas. If you turn left after passing the main harbor entrance, you head into North Harbour. The 60-slip Man-O-War Marina is the first major facility you encounter. The marina has services for boaters including fuel and dingy docks, a pavilion restaurant, dive shop, and bank. The restaurant is a fun place for lunch, serving delicious cracked conch and barbecued meats on weekends.

Albury's Ferry Service has a fleet of water taxis at the marina for trips to Hope Town, Marsh Harbour, and the surrounding cays. VHS channel 16 is the best means of communication here, as it is in all the other offshore cays.

A little farther into the harbor is the government wharf, which is flanked by two shipbuilding yards. The friendly settlement contains a grocery store, a couple of restaurants and delis, bakery, post office, and telephone station. The atmosphere here is peaceful and content. Just wandering around the narrow streets, all lined with brightly painted houses, is a pleasant way to pass some time. You can also walk across the island on coconut palm-lined paths to the gorgeous windward beaches.

Small boats, motorbikes, and golf carts are the main mode of transportation around the cay. Along the northern shore, on the leeward side, are several bonefish flats that are best accessed by boat. You have to take note of the tides, however, or you can become grounded as the tide falls. This is true for all boating anglers throughout this region. We have talked to plenty of people who have spent up to six hours stranded on a bar or flat because they didn't anticipate tidal movement.

Back on the mainland of Abaco, the highway south from Treasure Cay to Marsh Harbour is in great shape. The drive takes about 35 minutes. Taxi service is available for this trip, though we recommend renting a car if you prefer traveling by land. You can also reach Marsh Harbour by boat or ferry, either directly, or with stopoffs on the offshore cays.

Many people staying in Treasure Cay or on the offshore cays rent boats, and a number of good rental agencies are available. A 23-foot runabout is ideal for transportation, cay hopping, and reef fishing. In good weather the run from Treasure Cay to Marsh Harbour takes about 45 minutes.

Marsh Harbour is the third largest town in the Bahamas, and the center of commercial activity for Abaco. The settlement was established in the late 1700s. By the late 1800s and early 1900s, the settlement had grown prosperous from shipbuilding and sponging. Sponging declined after World War I and was eventually obliterated in 1938 by a blight that wiped out sponges throughout the Bahamas. Shipbuilding also declined and sent many residents off to Nassau in search of work.

By the late 1950s, several farming projects began to take hold, and tourism started to pick up. After Castro's revolution was successful in Cuba in 1959, even more sailors and vacationers began heading to the Abacos, and tourism led the way to new prosperity.

Today, the airport has convenient daily air service to Nassau and Florida. The main harbor offers easy access to a number of docks and marinas and the town itself.

Boaters entering the harbor along Pelican Shores can steer to the right through the dredged passage to the Government Customs Wharf or head straight in through the channel to the Conch Inn Marina and Hotel in the southeast corner. The marina has 75 slips and full boater services, though a number of the slips are taken by charter boats.

Part of this charter fleet features offshore boats for both reef and blue-water fishing. None of the crews are fly-fishing specialists, though they are enthusiastic and will be

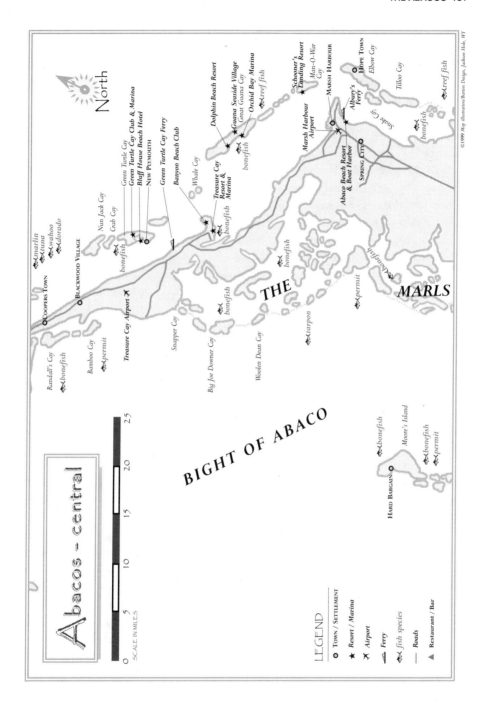

Abacos - central

SCALE IN MILES

0   5   10   15   20   25

North

LEGEND
○ Town / Settlement
★ Resort / Marina
✕ Airport
Ferry
fish species
— Roads
▲ Restaurant / Bar

marlin
tuna
wahoo
dorado

COOPERS TOWN
BLACKWOOD VILLAGE

Randall's Cay
bonefish

Bamboo Cay
permit

Nun Jack Cay
Grab Cay
bonefish

Snapper Cay

Treasure Cay Airport ✕

Big Joe Downer Cay

Woolen Dean Cay

Green Turtle Cay
Green Turtle Cay Club & Marina
Bluff House Beach Hotel
NEW PLYMOUTH

Green Turtle Cay Ferry

Banyon Beach Club

Whale Cay

Treasure Cay
Resort &
Marina
bonefish

bonefish

bonefish

tarpon

THE

BIGHT OF ABACO

Dolphin Beach Resort

Guana Seaside Village
Great Guana Cay
Orchid Bay Marina
bonefish

Schooner's
Landing Resort

Man-O-War
Cay
MARSH HARBOUR

Marsh Harbour
Airport

Abaco Beach Resort
& Boat Harbor

reef fish

Albury's
Ferry

SPRING CITY

Snake Cay

HOPE TOWN
Elbow Cay

Tilloo Cay

reef fish

bonefish

permit

MARLS

HARD BARGAIN

bonefish

Moore's Island

bonefish
permit

©1999 Map Illustration/Burton Design, Jackson Hole, WY

happy to put experienced anglers on fish. If you just want to catch fish with conventional gear, no problem, mon.

The Conch Inn Marina is operated by the Moorings, the charter yacht company. If you're looking to rent a boat and cruise the offshore cays, this is the place. The facility also features harborview rooms, a swimming pool, and dive shop.

Mangoes, a restaurant, bar, and boutique, has dock space for customers to tie up while eating lunch, dinner, or just shopping. If you're boating over from Treasure Cay, this would be a good spot to come ashore, enjoy some lunch, and walk around.

To the west is the Harbour View Marina, then Triple J Marine, the Tiki Hut restaurant, Long's Landing (where you can buy fresh seafood), and the government's Union Jack dock. There are three or four additional dinghy docks through this area for visitors to tie up and walk around town.

Straight across the harbor from Conch Inn is the Marsh Harbour Marina, home of the Royal Marsh Harbour Yacht Club, and Jib Room bar and restaurant. The yellow-and-white-striped roof makes this an easy landmark to spot. The two-story restaurant has views of the harbor, a fun atmosphere, a good variety of seafood, and special barbecues two nights a week.

If you're driving down from Treasure Cay, make sure you get a map from your rental car agency. You will have to negotiate several roundabouts on your way to the harbor, so remember that driving is on the left. The Conch Inn Marina and the Marsh Harbour Marina are well marked on all the maps we've seen.

The town of Marsh Harbour has just about anything you might need, including an Internet cafe. Still, using VHS channel 16 to communicate, especially if you want a taxi, will serve you better than a telephone. Cell phones have also become common with business people and taxi drivers.

The east side of Marsh Harbour can be easily reached by boat or car. If you're driving, keep going along the harbor past the Conch Inn and make a right turn following the signs for the Abaco Beach Resort and Boat Harbour. If you're headed to the main ferry dock, keep going straight out past the Abaco Beach Resort.

Sugarloaf Cay sits just off Marsh Harbour's eastern shore. Development here, and all around Marsh Harbour, is rampant, with new vacation homes and docks appearing everywhere. Albury's Ferry Service is located between the west end of Sugarloaf and Boat Harbour Marina. Albury's offers the most convenient ferry service to Hope Town and White Sound on Elbow Cay, plus other offshore cays from Man-O-War to Great Guana.

Boat Harbour Marina has 175 slips for boats up to 150 feet. Full services are available, including use of the Abaco Beach Resort's swimming pool and tennis courts. The resort hotel has spacious air-conditioned rooms and cottages, its own beach, Anglers' Restaurant, three bars, boat and bike rentals, dive shop, and boutiques. Grocery and liquor stores are nearby.

All resort facilities at the Abaco Beach Resort have been upgraded since 2002. With these improvements, the resort has become a perfect headquarters for anglers and vacationers. At least half a dozen billfish tournaments fill the resort each year. During the tournaments, the resort pulses with people in a party mood. The resort can arrange for guides or you can book your own independent guides. Do-it-yourself anglers can hang out in a comfortable resort atmosphere, and rent a boat to fish the flats from Marsh Harbour to Snake Cay and beyond.

Our favorite fly-fishing guide in the Marsh Harbour area is Justin Sands. Justin has a couple of Hell's Bay flats skiffs that he can trailer to various launching sites to fish either side of the island.

Elbow Cay, a 15-minute boat ride from Marsh Harbour, has become a mecca for boaters, sun worshippers, and fly-fishers. Hope Town is home to the most historic lighthouse in the Bahamas, the famous candy-striped tower built in 1863. When the lighthouse was built, the locals considered it a disastrous event, as this aid to navigation put a serious crimp in their salvage business.

Today the locals look more kindly on the landmark. They defeated an effort to automate the lighthouse, voting instead to keep the kerosene-powered system that requires winding every hour and a half throughout the night.

Hope Town is snuggled around a picture-book harbor dotted with pleasure boats. The streets are like wide sidewalks, with no automobile or golf cart traffic allowed. The houses are well tended, with fresh bright paint and lush flower gardens.

The Lighthouse Marina is just inside the harbor. Full services are available for boaters, including the only fuel service in Hope Town. Several hundred yards to the south is the long dock of the Hope Town Marina. The adjacent Club Soleil Resort features a restaurant and bar and comfortable air-conditioned rooms with balconies overlooking the harbor. If you want to talk about reef or offshore fishing, the Hope Town Marina is the place. You can charter a boat here or rent a boat and explore on your own.

A little farther south is the 12-slip dock and marina for Hope Town Hideaways owned by Peggy and Chris Thompson. The resort has two-bedroom waterfront villas with central air-conditioning, full kitchens, private docks, swimming pool, and beach all contained on a beautifully landscaped 11-acre property. The Thompsons also manage and rent the most luxurious houses on the island, including houses at Tahiti Beach.

Across the harbor, on the strip of land between the harbor and the oceanfront beach, is the main settlement of Hope Town. Two grocery stores, several bakeries, a liquor store, a variety of shops and restaurants, library, and post office are all easily accessed from various waterfront docks, including the Hope Town Harbour Lodge dock.

The Lodge itself is a classic, strewn over four levels and then running down the windward side to the beach. Accommodations include comfortable air-conditioned rooms with a choice of harbor or ocean view, and larger oceanfront suites. The swimming pool and pool bar are perched above the Atlantic beach. A thriving reef 30 feet off the sand is a favorite with snorkelers.

Hope Town has become an "in" place for groups of vacationers who return year after year, especially in April and May. If you plan to visit during this time, or during

Elbow Cay.

spring break, you'll need to make reservations well in advance. We've heard some boaters complain that the harbor has become over-crowded with boats, but we think there is just the right mix of "enough to do," with relaxing solitude, and access to prime fishing areas you can work on your own or with a guide.

South of Hope Town is White Sound, a quiet harbor with a bonefish flat stretching out from the southern tip of the boaters' leeward entrance. Golf carts are the main mode of land transportation from Hope Town to the White Sound and Tahiti Beach areas, though the two resorts, Abaco Inn and Sea Spray, provide van service to their guests from Nigh Creek. From Marsh Harbour, guests can use the Albury Ferry Service to reach the Abaco Inn or Sea Spray docks directly.

It is easy boating from Hope Town to White Sound and Tahiti Beach. We highly recommend that Elbow Cay vacationers rent their own boat. Island Marine, located on Parrot Cay, is one of the best boat rental companies. They also work through the Hope Town Harbour Lodge, and will deliver rental boats directly to your dock anywhere on Elbow, Man-O-War, or Great Guana Cays.

The Abaco Inn is our favorite place to stay on Elbow Cay. While there are many splendid tranquil spots throughout the islands, this strip of rock and sand is one of the most seductive, with views of the Sound on one side, and the blue-purple Atlantic on the other. The Inn has deluxe rooms, two spacious suites, a saltwater swimming pool, and a superb restaurant. And everywhere you look, it's shockingly beautiful.

At the southern end of the sound is Sea Spray Resort Villas and Marina. The pleasant one and two bedroom air-conditioned villas serve up inspiring views in a quiet tropical setting. Boaters and vacationers will find full services here, including fuel, boat and bike rentals, restaurant, bar, laundry, and villa catering. The resort was being renovated in the spring of 2004, and the marina enlarged, with the project expected to be completed by the winter 2005 season.

Elbow Cay's southern tip includes two points facing Tilloo Cay, while the exclusive Tahiti Beach faces Lubber's Quarters and the Sea of Abaco. Acres of coconut palms shade a number of casually luxurious homes available for rent here. Couples or families looking for a retreat that mixes fishing with laid-back vacationing should be more than happy here.

Fly-fishing boaters, including cay hoppers from Elbow Cay and Marsh Harbour, will want to explore the cays, flats, cuts, and mangrove-lined creeks south of Elbow all

between the cays, including deeper areas between
.ppers, jacks, mackerel, barracuda, and sharks. On
current is at its swiftest, you'll find these predators

a series of cays that follow the shoreline southward.
rd from the cays and a number of creeks lead into
of bonefish roam through the mangroves looking for
possible before heading back out to deeper water.
ambush points on the last part of the falling tide.
coming tide to cast to tailing fish.
gion is vital. It's better to get skunked than to end up
s—or maybe not, if you're a fishing fanatic. You need
ence in water levels between a spring and a neap tide.
If you fish this area on a neap tide, water levels won't change so dramatically. If you
come back a week later on a spring tide, you'll see lots of dry flats at low tide. Professional guides Jay Sawyer and Justin Sands run trips to the Snake Cay area when the
tides are right.

Long and lean, Tilloo Cay has some welcoming beaches for picnicking and several
wadable flats, the best we've fished being at the southern point. The Pelican Cays are
part of the Pelican Cay Land and Sea Park, which was founded by the Bahamas National Trust. The Trust's ongoing mission is to preserve the natural beauty of numerous
Bahamian cays, reefs, and seabeds. Boaters need to read the regulations for this area, as
dropping anchor in many parts of the park is forbidden.

There are several good wadable flats interspersed through the Pelican Cays, plus
some reef-type banks where we have seen large permit. These banks are on the windward side of the cays and are best fished in calm weather. We recommend that day
boaters pay close attention to the weather and pick the nicer days for exploring and
fishing.

Cruising boaters will be better served to explore the flats and creeks in smaller
tenders or dinghies. One area ripe for this type of adventure is the Bight of Old Robinson, which is north of Little Harbour. The Little Harbour area itself has a number of
creeks and cuts worth fishing a day or two. This is another area protected by the
Bahamas National Trust, so read the regulations carefully. Variety is what you're looking for here throughout this area. Bonefish, permit, different species of grouper, snapper, and jacks can provide lively action on flies, lures, and bait.

Little Harbour is known as the home of Randolph Johnston, the noted writer and
sculptor. Some of Randolph's most famous sculptures, including *Monuments to
Bahamian Women,* are on display in several galleries in Nassau. Johnston died in 1992
at the age of 88, but his family members, many of whom are artists also, still own much
of the land surrounding Little Harbour.

Boaters in this area should note that many cays around Little Harbour are privately
owned and require permission to come ashore. It is your responsibility to recognize

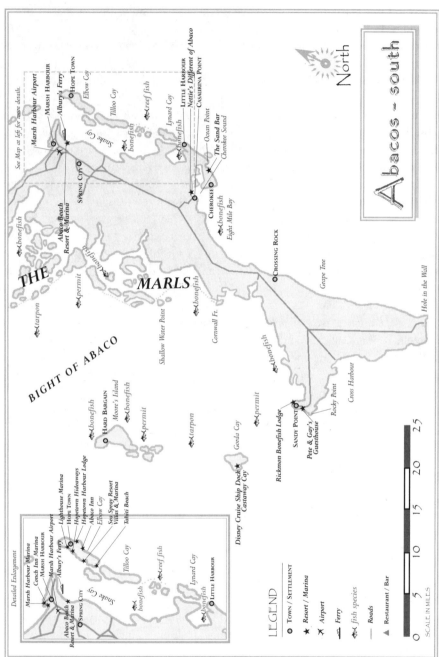

Abacos – South

North

©1999 Map illustration/Barton Design, Jackson Hole, WY

See Map at left for more details.

Marsh Harbour Airport
Marsh Harbour
Albury's Ferry
Hope Town
Elbow Cay
Tilloo Cay
reef fish
Snake Cay
bonefish
Lynard Cay
bonefish
Little Harbour
Nettie's Different of Abaco
Casaurina Point
Ocean Point
The Sand Bar
Cherokee Sound
Cherokee
bonefish
Eight Mile Bay
Spring City
Abaco Beach Resort & Marina
bonefish
bonefish
permit
tarpon

THE
MARLS

BIGHT OF ABACO

bonefish

Shallow Water Point

Cornwall Ft.

bonefish

Crossing Rock

Grape Tree

Hole in the Wall

bonefish
Hard Bargain
Moore's Island
bonefish
permit
tarpon
Gorda Cay
permit
Cross Harbour
Rocky Point
Sandy Point
Pete & Gay's Guesthouse
Rickmon Bonefish Lodge

Disney Cruise Ship Dock
Castaway Cay

Detailed Enlargement

Marsh Harbour Marina
Conch Inn Marina
Marsh Harbour Airport
Albury's Ferry
Marsh Harbour
Lighthouse Marina
Hope Town
Hopetown Hideaways
Hopetown Harbour Lodge
Abaco Inn
Elbow Cay
Sea Spray Resort Villas & Marina
Tahiti Beach
Tilloo Cay
reef fish
Snake Cay
bonefish
Lynard Cay
bonefish
Little Harbour
Spring City
Abaco Beach Resort & Marina

LEGEND

○ Town / Settlement
★ Resort / Marina
✈ Airport
⇌ Ferry
🐟 fish species
— Roads
▲ Restaurant / Bar

SCALE IN MILES
0   5   10   15   20   25

private property and not trespass. Remember that VHF Channel 16 is the best means of communication. It is easy to find people willing to help with directions and other information.

South of Little Harbour is the upscale resort development at Winding Bay. The Abaco Club on Winding Bay began development in 2003 and was in full swing in the spring of 2004 when we visited. This exclusive private resort covers 520 acres of varying terrain from high bluffs to long stretches of powdery white beaches. The resort includes an 18-hole golf course, clubhouse with pro shop and restaurant, cottage-style hotel rooms, two miles of beach, lavish private homes, and other amenities.

Continuing south, boaters can enjoy good trolling along the reef. Inshore there are a number of inlets and a large sweeping bay before rounding the point into Cherokee Sound. The Sand Bar Grill and Bar is in this bay—on the end of a 200-yard-long pier that stretches over glass-clear water with a white sand bottom. This open-air restaurant services cold Kaliks, grilled burgers, grouper, conch salad, and sizzling fries along with other Bahamian specialties.

If you are driving south from Marsh Harbour, the turnoff to the Sand Bar is easy to miss. There is a small sign out on the main highway at the turnoff to the settlement of Cherokee Sound. Take this road toward Cherokee Sound, a winding curvy strip of cement that skirts the edges of mangrove-lined creeks and bays cut into the coral. About a mile before the settlement you'll see another sign on your left. The road is very narrow and it ends at a locked gate. Park in one of the areas before the gate and walk in to the Sand Bar. You can't miss the magnificent pier that spans out over the water. This place is a must for lunch or afternoon drinks, and you can watch bonefish cruising all over the flats while drinking and eating. It would be a good idea to have a fly rod handy with the incoming tide. You can access the flats from the beach, or walk down the stairs at the end of the pier right into a school of bones.

Cherokee Sound is one of the oldest settlements on the island. The economy here is centered on commercial fishing, lobstering, and shipbuilding. The Sound is also home to Nettie Symon-ette's Different of Abaco, a bonefishing lodge and eco-tourism resort. Fly-fishers and vacationers who book with Nettie fly into Marsh Harbour, then are driven 20 minutes south on the Great Abaco Highway to Casuarina Point.

Bonefishers stay in the Sea Shell Beach Club section of the resort, which is spread out along a pristine

Loading up to go fish the Marls, out of Nettie's Different of Abaco.

white sand beach that stretches for miles north and south. Brightly painted, with Caribbean-style air-conditioned rooms, the Beach Club has a restaurant, bar, swimming pool, Jacuzzi, and a variety of bikes for exploring the area.

Packages are available for anglers and non-anglers. The bonefishing in Cherokee Sound is good, especially if you're looking for big fish. Anglers can fish with a guide or wade for miles on their own along the shoreline. The highlight of staying at Different of Abaco, however, is being able to fish the vast central section of the Marls. Located on the leeward side of the island, in the Bight of Abaco, this seemingly endless area of the Marls was only accessible by boat until Nettie opened it up to her guests with a private road and channel access.

The Marls habitat is one of the most fertile in the Bahamas. Miles of mangroves, creeks, cays, cuts, and flats blossom in every direction. Countless bonefish live in this protected area, and often seek refuge back in mangrove areas that are inaccessible. Anglers can catch high numbers of fish in the one- to three-pound range, plus larger fish ranging up to eight or nine pounds.

While there are wading flats, most fishing here is done from a poled skiff. Farther out, larger cays and deeper water lures bigger bonefish, permit, and an occasional tarpon in to feed on an array of crabs, shrimp, and baitfish over dark grass and coral bottoms.

From Cherokee Sound to Hole in the Wall, the southernmost tip of Abaco, the Atlantic shoreline is steep and rugged, with long breaks of deserted white sand beaches. A couple of new housing developments are popping up on some of these beaches, where you can find decent reef fly-fishing if the wind is down.

From Hole in the Wall, boaters can cross the Northeast Providence Channel to Spanish Wells, or make the 47-mile run to Nassau. Fly-fishers would want to head northeast along the edge of the Little Bahama Bank to Sandy Point.

The easiest way to reach Sandy Point, however, is by land or air. The highway down from Casuarina Point is in excellent condition. Travelers can fly into Marsh Harbour and rent a car for the drive, or take a charter flight to the Sandy Point airstrip from Nassau or Florida.

On the drive down to Sandy Point there are several places to stop and fish on your own, or if you have a boat, you can launch at Crossing Rock. This area is loaded with fish and receives very little pressure.

The settlement of Sandy Point sits on a finger of land between two creeks shaded by coconut palms. This is a quiet commercial fishing town with nicely painted houses and well-kept gardens. Pete and Gay's Guesthouse is located across the street from the main dock. The two-story bright blue building provides delightful views of the harbor from the rooftop lounge. Fuel is available up the street at the local Esso station and hardware store. A grocery store is within walking distance of the dock.

Bonefishing has been a significant contributor to the local economy in recent years, as has completion of the Great Abaco Highway. Pete and Gay's has 10 motel-style air-conditioned rooms and their restaurant serves some of the best Bahamian food found in the islands. Anglers can book rooms here on their own and have the management arrange guides, or prearranged bonefishing packages are available.

At the end of the settlement road, a few blocks beyond Pete and Gay's, is Rickmon Bonefish Lodge. The two-story whitewashed building is fronted by a large deck that is nestled into the white sand beach. The turquoise waters out front are irresistibly inviting, and the surface turns to sparkling pinpoints as the sun drops toward the horizon. This is one of the best places in the world to enjoy a drink and watch the sunset.

Rickmon's can take up to 18 anglers in nine double rooms and two single rooms. The restaurant and bar is a lively gathering place, and the fresh seafood is delicious. Ricardo Burrows, the head guide and owner, works with all the independent guides in the area, including Patrick Roberts. Anglers can book rooms or complete bonefishing packages that include transfers from Marsh Harbour.

Fly-fishers staying at Sandy Point can enjoy a fishery that produces good numbers of bonefish averaging three to six pounds, plus daily shots at larger fish, including double-digit monsters. Permit cruise the deeper edges of the Sarah Wood Bars near the outer cays like Gorda and Crab, and along the edges of the bank. On calmer days a run to Moore's Island, or maybe north to the Marls, is a fun option.

Local guides are long-time commercial fishermen who have worked hard to develop their bonefishing guide skills. Like the guides from Cherokee Sound, they have good eyes for spotting fish, a pleasant enthusiasm, and they are working to improve their fly-fishing skills. Guides use a variety boats, some with larger V-hulls for crossing deeper and rougher water, but less well suited for skinny water.

With the rising popularity of bonefishing, the Sandy Point area has become heavily fished. So have the flats around Moore's Island. While the fishing is still outstanding, the fish are now educated. Longer leaders and light flies are sometime necessary.

On the good side, the development of Gorda Cay (now called Castaway Cay) by the Disney Company has not hurt the quality of fishing around the cay, which is an ideal place to pursue permit.

Fishing Highlights

The Bight of Abaco runs from Sandy Point in the south to Little Abaco in the north, is flanked on the east by the Marls, on the west by a series of cays, and the east end of Grand Bahama. This area of the Little Bahama Bank is arguably the best overall shallow water fishery in the Bahamas.

There are no settlements on the west coast of Great Abaco from Sandy Point to Coopers Town, a distance of more than 50 miles. This means cruising boaters are on their own in this vast area. Navigating the Bight is a straightforward matter, though it requires diligent observation, especially in poor weather conditions. We recommend that exploring fly-fishers move through this area only in daylight.

The center of the Bight holds deeper water, roughly 10 to 18 feet, with varying sand and grass bottoms. As you move closer to any of the shorelines or cays, water depths can

When approaching bonefish in thin water like this, silence is indeed golden. (Brian O'Keefe)

drop quickly. This long and relatively wide patch of deeper water is the bad weather home for bonefish, permit, tarpon, and other shallow water gamefish and baitfish.

Abaco's northern location in the Bahamas means more northeast winter winds and greater chances for winter cold fronts. These cold fronts are most common from mid-November to the end of March, though they can occur from October into May. A strong cold front can last four to five days, while a weaker front can be through in a couple of days. Often, the day before a front will be beautiful, and bonefishing will be fabulous as fish feed aggressively before moving to deeper water in anticipation of bad weather.

After the cold front has passed, fish return to shallower water and flats. Water temperatures have generally cooled and fish begin feeding with vigor.

Moving north from Sandy Point, you reach Cedar Cays and then Big Mangrove Cay, which is the southern edge of the Marls. Ocean-type flats surround many of the outer Marls cays. Some of these irregular hard coral flats can be waded, but it's easier to fish from a boat. We like to fish crab flies, especially Yarn Crabs, over the coral and adjacent flats covered with turtle grass. A Borski Bonefish Critter with a weed guard is another favorite. Golden and snapping shrimp patterns with weed guards are productive over the turtle grass in skinnier water.

Entering the Marls proper is awe-inspiring. Without good local knowledge, it would be easy to get lost or to stick yourself on a bar. Much of the bottom is turtle grass interspersed with sand and coral. Mangroves are everywhere. Many of the green and brown clumps look like mating spiders with long legs arching toward the sky.

The closer you move toward the mainland, the softer the bottom becomes. The mangroves become denser. Creeks and cuts slash through the vegetation in every direction. Perfectly round bays and surprisingly large flats appear out of nowhere. Countless numbers of blue crabs, some the size of footballs, skitter across the dark grass and golden coral.

This mangrove root and grass bottom structure produces millions of swimming mantis, snapping shrimp, and grass shrimp. Grass shrimp especially love hanging around the latticework of mangrove roots, and they prefer water with a higher salinity. The salinity of the Marls changes with the amount of rain throughout the year. Factoring this into your fishing strategy and fly selection can be critical. The larger snapping shrimp prefer the turtle grass, and are a favorite food for tailing bonefish. The classic version of a Fernandez Snapping Shrimp works well because it lands softly and resists hooking up in the grass.

This unique habitat, combining abundant food and ample protection from predators, creates one of the best bonefish nurseries in the Bahamas. We have seen schools of bonefish here numbering in the thousands, with the largest fish about 10 inches long.

Bonefish are the number-one gamefish species in the Marls, and the number-one target for shallow water fly-fishers throughout Abaco. Bonefish size runs the spectrum from baitfish length to gigantic 15 pounders. The majority of Marls' fish run 1 to 4 pounds, with a decent number of fish up to 8 or 9 pounds. Larger average fish, including fish over 10 pounds, are found in deeper water around the outlying and offshore cays, and north of the Marls where access to deeper water is closer to the Abaco mainland.

The best months to fly-fish for bones are April through July, and October and November. March is also an excellent month also, but look out for cold fronts. August and September can be very good if no hurricanes are around. December through February is weather-dependent, and the most common period for cold fronts.

The highest concentration of bonefish is in the southern area of the Marls, though numbers are good all along the west coast. Marls' fish have a well-earned reputation for being super-aggressive. It is common to make a bad cast well away from your target, then watch one or more bonefish race over and gobble your fly. This may sound like fly selection is not that important, but we favor lighter flies without eyes, or with bead chain eyes. We rarely use lead-eyed flies such as Clouser's, which are our favorites in many other areas. Go with #4-6 Gotchas, Hoovers, Snapping Shrimp, Bonefish Critters, and Greg's Flats Fly as a basic selection.

We prefer to fish the Marls during a neap tide. Generally lower water levels don't allow fish to get as far back into the mangrove systems, making them more accessible throughout the day. During spring tides you have to be especially smart and quick to put yourself into position for success on an incoming tide. If you're fishing a spring tide, you'll usually have your best fishing during the last part of the falling tide. You can set up ambush points and then cast to those beautiful silver backs and blue tails as they come swaggering out of the creeks and mangroves.

Often, the time of day of the tide is more important than whether it's a spring or neap tide. There are times when the tide will be high for most of the daylight hours. If this is the case, you'll have to go into the mangroves after the fish. Guides familiar with this area know how to find fish in these conditions. You can get shots in clear areas, but these bones know a good mangrove root when they see one, and most will break you off. Fish shorter leaders and heavier tippets: up to 15-pound Mason or the fluoro-carbon brand you prefer. And use flies you don't mind losing.

Remember that all fish are creatures of habit, bonefish even more so. The guides from Nettie's and others who fish this area know bonefish behavior. Ask them questions so you can learn as much as you can about this behavior. If you're fishing on your own, make sure you know the tides, then consider access and ambush points, and you will probably have some success.

In working out the tides, you must factor in the barometric pressure as well as the wind. Both can hold a tide out longer, or bring it rushing in sooner. During windy conditions many areas of the Marls are well protected, which means good fly-fishing here when other areas might be unfishable. The bad news is that low pressure can drive fish out of the Marls' shallower areas and into deeper water covered with white caps. Hey, no one said bonefishing was a sure thing, which is one of the reasons it is our greatest fishing passion.

Continuing north of the Marls, bonefishing remains consistently good. From Norman Castle up to Basin Harbour and on past the backside of Coopers Town is a vast area that receives little pressure and produces much larger fish. Bones up here average four to five pounds. Double-digit fish are a real possi-bility. This is our favorite area of Abaco, and it is easily reached by anglers staying in Treasure Cay or on Green Turtle Cay. As we discussed in the Around the Island section, this is the home guiding water for O'Donald Macintosh and his sons. Justin Sands and other top inde-pendents fish here as well.

So how about permit? Anglers who fish the Marls can see the occasional permit while fishing for bones. If permit are your goal you should move out to the deeper water along the outer cays, or fish other areas of the island. Sandy Point has good numbers of large per-mit, especially along the sand-bottomed edges of the Little Bahama Bank, and north up near Cedar Cays. The cays between Gorda Cay and Moore's Island are also home to big permit. To the north, the leeward cays off Coopers Town have a number of deeper creeks and cuts that give permit access to many of the flats.

Sandy Point. (Brian O'Keefe)

The windward offshore cays, from Spanish Cay to Little Harbour, hold good numbers of permit. Fish concentrate around the ocean-side reefs and along bars and cays with access to deeper water. Fly-fishers in this area will have their best chance at hooking up during calm weather, though spinning rigs fished with live crabs are deadly any time. The best months for permit are April through July, though they are available year round. We especially like to fish for permit after a heavy rain. The rain-water reduces salinity and brings out the crabs in swarms. Our favorite permit flies include various #4 Yarn Crabs, a #2 Del's Merkin, a #4 Spawning Shrimp, and a #2 Gotcha Clouser.

There are resident tarpon in the Bight of Abaco, plus migratory tarpon that move along both coasts from April through August, but the numbers are not high as far as we know. We have talked with many boaters who report seeing tarpon roll all through the offshore cays region, but few have fished for them, and even fewer have jumped or landed any. Local guides have reported similar observations.

We have caught a few tarpon here and there in the northern Marls, and we've jumped some fish between Green Turtle and Elbow Cays, but in all these cases we were not specifically fishing for tarpon. We had a tarpon rod rigged and took the opportunity when we were lucky enough to see a fish.

If you just want to catch fish, fishing for snappers with fly or spinning gear is a blast. Mutton snapper are the real prize because they are great fighters and make a delicious meal. Grey snappers, or mangrove snappers as they are more commonly known, are everywhere, from the mangrove-infested Marls to the reefs of the offshore cays. Snapper fishing is good year round, with April through August being prime. April is the best month for mutton snapper. Clouser's Minnows in a variety of colors are our favorite flies for these feisty fish.

Barracuda are ferocious fish that are equally fun to catch on fly or spinning tackle, and they can deal with cold weather better than most other gamefish. The winter months are especially good, and many winter fishing days have been saved by pursuing barracuda. Wire shock tippet is essential against their razor-sharp teeth. If you choose to land a fish for photos, be extremely careful, as even the little guys can do serious damage to hands and fingers.

Sharks are great sport for anglers who feel like hooking up something big. We've talked with lots of people who just get that urge to feel the weight of a wide body. Go with a 10-weight for lemons and blacktips, and use six-inch-long 40- to 80-pound wire shock tippet to protect your leader. The best flies are Offshore Deceivers in red/black and chum colors.

Sharks prefer warm weather, and warm water, so April through October will offer the best flats fishing. In deeper water and around the reefs you can catch sharks year round. Most people understand extreme caution is necessary when landing sharks, and many people just break them off at the boat. Occasionally, anglers think it's cool to land a small shark for a photo. Be aware that sharks are like snakes! Their cartilage structure is relatively soft, and it allows them to completely bend back on themselves. This means if you are holding their tail they can easily whip around and bite your hand. One of our guides almost lost a hand this way, so be careful out there.

Billfishing for sails and blue marlin begins in March, picks up in April, and is prime May through July. There are very few fly-fishing savvy crews in the Bahamas, and most fishing is with conventional gear. If you have experience with fly-fishing for billfish, you should be able to get in some shots in June and July with traditional teasing methods.

June and July are the main months for a number of billfish and tuna tournaments, including the Green Turtle Cay Club Invitational and a leg of the Bahamas Billfish Championship out of Boat Harbour Marina. Good offshore boats are available for charter out of Treasure Cay, Green Turtle Cay, Marsh Harbour, and Elbow Cay, also.

The Bahamas Wahoo Championships hold one of the five legs out of Boat Harbour Marina and the Abaco Beach Resort in January. January and February are the best months for wahoo, which is our favorite offshore species in the islands. When these fish are concentrated, they will readily hit billfish flies and large surface poppers. Wire tippet is a must against their super-sharp teeth. And if you like to eat fish, fresh wahoo, or Ono as it is called in Hawaii, is as good as it gets.

July is Regatta Time, with continued excellent offshore fishing, and many related activities and parties on the offshore cays. Many anglers start thinking of trout in June and July, but this is a premier time to fish Abaco's flats and offshore waters.

April and May are prime months for dorado. You can often find scum and grass lines beyond the offshore cays where dorado hang out in good numbers. On these occasions you can cast surface poppers and large deceivers for fantastic action. Trolling will consistently bring up dorado during these months, and live bait will take the school fish on every cast.

Allison tuna show up in March, with good numbers beginning in April and prime fishing occurring May through July. This is definitely our favorite tuna to do battle with in the Bahamas, as they readily take flies and are commonly found hanging out with dorado. Our favorite flies include WBA Mullets and Abel Anchovies.

People often ask us to name our favorite Bahamian Out Island. We usually hedge a little, and qualify our answers based on what each island has to offer. We've already mentioned that Andros is our favorite island for pure fishing and hanging out. That said, we'll go out on a reef and say Abaco is our favorite overall when you put the big picture together.

Ease of access by air and boat combined with a variety of high-quality accommodations starts it off. Then you have the flats of the Marls, the offshore cays reef fishing and world-class blue water fishing, combined with a number of good guides, and a dizzying array of non-angling activities. Not a bad combination if you're looking for a vacation to satisfy a wide range of people.

Optional Activities

We don't know of any other Bahamian island where you can rent your own boat, take a short orientation session, and then head off over calm protected waters for secluded beaches, neon-colored reefs, quiet settlements on remote cays, or to superior fishing grounds, all on your own. You can have fresh cracked conch for lunch in a bayside restaurant, snorkel in a marine park, stroll through shops and galleries in a picture-book settlement, catch rays on beaches few people visit in a year, and do it all in one day.

Sailing is the number-one activity in Abaco, and it is a favorite destination for numerous regattas and sailing events. Regatta Time, an annual July event, attracts sailors from around the world who participate in a nine-day series of races. Contestants compete for trophies and bragging rights, but eating, drinking, and general partying seem to be of equal importance.

Diving and snorkeling are a close second to sailing in popularity. There are countless diving and snorkeling sites over coral reefs and around various wrecks, including the wreck of the USS Adirondack, a 125-year-old American warship lying off Man-O-War Cay.

If you want to combine boating and snorkeling you can visit Pelican Cay National Park, an underwater preserve; or Abaco National Park, a 20,000-acre site in southern Abaco that includes nesting habitat for the Abaco Parrot.

Treasure Cay is the ideal spot for people who want the largest variety of activities including an 18-hole championship golf course, tennis courts, marina, boat rentals, offshore fishing, dive packages, good restaurants, and powder-white beaches.

The Abaco Beach Resort and Boat Harbour Marina is another full-service resort where vacationers who want it all can set up shop. Abaco Dive Adventures, located at the resort, is the best dive operation on the island.

Lodging, Guides, and Services

Featured Lodges

Treasure Cay Hotel Resort and Marina

Treasure Cay A top choice for an all-round family or couples vacation. Accommodations range from marina-view rooms and suites, to villas and townhouses on one of the most beautiful white sand beaches in the Bahamas. Amenities include a swimming pool, restaurant, two bars, golf cart and boat rentals, golf, tennis, diving, and snorkeling excursions. Bonefishing guides and offshore charters can be arranged.

Season: October through July.

Suitable for: Anglers and non-anglers.

Optional Activities: Diving through the certified marina dive shop, snorkeling, an array of beach/water sports, golf, tennis, and excursions to the offshore cays.

What's Included: Deluxe accommodations, guided fishing, meals, and Bahamian taxes can be included in one package. Trips of any length are available.

Not Included: Airfare to/from Treasure Cay, optional gratuities, alcoholic beverages, and any optional activities not in your package.

Pricing: $$-$$$

Contact: Reservations and information, 800-327-1584; fax 954-525-1699.

Internet: www.treasurecay.com

E-mail: info@treasurecay.com

Abaco Beach Resort & Boat Harbour

Marsh Harbour   One of the premiere Out Island resort destinations, on 52 immaculately manicured acres overlooking the Sea of Abaco. Five minutes from the Marsh Harbour airport, a short ferry ride away from Hope Town on Elbow Cay. Accommodations and amenities include 82 ocean-front rooms, two swimming pools, one with a pool bar and restaurant, a fine dining restaurant (wonderful atmosphere and one of our favorites), two tennis courts, a water sports center with complimentary use of windsurfers, sea kayaks and mountain bikes, 7,500 feet of event space. Boat rentals and a dive shop are in the adjacent 190-slip marina. Fishing guides can be arranged. This place rocks during the half dozen fishing tournaments it hosts every year, and is one of the liveliest party spots in the islands. Complete packages are available, including taxi transfers from the Marsh Harbour airport.

Season: October through July.

Suitable for: Anglers and non-anglers.

Optional Activities: Diving, snorkeling, an array of beach/water sports, golf, tennis, and excursions to the offshore cays.

What's Included: Deluxe accommodations, guided fishing, meals, and Bahamian taxes can be included in one package. Trips of any length are available.

Not Included: Airfare to/from Marsh Harbour, optional gratuities, alcoholic beverages, and any optional activities not in your package.

Pricing: $$-$$$

Contact: Reservations and information, 242-367-2158 or 800-468-4799.

Internet: www.abacoresort.com

Nettie's Different of Abaco

Casuarina Point   Nettie Symonette's lodge offers the only easy access to the famed central and southern Marls regions, plus great wading flats in Cherokee Sound. The variety of bonefishing options is suitable for anglers of all ability levels. Air-conditioned accommodations are in the ocean-side Seashell Beach Club, located on a glorious eight-mile-long white sand beach. The restaurant, bar, and swimming pool are set amidst lush gardens. Delicious meals and experienced guides round out this low-key fishing package. It is possible to fish on arrival and departure days.

Season: October through June.

Suitable For: Anglers and non-anglers.   ·

What's Included: Airport transfers to/from Marsh Harbor, accommodations, all meals, guided fishing, and Bahamian taxes.

Not Included: Airfare to Marsh Harbor, alcoholic beverages, gratuities.
Pricing: $$-$$$
Contact: Reservations and information, 242-366-2150; fax 242-327-8152.
Internet: www.differentofabaco.com
E-mail: nettie@differentofabaco.com

Walker's Cay Hotel & Marina

Walker's Cay Located 110 miles east of Palm Beach and 45 miles northeast of Freeport, Grand Bahama, at the northern tip of the Abaco chain. Accommodations are in 62 hotel rooms and 4 villas. All accommodations are air-conditioned and have private balconies. On-island facilities include a 2,500-foot paved airstrip with customs and immigration clearance seven days a week. Amenities include two swimming pools, tennis court, dive shop, full-service 75-slip marina with commissary, two restaurants with bars, and a lounge. Walker's Cay specializes in offshore fishing, though they also have very good reef and flats fly-fishing options. They also specialize in diving and snorkeling.
Season: October through July.
Suitable For: Anglers and non-anglers.
Optional Activities: Diving through the marina dive shop, snorkeling, an array of beach/water sports, and excursions to the offshore cays.
What's Included: Deluxe accommodations, guided fishing, meals, and Bahamian taxes can be included in one package. Trips of any length are available.
Not Included: Airfare to/from Ft. Lauderdale, optional gratuities, alcoholic beverages, and any optional activities not in your package.
Pricing: $$-$$$
Contact: Reservations and information, 800-925-5377 or 242-353-1252.
Internet: www.walkerscay.com
E-mail: info@walkerscay.com

Rickmon Bonefish Lodge

Sandy Point At the end of the road on the water's edge, the two-story lodge has 11 double air-conditioned guest rooms overlooking the white sand flats. The restaurant and bar is a lively gathering place for home-cooked meals, and the large deck is the ideal place to sip an après-fishing Kalik. Owner Ricardo Burrows is one of the top guides on the island, and he works with the best independent guides in the area. Guides from Rickmon fish around the southern tip of the island, around Castaway Cay, up to Crossing Rock and into the southern Marls, and out to Moore's Island.
Season: October through July.
Suitable For: Anglers.
What's Included: Accommodations, guided fishing, meals, Marsh Harbour airport transfers, and Bahamian taxes. Trips of any length are available.
Not Included: Airfare to/from Marsh Harbour optional gratuities, alcoholic beverages.
Pricing: $$
Contact: Reservations and information, 242-366-4477; fax 242-366-4478.
Internet: www.rickmonbonefishlodge.com
E-mail: jeff@rickmonbonefishlodge.com

Additional Accommodations and Do-It Yourself Options

Pete and Gay's Guesthouse

Sandy Point Located at the main settlement dock, this motel offers splendid views of the harbor from the rooftop lounge, comfortable rooms, and tasty Bahamian meals. Complete bonefishing packages are available including accommodations, meals, airport transfers to/from Marsh Harbor, and Bahamian taxes. This is a popular fishing program at a value price.
Pricing: $$
Contact: Reservations and information, 242-366-4119; fax 242-366-4007.
E-mail: peteandgay@oii.net

Banyan Beach Club

Treasure Cay Deluxe air-conditioned one- and two-bedroom condos on the beach, with swimming pool, restaurant, bar, and all the amenities available at the Treasure Cay Resort. You can book accommodations only, or a complete bonefishing and meal package. We recommend renting a golf cart if you stay here.
Pricing: $$-$$$
Contact: Reservations and information, 888-625-3060 or 242-365-8111.
Internet: www.banyanbeach.com

Bahama Beach Club

Treasure Cay On Treasure Cay Beach, this luxury complex has two-, three-, and four-bedroom condos with central A/C, balconies, full kitchens, swimming pools, and all the amenities of the Treasure Cay resort a short walk away.
Pricing: $$-$$$
Contact: Reservations and information, 242-365-8500.
Internet: www.bahamabeachclub.com

Tangelo Hotel

Wood Cay, Little Abaco A top choice for do-it-yourself anglers and anglers on a budget. Comfortable oceanfront location with 12 air-conditioned motel-style rooms. Nice people and good food make this a fine place to stay. Wadable flats are nearby. If you fish on your own, you will need to rent a car. Bonefishing packages are available and can include airport transfer to/from Treasure Cay.
Pricing: $-$$
Contact: Reservations and information telephone/fax, 242-365-2222.
Internet: www.oii.net/tangelo

Spanish Cay Resort & Marina

Spanish Cay Quiet and secluded, this resort cay has five villa-suites, several one- or two-bedroom condos, and private homes for rent. The 81-slip marina can handle boats to 250 feet. The restaurant and swimming pool overlook the marina. A 5,000-foot paved runway is suitable for most private jets. Customs services are available. You can fish on your own, or bonefishing can be arranged with guides from Coopers Town. To reach this island you can fly in by private aircraft, or fly to Treasure

Cay Airport, take a taxi to Coopers Town dock, and then take the free Spanish Cay ferry to the island, about a 15-minute ride.

Pricing: $$-$$$$

Contact: Reservations and information, telephone/fax, 242-365-0083 or 888-722-6474.

Internet: www.spanishcay.com

Green Turtle Cay Club & Marina

Green Turtle Cay Thirty-four air-conditioned rooms and cottages are sprinkled across the lush manicured grounds of this renowned marina waterfront resort. The restaurant is well known throughout the islands for relaxing lunches and fine evening dining. Swim, dive, snorkel, relax, fish on your own, or with a guide. There are two bays you can walk to for bonefishing on your own, or take the ferry across to Treasure Cay and fish Coopers Town or the Marls with independent guides. Complete packages are available, including taxi/ferry transfers to/from the Treasure Cay airport.

Pricing: $$$-$$$$

Contact: Reservations and information, 242-365-4271 or 866 528-0539; fax 242-365-4272.

Internet: www.greenturtleclub.com

The Bluff House Beach Hotel

Green Turtle Cay Elegant yet laid back, this cozy resort's dining room is one of the best in the islands, and affords stunning views over the Sea of Abaco. The casual Jolly Roger restaurant on the marina is our favorite spot for lunch. Twenty-eight air-conditioned rooms, suites, and villas provide upscale travelers with all the amenities they expect. Guests enjoy easy beach access, bonefishing on their own, or with guide. The hotel can arrange all other activities. Complete packages are available, including taxi/ferry transfers to/from the Treasure Cay airport.

Pricing: $$$-$$$$

Contact: Reservations and information, 242-365-4247 or 800-922-3474; fax 242-365-4248.

Internet: www.bluffhouse.com

Guana Seaside Village

Great Guana Cay This seven-mile-long cay is located seven miles across the Sea of Abaco from Marsh Harbour and Treasure Cay, between Green Turtle Cay and Man-Of-War Cay. The eight-room beachfront inn has delightful restaurant and bar, swimming pool, boat dock, and access to miles of awesome beaches, swimming, and snorkeling. You can also catch bonefish on your own in a couple of the nearby bays. On Sundays, don't miss the great pig roast party at Nipper's Bar. Packages can include taxi/boat transfers from Marsh Harbor via Albury's Ferry service.

Pricing: $$

Contact: Reservations and information, 877-681-3091 or 242-365-5106.

Internet: www.guanaseaside.com

Orchid Bay Yacht Club and Marina

Great Guana Cay A luxury hideaway for boaters and vacationers, and a private home development. The resort has several seaside villas available for rental, a casual restaurant, bar, swimming pool, tennis court, and 32-slip marina. You can fish on your own around the cay, or hire a guide. Albury's Ferry service provides quick access if you don't have your own boat.

Pricing: $$$-$$$$

Contact: Reservations and information: 242-365-5175 or 404-237-7300.
Internet: www.orchidbay.net

Dolphin Beach Resort

Great Guana Cay Seven unique cottages painted in Junkanoo colors overlook the sea and beach and are filled with amenities—A/C, full kitchens, TV/VCR, CD player, and cool island furnishings. Also available are four cozy hotel rooms with kitchenettes. The Blue Water Grille serves delicious meals in an English pub atmosphere. Packages can include taxi/boat transfers from Marsh Harbor via Albury's Ferry service. Miles of beach are steps away. Snorkeling, diving, and fishing can be arranged.
Pricing: $$-$$$
Contact: Reservations and information, 242-365-5137 or 800-222-2646.
Internet: www.dolphinbeachresort.com

Schooner's Landing Resort

Man-O-War Cay Light and airy two-bedroom condos overlooking the water with kitchens, TVs, and VCRs. Renting a golf cart is the way to go to get around to the powder-white beaches, snorkeling sites, tennis, shops, and settlement activities. Guests fly to Marsh Harbour, and then take Albury's Ferry to the island dock. The resort staff will meet you at the dock, and then transfer you to the property. Fish on your own, or guides can be arranged to meet you at the Marsh Harbour dock.
Pricing: $$
Contact: Reservations and information, 242-365-6072; fax 242-365-6285.
Internet: www.oii.net/schooners

Hope Town Hideaway

Hope Town, Elbow Cay If you want to rent the best townhouses, villas, and homes on Elbow Cay, we recommend Hope Town Hideaway. They will take care of everything you need, from boat and golf cart rentals, to guided fishing trips, island-hopping excursions, scuba and snorkel trips, or whatever else you might want. Their 12-slip marina can take boats up to 70 feet. You can also book a nice two-bedroom villa with air-conditioning, full kitchens, and decks overlooking Hope Town harbor. Taxi/ferry transfers are available from the Marsh Harbour airport to Hope Town. The ferry ride is about 15 minutes.
Pricing: $$-$$$$
Contact: Reservations and information, 242-366-0224; fax 242-366-0434.
Internet: www.hopetown.com

Hope Town Harbour Lodge

Hope Town, Elbow Cay A tranquil multi-level Bahamian resort with a classy mix of hotel rooms and cottages overlooking the Sea of Abaco. The Butterfly House, a renovated 100-year-old piece of history, has a full kitchen, two bedrooms, two baths, and large decks, and will accommodate up to six people. Swimming pool, two restaurants, two bars, gift shop, and eye-popping snorkeling right out front. Taxi/ferry transfers are available from the Marsh Harbour airport to Hope Town. A wonderful place for a family vacation, and you can fish on your own or hire a guide. If you feel adventurous rent a boat and explore the wadable flats in the Snake Cay area.
Pricing: $$-$$$

Contact: Reservations and information, 242-366-0095; fax 242-366-0286.
Internet: www.hopetownlodge.com

Abaco Inn

Elbow Cay Set among coconut palms and seagrapes on a beautiful ridge of sand dunes, this is one of the most popular getaway spots around Abaco. Fourteen private cottage-type rooms and eight one-bedroom villas with kitchenettes nestled on the edge of the Atlantic Ocean. To the west are the sheltered harbor of White Sound and the Sea of Abaco. Sensational food is a trademark here, from elegant dinners to tropical lunches and leisurely breakfasts. The beach and surf are at your feet. You can swim in the pool or in the ocean, and all island activities, including fishing, can be arranged by the hotel. Taxi/ferry transfers are available from the Marsh Harbor airport to Hope Town or directly to White Sound. This is one of Kim's favorite places to hang out and relax.
Pricing: $$-$$$
Contact: Reservations and information, 242-366-0133; fax 242-366-0113.
Internet: www.oii.net/AbacoInn

Sea Spray Resort Villas & Marina

White Sound, Elbow Cay Located at the southern tip of White Sound Harbour, the resort encompasses six acres of well-groomed grounds tucked between the Atlantic Ocean and the Sea of Abaco, and is just three miles from Hope Town. One- and two-bedroom villas include island-style furnishings, full kitchens, air-conditioning, surrounding patio decks, and daily maid service. The Boat House restaurant serves delicious Bahamian-style meals. Swim in the freshwater pool or in the ocean. Surfing off Garbanzo Reef is a blast. A water sports and diving program is available, and any other activities can be arranged through the resort office. The marina was being expanded and enhanced in the summer of 2004, with completion expected by the fall. Complete packages are available. Taxi/ferry transfers are available from the Marsh Harbor airport to Hope Town or directly to White Sound.
Pricing: $$-$$$
Contact: Reservations and information, 242-366-0065; fax 242-366-0383.
Internet: www.seasprayresort.com

Independent Guides

The following are some Abacos guides we have fished with, or guides that have been recommended by our friends and readers:

O'Donald Macintosh, 242-365-0126, out of Coopers Town. O'D is one of our favorite guides. You can usually find him each morning in front of Florence's in Treasure Cay, but to be sure to get a booking call him in advance. O'D fishes the northern Marls and up north around Coopers Town. You can also book his two sons, Kirkland and Drexel.

Justin Sands, 242-367-3526 or 242-359-6890; justfish@batelnet.bs; www.thebahamian.com/justfish, out of Marsh Harbour. Justin has a dynamite Hells Bay skiff that can run in the skinniest water you've ever imagined. He can trailer his boat anywhere, but usually fishes the northern Marls, Snake Cay, and the Bight of Robinson. Like O'D, he is very popular and requires booking in advance.

Buddy Pinder, 242-367-2234, out of Marsh Harbour.

Patrick Roberts, 242-366-4286, one of the best out of Sandy Point.

Anglers staying on Great Guana Cay, Elbow Cay, Man-O-War Cay or in Marsh Harbour can fish with O'D or Justin. Either guide will pick you up at the Albury Ferry dock in the morning, fish you all day, then drop you back off at the ferry at the end of the day.

Rick Sawyer, 242-365-4261, or *Ronny Sawyer,* 242-365-4070, on Green Turtle Cay. Visit Captain Rick Sawyer's Web site at www.abacoflyfish.com. Rick has useful information on his site, and you can order custom-tied flies that are proven killers around Green Turtle Cay. Considering how spooky the fish can be on those flats, you want to be sure to have the best flies.

Joe Sawyer, 242-365-4173, out of Marsh Harbour for a day of reef fishing for grouper and snapper.

Services

The Port Authority: We recommend that boaters with any questions give the Port Authority a call at 242-393-1064. They can provide all necessary information including a complete list of Ports of Entry.

Diving and Snorkeling: Trips can be arranged by your resort or hotel, or at the nearest marina.
In Marsh Harbour: *Dive Abaco*, 242-367-2787; or *Abaco Dive Adventures* at the Abaco Beach Resort: 242-367-2963; Internet: www.abacodiveadventures.com.
In Treasure Cay: *Diver's Down*, 242-365-8465.
On Elbow Cay: *Dave's Dive Shop*, 242-366-0029.

Boat rentals: Check with your resort or hotel when you book.
In Treasure Cay: *J.I.C. Rentals* is a quality operation. 242-365-8465. The owner, John Cash, is very helpful and he knows everyone.
In Marsh Harbour: *Sea Horse Boat Rentals*, 242-367-2513.
In the Marsh Harbor/Elbow Cay area: *Island Marine*, 242-366-0282.

Restaurants: Our favorite Treasure Cay area restaurants are *Spinnaker's* at the marina and *A Touch of Class* and *Coconuts* on the main highway. You need reservations at Spinnaker's and Coconuts. For breakfast, you should definitely try *Florence's Cafe*. Florence bakes irresistible homemade cinnamon rolls fresh every morning, plus she puts together delicious box lunches for fishing and picnicking.

In Marsh Harbour, *Wally's* is one of our favorites for fresh seafood, spicy Bahamian specialties, and Key lime pie. *The Anglers' Restaurant* at the Abaco Beach Resort has a delightful atmosphere and a wide selection of dishes from grilled wahoo to charbroiled lamb chops. On the main marina drag, *Mangoes* is the place to hang out, eat a burger, and to see and be seen by the boating crowd.

On Elbow Cay, there are several good choices, but the *Abaco Inn* dining room is our favorite. For just hanging out, drinking, and simple food, the *Harbor's Edge* is the place.

Just north of Cherokee Sound, the *Sand Bar* restaurant and bar is on the end of a 200-yard-long pier that stretches over glass-clear water and white sand bonefish flats. The kick-back open-air atmosphere makes it hard to ever leave. Cold Kaliks, grilled burgers, fried grouper, fresh conch salad, and sizzling fries are served with other Bahamian specialties. This "secret" locals spot is easy to miss if you're not paying attention. There is a small sign on the main highway at the turnoff to the settlement of Cherokee Sound. Take this road toward Cherokee Sound, a winding curvy strip of cement that skirts the edge of mangrove-lined creeks and bays cut into the coral from the mouth of the Sound. About a mile before the settlement you'll see another sign on your left. This road is very narrow and it ends at a locked gate. Park in one of the parking areas before the gate and walk to the Sand

Bar. You can't miss the wondrous pier that skims out over the water. This place is a must for lunch or afternoon snacks and drinks. It would be a good idea to have a fly rod handy with the incoming tide. You can access the flats from the beach, or walk down the stairs at the end of the pier right into schools of bones.

Green Turtle Cay is well worth a visit for lunch or dinner—even if you're not staying there—just to eat at the *Green Turtle Cay Club* or the *Bluff House*. These are the two best restaurants in the Abacos for innovative food and a casually elegant romantic atmosphere.

In Sandy Point, you can stop in at *Pete and Gay's* Guesthouse or at *Rickmon's Bonefish Lodge* for a cold drink or lunch, though it's advisable to call ahead.

Car Rentals: There are a number of small agencies you can contact through your resort or hotel. At the Treasure Cay airport: *Corniche Car Rentals*, 242-365-8623. In Marsh Harbour: *H&L Car Rentals*, 242-367-2854; *Reliable Car Rentals*, 242-367-3015.

Taxi Service: Very good, with some fares regulated by the government. We advise asking about all fares ahead of time.

Shopping: There are a number of good shops in Marsh Harbour, especially around the marina. *Iggy Biggy* and *Mangoes Boutique* are two of Kim's favorites, and there is also the obligatory *John Bull*.

Grocery stores, liquor stores, pharmacies, and just about every other kind of shop you would need are available in Marsh Harbour. Treasure Cay also has most services, and there are a few stores in Coopers Town. The rest of the island has limited services, though resort cays such as Green Turtle and Elbow can take care of most requests.

Ferry Service: Often more important than taxi service on Abaco. *Albury's Ferry Service*: 242-367-3114. *Green Turtle Cay Ferry*: 242-365-4032.

Clinics: *The Marsh Harbour Clinic* is the best medical facility in the Abacos. Government clinics are available in the larger settlements.

Banks: Your best bet for banking is in Marsh Harbour, though bank services are available in Treasure Cay and on Green Turtle Cay on a limited basis.

New Developments

High-end development, the rage on many of the islands, is at its finest at the Abaco Club on Winding Bay. Development of this luxury resort community began in earnest in 2004, with completion of most facilities expected in 2005. The 520-acre property about 20 minutes south of Marsh Harbour includes a magnificent peninsula bluff that juts into the Atlantic, and over two miles of white sand beaches. When completed the resort will include an 18-hole Donald Steel "links" golf course, a "Great House" clubhouse with restaurant and bar, swimming pool, tennis courts, guest cottages, and lavish home sites.

There are ongoing rumors about a hotel company finally buying the old hotel site in Treasure Cay but we'll believe this when we see it. Development of private homes in Treasure Cay continues to boom and prices aren't getting any lower. More development is being focused on the offshore cays with emphasis on Great Guana Cay where the spectacular beaches are an irresistible lure.

Log onto our Web site at www.bahamasflyfishingguide.com for the most up-to-date information.

CHAPTER 7

BIMINI AND BERRY ISLANDS

Heading out to the fishing grounds, early morning.

Self-proclaimed "Sportfishing Capital of the World," Bimini actually consists of two distinct islands separated by a narrow channel that forms the entrance into North Bimini Harbour. North Bimini is a thin strip of land seven miles long and no more than 700 yards wide. This is where the action is, in the marinas and bars and hotels made famous by Ernest Hemingway, Zane Grey, Michael Lerner, and Adam Clayton Powell. South Bimini is the quiet cousin, with a 5,000-foot airstrip, two upscale hotels, and a full-service marina. The storied Fountain of Youth is supposedly somewhere near the airstrip.

The Biminis are only 48 miles east of Miami, making them the closest Bahamian islands to the United States, but they are a world away in terms of lifestyle and atmosphere. Shirts and shoes are not required. The saying, "so close, yet so far" has real meaning here. The proximity to Florida made the islands an ideal location for illegal activities. From pirates, to Confederates, to rum and drug runners, this was a place to rendezvous and hide. Today, fishing is the main topic of most conversations, though divers get in a word or two on occasion, usually bringing up the legend of the lost continent of Atlantis.

Alice Town, on the southern end of North Bimini, is the main settlement. All the hotels, marinas, bars, and shops are located along the Queen's and King's highways, which run parallel to each other. It's easy to walk wherever you want to go, though renting a scooter or golf cart can be fun. While some visitors arrive via Chalks-Ocean Airways, most people cruise into the harbor on boats. The Bimini Big Game Fishing Club and Marina is the happening place for anglers, and the headquarters for more than a dozen fishing tournaments throughout the year.

During tournaments the island really turns on, with nightlife going from so laid back you could fall asleep, to lots of serious partying and drinking. The Compleat Angler is often the epicenter of these wild times.

Over the years the locals have seen and done it all. People here take everything in stride—no problem, mon. Fishing and tourism keep the economy going for the population of 1,600 or so. As an official Port of Entry, the Biminis see a constant stream of boaters. During spring and summer, the Bahamas Boating Flings, which are organized flotillas, cruise over from Florida. These are regularly scheduled events, sponsored by the Bahamas Ministry of Tourism and the South Florida Marine Industries Association. A registration fee is required, no more than 30 boats are allowed, and vessels must be at least 22 feet long. To participate, call the Bahamas Tourist Office in Miami at 800-32-SPORT.

Chalks-Ocean Airways has daily scheduled air service to Alice Town from Miami's Watson Island terminal. Flights are also available from Ft. Lauderdale, and from Chalks-Ocean Airways terminal on Paradise Island, Nassau. A weight restriction of 30 pounds per passenger is usually enforced. The seaplanes land in the harbor, then waddle up onto a land-based ramp. Passenger vans meet all flights, and then drive you to your hotel. Western Air also flies daily to South Bimini from Nassau. Charter flights are available to South Bimini from all over Florida to South Bimini. When you land here, you take a water taxi to the hotels or marinas in Alice Town.

Around the Island

Whether by air or by sea, visitors usually arrive in Alice Town via the North Bimini Harbour. The Chalks-Ocean seaplane ramp and terminal are just inside the harbor next to a small customs office. Next is Freddy Weech's Bimini Dock, which can accommodate up to 15 boats. Just north is the government dock and Customs House.

The Sea Crest Hotel and Marina offers 18 slips, ice, electricity, and showers. The hotel is across the street, and has air-conditioned rooms and suites with satellite TV and oceanview balconies.

The Bimini Blue Water Resort, owned by the pioneering Brown family, was one of Ernest Hemingway's favorite places. You can contact the marina on VHF 68. Full services are available for boaters, along with 32 slips and a dockside pool. Accommodations are across the street in guestrooms that include balconies and satellite TV. The Anchorage Restaurant, which was once Michael Lerner's home, offers views of the west side of the island and serves fresh seafood. The restaurant will also make box lunches for fishermen.

GRAND ISAAC BANK

Paradise Point

Bimini Bay Guesthouse

East Wells

bonefish

North Bimini

BAILEY TOWN

ALICE TOWN

Bimini Big Game Fishing Club & Marina

Bimini Bluewater Resort & Marina

Compleat Angler Hotel

marlin

tuna

Entrance Point

wahoo

Pigeon Cay

bonefish

tarpon

dorado

permit

Bimini Sands Condos & Marina

Bimini Sands Beach Club & Marina

Nixon's
Harbour

Round Rock

South Bimini

reef fish

Turtle Rocks

North

Piquet Rocks

reef fish

Holm Cays

Gun Cay

North Cat Cay

LOUIS TOWN

Bimini Islands

South Cat Cay

Cat Cay Yacht Club & Marina

Wedge Rocks

Victory Cays

reef fish

GRAND BAHAMA BANK

Sandy Cay

Ocean Cay

Brown's Cay

LEGEND

Beak Cay

⊙ TOWN / SETTLEMENT

★ Resort / Marina

✈ Airport

Ferry

reef fish

fish species

Barren Rocks

— Roads

Square Rocks

▲ Restaurant / Bar

GRAND BAHAMA BANK

0 1 2 3 4 5   10

Riding Rocks

SCALE IN MILES

South Riding Rocks   ○ Castle Rock

©1999 Map illustration/Burton Design, Jackson Hole, WY

On up the harbor is the Bimini Big Game Fishing Club and Marina. The 100-slip marina offers full services to boaters and anglers, and just about anything else a visitor might need. Contact the marina on VHF 16. This self-contained resort includes the Clubhouse Restaurant for fine dining, the Tackle Box Bar for lunch, snacks, and light meals, deluxe accommodations, a swimming pool, gift shop, and the island's only tennis court. All rooms have air-conditioning, private baths, and satellite TV. Suites and penthouses are available. The restaurant serves everything from seafood to steaks. If you want to stay here, especially during a fishing tournament, you need to make reservations well in advance.

If you're looking to book a fishing guide for bonefish, backcountry, or offshore, the Big Game Club is the place. The more famous guides, like Bonefish Ansil and Bonefish Rudy, are booked well ahead during the prime fishing months of March through June. Not to worry, though, as there are plenty of other Bonefish Whoevers who can take you out, but if you're serious about your fishing, we suggest booking a guide well ahead along with your accommodations.

The post office, commissioner's office, and police stations are in the government building north of the Big Game Club. Additional services include a Royal Bank of Canada, Bimini Undersea for diving and bike rentals, the North Bimini Medical Clinic with a resident doctor and nurse, a straw market, several grocery stores and a number of shops. You can walk, bike, or golf cart to any place on the island, or take one of the Bimini buses that run up and down the island. Pay phones are scattered along the main roads, but they don't always work. Using a VHF radio is the most reliable way to communicate, though cell phones have become common.

Capt. Bob's is a favorite breakfast spot for its killer French toast. Opal's is an "in" spot with many local ex-pats for lunch. The Red Lion Pub and Restaurant is our favorite place for fresh Bahamian-style seafood in a kick-back atmosphere. The Compleat Angler offers calypso bands with dancing several nights a week. The historic bar features tables made of old rum kegs and hundreds of old fishing photos. The bartenders are geniuses when it comes to blending rum drinks. Hemingway had more than his share of Goombay Smashes here while he was working on his novel *To Have and Have Not*.

Most of the locals live in Bailey Town, to the north of Alice Town on Porgy Bay. Both settlements make a special effort to keep up their appearances, with fresh pastel colors applied to houses and shops of varying shapes and sizes on a regular basis.

North of the settlements on the western shore are long stretches of shell-covered beaches. The prettiest beach is at Paradise Point, which is the location of the famous Art Deco mansion built in the 1950s by George Lyons. The mansion was then owned by Rockwell International, and is now run as the Bimini Bay restaurant by Antoinette and Basil Rolle. Nearby is a new B&B called the Trev Inn.

Just off Paradise Point are the Atlantis Rocks, the underwater formation many people claim to be the remains of a temple from the lost continent. Whether this is true or not, this is an excellent dive site. The road continues north from here, ending at East Wells.

Porgy Bay and the Sound run up along the eastern shore of North Bimini, and separate the inhabited portion of the island from a large backcountry area of cays, mangrove creeks, and flats. This is where anglers will find some of the best fishing for big bonefish in the Bahamas.

Working back south, shallow open water with deeper flats and channels head to South Bimini, home to the Bimini Sands Condos and Marina, and the Bimini Sands Beach Club. These sister facilities include two marinas, deluxe condos and hotel units, two restaurants, two swimming pools, and a relaxing atmosphere that sinks into your bones and makes going home an arduous task.

Another nine miles south is Gun Cay. Between the two islands are many smaller cays and rocks, and the massive, partially sunken concrete ship, *Sapona*.

Another mile to the southeast is Cat Cay and the Cat Cay Yacht Club. This is a private club, so only members can stay overnight, but boaters can tie up during the day and enjoy a great lunch in the restaurant overlooking the marina. Some of the best off-shore fishing in the area is off Cat Cay.

Fishing Highlights

From a habitat point of view, you couldn't ask for a better location. The islands sit on the eastern edge of the Straits of Florida and the Gulf Stream, and on the northwest corner of the Great Bahama Bank. Thrilling smash-mouth offshore fishing for marlin, sailfish, tuna, wahoo, and dorado is a tradition, with some of the world's best known billfish tournaments operating out of the Bimini Big Game Club.

Stephen with bonefish.

Though several IGFA bonefish records have gone into the books here, the flats fishing has taken a back seat to the blue water challenges. From a conventional tackle perspective we understand this, but for fly-fishers, the flats fishing is the thing.

The main network of flats areas are northeast of Alice Town in a wilderness of mangrove-lined creeks and cays that require local knowledge to navigate. While bonefish over 10 pounds are always the talk here, you'll see good numbers of fish in the 4- to 6-pound range. If you want to go for the big boys, you'll have to be selective, as the larger fish often use the smaller fish for protection. An indiscriminate cast will almost always take the smallest fish in the group.

In talking with locals and regular boating visitors, it's clear that James B. Orthwein has been dubbed the "king of the flats" on Bimini for many past successes with double-digit monsters, including some IGFA world records. We understand his favorite guide is Bonefish Rudy, and his favorite fly is a Jim's Golden Shrimp. We recommend Dick Brown's books *Fly Fishing for Bonefish* and *Bonefish Fly Patterns* for a comprehensive reference to Mr. Orthwein's flies.

When we fish for big bones we like flies that get down quickly. A #2 Gold Shiner Clouser Minnow would be our first choice in most situations, though a #2 Gotcha Bunny or Spawning Shrimp to match the bottom color would be close second choices.

Bimini bonefish guides commonly take out spinning anglers who use a variety of small jigs tipped with shrimp. This is a guaranteed way to catch bonefish even during periods of bad weather. If you have children who want to catch bonefish, but can't manage a fly rod, this is an ideal way to introduce them to the sport. This is also the time to introduce them to catch-and-release fishing, which is promoted by most guides on Bimini.

Other flats species include barracuda, sharks, permit, jacks, and tarpon. Tarpon fishing can be excellent from April through July, with June the prime month. Our favorite tarpon flies include a Shallow Water Cockroach and a Red/Black Sea Bunny. June is also the month with the most rainfall and lightning. Most guides know to get out of the way of these powerful thunderstorms, but sometimes the storms develop too quickly to avoid. Don't let your enthusiasm for catching fish get the best of your judgment. You need to head for cover when those ominous black clouds start spitting lightning bolts.

Offshore, the best months for billfish are April through July, though billfish cruise these waters most of the year. The Hemingway Championship is held in February or March, Bacardi Rum tournament in March and April, and the Big Game Club Bimini Festival in May.

A variety of tuna, including giant bluefin, blackfin, and yellowfin, are best April though June, with May the prime month. Wahoo and kingfish are the prime winter species, with January and February best. The Bahamas Wahoo Championships are held throughout the islands from November through February, with the Bimini leg usually in November.

Reef and wreck fishing for sharks, barracuda, jacks, snappers, and grouper is good year round. Using chum will get the fish in the feeding mood, then you can toss out flies, lures, or bait and have a field day. Most restaurants on Bimini will be happy to cook your catch. Charter boats are available for hire through the Bimini Big Game Club and the Bimini Blue Water Marina.

Optional Activities

Ah, the boating life for me is the inner voice of the Biminis. The atmosphere here is a combination of the old pirating days mixed with modern nostalgia. People who leave Florida as intense American entrepreneurs transform themselves into barefoot deckhands in a mere 48-mile crossing.

While fishing is the dominant activity around Bimini, just hanging out, relaxing, and socializing is a major part of daily life, especially on weekends. Long lazy beaches offer sunning, swimming, and snorkeling. If you need some exercise, you can jog or bike up the King's Highway to East Wells.

Diving enthusiasts can choose from a variety of sites rich in marine life. The Bimini Wall, Rainbow Reef, the Bimini Barge, Little Caverns, and the Atlantis Rocks are among the most popular dives. Most hotels can set up a dive package, though Bimini Undersea is the main diving operation, and you can book directly with them. Guided snorkeling and swimming with dolphins can also be arranged. Snorkeling around the concrete wreck of the *Sapona* and all through the surrounding area is very good. All necessary equipment is available for sale or rent. Boston Whalers can be rented by the day or half day from Weech's Bimini Dock.

If you're looking for nightlife, make your visits on the weekends or during the bigger fishing tournaments.

Lodging, Guides, and Services

Featured Lodges

Bimini Big Game Fishing Club and Marina

North Bimini This self-contained resort offers full marina services and deluxe accommodations in a casual fun atmosphere. Thirty-three air-conditioned rooms feature two double beds, private bath, and enough room to spread out your fishing and diving gear. Twelve larger cottages include a dining area and refrigerator. Two penthouse suites provide outstanding views of the marina and harbor beyond. All rooms have satellite TV.

Amenities include a freshwater swimming pool, fine dining restaurant, poolside and sports bars, event barbecues, and duty-free liquor store. Meeting rooms are available for up to 30 people. Baby-sitting and laundry service can be arranged.

The marina has 100 slips, 110- and 220-amp electrical, satellite TV hookups, fresh water, ice, and Texaco diesel and gas products.

Everything in Alice Town is within walking distance, including the west shore beaches. Guided flats, reef, and offshore charters are arranged, along with diving and snorkeling packages. Calling well ahead for reservations is a must.

Season: October through July.

Suitable For: Anglers, divers, and non-anglers.

What's Included: Fishing and diving packages, including meals, are available through the resort.

Not Included: Air or boat transportation to the islands, alcohol, gratuities. Any optional activities you choose. Most people book accommodations and fishing, and then do everything else on their own. We recommend booking your fishing guide or charter boat well in advance.

Pricing: $$-$$$

Contact: Reservations and information, 800-737-1007 or 242-347-3391; fax 242-347-3392.

Internet: www.biminibiggame.com

E-mail: reservations@biminibiggame.com

Bimini Sands Condos and Marina

South Bimini   Overlooking the Straits of Florida, this luxury property rents one- or two-bedroom condominiums in two-story red-roofed buildings at the water's edge. The pool, beach, and marina make this a sun worshiper's getaway, and a good spot for a family vacation. The Petite Conch restaurant serves three meals a day, blending Bahamian dishes with steaks, burgers, and fries. The property includes a 150-slip full-service Texaco Starport marina and a convenient customs office so guests with boats can tie up and clear their paperwork without traveling to North Bimini. An all-night water taxi shuttles you to North Bimini to dine and party.

Pricing: $$-$$$

Contact: Reservations and information, 242-347-3500.

Internet: www.biminisands.com

E-mail: bimini@biminisands.com

Bimini Sands Beach Club Hotel and Marina

South Bimini   Adjacent to Bimini's southern tip, the Beach Club is the sister property of the Bimini Sands Condos. Ocean- and marina-view rooms have light-colored interiors and thoughtful touches—such as good lighting, flowers, and throw rugs on gleaming terrazzo tile floors. The beach club offers a reception-lounge area with large couches placed in front of a working fireplace, a billiard room, a tiny bar that overlooks the sparkling pool, and a restaurant with superb Bahamian cuisine and unparalleled views of the surrounding waters. The marina has slips for 53 boats.

Pricing: $$-$$$

Contact: Reservations and information, 242-357-3500.

Internet: www.biminibeachclub.com

E-mail: bimini@biminisands.com

Additional Accommodations

Bimini Blue Water Resort and Marina

The hotel portion of the resort is atop a hill on the western side of the island, while the marina is on the eastern harbor. Nine rooms have private balconies and baths. Anchorage suites feature two bedrooms, a sitting room, and private balconies. You can also rent the three-bedroom Marlin Cottage with a full kitchen, where Hemingway wrote much of his novel *Islands in the Stream.* The west-facing cottage provides a spectacular sunset view. You can swim off the beach or in the freshwater pool. The

Anchorage Restaurant also presents great views of the ocean along with some of the best seafood on the island. The 32-slip marina offers full services and monitors VHF Channel 68.

Pricing: $$-$$$

Contact: Reservations and information, 242-347-3166; fax 242-347-3293.

Sea Crest Hotel and Marina

Three-story hotel with 11 motel-style rooms with satellite TV and balconies, plus one two-bedroom, and one three-bedroom suite. Short walk to the beach. Special off-season rates are offered October through February. Golf carts are available for rent. The marina monitors VHF Channel 68.

Pricing: $-$$

Contact: Reservations and information, 242-347-3071; marina 242-347-347; fax 242-347-3495.

Internet: www.seacrestbimini.com

Weech's Bay View Rooms and Marina

Five simple air-conditioned rooms and one apartment. Full marina services with the exception of fuel. VHF Channel 68. Close to the beach.

Pricing: $-$$

Contact: Reservations and information, 242-347-3028; fax 242-347-3508.

Compleat Angler Hotel

This place is a piece of history. Twelve comfortable air-conditioned outside rooms open onto a common walkway facing the bar and street. Guests can use the pool at the Blue Water Resort. If you like getting to sleep early, you might have a problem during fishing tournaments because the downstairs partying gets pretty loud.

Pricing: $-$$

Contact: Reservations and information, 242-347-3122; fax 242-347-3293.

Independent Guides

Bimini is famous for its long tradition of independent guides. Many of these guides have world records under their belts, and all have seen countless double-digit monsters hooked and lost. Fishing with any of the following guides can be a memorable experience. They can be booked directly or through the Bimini Big Game Club.

Bonefish Ansil: 242-347-2178 or 242-347-3098
Bonefish Ray: 242-347-2269
Bonefish Ebbie: 242-347-2053
Bonefish Tommy: 242-347-3234
Bonefish Rudy: 242-347-2266

Services

Air Service: *Chalks-Ocean Airways* has daily scheduled flights aboard Mallare seaplanes from Miami and Ft. Lauderdale. Contact: 800-424-2557 or 242-347-3024. Internet: www.flychalks.com.

Bimini Island Air, 954-938-8991, from Ft. Lauderdale Executive Airport, and *Island Air*, 954-359-9942, from Ft. Lauderdale Jet Center are both offering service to Bimini.

Western Air offers service to Bimini from Nassau. Call 242-347-4100 or 242-377-2222; Internet: www.westernairbahamas.com.

Diving and Snorkeling: *Bimini Undersea Adventures* offers full diving and snorkeling services and excursions, including sales and rentals. Also rents bicycles. Call ahead for rentals during prime times. Contact: Reservations and information, 800-348-4644 or 242-347-3089; Internet: www.biminiundersea.com

Rentals: *Compleat Angler Golf Cart Rentals,* contact: 242-347-3122.

Events and Activities: The Biminis host a series of fishing tournaments and boating events throughout the year, including the *Mid-Winter Wahoo Tournament* (November, February), the *Annual Bacardi Rum Billfish Tournament* (March), the *Bimini Break and Blue Marlin Tournament* (April), the *Bimini Festival of Champions* (May), *Annual Bimini Native Tournament* (August), the *Bimini Family Fishing Tournament* (August), and the *Small BOAT—Bimini Open Angling Tournament* (September). The island also hosts an annual *Bimini Regatta*, which takes place in the spring. For information on dates, tournament regulations, and recommended guides, call the Bahamas Tourist Office in Florida (800-327-7678) and ask for the sportfishing section.

The *Bimini Museum*, sheltered in the restored (1920) two-story original post office and jail—a short walk from the seaplane ramp—displays numerous artifacts including Adam Clayton Powell's domino set, Prohibition photos, rum kegs, plus a fishing log and rare fishing films of Ernest Hemingway. Contact: 242-347-3038. Hours: Monday through Saturday, 9 A.M. to 9 P.M.; Sunday, noon to 9 P.M.

Government: *Bimini Tourist Office.* Contact: Telephone 242-347-3529; fax 242-347-3530.

Clinics: *North Bimini Medical Clinic,* 242-347-2211.

Marinas: Most of *Cat Cay Club and Marina* is private, for members only, but boaters can stop in the marina to clear customs or to have lunch. The marina offers full services to boaters, a gift shop, and a small grocery store with a good array of provisions. Reservations and information: 954-359-8272 or 242-347-3565. The marina monitors VHF Channel 16.

New Developments

There is continued talk of building a large casino resort on either North or South Bimini but this talk has been going on for years. For updated information, stay tuned at www.bahamasflyfishingguide.com.

Berry Islands

About 70 miles east of Bimini, a cluster of 30 islands and a hundred cays form the crescent shape of the Berry Islands. With a physical mass totaling about a dozen square miles, these droplets of land rest on the northeastern edge of the Great Bahama Bank, sandwiched between the sapphire-blue waters of the Northwest Providence Channel and the Tongue of the Ocean. Starting with Great Stirrup Cay in the north, the islands extend some 30 miles to Chub Cay in the south, which is 35 miles north of Nassau and 12 miles from the Joulter's Cays on north Andros.

These largely uninhabited islands offer tranquil secluded anchorages, several small resorts for diving, snorkeling, bonefishing, and offshore fishing for blue and white marlin, sailfish, wahoo, and kingfish.

At 10 miles long and a mile and a half wide, Great Harbour Cay is the largest island in the chain. Most of the island's 600 or so residents live here, in Bullock's Harbour settlement. The local economy is based on commercial lobstering, conching, and fishing, with some farming and stock-raising, as well. Tourism, centered on diving, fishing, and boating, is also a significant factor on Great Harbour and Chub Cay.

The locals in Chub Cay will tell you that there are more millionaires per square mile in the Berry Islands than almost anywhere on the planet. When you look around at all the private islands and cays, it's not hard to believe that this is true.

While most visitors arrive by boat, there are two airports, one at Great Harbour Cay and one at Chub Cay. Tropical Diversions Air is the number-one charter company operating flights to both cays from Ft. Lauderdale. A number of other charter companies fly in from Miami, Ft. Lauderdale, and West Palm Beach.

Around the Islands

Both Little Stirrup Cay and Great Stirrup Cay have become day stops for at least two cruise ship companies. Royal Caribbean Cruise Lines occupy Slaughter Harbour for its day operations, which include jet skiing and parasailing. Bertram Cove on the north side of Great Stirrup is also cruise ship central. Local vendors have sprouted from the sand to sell T-shirts, baskets, and other souvenirs.

Good bonefish flats, wadable at low tide, extend south of Great Stirrup to Snake Cay and Goat Cay. There is also a pleasant anchorage for boaters on the northeast side of Goat Cay. This would be a fine base from which to explore the flats between Lignum Vitae Cay and the north end of Great Harbour Cay. The water in this area is usually one to two feet deep, and some areas go dry at low tide. Using a dinghy or sea kayak would be ideal, fishing both from the watercraft and by wading.

A maze of mangroves and creeks continues south past Cistern Cay on the way to Bullock's Harbour. This area holds consistent numbers of bonefish, with fishing best on the incoming tide. Boaters must stay well off this area, however, as many of the sand banks go dry at low tide.

The entrance to Great Harbour Cay Marina is through an 80-foot wide channel on the bank side in the center of the island. The 70-slip marina and resort offers full services to boaters including a grocery and liquor store. All Tropical Diversions Resort guests have the use of the freshwater swimming pool and the nine-hole golf course.

Visitors arriving by air are met at the airport and transferred to the resort. Accommodations are in privately owned villas and townhouses that have satellite TV, sundecks; some are air-conditioned—be sure to ask for air-conditioning when making

Cruise Ship Beaches

Great Stirrup Cay

Little Stirrup Cay

bonefish

Goat Cay

Lignum Vitae Cay

bonefish

marlin
dorado
tuna
wahoo

Cistern Cay

Petit Cay

Great Harbour Cay

bonefish

BULLOCK'S HARBOUR

Tropical Diversions Resort & Marina

Hawksnest Cay

Bamboo Cay

Haine's Bluff

Anderson Cay

bonefish

Sheep Cay

Haine's Cay

Turner Cay

Kemp Cay

Water Cay

Ceasar Cay

Fanny Cay

Soldier Cays

bonefish

bonefish

reef fish

Market Fish Cays

Ambergris Cays

Pigeon Cay

Money Cay

permit

Hoffman Cay

GREAT BAHAMA BANK

North

bonefish

Saddle Back Cay

reef fish

Devil's Cay

Berry Islands

Little Harbour Cay

bonefish

Comfort Cay

Flo's Conch Bar
& Restaurant

Guano Cay

0 1 2 3 4 5 6 7 8

SCALE IN MILES

High Cay

Alder Cay

LEGEND

Sandy Cay

Cormorant Cay

⊙ TOWN / SETTLEMENT

★ Resort / Marina

Bond's Cay

✈ Airport

Ferry

bonefish

fish species

Roads

Fish Cays

▲ Restaurant / Bar

Cockroach Cay

Little White Cay

reef fish

tarpon

South Stirrup Cay

bonefish

Frazer's Hog Cay Resort

permit

Crab Cay

Frazer's Hog Cay

Cat Cay

marlin
dorado
tuna
wahoo

Chub Cay Club & Marina

Chub Cay

Bird Cay

Whale Cay

Diamond Cay

© 1999 Map illustration/Burton Design, Jackson Hole, WY

your reservations. Guests can stock up on food and cook in their units or eat out at a variety of restaurants. If you plan to shop for provisions, be sure to check the freight boat schedules and be at the grocery stores soon after it arrives.

One of the most popular places for lunch and dinner is the Tamboo Club at the marina. They put on an exceptional seafood buffet a couple of nights a week. Another favorite restaurant with boaters is the Wharf, also located on the marina. Salads, burgers, and sandwiches are served at lunch, while seafood specialties change every night.

Our favorite part of Great Harbour Cay is the eastern shore, where you'll find one of the most inviting beaches in the Bahamas. The white sand runs from south of the airstrip to the northern tip of the island. The Beach Club restaurant, near the airport, is the best place on the island for lunch. You can fish the incoming tide on mangrove flats south of the airport, take a swim, enjoy some snorkeling, and have a great lunch or afternoon drinks, all in the same day.

Great Harbour Cay is one of the best locations in the islands to fish on your own. Percy Darville is the man to contact to point you in the right direction. Mr. Darville can arrange for boat rentals; then, if you get frustrated, he can arrange for a guide.

The flats south of Great Harbour are best fished on the incoming tide, though the seemingly endless mangrove areas between Anderson Cay and Haine's Cay are very good during the last of the falling tide.

Miles of shallow banks, flats, and cuts continue east and south. The banana-shaped Ambergris Cays have rarely fished flats on their western side, and deeper water on the east running out to the Solider Cays and Market Fish Cays. Using chum, you can catch sharks, barracuda, jacks, and snappers in this deeper water until your arms ache. On the tide, you can wade for several hours for bonefish that average five to six pounds. The east side of the cays, and down around Ambergris Rock, are also good permit areas, with 25- to 45-pound fish working most consistently on the spring tides.

There is a pleasant anchorage for boaters in the lee of Market Fish Cays, with good fishing for jacks, snapper, and grouper in the cuts. This type of fishing continues consistently down through the Holmes Cay, Hoffman Cay, and Devil's Cay section. The bonefish flats are inside, on the bank.

A favorite spot for boaters is Little Harbour Cay. This is a private island but you can get permission to use the dock and visit the island from Chester Darville and his family. The Darville family dock and a dazzling little harbor are located in the lee off the southern end of the cay. The cay itself is hilly and covered with dense vegetation. You can contact the Darvilles on VHF Channel 68. We recommend Flo's Conch Bar and Restaurant for great lobster, grouper, fried conch, conch salad, cold Kaliks, and island cocktails. You'll need to call at least three hours in advance for reservations.

There are a number of privately owned houses on the island, and we're told they do not welcome visitors, which is the case on many of the private islands to the south. Just across from the southern end of Little Harbour is Cabbage Cay. A small white sand flat on the west side can produce excellent bonefishing for a couple of hours each day, with the best times being morning or late-afternoon incoming tides. Just north is

Guana Cay, Comfort Cay, and some smaller cays form another white sand flat in their center. We've caught fish here each time we've tried it on incoming and falling tides.

Continuing south, Frozen and Alder Cays are private property. The owners here have been busy with all kinds of construction, including large docks that have brought some boat traffic to the area. Access to hot offshore fishing, especially for billfish and tuna, is only a couple miles off these cays. To the south, Bond's Cay is also private, as are Little Whale and Whale Cays. Whale Cay has been significantly developed in the past three years. Little Whale Cay was originally developed by Wallace Groves, the founder of Freeport. The bird population on this cay includes peacocks, golden pheasant, ducks, geese, and flamingos. The reef fishing off these cays is first-rate. If you want to hook up a big shark, bull, or blacktip, this is one of the best places to try it.

On the bank side of these private cays are countless flats dissected by cuts and creeks running out to Cockroach Cay, Cormorant Cay, Fish Cays, and many other nameless cays. To the south and west, the chain ends with Bird Cay, Frazer's Hog Cay, and Chub Cay. That's a lot of cays, and they create ideal habitat for big bonefish and permit. This area is one of our top recommendations for anglers who want to fish on their own.

Bird Cay is a millionaire's haven, with elegant homes, roads, and landscaping that includes groves of coconut and citrus trees. Across the channel is Frazer's Hog Cay, which is actually the eastern part of Chub Cay. Frazer's Hog Cay Resort is located to the east of the island's airstrip. This small resort specializes in taking it easy. If you really need to do something, diving, snorkeling, fishing, and water sports are available.

The Chub Cay Club and Marina is located on the southwestern tip of the island. This is a port of entry with a customs office at the airstrip. Once a privately owned resort, the Club is now open to the public. The well-designed marina can accommodate almost a hundred boats, and offers full services that include a restaurant, grocery and liquor stores, and gift shop.

Visitors arriving by air are met at the airstrip and driven to the resort. Deluxe air-conditioned rooms are built around a large swimming pool. One- to three-bedroom villas are situated on a gorgeous southwest-facing beach. A good anchorage for boaters is just off this beach. Another longer beach is around a rocky point to the east, where you can enjoy snorkeling in glass clear water. Two tennis courts, a diving operation, and bike rentals are available.

Bonefishing packages have been offered on and off. Boaters and visitors can hire a fishing guide or arrange an offshore charter through the Club office. We've fished the area on numerous occasions, running across from north Andros on calm days, and a few times while staying in one of the villas. While we've seen good numbers of fish, the impressive thing here is the size of the bonefish. Fish average five to seven pounds, with plenty of fish pushing double digits. This is also a prime area for permit, especially in late spring and summer.

Fishing Highlights

Flying over the Berry Islands is always exciting and enticing. It's the same flying over the Joulter's. The white flats go on forever, sliced up by blue cuts and creeks and green cays that create the best possible habitat for big bonefish and permit. A shallow lee bank runs the length of the chain, from Little Stirrup Cay to Chub Cay. These banks are packed with shrimp and crabs. Blue water traverses 75 percent of the chain. Miles of coral reefs are home to countless baitfish. And very few people ever fish here.

Bonefish are the primary flats gamefish, with the average size being five pounds throughout most of the chain. Many of these fish are dark-green-backed ocean fish that will take 200 yards of your backing on the first run. If you hook up an ocean fish over eight pounds, you can count on runs like this.

There are not many guides in the islands who understand the intricacies of this fishery. The area is so vast, with so much structure for fish to follow, that this type of understanding takes years of observation. Certain areas are well known, while other flats go unfished for years at a time. The mangrove areas south of Great Harbour Cay hold higher numbers of smaller fish, telling us this is a nursery area, though big fish also cruise the region. Many of these fish tend to be lighter in color.

We prefer to fish the Berrys on a neap tide. These lower tides create miles of wadable flats. Big bones nor-

Bonefish are plentiful in the waters off Bimini.

mally prefer spring tides, but here the bigger fish have plenty of deeper water channels to use for accessing super-shallow flats. Our favorite fly for these tailing fish is a White or Tan Yarn Crab. We also take fish consistently on these light-colored bottoms with Gotchas, Hoovers, and Sililegs. The prime bonefishing months in the Berrys are March through June and October and November.

Your chances for catching a permit are best in the southern Berrys, from Chub Cay west to the Rum Cay area. The fish we've seen averaged 25 pounds, with some monsters pushing 50. Best months are April through August, with the fall also good. Our favorite permit fly here is a White Yarn Crab with brown rubber legs and heavy lead eyes. If you find a permit following a big stingray in this environment, you'll have an excellent chance for a hookup.

Tarpon fishing in the Berrys is fair from April on through the summer, though we suspect it could be very good if the guides tried harder to figure it out, or if some boating anglers took an interest and put in some time. The few times we've seen tarpon on the flats around South Stirrup Cay, they've attacked our flies with abandon. These fish averaged about 80 pounds, with a couple pushing 100. A Shallow Water Cockroach is all we've tried, so until we get a refusal, we'll just stick with it.

Like the Biminis, the Berrys are best known for their reef and offshore fishing. If you're looking to catch an amberjack in the 50-pound class, you'll have ample opportunity from November through May, with April the best overall month. April is also prime time for mutton snappers over the reefs. If you catch a few of these hard fighters, keep one for the dinner table.

Offshore fishing is the specialty out of Great Harbour Marina and Chub Cay Marina. The winter months are prime for wahoo and kingfish, with some dorado and tuna. Starting in April, the dorado and tuna really pick up, with May the best time. Allison tuna are our favorites, though dealing with the ones over 50 pounds are pretty tough on a fly rod. The best flies are mullet patterns and Carter Andrew's Snak-Pak series, though a variety of Offshore Deceivers and other similar patterns will take fish.

Blue and white marlin and sailfish are available from January on, with May and June the best marlin months. Several tournaments are held out of each marina during these prime months, but you don't have to be serious to enjoy this fishery. Cruising boaters can toss out trolling rigs almost anywhere throughout the chain and hook up something.

Optional Activities

Sailing, boating, and just enjoying the remote beauty of the islands is the attraction here, though the diving and snorkeling doesn't get much better. In the Chub Cay area, the water is so clear you can easily see small crabs moving on the bottom 20 feet below the surface. Undersea Adventures out of Chub Cay operates a diving program. Reef, wall, and cave sites are suited to the most adventurous divers, while beginners can enjoy calm areas loaded with fish. Night dives are also available.

Secluded beaches can be found on almost every cay. If you're looking for a piece of sand all your own, you'll find it here, even on Chub and Great Harbour.

Lodging, Guides, and Services

Featured Lodges

Tropical Diversions Resort & Marina
Great Harbour Cay   This is an ideal spot for couples and families, and a convenient location for boaters to hang out for extended periods. Anglers looking for variety, and a chance to fish on their

own, will have lots of options. The resort's villas and townhouses are nicely appointed, and since they are individually owned, they are all different. Air-conditioning is available, and all units include satellite TV, and sundecks, but no telephones. The resort includes three restaurants, a bar, 9-hole golf course (though it's not in good shape), boat and bike rentals, and a beautiful beach. The full-service marina monitors VHF Channel 68. A couple of grocery stores and a liquor store are nearby, as are other restaurants and bars.

Season: October through July.

Suitable For: Anglers and non-anglers.

What's Included: Fishing packages are available, including meals and airport transfers, though most people book accommodations first, then other activities separately.

Not Included: Airfare to/from Great Harbour, meals, and optional activities. Flats, reef, bottom, and offshore fishing can be arranged through the resort.

Pricing: $$-$$$

Contact: U.S. reservations and information, 800-343-7256 or 242-367-8838; fax 242-367-8115.

Internet: www.tropicaldiversions.com

E-mail: info@tropicaldiversions.com

Chub Cay Club and Marina

Chub Cay This is our favorite place in the Berrys. The marina is one of the nicest in the Bahamas. The marina monitors VHF Channel 68. Boaters should call ahead for slip space. The 16 deluxe air-conditioned rooms around the larger of two pools will make most people very comfortable. If you need something bigger and more remote, you can rent one of the nine villas on the beach just south of the marina. The villas include large living rooms and full kitchens. You can walk right off your deck onto the white sand beach to take a swim in the tranquil bay. Two tennis courts and bike rentals are available. The Club dining room serves fresh seafood every evening, with most dishes prepared with a distinct Bahamian flare. That means spicy and delicious. Fresh lobster is available in season. We suggest making reservations for dinner. Three bars make it convenient to get a cold Kalik or rum drink from noon until whenever. The grocery store is usually well stocked, though shopping right after the freight boat arrives is a smart thing to do.

Season: October through July.

Suitable For: Anglers and non-anglers.

What's Included: Fishing and diving packages can be arranged, including meals and airport transfers, though most people book accommodations first, then other activities separately.

Not Included: Airfare to/from Chub Cay. Tropical Diversions charter flights. Meals and optional activities. Flats, reef, bottom, and offshore fishing can be arranged through the Club. Full and half-day diving and snorkeling excursions are available through the dive shop. Guides David Lightbourne and Felix Russell have received good recommendations from our readers. A 36-foot Hatteras, the *Passage,* has received good reviews for full and half-day reef and offshore charters.

Pricing: $$$

Contact: Reservations and information, 800-662-8555 or 242-325-1490; fax 242-322-5199.

Internet: www.chubcay.com

E-mail: chub@chubcay.com

Additional Accommodations

Frazer's Hog Cay Resort

If you're looking for peace and quiet you'll find it here on the east end of Chub Cay. The emphasis is on a natural Bahamian experience. Comfortable rooms feature ceiling fans and private bath. The open-air restaurant is on the beach and specializes in fresh grilled seafood. Fishing, diving, snorkeling, and water sports are the main activities.

Pricing: $$

Contact: Reservations and information, 242-328-8952; fax 242-356-6086.

E-mail: fhcresort@bahamas.net.bs

Independent Guides

Captain Percy Darville has been involved in a number of package bonefishing operations over the years. He can assist anglers interested in fishing on their own, or he can arrange for bonefish guides. Contact him through the Great Harbour Marina. We suggest contacting Mr. Darville as far in advance of your arrival as possible. Contact: 242-367-8119 or 242-367-8005.

Services

Air Service: *Tropical Diversions Air* has the best service. They fly Cessna 402s, Aztecs, and Navajos. Charter flights from Ft. Lauderdale to Great Harbour Cay. Reservations and information: 800-343-7256 or 954-629-9977; Internet: www.tdair.com.

Diving and Snorkeling: *Undersea Adventures,* operated by dive master Bill Nelson out of Chub Cay. Morning, afternoon, and night dives are available. Packages are available. Reservations and information: 800-327-8150 or 242-323-2412.

Rentals: *Elorne Rolle's Happy People on the Great Harbour Marina* rent cars, boats, motorbikes, and bicycles. Reservations and information, 242-367-8117.

New Developments

We've heard all kinds of rumors about new mega-resorts, more cruise ships taking over private cays, and a bonefish lodge or two, but nothing is confirmed. Major developments are definitely in full swing on a number of the private islands, but we don't know if these will remain private or be opened to the public. Stay tuned to our Web site at www.bahamasflyfishingguide.com for updated information.

CHAPTER 8

ELEUTHERA, SPANISH WELLS, AND HARBOUR ISLAND

If you get lost, just ask for directions. The people here will go out of their way to help you.

At its closest point Eleuthera lies 30 miles northeast of Nassau, and less than 30 miles east of the northern Exuma Cays. The island spans about 100 miles from north to south, ending in a Y shape formed by Powell Point, Rock Sound, and Bannerman Town. While long, the island is also skinny, with an average width of less than two miles.

The terrain is a combination of tall white-faced cliffs, coral sand beaches, forests, green hills, and pristine valleys dotted with lakes. All of this is surrounded by aquamarine seas, with the deeper blue of the Atlantic Ocean pouring in over the windward reef.

The story of the Eleutherian Adventurers is well known throughout the Bahamas. Led by Captain William Sayle, a former governor of Bermuda, 70 souls seeking religious freedom set out in search of a new homeland. They originally landed in 1648 near Governor's Harbour, then discord within the group caused Sayle and some of his followers to sail north. Their boat eventually ran aground on the dangerous northern reefs, but the party struggled ashore at a location that came to be known as Preacher's Cave. Some of the group found their way to what is now Spanish Wells. Life was harsh, with starvation a constant threat.

The entrance to Pink Sands Hotel, Harbour Island.

These settlers named the island Eleuthera, from the Greek word for freedom, and continued their determined battle to survive. Sayle, realizing his new homeland needed help, sailed off to the Colonies to look for support.

Though most of the original settlers returned to England by 1650, Sayle's mission was ultimately a success. Eleuthera became known as the "birthplace of the Bahamas," and was probably the first true democracy in the Western Hemisphere.

Loyalists arrived with their slaves after the Revolutionary War. They built colonial-style homes and based their economy on agriculture and shipbuilding. As with the Abaconians, salvaging wrecked ships off the reefs became an important part of their livelihood.

Growing pineapples proved to be big business for a long period of time, with many tons shipped to the United States and England. Though the pineapple business is not what it was, it is still important to Eleuthera's economy today. Tomatoes, citrus fruits, corn, and other crops are also routinely shipped to the markets in Nassau.

Spanish Wells, the settlement on St. George's Cay off northwestern Eleuthera, was made famous by the Spanish Conquistadors, who stopped here to load up with fresh water for the final leg of their journey back across the Atlantic Ocean. Residents of the settlement are expert seamen and accomplished farmers, working crops on the mainland of Eleuthera. Today, harvesting crawfish and servicing the many visiting boaters are the key elements in the community's prosperity.

Harbour Island, or Briland as residents call it, is just off the northeastern coast of Eleuthera. The island is only three miles long and half a mile wide, yet it has played an important role in Eleuthera's development. By the late 1800s, Dunmore Town, its main settlement, had grown into a renowned shipyard and sugar-processing site. The sugar business gave rise to the rum business, which made the island especially popular during prohibition in the United States.

The Pink Sands Hotel and the Dunmore Beach Club helped create a long-standing resort atmosphere for refined elegance and quiet charm, yet for years you had to be "in the know" to realize this was an option on Harbour Island. Through modern renovations and promotional efforts, both resorts are now better known, though the pampered feeling given to guests hasn't changed at all, nor has the vivid pink sand beach.

The current population of Eleuthera is a little more than 10,000. Without as many sailing and resort options as Abaco, Eleuthera is quieter and unassuming. Development on the island is geared more toward private residential communities than toward resorts. Harbour Island and a redevelopment of the Club Med property in Governor's Harbour are exceptions, but they still fit in with the overall remote feeling of the island.

Like most Out Island Bahamians, the people here are self-sufficient, welcoming, and accommodating. Nothing seems too difficult if you ask politely. No problem, mon. Excellent seafood can be readily found in many local restaurants. So can some of the best johnnycake anywhere, but the special treat on Eleuthera is pie, the best coconut and pineapple pies in the world.

Taxi service on the island is very good, or you can choose to rent a car. We highly recommend renting a car and doing some exploring and fishing on your own. To reach some of the best beaches you'll need four-wheel drive. If you're really ambitious, you can cover the island from top to bottom in about three and a half hours. Miles of pink and white sand beaches are mixed with rugged cliffs on the windward side of the island. Calm bays and bonefish flats are sprinkled in the lee. Pleasant colonial villages with brightly painted houses overlook pineapple plantations and white-capped waves crashing over the outer reef.

Think of the Old South, of the graceful illusion created in *Gone With the Wind* before the war, and you'll have a feel for Eleuthera, something that is subtly different from any other of the Bahamian islands.

Diving and snorkeling are top activities throughout Eleuthera, but surfing is also a top draw. We often encounter surfers in the North Eleuthera Airport when we're on our way to or from Harbour Island. We have received consistent reports of good surf between Glass Window and James Point, with Surfer's Beach the most popular overall.

Biking and hiking are popular as well, with beautiful rolling terrain surrounding good roads and trails. If you want privacy, you'll find plenty of remote beaches, many with pink sand, where you can swim and picnic in idyllic conditions.

American Eagle flies daily from Miami to Governor's Harbour. Bahamasair flies daily from Miami and Nassau to North Eleuthera, Governor's Harbour, and Rock Sound. Continental Express/Gulfstream flies daily from Miami and Ft. Lauderdale to North Eleuthera. US Airways Express flies daily from Ft. Lauderdale to North Eleuthera and Governor's Harbour. Be sure to check with your resort or hotel for the nearest airport, as this will save you time and taxi fare.

Arriving and departing visitors will want to carry plenty of small bills for taxi and water ferry services. After landing at North Eleuthera or Governor's Harbour, it is common to spend $25 to $50 reaching your accommodations. These transfers are often taxi, water ferry, then another taxi, which is the way you reach Harbour Island.

We recommend soft luggage that is water-resistant. You should also have a rain jacket handy for bad weather and ferry crossings. If the weather is calm, have insect repellent ready to apply while you're waiting for your luggage.

Around the Island

Decisions, decisions!

There are several ways for boaters to approach northern Eleuthera. One is across the Northeast Providence Channel from Abaco. Another is across the channel from the Berry Islands. The most common route is northeast from Nassau, past Rose Island, Six Shilling Cay, Current Island, and other smaller cays, to the triangular-shaped landfall of North Eleuthera.

Most vacationers fly. If your destination is Harbour Island or Spanish Wells, you should fly into North Eleuthera airport. Then you'll take a short taxi ride, followed by a ferryboat ride to either island.

Flying between North Eleuthera and Nassau has always fascinated us. As we look down over the series of cays, we can see white sand flats everywhere around North Eleuthera. The southwestern point, called Current settlement, is particularly noticeable from the air. The settlement is one of the oldest on Eleuthera. When you talk with the locals, they will tell you stories about the first arrivals, American Indians who were driven out of Cape Cod after a bloody slaughter.

There is not much to see in Current settlement, but if you're looking for good fishing, diving, or snorkeling, you'll find it here. The road into the settlement runs along several miles of bonefish flats that are easy to access and wade. Fishing the incoming tide will usually give you good shots at single tailing bonefish, though you'll also see schools of fish as the tide rises. The mail boat stops at the settlement dock once a week. On either side of the dock you can see the ruined remains of a small resort lodge and a marina that were destroyed by the hurricane in 1995.

For a small charge, local boaters can take you across the cut to Current Island, where there are several flats adjacent to the best boat harbor. Current Cut provides one of the best drift dives in the Bahamas. The deep violet water is glass clear and there are swarms of brightly colored fish cruising over the coral. The snorkeling in this area is also sensational.

A couple of local guides offer good bottom and reef fishing no more than five minutes from the dock. These guys also know where to find bonefish in the bays and around the cays up toward Spanish Wells. They'll show you the fish, and then the rest

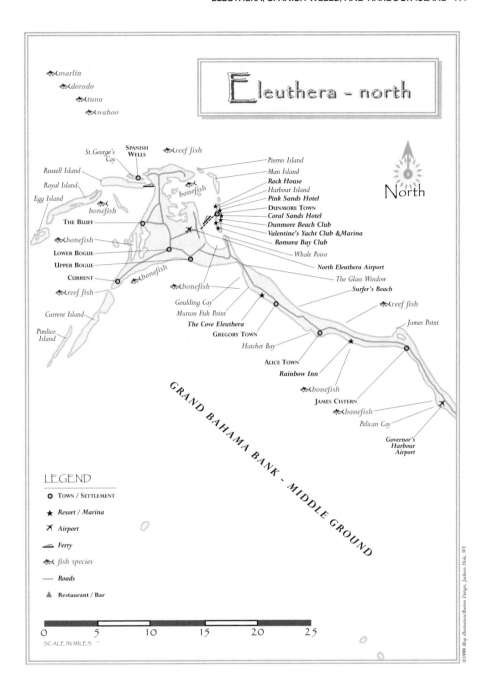

marlin
dorado
tuna
wahoo

Eleuthera - north

St. George's Cay
SPANISH WELLS
reef fish

Russell Island
Royal Island
Egg Island

Pierres Island
Man Island
Rock House
Harbour Island
Pink Sands Hotel
DUNMORE TOWN
Coral Sands Hotel
Dunmore Beach Club
Valentine's Yacht Club & Marina
Romora Bay Club

bonefish

bonefish
THE BLUFF

bonefish
LOWER BOGUE
UPPER BOGUE
CURRENT
reef fish

Current Island

Pimlico
Island

North

Whale Point
North Eleuthera Airport
The Glass Window
Surfer's Beach

bonefish
Goulding Cay
Mutton Fish Point
The Cove Eleuthera
GREGORY TOWN

bonefish

reef fish
James Point

Hatchet Bay

ALICE TOWN
Rainbow Inn

bonefish
JAMES CISTERN
bonefish
Pelican Cay

Governor's
Harbour
Airport

G R A N D   B A H A M A   B A N K   -   M I D D L E   G R O U N D

LEGEND

- ◎ TOWN / SETTLEMENT
- ★ Resort / Marina
- ✈ Airport
- Ferry
- fish species
- — Roads
- ▲ Restaurant / Bar

0   5   10   15   20   25
SCALE IN MILES

©1999 Map illustration/Burton Design, Jackson Hole, WY

is up to you. The management at the Cove Eleuthera can set up anglers with a guide at reasonable rates.

From the Current, boaters either travel north to the Egg Islands, Royal Island, and Spanish Wells, or east to Hatchet Bay. Royal Island is gorgeous, with a protected leeside harbor, and some pristine beaches facing the reef. Services on the island are either unreliable or non-existent as far as we know, but well-stocked boaters can explore productive bonefish flats from here, including flats and reefs around the Egg Islands. The bonefish in this area rarely get fished and are usually aggressive to any fly they see.

Spanish Wells makes a better overall base for this area, as full services are available in the settlement. Most boaters enter the harbor between Russell Island and Charles Island, though a second entrance is available between Charles Island and St. George's Cay. Ferryboats from the mainland use this second entrance.

Spanish Wells Marine is located in the center of the harbor at the concrete dock that is used by the mail boat. Spanish Wells Yacht Haven is farther along inside the harbor, and is recommended for recreational boaters. Fuel and petroleum products are available here along with electrical and TV hookups, water, and a laundromat. The Harbour View restaurant has a bar with pool table and tasty seafood. In season, August through March, the fresh lobster here is outstanding.

There are several comfortable rooms for rent at Yacht Haven. A small "resort," called Adventures Resort, has rooms and kitchenette units, and they can arrange golf carts, bikes, and water sports. A few small restaurants, including the Gap, serve Bahamian fare, burgers, and light meals. The community is well maintained and prosperous, but it can seem like a ghost town even in the prime season of December through April. Local guides, including Woody Perry, are available to take anglers bonefishing or reef fishing. Some of the best bonefishing is across the channel along the mangrove-lined shore of North Eleuthera.

Boaters can continue on from Spanish Wells to Harbour Island via Ridley Head Channel and Devil's Backbone, but it is highly recommended that you hire a local pilot for this trip due to dangerous coral heads and reefs.

We'll leave that route to adventuresome seafarers. We fly into North Eleuthera Airport, and then take a five-minute taxi ride to the ferry dock, and a five-minute boat ride to Dunmore Town. No matter where you're staying on the island, a five-minute taxi ride will put you at your place of residence. The Pink Sands Hotel, Coral Sands Hotel, Dunmore Beach Club, and Romora Bay Club all provide accommodations and guest amenities that range from nice to luxurious.

With brightly painted houses and white picket fences, Dunmore Town is not only one of the oldest settlements in the Bahamas, but one of the most charming. The concrete government wharf is the center of activity, as it is the ferry landing and the mail boat dock. This is also where we meet our bonefishing guides each morning. Legendary "Bonefish Joe," Joe Cleare, is the dean of guides. Stanley Johnson, Jermaine Johnson, Vincent Cleare, Stuart Cleare, Patrick Roberts, and Vincent Flucker round out the guiding team we use most often.

Fishing for tarpon, creek on West Side, Andros.

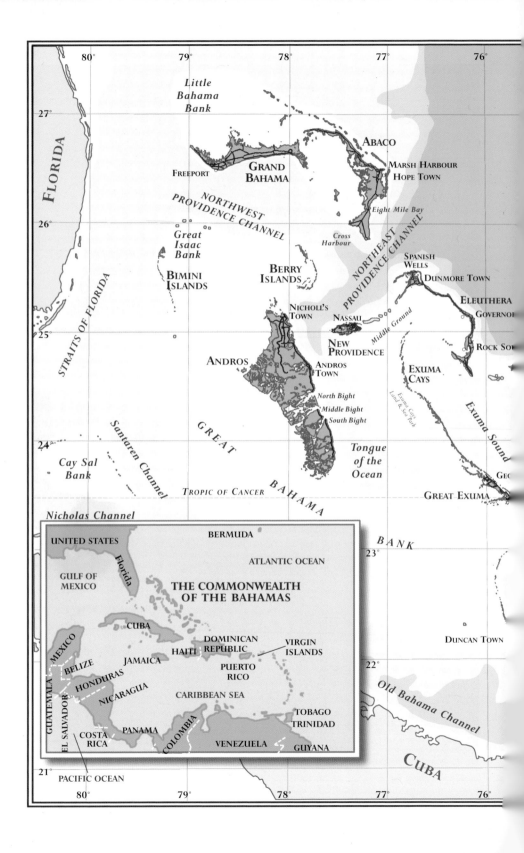

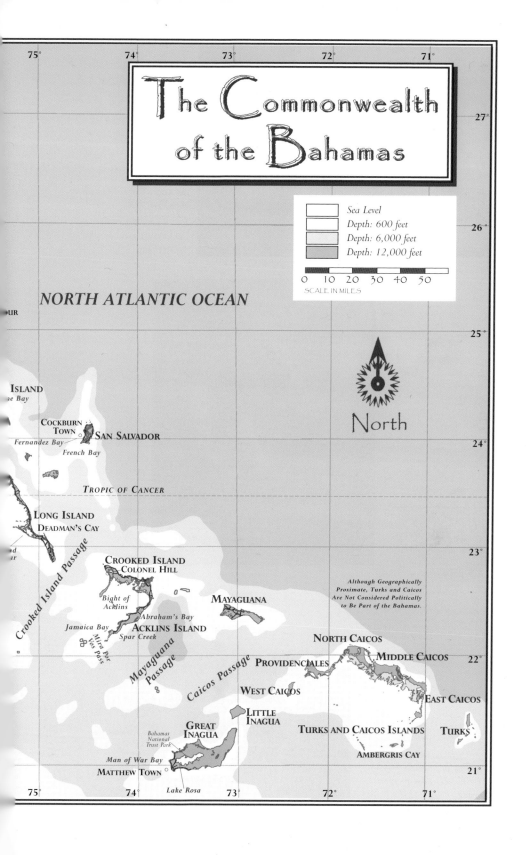

The Commonwealth of the Bahamas

	Sea Level
	Depth: 600 feet
	Depth: 6,000 feet
	Depth: 12,000 feet

0   10   20   30   40   50
SCALE IN MILES

NORTH ATLANTIC OCEAN

North

ISLAND
ie Bay

COCKBURN TOWN ○ **SAN SALVADOR**
Fernandez Bay
French Bay

TROPIC OF CANCER

LONG ISLAND
DEADMAN'S CAY

Crooked Island Passage

CROOKED ISLAND
COLONEL HILL

Bight of Acklins

MAYAGUANA

Jamaica Bay
Abraham's Bay
ACKLINS ISLAND
Spar Creek
Mira Par Vos Pass

Mayaguana Passage

Caicos Passage

NORTH CAICOS

MIDDLE CAICOS

PROVIDENCIALES

WEST CAICOS

EAST CAICOS

Although Geographically Proximate, Turks and Caicos Are Not Considered Politically to Be Part of the Bahamas.

LITTLE INAGUA

GREAT INAGUA
Bahamas National Trust Park

Man of War Bay
MATTHEW TOWN ○
Lake Rosa

TURKS AND CAICOS ISLANDS

TURKS

AMBERGRIS CAY

Brian O'Keefe

An aerial view of Grand Bahama. Flying into the islands can be as exhilarating as actually being there.

Stephen Vletas with guide Bertram Brown, Banyan Beach Club, Abaco.

Fishing the buoy off Andros. Kim Vletas and a gorgeous dorado.

Brian O'Keefe

Brian O'Keefe

Fishing for mutton snappers in the rocks.

Whichever island you choose, you'll be sure to land an impressive catch.

Jon Covich

The Bahamian waters offer endless flats for superb bonefishing.

The Bahamas are filled with color—even these picnic tables at Rickmon's Lodge, Sandy Point, Abaco.

A strategically placed hammock at Bair's Lodge on Andros invites anglers to take a restorative nap between fishing excursions.

The crystal blue sky, powdery white sand, and sparkling turquoise waters of Cape Santa Maria invite anglers and non-anglers to sit back and relax.

Tarpon, Andros.

The flats of the Bahamas provide anglers with spectacular fly-fishing.

The smile of this angler's face says it all—this bonefish made her day.

Grace Bay, Providenciales, in the beautiful Turks and Caicos.

The Blue Bar and Restaurant on the beach at Pink Sands Hotel.

Some of the best fishing is just northwest across the harbor, on wide-open white sand flats where the incoming tide tempts tailing fish on a consistent basis. As the tide moves in the fish cruise the many mangrove shorelines and creeks with darker bottoms of sand, coral, and grass. One particular creek winds through the mainland for miles, with a current like a river during a spring tide. You can also fish the outside cays like Jacob Island, Man Island, and many smaller ones, all of which have bays and bars of white sand that make spotting bonefish unusually easy.

While we consider the bonefishing good here, Harbour Island is the ultimate Bahamian location for pampered beach vacationing in luxury accommodations. The three-mile pink sand beach facing the Atlantic Ocean is protected by a reef that makes swimming fun for all ages. If you like body surfing or boogie boarding, the reef break is just right. Several of the hotels, including the Pink Sands, have lighted tennis courts. The food on the island is usually well prepared and delicious.

Anglers and non-anglers can take equal pleasure in pursuing their own types of relaxation. You can walk anywhere on the island, though many visitors rent golf carts. If you get lost, just ask for directions. You'll find the people here will go out of their way to help you.

For boaters, Harbour Island is a port of entry. Valentine's Resort & Marina is located a couple hundred yards south of the government wharf. Full services are available including two restaurants, a bar, pool, guest accommodations, and a certified dive center. A new condo resort, Villas at Valentine's is scheduled for completion in the winter of 2005. Valentine's has become a popular spot with the upgrade of all its facilities, so we suggest you call ahead for reservations. Along with the Romora Bay Club poolside bar, the bar at Valentine's is the best place on the island to watch the sunset.

The Romora Bay Club offers an outstanding dive service with a PADI-trained staff that specializes in specially arranged trips to meet individual needs.

The Harbour Island Club & Marina is south of Romora Bay. Forty slips offer full services including showers and a laundromat. The restaurant here serves a good lunch and is another nice spot from which to watch the sunset.

Unlike Abaco, Eleuthera doesn't have a long string of offshore windward cays. The deep ocean pushes in close against the protective reef that has been a hazard to sailors for centuries. For this reason, cruising boaters usually choose to navigate through the Bight of Eleuthera and along the western shoreline where a number of bays create pleasant anchorages.

Visitors driving south from North Eleuthera Airport will pass the settlements of Lower and Upper Bogue before reaching a unique bridge known as the Glass Window. Sailors gave this spot its name because they could see under the span of land connecting North Eleuthera with the southern part of the island. Their view from the tranquil waters of the Bight was of the turbulent Atlantic beating across the reef.

It is believed that violent seas washed the natural span away in the early 1900s. In 1991, a storm surge pushed a modern two-lane bridge seven feet to the south, reducing it to one lane.

The pleasant drive through this area affords views of 60-foot cliffs dropping straight down to the roiling sea on one side and glass-clear green water rippling over white sand on the other. About a mile north of Gregory Town is the turn-off to The Cove Eleuthera. Situated on the leeward side of the island, this intimate tranquil resort offers stunning ocean views over three rocky promontories that protect two small coves and a delightful white sand beach. Called "Pineapple Cove" by the locals, the resort has air-conditioned rooms with private terraces overlooking the water, a casual restaurant and bar, beautiful swimming pool, and two unlighted tennis courts. The snorkeling here is exceptional, as is the sea kayaking.

Management and staff are among the most friendly people we've met in the islands. They can help vacationers arrange fishing, diving, snorkeling or point you in the right direction to explore the island on your own. The best nearby bonefishing areas run from the Current settlement to Goulding Cay to Rainbow Bay and Pelican Cay.

Gregory Town is a quiet little settlement surrounded by pineapple fields. Amazingly, the town harbor holds

Bungalow at The Cove Eleuthera.

a good number of bonefish at low tide. Surfer's Beach is just two miles away over a road that requires a four-wheel drive vehicle. Elvina's Restaurant and Bar is the main surfers' hang-out, with good seafood, coin laundry, and satellite television. You can also rent cars here. Rebecca's General Store is Ponytail Pete's surfing headquarters, where this friendly local surfer dude posts surf conditions and tide reports. Pete's tide reports are essential for anglers fishing on their own.

For boaters and land-based visitors, the next stop down the road is Hatchet Bay. Marine Services of Eleuthera has moorings and some dock space plus fuel, electricity, and water. Rolle's Harbour View Restaurant serves spicy conch chowder and hosts lively weekend nightlife on an irregular basis.

There are miles of secluded beaches to explore on your own.

Alice Town is the settlement on the south side of the bay. There are a couple of grocery stores with limited supplies, a laundromat, liquor store, and a telephone office.

The 15-mile drive down to Governor's Harbour will take you past the Rainbow Inn, the settlement of James Cistern, the airport, and many miles of awesome pink sand beaches sheltered by high limestone bluffs. Unless you rent a car and explore on your own, all of this will be lost, as many of these striking beaches are not visible from the highway. We like to take a picnic lunch and make a day of touring different beaches and flats. There are flats on both sides of the island throughout this area, so regardless of the wind direction, you can find a lee. You can also find superb snorkeling, even for beginners, while swimming and just catching rays is a great way to kick back.

But let's face it—we like to fish too. The reef fishing here is excellent for snappers, jacks, and grouper, but the weather has to be calm to fly-fish. Clouser's Minnows and baitfish imitations are the way to go. Tossing plugs and spoons on spinning gear is always deadly, even in a light wind.

For bonefishing, the last of the falling and first of the incoming tides are best. The tide on the ocean side of the island is two hours earlier than the tide on the leeward side. This gives anglers several different prime times to fish during a day. We recommend good wading booties to fish the outside ocean flats and reef areas safely.

Between Hatchet Bay and James Cistern, is the Rainbow Inn, which is home to one of the best restaurants on the island. Ribs on Wednesday night and steaks on Friday are local events and often include Dr. Seabreeze strumming island tunes on his guitar. Fish chowders, plus steamed and boiled fish are Bahamian delicacies you have to try. Great views and amazing sunsets can be enjoyed from the restaurant or bar. This is one of our favorite places to watch the orange end of a perfectly relaxing day while sipping Goombay Smashes, Kim's favorite Bahamian rum drink.

Comfortable air-conditioned accommodations here are spacious, and make this a prime location to spend a few days and explore the island. Be sure to ask the staff about things to do, as they can help you plan day trips. They will also give you a free copy of "Bone Fish Graham's" personal guidebook to bonefishing on Eleuthera. We suggest you read it carefully.

Six miles north of Governor's Harbour, just five minutes from the airport, on the lee side of the island, rests Coco di Mama, a 12-room deluxe resort arranged in colorful colonial-style cottages. The main lodge has a wonderful restaurant and bar and satellite TV. This resort has become our top recommendation for anglers who want to fish on their own and travel with non-fishing companions. This "center of the island" location makes it perfect for exploring and fishing the island at your leisure.

Just before reaching Governor's Harbour you'll see a high pointed bluff either from the highway or from the water. Balara Bay is on the northern side of this bluff, and there are some good bonefish flats here between the tree-lined shore and Levy Island. These flats can be waded on lower tides. The bottom structure is a combination of coral and sand.

Governor's Harbour offers easy access for boaters, with plenty of deeper water over grassy bottoms, though this is not a good rough weather anchorage. Driving in from the north you can see across the harbor to Cupid's Cay, which many locals claim was the original settlement of the Eleutherian Adventurers. If you need to stock up on groceries or other supplies this is a good place. Most services are available, including a post office, telephone office, government clinic, bank, movie theater, and car rentals. If you don't mind a local audience while you fish, you can catch bonefish right in the harbor during the lower tidal stages.

The Duck Inn is our choice as the best place to stay in Governor's Harbour. The self-catered deluxe air-conditioned cottages overlook the harbor, the ocean, and Cupid's Bay. The Inn works closely with a network of reliable independent fly-fishing guides, Eleutherabonefish.com and Exumabonefish.com.

Across town, the old Club Med Resort remains closed as of summer 2004.

Driving south, Queen's Highway will take you to Palmetto Point. The place to stay on North Palmetto Point is Unique Village, set on a small green rise between a lush forest and a pink sand beach. Hotel rooms and villas are spacious and comfortable. Villas have full kitchens. All rooms have ocean views. The restaurant serves good local fare and you can choose a meal plan option, or not. The Sunday brunch buffet sometimes features Dr. Seabreeze on his guitar, and the bar shows sports programs on satellite TV.

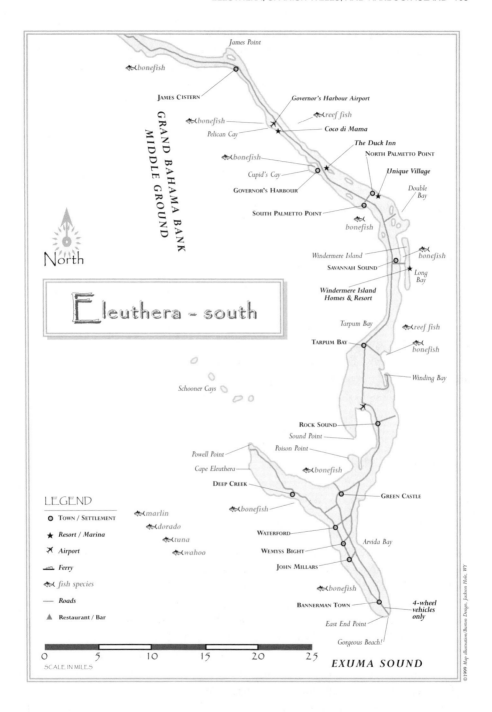

This is a comfortable base for exploring the southern region of Eleuthera and its many bonefishing options. Renting a car is a must to reach wadable flats and miles of secluded beaches. There is a good white sand flat marked by a high mangrove cay just north of the Palmetto settlement pier. You can walk all the way out and around this mangrove on a low neap tide. Larger bonefish like the darker deeper edges out past this mangrove.

Savanah Sound and Windermere Island are about five miles south of Palmetto Point on the Atlantic side of the island. An expansive white sand flat stretches out from the settlement and is rimmed with powdery beaches. You can park near the beach and fish this flat on your own. Working the incoming tide is best, and because of the size of the area, you should plan to spend at least half a day here.

The bridge that crosses to Windermere Island is guarded and you have to ask permission to visit, which is usually not a problem. Windermere Island is one of the oldest and most exclusive private island developments in the Bahamas. Glistening pink sand beaches run the five-mile length of the island and are washed by the warm Atlantic shallows that pour in over the black coral reefs.

A private club, usually open from late November to mid-May, services members and guests. The club has a restaurant, bar, tennis courts, and swimming pool. Accommodations on the island are in the club's suites, cottages, and condos, or in private homes. Most of the accommodations are on the beach, and many of the private homes are elegant island masterpieces. Windermere Island Homes manages all reservations for the island, though some property owners rent their houses or apartments directly.

Tarpum Bay is the next settlement south. What a pretty little place this is, with white-walled buildings and shallow clear water covering golden sand stretching out from the shoreline. There is a well-stocked grocery store and hardware store near the main dock. Even though you will have your own car, don't forget the taxi drivers. These guys know everything about everything and are happy to talk to you. Sometimes we just park our car and have them drive us around.

This is how we were originally reminded not to forget the windward side of the island between Palmetto and Rock Sound. "You been out to the ocean side, mon? All kinds of fish out there, mon." This was in response to a question we asked about fishing the Bight side. The ocean side has at least half a dozen bays and coves where bonefish feed on the tide. And the reef fishing is consistently good during calmer conditions.

Drive 10 to 15 minutes south and you'll be in Rock Sound. Boaters and land-based do-it-yourselfers will love the Market Place supermarket here. Fresh fruit, seafood, and other staples are in good supply. If you aren't cooking for yourself, stop in at Sammy's Place, just out of town toward the airport. The food is home-cooked delicious and reasonably priced. We've also heard good reports about a newer restaurant, North Side Beach & Restaurant on the eastern side of town.

The main road runs through the settlement along the water where a number of commercial fishing boats and Boston Whalers are tied up. Stop by here in the afternoon and you can work out a fishing guide, or ask one of the taxi drivers to recommend a guide. Most likely, the driver will steer you to one of his cousins.

South of Rock Sound is the currently closed Cotton Bay Club. The Robert Trent Jones golf course, however, is open to the public.

Most boaters travel from Rock Sound across to Powell Point, which begins the journey to the Exuma Cays or back to Nassau. We like to drive all the way south to Bannerman Town where there are beautiful flats and creeks and lots of bonefish. On occasion we take the right fork to Greencastle, then head to Deep Creek and Cape Eleuthera. There are miles of mangrove-lined flats around Deep Creek and a maze of creeks at Cape Eleuthera that hold bonefish and tarpon.

If you drive down to Bannerman Town or Deep Creek be sure to take along a picnic lunch and a cooler with drinks because there are no reliable food services in the area. Good wading shoes are a must because you will often have to walk through mucky mangrove areas to reach the fishable flats, bays, and creeks. This is sometimes difficult walking with areas of soft bottom but there sure are a lot of nice-sized fish. If you have a four-wheel drive vehicle, you can drive to the end of the road past Bannerman Town. Your reward will be one of the most spectacular deserted beaches in the Caribbean.

Another thing to remember is gasoline. Don't run out. Our motto is "never pass an open gas station without filling up, even if you only need a couple of gallons." You can't rely on gas stations being open even during regular business hours, and sometimes it is impossible to find gas anywhere on the weekends.

Fishing Highlights

The most surprising thing about Eleuthera is that it is the only major Out Island without an established bonefishing lodge. There are, however, several good options for anglers who want easy access to experienced guides. One is staying at the Duck Inn in Governor's Harbour and fishing with the Eleuthera Bonefish guides, and another is staying on Harbour Island where you can book some of the island's independent guides. Staying at Cove Eleuthera will also give you access to these same guides from Harbour Island. We recommend booking independent guides well in advance of your trip, either through your hotel or with one of the few agents who work with these guides.

The North Eleuthera fishery covers a sizable area of productive flats and creeks on both sides of the mainland. Boaters fishing on their own, exploring in skiffs or dinghies, have better access to the Spanish Wells side, due to the geography and lack of accommodations. The dangerous yet alluring reefs that guard North Eleuthera and drop off into the Northeast Providence Channel create a home for countless baitfish, and provide nearby deep water for larger flats gamefish. The dense mangrove shorelines of the mainland provide habitat for smaller fish and a variety of shrimps and crabs.

View from The Cove Eleuthera.

There are many areas of wide-open white sand flats within the shallow water area created by the mainland, the southwest reef, Royal Island, Russell Island, and St. George's Island. The areas from the Lobster Cays and up past Ragged Cays are some of the best. These flats are a short run from the settlements of The Bluff or the Current.

Just south of The Bluff is an expansive mangrove-lined bay that is often stacked with bonefish, and the entire shoreline can produce fine fishing. Easy runs also put boats over some wild reef fishing for jacks, snappers, grouper, and mackerel. The drawback is protection from the weather, which is minimal with the wind anywhere in the north, and this is the prevailing wind direction during cold fronts. The exception is when the wind is from the east, or northeast, and then anglers can gain protection for bonefishing along the mainland shorelines.

On the Harbour Island side, the habitat is similar, though there are many more shallow-water back bays and mangrove systems that hold even higher numbers of bonefish. This area is more closed in, which provides some protection from the wind, but is more exposed to the northeast, which evens that score. During bad weather conditions, casting will be difficult as usual, but there are lots of light sand areas where visibility is still good enough to catch some fish.

We prefer to fish an incoming tide on both sides. The bonefish are really dialed in to move from the deeper water into the mangroves, and they are often very quick about it. Timing is critical if you want to catch them tailing over sandy bottoms. Once the fish get into the creeks and spread out through the mangrove flats they are actually easier to hook up, but you might break off more than you land.

Bonefish are the number-one flats species on Eleuthera. The highest concentration of fish live at the northern and southern tips of the island where there is more protected habitat and more food. The creeks and bays and mangrove structure from Rock Sound to Deep Creek and Bannerman Town is much like it is in the north.

The long skinny strip of land connecting the north and south is unique in its own way. It is easy to cross between the Bight and ocean flats and therefore easy to escape the wind. The Bight-side tide is two hours behind the ocean tide so you have at least two periods of prime fishing throughout the day. The Bight side holds more bonefish. The windward side has bigger fish. The nice thing about this area is that the good flats are obvious, and many are easily accessed from land. As Bone Fish Graham says, "you don't need a boat or a guide here; you can do it on your own."

Our favorite flies for sandy bottoms are Gotchas, Crazy Charlies, Hoovers, Spawning Shrimp, Yarn Crabs, and Sililegs. The most finicky fish live in the north, and on some of the most fished flats like those at Pelican Cay and Savannah Sound. Be aware that in some of these areas you will need to fish long (12-foot) fluorocarbon leaders with 8- to 10-pound tippet. A good fly to start with when fishing a flat for the first time is a #6 pink Hoover or Gotcha. For tailing fish go with a #6 Tan Yarn Crab. It's fun to watch bonefish pounce on this fly like a cat on a mouse. Over grass and broken coral we like to use flies with weed guards. One of our favorites is Greg's Flats Fly.

While we have cast to a few permit in the north, we have never hooked up. Several of our friends and clients have caught permit up to 35 pounds out of Harbour Island, but most were on live crabs. Bonefish Joe and the other guides say the best permit fishing is around the outer cays and over the reefs from April through July.

Other people we've talked with from Gregory Town to Rock Sound have seen permit occasionally, but the only ones reported caught were on live crabs. The commercial fishermen out of Rock Sound love to tell stories about seeing huge schools of permit around the Schooner Cays and all along the Exuma Sound banks.

We've seen permit inside the windward reefs in a number of places while snorkeling and while fishing for jacks but have never had a cast to one. Permit are permit, and they remain as elusive on Eleuthera as elsewhere.

Migratory tarpon move through the Bight of Eleuthera from April through October. In talking with boaters and with people up and down the island it seems like the best spot for tarpon would be around Current Island; setting up ambush points throughout the Current

Fishing reel.

Cut channel. This is the place where tarpon move in and out of the Bight most consistently. Another good location would be in the Deep Creek and Cape Eleuthera area. We've seen resident tarpon in some of the creeks and the migratory tarpon move through in season.

Sharks and barracuda are everywhere, especially around the reefs. So are jacks, grouper, snappers, mackerel, and zillions of baitfish. If you just want to catch fish, the reefs are the place. Our favorite flies are Edgewater Poppers, Clouser's Minnows, Sea Habits, Snak-Pak Mackerels, and Abel Anchovies.

Local fishermen from Hatchet Bay to Rock Sound love to go reef fishing. Pick a calm day, hire one of these guys, and you'll have some of the best action you can imagine. If you promise to let your guide keep the catch, he'll bring the bait and chum. Even if you don't promise, you'll have to be quick to release any of the snapper, mackerel, or grouper.

Offshore fishing is very good out of North Eleuthera. Valentine's Marina on Harbour Island is headquarters for a leg of the Bahamas Wahoo Championships in January, and the Bahamas Billfish Tournament final leg in June.

November through March is wahoo time, with January and February prime. Boats are available for charter from Valentine's and Harbour Island Marinas.

Allison tuna and blue marlin are in the waters off North Eleuthera year round, but June and July are the prime months. July is also regatta time, which means lots of boaters and parties. While this is off-season for general tourism, this is a great time to visit as rates all the hotels are at their lowest, and weather is generally at its best.

When we evaluate the overall fishing opportunities on Eleuthera, we have to give it high marks for uncrowded, unspoiled flats, good numbers of bonefish, and outstanding reef fishing. For adventurous fly-fishers looking to explore on their own this island is one of the best options.

Optional Activities

Eleuthera is the sort of place where optional activities are often ignored in favor of laying on the beach and reading a book. Those who get motivated usually decide that general exploring is the best option. The best way to see the island is by renting a car, though biking, hiking, and sea kayaking will give you access to some gorgeous remote locations.

Preacher's Cave on the northernmost coast is a standard point of interest, as are many other caves, including the ones at Hatchet Bay. Most explorers end up at one spectacular beach or another, swimming and snorkeling inside the ocean-side reefs. Diving programs are available, with the best ones out of Harbour Island.

Golf is available at the Robert Trent Jones course south of Rock Sound, and if you need to work up a serious sweat, you can play tennis during the day at a variety of locations.

If you somehow get tired of fishing, you can always go swimming—or just catch a few rays!

Lodging, Guides, and Services

Featured Lodges

Pink Sands Hotel

Harbour Island   This is Kim's favorite hotel in the Bahamas. This Island Outpost resort has 26 rooms in 18 cottage-style buildings. Large deluxe air-conditioned rooms and suites include wet bars, refrigerator, toaster, coffeemaker, CD player, Italian-tiled bathrooms, and private terraces. The open-air lobby is bright and comfortable and includes a long hardwood bar, pool table, and cocktail area. A living room/library has satellite TV and board games. The outdoor dining area is casual and elegant and the food is simply superb. A beachside restaurant serves delicious lunches, or you can order lunch on the beach. And the pink sand beach? Yep, it's pink and magnificent. If you don't want to swim in the ocean, try the freshwater pool, next to three lighted tennis courts. The hotel can arrange for bonefish guides or offshore fishing, or you can book independent guides on your own. This is the best place in the Bahamas for "luxury" bonefishing. Diving and snorkeling excursions are also available.
Season: Mid-October through July. (Low season rates available in October, early November, and in the summer. These are great fly-fishing months.)
Suitable For: Anglers and non-anglers, or anyone who wants a luxurious beach vacation.
What's Included: Complete packages include accommodations, Bahamian taxes, breakfast, and dinner.
Not Included: Airfare to/from North Eleuthera airport, taxi/boat transfers, guided fishing and other optional activities.

Pricing: $$$$

Contact: Reservations and information, 800-688-7678 or 242-333-2030; fax 242-333-2060.

Internet: www.islandoutpost.com

E-mail: outpost800-@aol.com

The Cove Eleuthera

Gregory Town This resort sits on 30 isolated acres overlooking the Atlantic Ocean. Twenty-seven air-conditioned rooms are bright and comfortable. The restaurant and bar are adjacent to the swimming pool and large surrounding deck. Picture-perfect snorkeling in a protected bay is right out front off a white sand beach. If you need some exercise, there are two non-lighted tennis courts. There are miles of wadable bonefish flats nearby. You can fish on your own or the hotel can arrange for a guide. You can fly into either North Eleuthera or Governor's Harbour, but we recommend North Eleuthera, and we definitely recommend renting a car. Sea kayaks, bicycles, snorkeling gear, beach towels, and coolers are provided to guests at no charge.

Season: October through July.

Suitable For: Anglers and non-anglers.

What's Included: Packages are available, including special honeymoon packages.

Not Included: Airfare to/from North Eleuthera airport, taxi transfers, guided fishing and other optional activities. Regulated taxi fares are $27 from North Eleuthera, and $42 from Governor's Harbour.

Pricing: $$

Contact: Reservations and information, 242-335-5142 or 800-552-5960; fax 242-335-5338.

Internet: www.thecoveeleuthera.com

E-mail: ann@TheCoveEleuthera.com

Rainbow Inn

Governor's Harbour A delightful small oceanfront resort that specializes in friendly personal service. The location makes it ideal for exploring all of Eleuthera. Comfortable air-conditioned rooms are suitable for couples, families, or hard-core anglers, and include mini-kitchens and CD players. The restaurant is one of the best on the island, and the bar is a magical place for watching the sunset. If you're looking for a place to fish on your own, or simply do nothing at all, this is one of the best choices in the Bahamas. The resort has a swimming pool, seaside tennis court, and they can arrange for rental cars and fishing guides. Also, anglers here get a free copy of "Bone Fish Graham's" guide to fly-fishing Eleuthera.

Season: November 15 through August.

Suitable For: Anglers and non-anglers.

What's Included: Eight-day/seven-night packages include air-conditioned tropical studio apartment with mini-kitchen, breakfast and dinner daily, wine and drinks with dinner, unlimited tennis, use of bicycles and snorkeling equipment, car rental for the week. Non-package rates are available for accommodations only. Stays of any length are available.

Not Included: Airfare to/from Governor's Harbour airport, taxi transfers if applicable, guided fishing, and other optional activities.

Pricing: $$

Contact: Reservations and information, telephone/fax, 242-335-0294 or 800-688-0047.

E-mail: vacation@rainbowinn.com

Internet: www.rainbowinn.com

The Duck Inn

Governor's Harbour John and Kay Duckworth's Inn has three self-catered, deluxe cottages with gardens looking out on the harbor, the ocean bay, and Cupid's Cay. The three cottages are surrounded with orchids and fruit trees and all have fully equipped kitchens with dining areas and verandahs. Each colonial cottage is decorated with wood floors and antique furnishings, and includes A/C, ceiling fans, and maid service. Bicycles, boat rentals/charters, bonefishing, kayaking, can be part of your package or you can choose your activities after arrival. This is a good location to explore Eleuthera, with convenient access to markets, gas station, shopping, and restaurants. We recommend this location for anglers looking for a "do-it-yourself" trip.
Season: November 15 through August.
Suitable For: Anglers and non-anglers.
What's Included: All-inclusive bonefishing packages are available or you can just book a room.
Not Included: Airfare to/from Governor's Harbour airport, taxi transfers if applicable, guided fishing, island excursions, rental cars, and other optional activities.
Pricing: $-$$
Contact: Reservations and information, 242-332-2608.
Internet: www.theduckinn.com
E-mail: duckinn@batelnet.bs

Coco di Mama

Governor's Harbour Five minutes from the international airport (US Airways has direct flights from Miami), on the lee side of the island, this charming beachfront resort has 12 deluxe air-conditioned rooms in three colorful colonial-style cottages. The main lodge, designed with a colonial and Bahamian flare, features a wonderful restaurant and bar with satellite TV. You won't find a better place to watch the sunset or to just hang on the beach and do nothing. The location in the center of the island makes it ideal for anglers looking to explore and fish on their own. Car rentals are available to get you to remote flats and beaches and there are wadable flats nearby.
Season: November 23 through August.
Suitable For: Anglers and non-anglers.
What's Included: Accommodations and meals, though activity packages can be arranged.
Not Included: Airfare to/from Governor's Harbour airport, taxi transfers if applicable, guided fishing, diving, and other optional activities.
Pricing: $$
Contact: Reservations and information, 242-332-3150.
Internet: www.cocodimama.com
E-mail: info@cocodimama.com

Additional Accommodations

Rock House

Harbour Island This historic complex overlooking the harbor has been elegantly renovated into a posh hotel. The nine rooms and two suites have different motifs to go along with appropriate names such as the "Monkey Room" or the "Seahorse Room." Each room has a mini-bar, VCR, and a private cabana situated around the swimming pool. The only complete gym on the island is part of the resort. The chic restaurant serves marvelous seafood with all the trimmings. Internet service is available.

Pricing: $$-$$$$
Contact: Reservations and information, 242-333-2053.
Internet: www.rockhousebahamas.com
E-mail: reservations@rockhousebahamas.com

Dunmore Beach Club

Harbour Island A tradition on Harbour Island, this resort is a little stuffy for us, though they have a long list of repeat clientele. Comfortable rooms are set in beautiful gardens on the hillside overlooking the ocean. Amenities include a swimming pool and tennis court. Excellent meals are served in the clubhouse. Men must wear jackets for dinner. The Club is down the beach from the Pink Sands and next door to the Coral Sands.
Pricing: $$$$
Contact: Reservations and information, 242-333-2200 or 877 891-3100; fax 242-333-2429.
Internet: www.dunmorebeach.com

Coral Sands Hotel

Harbour Island Next door to the Pink Sands, and perched on the bluff overlooking the Atlantic, this hotel has been significantly upgraded over the past five years and is our top choice as an economical vacation option on Harbour Island's pink sand beach. Twenty-seven deluxe air-conditioned rooms overlook the ocean, and luxurious suites are available in the new Lucaya building. The restaurant, bar, and sundeck provide shaded comfort above the beach for breakfast, lunch, and dinner. The large swimming pool, set in a lush garden, is a nice alternative to the ocean, and a tennis court is available. Fishing, diving, and snorkeling excursions can be arranged.
Pricing: $$-$$$
Contact: Reservations and information, 242-333-2320 or 800-468-2799; fax 242-333-2368.
Internet: www.coralsands.com

Bahama House Inn

Harbour Island If you are a B&B fan, this renovated eighteenth-century two-story pink colonial house surrounded by lush gardens may be for you. Seven spacious rooms have air-conditioning, hardwood floors, four-poster beds, ceiling fans, and private entries. The library has satellite TV. You can enjoy spectacular sunset views from the second story verandah. Breakfast is included in the rate.
Pricing: $-$$
Contact: Reservations and information, 242-333-2201.
Internet: www.bahamahouseinn.com
E-mail: bahamahouseinn@coralwave.com

Romora Bay Club

Harbour Island The casual and comfortable resort is on the harbor. The bar is the best place on the island to watch the sunset. Island-style air-conditioned accommodations, a good restaurant, a large swimming pool, tennis court, and a nearby dive center are the highlights. A nearby three-bedroom villa is available for rent and it includes use of all the Club's facilities.
Pricing: $$$
Contact: Reservations and information, 242-333-2325.
Internet: www.romorabay.com

Valentine's Resort & Marina

Harbour Island   Twenty-one air-conditioned rooms combine with the 39-slip marina to create a center of activity on the west side of the island. Amenities include a swimming pool, tennis court, bicycles, and a dive center. Fishing trips, flats and offshore, can be arranged. The marina monitors VHF Channel 16. The new (scheduled for completion in the winter of 2005) Villas at Valentine's are luxury one-, two-, and three-bedroom condos for sale.
Pricing: $$-$$$$
Contact: Reservations and information, 242-333-2142; fax 242-333-2135.
Internet: www.valentinesresort.com

Unique Village Hotel & Villas

North Palmetto Point   South of Governor's Harbour, the resort's 14 air-conditioned rooms and villas are spacious and overlook a beautiful stretch of beach. The restaurant serves good steaks and seafood. The bar has satellite TV and ocean views. Island excursions and car rentals can be arranged.
Pricing: $$-$$$
Contact: Reservations and information, 242-332-1830 or 888-820-8471.
Internet: www.uniquevillage.com

Windermere Island Homes

Windermere Island   A private island retreat with upscale accommodations ranging from suites and apartments to luxurious homes on five miles of pink sand beaches. During the November to May season, a private club is operated for members and guests. The club has a fine restaurant, bar, swimming pool, and tennis courts.
Pricing: $$-$$$$
Contact: Reservations and information, 888-881-2867.
Internet: www.windermereislandhomes.com
Please Note: Eleuthera is virtually all do-it-yourself in terms of bonefishing. Depending on your needs, any of the listed accommodations will be suitable for anglers looking to explore and fish on their own.

Independent Guides

Most of the independent guides on Eleuthera work out of Harbour Island. Many offer morning half-day trips. Be aware that Harbour Island guides charge more than any other guides in the Bahamas, often $400 to $500 per day for a full day. During the main winter season you will need to reserve your guide well in advance of your trip. You can do this directly or through your hotel.

Legendary "Bonefish Joe" Cleare, Harbour Island: 242-333-2663.

Woody Perry, Spanish Wells: 242-333-4433 or VHF Channel 16.

Jermaine Johnson, Harbour Island: You can communicate with Jermaine easily through his Web site (www.bonefishjermaine.stop.to) or by phone: home 242-333-3205; mobile 242-464-0760. You can also e-mail him at bonefishjermaine@yahoo.com.

Other guides who receive frequent recommendations include *Patrick Roberts, Stanley Johnson, Vincent Flucker, Gladstone Petty*, and *Paul Petty*.

www.EleutheraBonefish.com: This is the best Web site for fly-fishers specifically interested in fishing with a guide on Eleuthera. The site recommends staying at the Duck Inn, one of our top recommendations as well. Tide information for the Atlantic and Caribbean is available with suggestions on how to use the tides to your advantage.

Services

Offshore Fishing: Your resort or hotel can book offshore boats.

Out of Harbour Island, contact *Valentine's Marina* for reservations and information, 242-333-2309.

Out of Hatchet Bay, *Captain Gregory Thompson* runs a 32-foot Stamas Sportfisher. Contact him at 242-335-5357.

Diving and Snorkeling: Out of Rock Sound *South Eleuthera Divers* covers the south part of the island. We recommend booking dive trips well in advance here. For reservations and information, call Tim Riley at 242-334-2221.

Out of Harbour Island: *Valentine's Dive Center* is the best operation for North Eleuthera and the surrounding area. Equipment is available for sale or rent. Dive packages, or daily dives, including certification, are available for all ability levels. You should book well in advance during the season. Your hotel can book diving or snorkeling for you. Reservations and information, 242-333-2309; Internet: www.valentinesresort.com

Car Rentals: It's best to arrange this in advance. Most hotels and resorts are happy to make these reservations for you. Some packages include car rentals. Most car rental companies are located in Governor's Harbour, but rentals can be delivered with advance notice.

Cecil and Stanton Cooper, Sunshine Tours, Governor's Harbour: 242-332-1620 or 242-332-1575; Internet: www.thebahmian.com/sunshinetours/.

Butch Johnson, Governor's Harbour: 242-332-2648.

Arthur Nixon: 242-332-2568. Mr. Nixon also conducts tours of the island. If you want to know everything about everything on Eleuthera, this is the man to talk to.

Boat, Golf Cart, and Other Rentals: It's best to make these arrangements through your resort or hotel in advance.

On Harbour Island: *Big Red Rentals* rents snorkeling gear, golf carts, and small boats. Contact them at 242-333-2045.

Restaurants: On Harbour Island we like to stay and eat at the *Pink Sands Hotel*. Our feeling here is, why leave perfection? However, we do try different places. Some of our favorites include *Ma Ruby's* for tasty seafood, and her famous Jimmy Buffet–inspired, "Cheeseburger in Paradise," plus killer Key lime pie; *Angela's Starfish* for fresh conch ceviche; the *Dunmore Deli* for good boxed fishing lunches. Definitely have sunset drinks at *Romora Bay*. And try *Sip Sip* for fresh seafood with an Asian flare. If you're cruising around Eleuthera, stop for a meal at the *Rainbow Inn*. We especially recommend sunset rum drinks and dinner.

Out of Palmetto Point, try the *Unique Village* restaurant for lunch, dinner, or Sunday brunch.

Golf: *Cotton Bay Club Golf Course at Rock Sound.* This is an 18-hole, par 72, 7,000-yard Robert Trent Jones–designed course. Rates are available for 9- or 18-holes. Contact: 242-334-6101.

Banks: *Barclay's Bank*, in Governor's Harbour, is open Monday through Friday, 9:00 A.M. to 1:00 P.M. *Royal Bank of Canada*, on Harbour Island, is open Monday through Friday, 9:30 A.M. to 3:00 P.M.

Clinics: Government medical clinics are located on Harbour Island and Spanish Wells, in Governor's Harbour and Rock Sound.

Government:

Harbour Island Tourist Office: 242-333-2621; fax 242-333-2622
Eleuthera Tourist Office: 242-332-2142; fax 242-332-2480

New Developments

There is ongoing talk about new developments and mega-resorts, but we haven't seen anything concrete in the works. In fact, Eleuthera is littered with abandoned resort and housing developments. Many of the roads leading to spectacular remote beaches were put in to reach these developments that just never happened. Breeze Away Estates is a classic example. This development is still advertising with full-page full color ads, but the roads are overgrown, there is no sign of any activity. Potential buyers should be cautious.

There are a number of private homes being built around the island and several small resorts in the works.

Log on to our Web site, www.bahamasflyfishingguide.com, for updated information.

CHAPTER 9

NEW PROVIDENCE AND NASSAU

The impressive underwater aquarium at the Atlantis Hotel.

New Providence Island is a name not many people know outside the Bahamas, yet it is the Bahamian national capital and home to about 190,000 residents, or roughly two-thirds of all Bahamians. Twenty-one miles long and seven miles wide, it's one of the country's smallest inhabited islands.

Better known as the city of Nassau, the island has been the thriving hub of the Bahamas since the days of the legendary pirate Blackbeard. Its centralized location between Andros and Eleuthera, easy access to deepwater sea-lanes, and its renowned harbor have made it an international transportation and banking center. Banking laws in the Bahamas rival those in Switzerland, and there is no inheritance tax, sales tax, or income tax.

For years Nassau was nothing more than a short overnight stop for us on our way to the Out Islands. That changed in 1995 when Sun International opened the Atlantis Hotel and Casino on Paradise Island. We decided to stay a night to see the resort, and impulsively, we chose to eat diner at Graycliff, an elegant restaurant and hotel set in an old colonial mansion. The maître d' and staff are dressed in tuxedos and jackets are preferred for men, though in the off season this rule is not enforced. It may sound fancy and stuffy but it's actually relaxing and exquisite.

The Cuban cigar master who invented the Cohiba for Castro often sits at a mahogany table in the polished wood-floored entry rolling fresh tobacco into perfect cigars. Cocktails and hors d'oeuvres are served in the living room. This is also where you peruse the two-inch-thick wine list. If you want a bottle under a thousand dollars, skip the first half of the list. You place your dinner order here before moving into one of the small air-conditioned dining rooms. We couldn't resist ordering chocolate soufflé for dessert.

The food and service is everything you would expect in one of the world's best restaurants, though Graycliff is more than just a restaurant and hotel. It is a destination all its own, one we have now made a habit of visiting on most trips through Nassau.

If you're into food, Nassau has something for every appetite. If you want down-home Bahamian johnnycake, conch salad, steamed fish, rice and peas, no problem. If you want fast food, there's pizza, McDonald's, and more. Many casual restaurants serve varied menu items. For fine dining, Graycliff is just the beginning.

Other international gourmet experiences can be enjoyed at Buena Vista, the Sun and . . ., Five Twins, the Bahamian Club, Dune, Chez Willie's, and the Ocean Reef Club.

For the past several years our favorite restaurant overall has been Cafe Matisse (www.cafe-matisse.com). Owner Gregory Curry blends superior service with delicious fresh food—everything from rack of lamb to grilled grouper to homemade pasta and Key lime pie—in a convivial atmosphere. The downtown location on Bay Street makes it convenient to reach from most resort locations on the island.

For a casual evening meal overlooking the harbor and the Yacht Haven Marina, we like the Poop Deck Restaurant and Bar. Order the fresh seafood here. For authentic Bahamian food, try Mama Lyddy's Place. This restaurant does not take credit cards, which is something you should always be aware of, especially in the Out Islands. For a half-dozen other good casual eateries, take a stroll through Atlantis. You will find something for any taste, from massive buffets to traditional tuna sandwiches.

No matter where you go on New Providence, you will see advertisements for Atlantis, and the fact is, the Atlantis Resort dominates the island and brings more tourism to the Bahamas than all other resorts combined.

While some mega-resorts around the world lack one thing or another, Atlantis lacks nothing. Our favorite attraction is the seemingly endless saltwater aquarium that sprawls through the resort to be viewed from every conceivable angle.

One shallow water section is loaded with bonefish, cruising the flats just as they would off Andros. If there hadn't been so many people around we might have put our fly rods together. The deeper-water sections contain sharks, barracuda, snappers, jacks, tarpon, and countless other species of tropical fish.

Then there are the permit, hundreds of them. It's a mesmerizing sight. You can watch them from above, but the best view is from the tunnels where you see them at eye-level through thick glass. Their eyes never stop moving, darting and inspecting. It makes you nervous just watching them, and makes you realize why they are so hard to catch on a fly. Attracting their attention is no problem, but getting them to commit to eating is one of the toughest things in fly-fishing.

We stayed at Atlantis in 1995, and it made an impression. Just picture a glitzy Las Vegas hotel, say the Mirage, set it down in a tropical paradise with water running through it, and you have Atlantis.

That was Atlantis then, with about a thousand rooms. In December 1998, Atlantis opened its Royal Tower and Marina, which more than doubled room capacity and created the most mind-boggling outdoor water theme park in the world. They also began the Harborside Resort complex, an upscale townhouse development across the marina from the Royal Tower. The first three phases sold out by mid-2004, and two new phases began construction at that time.

We understand that some locals don't like the progress being made on New Providence, and especially on Paradise Island. In spite of the city's crowds and traffic, there are still places on the island that remain untouched and peaceful. Wanting to preserve this makes sense, but progress has improved the economy for most people on New Providence. Thousands of well-paying jobs have been created. The city is cleaner and it feels safer than ever before. Crime is certainly no worse than in any U.S. city of the same size.

Downtown is a hopping place. The atmosphere is fun and energetic. The Prince George Wharf is a beehive of activity centered on the cruise ship industry. The cruise ship companies bring in more than one million visitors a year. The Hilton British Colonial Hotel at One Bay Street has become our favorite place to stay. With a complete remodel finished in 2000, the elegant hotel is ideally located to accommodate business and leisure travelers.

Trendy clubs and cigar bars mingle with upscale restaurants that draw affluent travelers, while spring-breakers go wild, and cruise ship passengers shop until they drop. Compass Point Resort is a celebrity magnet on the opposite end of the island, as is the exclusive gated community at Lyford Cay.

Bahamian culture is on display with the Junkanoo Expo leading the way. Restored museums tell of Nassau's history, poetry readings are hip, and art fairs take place almost every week.

Outdoor enthusiasts will not be bored on New Providence. Three public golf courses are highly rated. The private Lyford Cay Club course is also well regarded, but you have to be a member, or guest of a member, or staying at the club to play. Most of the major resorts have tennis courts and health clubs. Water sports are the main attraction, with snorkeling and diving trips put on by a number of vendors, though there is good snorkeling that you can do on your own.

Cable Beach is wild with jet skis, parasailing, water skiing, beach volleyball, and any other type of beach activity you can think of.

While none of this is the Bahamas we crave, it is fun and exciting for many people. We're glad to see this segment of tourism thriving around New Providence and Paradise Island.

This sense of enthusiasm is drawing thousands of visitors, making tourism by far Nassau's leading industry. We rarely visit the Bahamas now without spending a night

It's a quick hop from New Providence to Andros . . . and to bonefish like this one.

or two in Nassau. Many of our client couples use Nassau as a way to compromise on a "fishing" vacation. Four nights in Nassau traded for four days of bonefishing on one of the Out Islands makes a balanced trip, though most of the anglers we know try to shift this balance in favor of the fishing.

There is good off-shore and reef fishing out of Nassau with conventional gear. Experienced fly-fishers with their own equipment could catch fish too, but don't count on any help from the charter boat crews.

For serious anglers who are dying for some quality flats fishing, it is possible to travel to Andros for the day. You need to arrange an early-morning charter flight to Andros Town Airport, or you can go on Western Air. An independent guide can meet you at the airport for your day of fishing and have you back to the airport in time for the ten-minute flight back to Nassau.

Nassau's International Airport is a comfortable modern facility and the hub of Bahamasair and Western Air. Delta, Comair, American Eagle, Continental/Gulfstream, US Airways, Air Canada, Air Jamaica, and different charter jets fly here daily. Visitors arriving on commercial airlines land here. Passengers clear customs, retrieve their luggage, then take a taxi to their island accommodations, or transfer over to the domestic terminal for a flight to the Out Islands.

If you're staying on the island, service personnel outside the international terminal will get you a taxi in orderly fashion. The government regulates zone fares so you'll know what the fare is in advance. If you're going to the domestic terminal, we suggest using a porter to help with your luggage. It's a five-minute walk, and if you pack like we do, it's worth the tip money to have assistance.

The domestic terminal is basic, but it was upgraded in 2002 to include the reservation desk for Western Air, an expanded area for charter companies and for Bahamasair, and a larger departure lounge with a restaurant and bar. Outside the departure lounge are a couple of convenience stores and a well-stocked liquor store. We often buy liquor here to take with us to the Out Islands.

Bahamasair schedules don't always match up well with international flights. You can have long layovers coming and going. Western Air has the best service to Andros and is now offering service to Grand Bahama and Bimini, but layovers are still a factor.

Our favorite way to have some fun is to take a five-minute taxi ride ($10) to Compass Point, an upscale jazzy resort located near Love Beach. They have an open-air restaurant on the water, a swimming pool, dock, and adjacent beach. They serve delicious eggs Benedict at breakfast, and have a wide variety of dishes on the menu throughout the day.

If you have a really long layover (at least four hours), you can go to Bay Street. Tell the driver to drop you at the Hilton British Colonial Hotel. This is also our top recommendation if you are staying overnight on your way to one of the Out Islands. From here you can stroll down Bay Street, a shopping mecca, and have lunch at Cafe Matisse. Depending on the length of your layover, you could make a dash to Paradise Island to see the Atlantis aquarium. Be advised that even with the new Paradise Island bridge, traffic jams can create an hour's drive back to the airport.

We recommend making use of your taxi rides by talking with the drivers. They know everything that's going on in the city, and can make some great suggestions for things to do and places to eat. Most will offer to pick you up for the return trip to the airport. Ninety-nine percent of the time they will be where you say, right on time.

Flights returning from the Out Islands to Nassau will arrive at the domestic terminal. You will retrieve your luggage here then trek to the international terminal. The check-in area of the international terminal is considerably farther than the arrival area so we recommend using a porter. The porter will also get you a cart that you will need to take your luggage through customs.

After checking in with your airline, you clear U.S. Customs, then turn over your luggage and proceed upstairs to the waiting lounge for your flight. Since 9/11, the customs-screening procedures have been beefed up and they take more time. You absolutely must arrive at the airport at least two hours prior to your departure time or you might miss your plane.

The international departure lounge has a restaurant, bar, and gift shop.

Around the Island

Nassau International Airport is in the northwest section of New Providence, which is a roughly oval-shaped island laid out west to east. Most visitors staying on the island, or transferring to the Out Islands, arrive here. You drive north out of the airport, then have a choice to turn right (east) toward Cable Beach and downtown, or left (west) to Love Beach, Compass Point, Old Fort Bay and Lyford Cay. Most people hang a right.

The drive along West Bay Street gives you a pleasing view of the blue-green water inside the reef. Ten minutes later you hit the beginning of Cable Beach. Sandals Royal Bahamian Resort and Spa, on the beach side of the street, is an all-inclusive couples-only deluxe facility that includes an outstanding health club and spa.

Down the road a short piece is the Radisson Cable Beach Casino and Golf Resort. This is a super-popular package hotel and it's wild during spring break. Guests receive special rates at the Cable Beach Golf Club, and tennis enthusiasts have

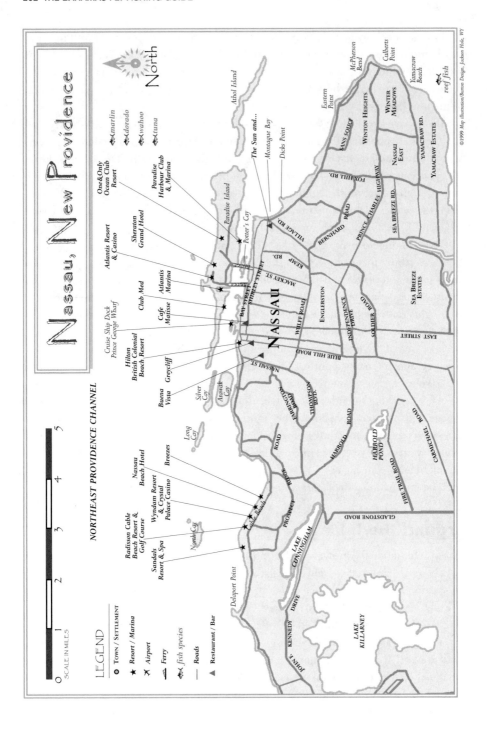

Nassau, New Providence

©1999 Map Illustration/Buenos Design, Jackson Hole, WY

18 courts to choose from. An underground walkway and mall connects to the Wyndham Nassau Resort and Crystal Palace Casino. The Wyndam purchased this property from Marriott in 2003 and now offers all-inclusive packages.

The Crystal Palace is one of the most garish-looking structures you'll ever see, with five gaudy purple-pink towers dominating the skyline. The hotel has the second largest casino on the island, a number of good restaurants, a large pool and beach area, and a top health club.

Next is the Nassau Beach Hotel. Though this hotel has undergone several renovations, it needs more work. Still, it's a good value, has a large pool, beachside bar, beach, Johnny Canoe's restaurant, tennis courts, and it's located in the heart of the action on Cable Beach.

Breezes Bahamas is next-door. This SuperClub resort is an all-inclusive facility for couples and singles, and is more moderately priced than Sandals. If you enjoy non-stop action, this is the place to find it. If you want a quiet relaxing vacation, don't book here.

Continuing east, West Bay Street winds along the shoreline. In 15 minutes you reach the edge of downtown, which is noticeable due to the increased traffic and McDonald's. The Hilton British Colonial Beach Resort is on the northwest corner of where West Bay Street becomes Bay Street. Traffic continuing east must divert to Shirley Street because Bay Street is one-way heading west. Driving in this area can be a nightmare during rush hour so we suggest taking a taxi or a public bus, then setting out on foot.

Bay Street is the shopping mecca of the Caribbean. Prince George Wharf, the cruise ship headquarters, and Rawson Square, merge in a hive of big-city bedlam. A dozen blocks later traffic is still congested, but a semblance of order returns as you reach the new and old bridges to and from Paradise Island. The new bridge is first. It is one-way going onto the island. The old bridge is one-way coming back to Nassau.

Paradise Island is its own universe that spins around the star of Atlantis. Club Med is tucked away in a 21-acre compound on the southwestern side of the island. You can't miss the massive Atlantis compound if you just keep going straight after clearing the new bridge toll-gate. Kim suggests driving over at night—Atlantis is an epic sight when it's all lit up.

Atlantis is broken up into three sections: the Beach Tower, Coral Towers, and the Royal Towers. You need to know which section of the hotel you're staying in, and check in there, or you will be walking, and walking, and walking to reach your room.

It's fair to say that as a beach resort, Atlantis has it all. The complex of pools, streams, water slides, lagoons, and beaches is the most amazing on the planet.

The same goes for the marina, with luxury dock facilities and services for more than 60 yachts up to 220 feet in length. "Luxury" services here means concierge and other guest services that are equal to those of the hotel are available to boaters. On the Nassau side of the marina is the Harborside Resort at Atlantis, a townhouse development with units for sale.

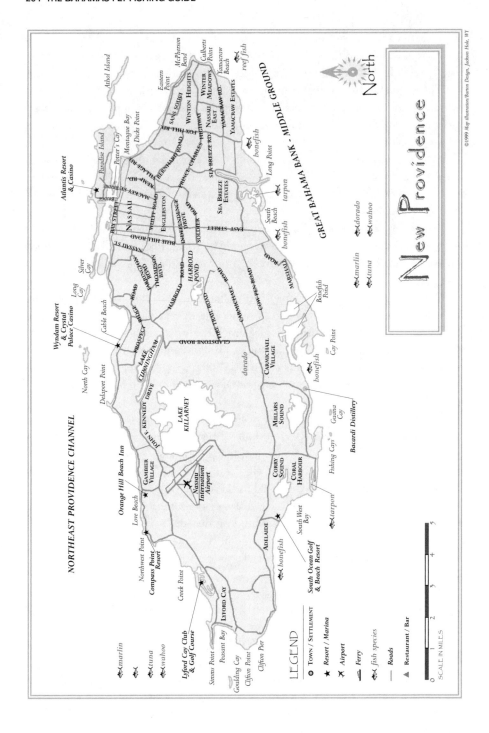

New Providence

Overshadowed by its neighbor, The Sheraton Grand Hotel is definitely a step down from Atlantis but still a good beachfront option on Paradise Island. As a matter of perspective, it's a shorter walk from the Sheraton to the Atlantis Beach Tower, than from the Atlantis Beach Tower to the Royal Tower.

The Sheraton has spacious guestrooms, a fine stretch of beach, pool area, and a water-sports activity center that rivals those on Cable Beach.

Farther down Paradise Island Drive is the Sol Kerzner's One&Only Ocean Club Resort. This is the most elegant and sophisticated hotel on the island, with manicured grounds featuring fountained courtyards and quiet gardens. When you're lounging around the peaceful pool area, it's hard to believe Atlantis is a five-minute drive away. The beach has a remote luxurious feeling. Large guestrooms include private verandahs, tasteful Caribbean furnishings, and posh marble bathrooms. Suites and villas are magnificent, and they come with a matching price tag. If you're trying to bribe someone into going on a fishing trip, a stay here before or after should do the trick. The Ocean Club's 18-hole golf course and nine tennis courts complete the exclusive country club atmosphere.

For boaters cruising into New Providence from the north and northwest, the hotels of Cable Beach and the Coral World tower are obvious landmarks, but this is an extremely confusing area, and should be navigated during the day using considerable caution. As this is the entrance for cruise ships into Nassau Harbour, remember that size matters. In general, this is a very busy harbor and all vessels are required to seek clearance with the harbor control when entering, leaving, or changing position. VHS Channel 16 is the best method of communication.

Recent changes in the harbor include the Paradise Island Bridge, west of the old bridge, and the Atlantis marina. The marina entrance is to the north just before you reach the new bridge. In addition to all the services available at Atlantis, the marina provides complete protection from wind and tides.

After passing under both bridges and rounding the east end of Potter's Cay, you reach Nassau Yacht Haven with full services and space for up to 100 boats.

Across the harbor on Paradise Island is Hurricane Hole Marina. Full services are available for boaters, including a good restaurant for lunch, and walking access to a number of shops, or to the Atlantis complex.

Back on the Nassau side, the Bayshore Marina is east of Yacht Haven. One hundred fifty slips are available in this modern marina.

Cruise ships are a common sight in Nassau Harbour.

Continuing east, the Nassau Harbour Club Hotel and Marina, and the Harbour View marina provide still more services and accommodations to boaters and vacationers.

At the eastern end of Nassau Harbour is Montagu Bay, which is sheltered by Paradise and Athol islands. Boaters cruising to and from Spanish Wells and the Exumas most often use this route. South of the bay is East Point. The reefs and coral heads in the area produce good fishing for snappers, jacks, grouper, mackerel, and amberjack.

The south shore of New Providence is relatively undeveloped. From Port New Providence to Coral Harbour are some nice beaches and the only flats on the island. These flats can be waded on the incoming tide. Fishing a neap tide is your best bet. Fly-fishers rarely fish these flats and the bonefish average five pounds. Fishing these flats is more productive from a boat, and we have heard that some guides from Andros might now be guiding here on occasion.

Whether that is true or not, we want to make the point that if fly-fishing is even the slightest glimmer of an idea in your vacation plans, don't book a trip to Nassau or Paradise Island. Instead, go to Grand Bahama and stay at the Westin and Sheraton Resorts of Our Lucaya, or at Pelican Bay. There you can combine high-profile resorts with quality flats fishing.

Around Cay Point are more flats but access from shore is difficult. The Bonefish Pond, aptly named, is in the lee of Cay Point, and it stretches west toward the entrance to Millars Sound. This is all good bonefish habitat with hard coral bottoms and plentiful blue crabs but the fish numbers are sparse. The Bacardi Distillery is nearby on the road leading to Coral Harbour.

The harbor itself is the base for the Bahamian Defense Force. The residential development is a quiet, luxury community set amidst palm trees and winding man-made canals. The canals provide sea access for the homeowners, and are also home to resident tarpon.

West of Coral Harbour is the small village of Adelaide, one of the first black settlements established after the abolition of slavery. This whole South West Bay area is a quiet serene surprise. If have to go fishing on your own on New Providence, this is definitely the best area to give it a shot. We have caught some nice-size tailing fish here on several occasions, and have seen some double-digit giants.

Just west of Adelaide is the South Ocean Golf and Beach Resort. This pleasant out-of-the-way resort has a colonial plantation feel with bright comfortable rooms in the main section, and more elegant accommodations across the road on the beach. The 18-hole golf course is the best on the island. Tennis facilities, a dive center, two restaurants, and accompanying bars create a self-contained destination.

At the west end of the island is Clifton Point, Pleasant Bay, then exclusive Lyford Cay, which is a private residential community that features a golf course, luxury guest accommodations, and an impressive marina.

Turning the corner past Lyford you're on West Bay Street again and a short drive from the Compass Point Resort. The small colorful facility is an island classic featuring Junkanoo decorations and rooms complete with fax machines and CD players.

This is an ideal resort for those who want to be away from bustling Paradise Island and Cable Beach. Adjacent Love Beach offers some of the best snorkeling on the island.

Fishing Highlights

The pool at the Compass Point Hotel.

As we have said in several places already, if you want to fish on your vacation, you should not book a trip to New Providence. There are just too many other options on other islands, including full-scale resorts on Grand Bahama, and the new Four Seasons Resort on Exuma.

That said, the unique thing about the Nassau fishery is that bonefish are not the primary species. Offshore is the draw, with the Northeast Providence Channel and the Tongue of the Ocean drop-offs minutes from the island.

Full and half day charter boats are available out of Nassau Harbour. Prices range from $400 for a half day to $750 and up for a full day. The major resort hotels have concierge desks that can book you a boat, or you can call the Nassau Yacht Haven directly.

White marlin and sailfish move into the Tongue of the Ocean in numbers in late March and April. Blue marlin turn up a little later, with May through July being prime.

Allison tuna are in these waters year round, with March through July the best months. From the Andros side of the Tongue we've had our best tuna fishing in May. With an average size here of about 50 pounds, these tuna can tear you up. A 10-weight rod is the minimum needed to do battle with these fireballs, but you should really have a 12-weight. Our favorite flies include Abel Anchovies, Sea Habits, Snak-Pak Mackerels, and Black Sardinas.

Dorado tend to run with the tuna, with the highest concentrations of fish occurring April through June, though October and November can be good as well. Average fish run about 20 pounds, but we've caught fish over 50 pounds in May on the Andros side of the Tongue. A 10-weight fly rod is the minimum. Best flies include Mullets patterns, Edgewater Poppers, and Offshore Deceivers.

The best winter sport is for wahoo. November through April is the range, with January and February producing the highest numbers of fish. It is possible to hook more than 20 fish a day during the prime months on conventional tackle. Wahoo readily hit flies, but you need to have a good teasing partner to make this work. You also need at least 40-pound wire shock tippet.

A dorado on fly.

Our favorite reef species here is amberjack. These brutes concentrate around the reefs and wrecks from March through the summer months. Fishing with conventional gear is the surest way to hook fish, but using chum can produce action on flies. Chum will also bring up everything else around the reef, including sharks, jacks, snapper, and grouper. You can't beat this kind of fishing if you want variety and a lot of action.

While the offshore and reef fishing can be excellent off New Providence, this is not the fishing reason to travel to the Bahamas. Andros Island is a 10-minute flight away, and less than an hour by boat. Even if you're on a non-fishing vacation, Andros will tug at your fishing soul while you lie on the beach or cruise through one of the casinos. It's so close, so how can you resist?

Optional Activities

Atlantis is its own center of activities. There is enough to do here for days without leaving—exactly what Sun International intended when they built the place. Beach and water-sports aficionados can go berserk. The only drawback to sun worshippers is a winter cold front. These can come through at any time from December through February. We recommend a visit to Atlantis to see the saltwater aquarium. Plan on at least two hours, and you might as well have lunch as you wander through the massive property.

Gambling is a major draw for Nassau. The casino scene at Atlantis ranks with any Las Vegas facility. Wyndam's Crystal Palace isn't shabby either. Both hotels have sports book betting and cabaret-style shows.

Atlantis, Sandals, and the Crystal Palace have the best resort fitness clubs and spas. The Palace Spa is also open to the public, and has the most extensive exercise facilities. Massages are available in all the better hotels.

In general, the major resorts have concierge desks where you can book any type of island activity you choose, including guided tours.

There are a number of island tours available. Many begin at downtown Parliament Square; the traditional center of the Bahamian government. The pastel buildings were erected in the early 1800s by Loyalists, and include the Houses of Parliament, the old Colonial Secretary's Office, and the Supreme Court.

Rawson Square, the Pompey Museum, the Junkanoo Expo, Bay Street, the Hilton British Colonial Hotel, and Arawak Cay are often included in tours of this nature.

The Pompey Museum of Slavery and Emancipation was used as an auction house for slaves during the eighteenth century. Now this government-funded museum displays the history and lifestyles of African Bahamians from the slave trading days to post-emancipation. There is also a fine collection of the island's contemporary art.

The Junkanoo Museum is a celebration of the Bahamas national carnival spirit. This is a fun lively place featuring colorful, intricately designed costumes and masks. Be prepared to learn the Junkanoo dance before you leave.

The mini-tour of the Bacardi and Company rum distillery includes sampling various rum products. If you like making your own mai tais or Goombay Smashes we suggest taking home some coconut rum.

For some history about pirating days, take the tours of Fort Charlotte, built in 1789 by Lord Dunmore and named in honor of the wife of King George III. The fort features a commanding view over Nassau and was meant to guard the western entrance of the harbor. This is a full-service fort, with moat, drawbridge, ramparts, and dungeons. Also don't miss Fort Montagu on East Bay Street, the oldest of the surviving forts. It overlooks the eastern entrance to the harbor and was built in 1741 in anticipation of a Spanish attack that never materialized.

A number of tours are available to nearby cays and islands. The 44-foot powerboat Midnight Express heads to the Exuma Cays for snorkeling, barbecuing, stingray and shark feeding, plus beach activities. On a calm day the water crossing is spectacular.

An excursion to nearby Rose Island is one of the best beach-oriented day trips. The long beach has plenty of room for relaxation and privacy, and you can take a fly rod along to fish for jacks and snappers along the reefs. Snorkeling, fish feeding, sea kayaking, beach volleyball, and barbecue lunches are featured activities.

Many diving and snorkeling trips are available to various cays, reefs, wrecks, and blue holes, and dolphin encounters are also available.

If you're interested in the conservation movement in the Bahamas, we recommend a visit to the Retreat, which is headquarters for the Bahamas National Trust. The Retreat is an 11-acre property with verdant gardens and an extensive collection of palm trees. You can become a member or make a donation if you wish.

Lodging, Guides, and Services

Featured Lodges

Atlantis Resort Casino and Marina

Paradise Island   The Royal Towers section is the crown jewel of this monstrous lavish resort that has more than 2,000 guest rooms. The Coral Towers section includes the Reef Club, which is a VIP section of luxurious rooms with private concierge service. This section also contains more than 60 one-bedroom suites in villas facing the beach and one of the pool areas. The Beach Tower is the original section of the hotel, but it was renovated to fit in with the luxury surrounding it.

The inner harbor marina is one of the ritziest on the seven seas. Marina guests are entitled to full hotel privileges, which include: acres of swimming pools and water slides; snorkeling lagoons and beaches; more than 30 restaurants and bars; the Entertainment Complex, with its 50,000-square-foot casino; a full-service resort spa featuring indoor/outdoor beauty treatments and a state-of-the-art workout facility; and championship golf and tennis located nearby.

Season: Year round.

Optional Activities: Indulge in all the resort amenities, or have one of the concierge desks book an outside excursion such as offshore fishing, diving, golf, or island tours.

What's Included: Complete vacation packages are available including air, accommodations, and meals.

Not Included: Air fare to/from Nassau International Airport, or to the Paradise Island floatplane dock, airport transfers, meals, and any optional activities you choose. It is at least a 30-minute taxi ride from Nassau International Airport to the resort, longer if there is traffic.

Pricing: $$$-$$$$

Contact: Reservations and information, 888-528-7155 or 242-363-3000.

Marina: 242-363-6068.

Internet: www.atlantis.com

One&Only Ocean Club Resort, Bahamas

Paradise Island If you're looking for pampered elegance and privacy just minutes from Nassau and Atlantis, this is the place for you. This stylishly sophisticated property is the best choice on New Providence for the discriminating traveler. The service and amenities offered here rival the best beach resorts anywhere. Dining in the Courtyard Terrace is superb and perhaps the most romantic dinner spot on the island. Equally lavish meals are served in the oceanfront Dune Restaurant. The adjacent golf course and tennis courts, highlighted by dramatic beaches and seascapes, create a virtual paradise.

Season: Year round.

Optional Activities: You can take advantage of the amenities at Atlantis, or have the concierges book an outside excursion such as offshore fishing, diving, golf, or island tours.

What's Included: Complete vacation packages are available including air, accommodations and meals.

Not Included: Airfare to/from Nassau International Airport, or to the Paradise Island floatplane dock, airport transfers, meals, and any optional activities you choose.

Pricing: $$$$

Contact: Reservations and information, 242-363-2501; fax 242-363-2424.

Internet: www.oneandonlyresorts.com

Hilton British Colonial Beach Resort

Downtown, Bay Street Our favorite place to stay in Nassau, this casual yet luxurious grand hotel is located at One Bay Street, 20 minutes from the international airport, and in the middle of everything. You can walk out of the hotel and start shopping until your credit card melts. Many of the island's best restaurants are five minutes away. The 289 air-conditioned rooms and luxury suites have high-speed Internet connections, desks, large bathrooms, and mini-bars. Amenities include a swimming pool, beach, water sports, three tennis courts, a business center, Azure Spa, and fitness center.

Season: Year round.

Optional Activities: Golf, tennis, snorkeling, diving, offshore fishing, gambling, water sports, great dining, shopping, or island tours.

What's Included: Packages are available, though most people just book a room and then do everything else on their own.

Not Included: Airfare to/from Nassau International Airport, airport transfers, meals, and any optional activities you choose.

Pricing: $$$

Contact: Reservations and information, 242-322-3301 or 800-HILTONS; fax 242-302-9010.

Internet: www.nassau.hilton.com

Radisson Cable Beach Casino and Golf Resort

Cable Beach This high-rise mega-resort is conveniently located only 10 minutes from the international airport on a white sand beach. The resort has 700 air-conditioned rooms, six restaurants, numerous bars, a huge swimming pool area, an 18-hole golf course, health club, 18 tennis courts, racquetball, shopping, meeting rooms, and is adjacent to the Wyndam Crystal Palace casino. You can walk through an underground shopping arcade right into the Crystal Palace. Be aware that during spring break this place rocks with young partying vacationers.

Season: Year round.

Optional Activities: Golf, tennis, snorkeling, diving, offshore fishing, gambling, water sports, great dining, or island tours. You might even want to relax and do nothing.

What's Included: Complete vacation packages are available including meals, accommodations, drinks, activities, golf course fees, taxes, and gratuities.

Not Included: Airfare to/from Nassau International Airport, airport transfers ($15 one-way), meals, and any optional activities you choose.

Pricing: $$$

Contact: Reservations and information, 800-214-4281 or 242-327-6000; fax 242-327-6987.

Internet: www.radisson-cablebeach.com

E-mail: info@radissonbahamas.com

Compass Point

Northwest New Providence One of the most colorful in the Bahamas—literally. Painted in brilliant Junkanoo colors, the 21 cottages and cabanas are only steps from the white sand beach. Each room has island furnishings covered in handmade batik, private sundecks, a coffeemaker, fax machine, CD player, and an array of bathroom amenities. Some rooms include a kitchenette and VCR. Love Beach, which is snorkeling nirvana, is just a short walk down the sand. Additional amenities include a restaurant and bar, tennis court, swimming pool, and dive shop. Blue-water fishing can be arranged. The resort is a five-minute taxi ride from the airport, so if you have a daytime layover this is a perfect spot for breakfast or lunch.

Season: Year round.

Optional Activities: Golf, tennis, snorkeling, diving, offshore fishing, gambling, water sports, great dining, shopping, and island tours.

What's Included: Packages with meals are available. Most people book optional activities on their own.

Not Included: Airfare to/from Nassau International Airport, airport transfers, and any optional activities you choose.

Pricing: $$$-$$$$
Contact: Reservations and information, 877-364-1100 or 242-327-4500.
Internet: www.islandinns.com
E-mail: info@islandinns.com

Orange Hill Beach Inn

Northwest New Providence Set on a hilltop overlooking the ocean, the hotel is steps from a sandy beach and the crystal-clear water. There are 32 air-conditioned rooms, a restaurant, bar, satellite TV, and a coin-operated laundry. For more than 20 years the hotel has catered to divers and vacationers looking for value-priced accommodations. This is the best place to overnight if you get in to Nassau late, and are leaving early the next morning for a fishing trip to the Out Islands.
Season: Year round.
Optional Activities: Golf, tennis, snorkeling, diving, offshore fishing, gambling, water sports, great dining, shopping, and island tours.
What's Included: Most people just book a room here.
Not Included: Airfare to/from Nassau International Airport, airport transfers, and any optional activities you choose.
Pricing: $-$$
Contact: Reservations and information, 888-399-3698 or 242-327-7157.
Internet: www.orangehill.com

Additional Accommodations

Sandals Royal Bahamian Resort & Spa

Cable Beach Luxury all-inclusive couples retreat. Large opulent air-conditioned rooms, tons of food, rum drinks galore, and plenty of activities to work it all off. The health club and fitness center is the best on the island, and is only available to guests. Four hundred rooms, two swimming pool areas, private beach, six restaurants, a dance club, and pampering service. Two-night minimum stay.
Pricing: $$$$
Contact: Reservations and information, 800-726-3257 or 242-327-6400
Internet: www.sandals.com

Breezes SuperClubs

Cable Beach A SuperClubs all-inclusive resort. Families are welcome here. Four hundred air-conditioned rooms, lots of restaurants and bars, five swimming pools, three tennis courts, and a complete beach sports center.
Pricing: $$$
Contact: Reservations and information, 877-467-8737 or 242-327-5356.
Internet: www.superclubs.com

Wyndam Nassau Resort & Crystal Palace Casino

Cable Beach Five gaudy purple and magenta towers make up this huge resort and casino, located between the Radisson and the Nassau Beach Hotel. Most of the 1,000 rooms, suites, and supersuites overlook the ocean. The supersuites are located on special Crystal Club floors, with individual concierge service. The health club features daily aerobics classes. The casino is the center of activity, with 12 surrounding restaurants and a shopping arcade. The massive pool area is on the beach, and the pool staff runs a complete water sports program. The concierge staff can arrange any activity on the island.

Pricing: $$$

Contact: Reservations and information, 800-222-7466 or 242-327-6200; fax 242-327-6308.

Internet: www.wyndam.com

Nassau Beach Hotel

Cable Beach This 400-room hotel is in the center of the Cable Beach action. It's more low key than its glitzy neighbors, yet you can walk to those hotels in minutes. The swimming large pool area is a lively spot and it's adjacent to the beach. The beach bar is a kick-back spot for early evening drinks. Johnny Canoe's restaurant is a fun, casual place to eat.

Pricing: $$-$$$

Contact: Reservations and information, 888-627-7282 or 242-327-7711.

Internet: www.nassaubeachhotel.com

Graycliff Hotel, Restaurants, Cigars

Downtown Nassau This small exquisite hotel was converted from a colonial mansion, and the restaurant is our favorite in Nassau. Fourteen rooms and suites are individually furnished and include all modern conveniences. Amenities include a swimming pool, sauna, and small health club. The Humidor Restaurant, a more casual yet classy sister restaurant to Graycliff, is on the property, as is the Graycliff Cigar Factory. The cigar factory has an elegant smoking room to sample the fine cigars with a snifter of fine cognac.

Pricing: $$$-$$$$

Contact: Reservations and information, 800-688-0076, 242-302-9150, or 242-326-6188.

Internet: www.graycliff.com

South Ocean Golf & Beach Resort

South New Providence Almost 300 air-conditioned rooms set in a colonial plantation-style resort on one of the best beaches in the Bahamas. The 18-hole golf course is said to be the best in the islands. Three restaurants, two swimming pools, four tennis courts, several bars, and a dive shop complete the amenities. Located about 30 minutes from downtown and 10 minutes from the international airport. All-inclusive packages are available. For anglers who want to fish on their own on New Providence this is by far the best place to stay. Productive flats you can wade on your own are nearby.

Pricing: $$-$$$

Contact: Reservations and information, 242-362-4391; fax 242-362-4810.

Internet: www.southoceanbahamas.com

Services

Diving, Snorkeling, Adventures: A number of operations offer full services including rental equipment and PADI certification programs. We suggest booking diving and snorkeling trips through your resort or hotel.

Dive Dive Dive, Ltd teaches beginners in the pool, and then takes you to a variety of sites around the island. Contact: 242-362-11401; Internet: www.divedivedive.com.

Bahama Divers, Ltd will pick you up at your hotel for PADI certification or any variety of diving options. Contact: 242-393-5644 or 800-398-3483; Internet: www.bahamadivers.com.

Nassau Scuba Centre is recommended by the people at Orange Hill. Contact Ed Moggio at 800-805-5485 or 242-362-1964; Internet: www.divenassau.com.

Exuma Powerboat Adventures offers full-day trips to the Exuma Cays for nature walks, picnics, and snorkeling. Contact: 242-327-5385.

Seaplane Safaris can arrange for you to take a floatplane to the Exuma Cays, including the Exuma Land and Sea Park, for hiking, beachcombing, picnicking and snorkeling. Contact: 242-393-2522.

Restaurants: We've mentioned a number of good restaurants. A separate book could be written on this topic so we'll just give you our favorites here. And actually, there are several free restaurant and shopping guide books available at the international airport right past the customs clearance area, and these books are also available at most hotels, and in various downtown stores.

Graycliff is our favorite for a special dining experience. The atmosphere, service, food, cigars, wine, and cognacs are all world class. Jackets required, but they often make exceptions.

Buena Vista and *The Sun and . . .* are in the same league with Graycliff. You could make a case for them being just as good, or some would say better. Jackets required. The Sun and . . . is very strict about the jacket requirement. You will not get in there without a jacket. Also, no tennis or running shoes are allowed.

Cafe Matisse is our favorite overall restaurant for all-around dining. You can have the best lunch in town here, or enjoy a memorable meal every evening. Located behind the courthouse on Bay Street, it's a five-minute walk from the Hilton British Colonial Hotel.

Johnny Canoe's is a casual place to eat in the Cable Beach area, though there are so many restaurants tucked away in the hotels that you're bound to find something you like.

On Paradise Island there are many good restaurants, mostly in or around the Atlantis complex. *Five Twins* is our favorite at Atlantis, located off the casino overlooking the marina. Five Twins serves excellent Chinese and continental cuisine in a regal setting. Reservations are mandatory and jackets-optional attire is enforced. There is also a superb sushi bar in the Five Twins, along with a cigar bar and lounge. The *Bahamian Club Steakhouse* serves superior beef and fresh seafood in an elegant club atmosphere. Resort evening attire required. *Mama Loo's* offers good Asian food with a Caribbean flair served in a tropical setting. Resort evening attire required. The *Water's Edge* serves a nice variety of Italian, French, Greek, and Spanish cuisine. Resort evening attire for dinner. The *Courtyard Terrace* at the Ocean Club is another favorite dinner spot on Paradise Island. Dine under the stars while listening to soft calypso music. This is a very romantic setting, with superb continental cuisine combined with a distinctive island touch and superior service. Jackets required. Reservations are mandatory.

Dune is a designer beachfront restaurant at the Ocean Club, a place to see and be seen by the beautiful people. Nouvelle cuisine is the thing here.

Guide to Attire: "Casual attire" means just about anything goes, including shorts, T-shirts, jeans, sundresses, and similar apparel. Bathing suit cover-ups are required.

"Resort casual attire" means nice T-shirts or polo shirts, dress shorts, slacks or jeans, sundresses or skirts, and similar apparel.

"Resort evening attire" means polo or button-down shirts, slacks, sundresses or skirts, and similar apparel.

"Jackets optional" means no shorts, jeans, or T-shirts.

"Jackets required" means just that, with no shorts, T-shirts, jeans, or tennis/athletic shoes. Most of the best restaurants are serious about this attire business, and will not let you in no matter how much you protest, or how much money you offer them. During the off-season, however, they may be more lenient.

Golf: *Cable Beach Golf Club, Paradise Island Golf Club*, and *South Ocean Beach and Golf Resort* are open to the public. You should always call ahead to reserve a tee time. You can call these clubs directly, or your hotel can make the reservations for you.

Tennis: *The Nassau Cable Beach Hotel, The Radisson Grand Resort on Paradise Island*, and the *Atlantis* resort rent their courts to the general public, otherwise you need to be a guest of the hotels with tennis facilities.

Shopping: Bay Street is the place. Start at the British Colonial Beach Resort and head east. You'll find just about every name brand store you can think of, plus the massive *Nassau Straw Market*. Don't get lost. Shops are open Monday through Saturday from 9:00 A.M. to 5:00 or 6:00 P.M. Shops are allowed to be open on Sunday, but few take advantage of this opportunity.

Additional special-interest tours and activities can be arranged through your hotel. Every major hotel has a concierge desk with hundreds of brochures describing the available activities.

Car Rentals: All the major agencies are on the island—*Hertz, Avis, National, Dollar*, and others—have Nassau offices, and many have offices in the major resort hotels. We recommend booking a car rental ahead of time, though you do not need a car unless you really want to drive around the island. Traffic can be a nightmare. Taxi service and bus service is very good.

Taxi Service: While taxi service is very good, there is a huge difference between taxi drivers and the vehicles they use. We prefer the more comfortable air-conditioned models. Our favorite taxi driver is *Orville Mott Coleby*, Taxi # 911. "Mott" is friendly, knowledgeable, reliable, and always punctual. We call him whenever possible, and always to pick us up at our hotel for airport transfers.

Banks: Nassau is a major financial capital, so a variety of banks are open Monday through Thursday 9:30 A.M. to 3:00 P.M., and until 5:00 P.M. on Friday. ATMs are available.

Medical Facilities: *Princess Margaret Hospital* is a major medical facility operated by the government. *Doctors Hospital* is privately owned. Both are on Shirley Street.

Government: *Bahamas Ministry of Tourism* is located behind the Hilton British Colonial Hotel. You can contact the Tourism Help Line at 242-325-4357.

New Developments

Things are hopping in Nassau. Private development of homes and luxury condos is booming across the island.

The biggest news is the continuing development at Atlantis. It seems like no matter how big they get, they want to be even grander. A new Mayan tower and water park complex is under construction adjacent to the Royal Tower. This complex will be even more massive than the Royal Tower and will double the number of rooms the resort offers, bringing the total to around five thousand. The Mayan expansion is scheduled to open in 2006.

A fourth and fifth phase of luxury townhouses was being built in the Harbourside Resort at Atlantis in summer 2004 with many of the units already pre-sold at that time.

As of summer 2004, the One&Only Ocean Club was preparing to build new luxury villas and homes for sale.

Western Air continues to expand their air service to the other islands. They have done such a great job of flying on time that they have put Bahamasair out of business on Andros Island. They have also expanded service to Bimini and to Grand Bahama and have plans for additional routes to other islands. You can visit their Web site at www.westernairbahamas.com.

Log on to our Web site at www.bahamasflyfishingguide.com for updated information.

CHAPTER 10

EXUMA CAYS, GREAT EXUMA, AND LITTLE EXUMA

The view from Stocking Island, in Exuma.

The Exuma Cays begin in the north with Beacon Cay, a little more than 30 miles southeast of Nassau. This exquisite string of cays then traverses glass-clear tropical waters colored vivid blues and greens for over 90 miles to Great Exuma, Little Exuma and, finally, Hog Cay. The cays come in varying shapes and sizes, some with wavy green hills, trees, and thick vegetation, and others that are low, flat, and bare.

These cays compose the centerpiece of Exuma's claim to the title of the "Sailing Capital of the World." Boaters can find countless anchorages and harbors that are gorgeous, stunning, mesmerizingly beautiful—just pick your favorite adjective. Like the offshore cays of Abaco, there is a feeling here you want to keep with you always: it is peace and serenity and wonder.

That feeling is reflected in the people, though settlements are few and well spread out until you reach Great Exuma. About 4,000 people live on this strand of emerald islands sandwiched between the Tongue of the Ocean and Exuma Sound and fed by the Great Bahama Bank.

American Loyalists who wanted to remain true to the British king after the American Revolutionary War settled the Exumas in 1783. These people reconstructed their former way of life in the Exumas, complete with cotton plantations, farms, and slaves.

Lord John Rolle was a preeminent landowner and one of the most powerful Loyalists. He imported the first cottonseeds to the islands and owned more than 300 slaves. In 1835, Rolle freed his slaves and ultimately bequeathed to them more than 2,000 acres of Crown land along with his name. This land has been passed down through the generations, and we understand the land can never be sold outside the Rolle clan.

British traditions and lifestyles have remained strong through the years, with the original Club Peace & Plenty in George Town being a favorite vacation spot for the Royals. After landing at George Town Airport on Great Exuma, known locally as Moss Town, it's more than likely your taxi driver will have a British accent.

The Exumas are a breathtaking sight from the air. When flying to Long Island or Crooked Island you are rewarded with a view of deserted coves, white sand beaches, flats that stretch for miles, and dark coral heads swaying beneath crystal-blue water. Parachuting has crossed our minds more than once.

The locals like to say there are 365 cays, one for each day of the year. Many of our boating friends agree that there are at least that many. Diving and snorkeling doesn't get any better, and fishing is almost too easy at times.

The showcase of the cays is the Exuma National Land and Sea Park administered by the Bahamas National Trust. The park boundaries run from Wax Cay Cut in the north to Conch Cut in the south, an area about 22 miles long and 8 miles wide. The park is home to the Bahamian iguana and mockingbird, terns, and numerous other seabirds. Many of the smaller cays only poke their sand above water at low tide.

Fishing is a way of life throughout these remote cays. People take from the sea what they need to live. On Great and Little Exuma farming and tourism combine with fishing to create the local economy. Most fruits and vegetables are brought into these islands, and in the more remote areas, supplies can often run low. Boaters and vacationers should be aware of this and stock up accordingly.

George Town is the administrative center of the Exumas; a thriving settlement with one of the best straw markets in the Out Islands. Elizabeth Harbour is a premiere anchorage and when combined with nearby Stocking Island anchorages, it provides haven for up to 600 boats during Regatta Time.

Club Peace & Plenty is a tradition in George Town. This venerable waterfront hotel—renovated in 2002 and 2003—is a center of activity and the ferry headquarters for visitors going to Stocking Island. Joined by the Beach Inn and the Bonefish Lodge, the Peace & Plenty family of accommodations and restaurants is an important part of the land-based tourism to Great Exuma.

With the main highway completely resurfaced throughout Little and Great Exuma, exploring the islands by land is almost as easy as it is by water. Prime bonefish flats lie on both sides of the islands and are accessible in many areas. There are a number of houses for rent on secluded beaches for people who prefer to do things on their own. If you pick the right house you can catch bonefish in your front yard and snorkel over nearby reefs.

Peace and Plenty Beach Inn on Exuma.

The Four Seasons Resort at Emerald Bay, a long-delayed project, finally opened its doors late in 2003, bringing true luxury accommodations to Exuma for the first time. The self-contained resort has deluxe rooms, magnificent suites, restaurants, bars, and pools, all on the Atlantic-side beachfront.

American Eagle flies non-stop daily from Miami to George Town. Lynx Air, Air Sunshine, and Island Express fly into George Town from Ft. Lauderdale and other Florida airports. Bahamasair has daily service from Nassau. If you have four to six people in your party, a private charter from Ft. Lauderdale or Nassau becomes economical and is definitely more convenient.

Around the Island

Boaters leaving Nassau Harbour usually head for Allan's Cays and Leaf Cay as their first stops. There are several anchorages and a variety of flats. We like the flats on the northwestern side of Leaf Cay. Bonefish often feed here on the incoming tide, then work their way through the cut between the cays at varying stages of the tide. Hard-bottom flats make wading easy, but you cannot cross the channel from Leaf Cay to Southwest Allan's Cay unless you want to swim.

Leaf and Southwest Allan's Cays have white sand beaches and calm coves ideal for snorkeling. Both cays also have populations of curious iguanas. If you decide to catch some rays on one of the beaches, you will probably attract some company. Unfortunately, you're also likely to see a lot of trash in this area, dumped here by inconsiderate boaters.

Continuing southeast, Highborne Cay is a popular spot for sailors. A 26-berth marina has fuel, water, showers, and telephones. Our boating friends tell us you need to call ahead for reservations during popular sailing months. A new marina grocery stocks food and supplies. Rental houses are available on a nearby private cay, and the eastern beaches are right out of a fairy tale.

South of Highborne are many small cays and rocks, then Long Cay and Norman Cay. To the west of Norman Cay is an immense sand bank that goes dry during low tides. This is an outstanding wadable flat during the last of the falling and first of the incoming tides. Bonefish move in here from the deeper surrounding water and the visibility is usually very good. A Pink Hoover or a small Kwan pattern is the ticket here.

Exuma Cays

North

Salt Rocks

Ship Channel Cay

Allan's Cays

bonefish

Marina

Highbourn Cay

Long Cay

bonefish

Norman's Cay

bonefish

(Private)

Wax Cay
Little Wax Cay

Hungry Hall

Elbow Cay

Shroud Cay

Hawksbill Cay

Cistern Cay

Exuma Cays Land & Sea Park

marlin

tuna

dorado

wahoo

EXUMA SOUND

Park Headquarters

Waderick Wells Cay

Halls Pond Cay

Soldier Cay

O'Brien Cay

Little Bell Cay

Bell Island

Marina

Compass Cay

Joe Cay

Pipe Cay

Thomas Cay

Over Yonder Cay

bonefish

Sampson Cay Club & Marina

Fowl Cay

Little Majors Spot

Majors Spot

Staniel Cay Yacht Club

bonefish

STANIEL CAY

Harvey Cays

Happy People Marina & Hotel

Bitter Guana Cay

BLACK POINT

Goulin Cay

Airport

Great Guana Cay

reef fish

Farmer's Cay Yacht Club & Marina

LITTLE FARMER'S CAY

Big Farmer's Cay

Cave Cay

reef fish

bonefish

MUSHA CAY

Rudder Cut Cay

Little Darby Island

Darby Island

Lignum Vitae Cay

Young Island

Bock Cay

bonefish

Norman's
Pond Cay

Lee Stocking Island

Williams Cay

Rat Cay

bonefish

Barraterre
Bonefish Lodge

Brigantine Cays

BARRATERRE

GRAND BAHAMA BANK - MIDDLE GROUND

LEGEND

- ⊚ TOWN / SETTLEMENT
- ★ Resort / Marina
- ✈ Airport
- ⛴ Ferry
- 🐟 fish species
- — Roads
- ▲ Restaurant / Bar

0   5   10   15   20   25
SCALE IN MILES

©1999 Map illustration/Burton Design, Jackson Hole, WY

Norman's Cay is V-shaped, with the largest landmass at the southwestern edge of the inverted V. A number of private homes are located north of the private airstrip. Boaters approach the inner anchorages from both sides. The best bonefishing flats are on the Exuma Sound side, and though there are some good wading spots, a dinghy can get you into fish more consistently.

The northern boundary of the Exuma Cays Land and Sea Park begins in the center of Wax Cay Cut. To the south, Shroud Cay is a maze of mangroves and creeks that create perfect habitat for a variety of seabirds. Next is Hawksbill Cay, a deserted cay with long stretches of pristine beaches on its western shoreline; a great place to catch some rays. If you want to be more active, you can take a hike to Loyalist plantation ruins.

Warderick Wells Cay is the headquarters for the park warden and a small staff of volunteers. The Royal Bahamian Defense Force is also stationed here permanently to enforce the strict park conservation laws. It is your responsibility to know these laws. Copies of the laws, trail maps, and reference books on wildlife, coral, and plants life are available at the headquarters. You need to call ahead on VHS Channel 16 to let the warden know you are coming ashore.

Remember that fishing, shelling, picking plants, or any type of taking of the natural resources is prohibited in the park boundaries.

Conch Cut marks the southern end of the park, with Compass Cay next in line. A creek and mangrove swamps split this large cay down the middle. The Compass Cay Marina has 14 slips and four moorings; water and electricity are available. The marina store stocks a few food items, sells books and T-shirts, and you can buy a map of the area. Depending on demand, and the mail boat schedule, this and other stores throughout the area can be depleted.

Compass Cay has several rental houses. They are air-conditioned, clean, neat, and the views are sensational. The cay has miles of hiking trails and some of the best beaches in the islands. There are also a variety of flats for good bonefishing, including those around the creek adjacent to the marina. Some of these flats receive a fair amount of fishing pressure so you should use longer (10- to 12-foot) fluorocarbon leaders and smaller flies. This will be the case for most of the flats from here down to Staniel Cay.

The Pipe Cay and Pipe Creek area is composed of many small islets that form miles of shallow water flats. Exploring this region in a dinghy is the way to go. You'll be able to reach wadable flats on varying stages of the tide.

While cruising between the cays, or in and out of the many cuts, boaters trolling lures or cut bait can enjoy consistent action. Good tidal flows rip through most cuts, creating ambush points for jacks, snappers, barracuda, and other gamefish. Fishing an intermediate sinking line with short leaders and Clouser's Minnow or baitfish patterns can produce a lot of action. Casting plugs and spoons on conventional tackle is also deadly.

Sampson Cay is similar to Compass Cay in that its two main landmasses are divided by creeks and mangrove mazes. The completely renovated (2003) Sampson

Cay Club and Marina occupies an idyllic spot in a protected harbor on the southwestern side of the island. The turquoise water is ringed with white sand beaches. The marina has almost 2,000 feet of docks that can accommodate boats up to 180 feet. All services for boaters are available. Other amenities and services include a store, restaurant, bar, and rental cottages. Fully furnished villas and houses are also available. The restaurant is a relaxing place to meet fellow travelers from all over the world. Delicious seafood and a variety of eclectic dishes are served nightly. Reservations are a must during the season.

Many of the cays from Allan's to Staniel are private, and you may not go ashore without an invitation. It is your responsibility to know the private cays, and to respect private property.

One private cay of note is Fowl Cay, a picture postcard that has been turned into an upscale resort by Stuart and Libby Brown. The resort facilities on this 50-acre cay, which is one and a quarter miles from Staniel Cay, include three rental houses, a main clubhouse with a 24-seat restaurant, freshwater swimming pool, tennis court, and dock.

The Browns' private residence is on the east end of the island overlooking the Fowl Cay Cut. Two managers live full-time on the island, and they are ready to welcome your family or small group. Transportation on the island is via golf cart, while boats are used to access the island and its surrounding cays. Rental houses include the use of a 17-foot 65-hp outboard runabout. If you are in the market for a do-it-yourself vacation with style, Fowl Cay is one of our top recommendations.

We've talked with people who say this area of the Exumas has been "discovered," and that was clearly the case during our visit in 2004. There are noticeably more boats in the area, but also, it seems as if some sort of building project is under way on many of the cays. Fortunately, most of the development is being done by private homeowners, so the projects are relatively small and usually blend with the environment.

And speaking of "developed," Staniel Cay is the most developed cay in the chain, though that is a relative term. The local village has a population of about 100, and you won't find any traffic jams. Golf carts, bicycles, and your own two feet are the main modes of transportation on the three-square-mile island. The 3,030-foot airstrip is adjacent to the village, while the Happy People Marina and Hotel sprawls along the waterfront. This operation was closed as of this writing due the passing away of Kenneth and Theaziel Rolle. Please check our Web site for updates.

Two island-style grocery stores—one painted blue and the other pink—are conveniently located in the village. Both keep a decent supply of food items, though when demand is high many products can disappear until the resupply boat arrives. Berkie Rolle's Isles General Store offers convenient access for dinghies on the creek south of the village. Basic marine supplies are available, along with LP gas, some dive equipment, food, and small boat rentals. If you're looking for fresh baked bread, you can buy it here every morning except Sunday.

Farther into the harbor, with boating access through a dredged channel, is the Staniel Cay Yacht Club. This place is a lively flurry of activity during the season. The

Stephen celebrates a catch.

dock can accommodate up to 18 boats. Services include water, ice, electricity, and telephones. The Club has six air-conditioned cottages and a hopping restaurant and bar. The cottages are brightly painted and distinctively decorated and each includes a small refrigerator, coffeemaker, and purified water. Several of the cottages have porches that overhang the water. The porches face west, making for spectacular sunset views. Package rates including a meal plan are available. The restaurant serves fresh seafood, steaks, and pork. Thirteen-foot Boston Whalers are available for rent, as are golf carts and bicycles. Guests arriving via charter flights are met at the airport and transferred to the Club. Guides can be arranged for snorkeling, sightseeing, and fishing.

The beaches around Staniel Cay are idyllic and can be accessed via land or water. We recommend that land-based visitors rent a boat and do some exploring on their own. There are countless snorkeling locations and many wadable bonefish flats. For anglers looking to do it "on their own," this is a good location. Many people fish this area, however, so expect to see some spooky fish. Wadable flats surround Big Majors Spot, Little Majors Spot, and other nearby cays. If you like tailing fish don't miss the incoming tide when it occurs early morning or late afternoon. A small Mantis Shrimp or a Yarn Crab are our favorite flies here.

Fishing in the cuts, over the reefs, and offshore can be excellent. Snappers, jacks, and barracuda are abundant in all the traditional ambush points, especially when the tide is really moving. Offshore, marlin, sailfish, wahoo, dorado, and yellowfin tuna are the highlights.

Staniel Cay has developed a fun atmosphere over the years. For people who spend any time here, it's easy to get to know everyone. Beach cookouts, an annual bonefish tournament, and numerous regattas are just a few of the community activities that bring people together to enjoy this tranquil location.

Boaters use Big Rock Cut to access Exuma Sound. Next stop southeast of Staniel is Bitter Guana Cay, then Great Guana Cay. Black Point settlement is located on the northwest coast of Great Guana. With more than 300 residents, this is the largest settlement in the Exuma Cays, and another good spot for adventurous anglers who want to pursue bonefish on their own. The settlement has a post office, clinic, laundromat, a couple of grocery stores, a general store, several good restaurants and bars, and an airstrip.

The Scorpio Inn and Lorene's Café both serve good Bahamian fare at reasonable prices and freshly baked breads are a specialty. We have spoken with anglers who have enjoyed fishing with Simon Smith and Wentzel Rolle. They stayed in one of Simon's three air-conditioned apartments that are managed by his wife, Diane, and reported the rooms to be clean and comfortable, and the fishing outstanding. Anglers can also rent a Boston Whaler from the Smiths' to explore and fish on their own.

Off the southern tip of Great Guana Cay are Little Farmer's Cay, Big Farmer's Cay, Little Galliot Cay, and Cave Cay. This area has exceptional bonefishing and reef fishing. The tidal currents are strong through Farmer's Cay Cut and Galliot Cut, concentrating baitfish and therefore, gamefish. Portions of the Galliot Bank go dry during low tides, making this a prime spot for wading.

The Farmer's Cay Yacht Club and Marina is at the point of the bay on the northeast side of Little Farmer's Cay. The dock juts out from the white sand beach to accommodate up to eight boats. Fuel, water, ice, electricity, telephones, and a restaurant and bar are available here. A marina and resort expansion began here at the end of 2003. The marina will eventually accommodate up to 40 boats. Other facilities will include 10 deluxe villas, a swimming pool, and a cafe with Internet access. We've been told these facilities are scheduled to open in 2005.

A small clinic is in the settlement, and it can be reached on foot from the Club or from the town dock. Ocean Cabin, operated by Terry Bain, has private moorings, a restaurant, a liquor store, and a rescue and towing service. If you need a local guide, someone in the family can help. Hallan Rolle and his family are also helpful guides, plus they arrange snorkeling and diving excursions. If you want guided fishing, we've heard good things about Stanley Rolle.

There are a number of deserted white sand beaches in the area that are ideal for picnicking and snorkeling. Cave Cay is especially beautiful, with dramatic cliffs and green hills, but the island is private and visits ashore require an invitation. You can fish the flats around the island on your own during the lower tidal stages.

To the south across a cut is Musha Cay, one of the most luxurious private island resorts in the world. And this isn't hype. The private resort facilities on this cay are casually elegant, luxurious, and beyond. A staff of 32 attends to a maximum of 24 guests. Accommodations range from the 10,000-square-foot Manor House to the romantic beachfront Pier House. Fine dining is in the Landings waterfront restaurant, with all meals prepared especially for you and your group.

Groups are not mixed at Musha Cay. When you reserve the cay, it's all yours. All accommodations are air-conditioned and include satellite TV and CD players. Amenities range from lighted tennis courts to freshwater pools, state-of-the-art gym, in-room massages and a variety of water toys. Guided bonefishing, snorkeling, and diving excursions can be arranged.

Continuing south toward Great Exuma, many of the cays are private property, including Rudder Cut Cay, Darby Island, and Little Darby Island. Permission is needed to go ashore, but there are wadable flats that can be accessed by small boats and dinghies.

Bock Cay, Norman's Pond Cay, Lee Stocking Island, Williams Cay, Rat Cay, and Pigeon Cay continue the chain of cays leading to Great Exuma. To the west, Bock Cat Cay, Allen Cay, and the Brigantine Cays form a smaller chain leading to Barraterre Island. Between these cays lies a mini-sound that forms prime bonefish habitat. Sand bottoms, laced with crunchy coral and patches of turtle grass, create ideal conditions for wade fishing on an incoming tide. On a calm day, you can see wakes and tails in every direction on many of these flats.

Lee Stocking Island is home to the Caribbean Marine Research Center field laboratory, where scientists study marine resource management and marine food production. This is a branch project of the National Undersea Research Program administered by the National Oceanic and Atmospheric Administration (NOAA).

The settlement dock at Barraterre is located on the eastern shore. The Fisherman's Inn, operated by Norman Lloyd, is the place to hang out here. The restaurant serves breakfast, lunch, and dinner. Delicious dinners include conch, lobster, grouper, and snapper. Make sure to call ahead for reservations on VHS 16. A taxi transfer can be arranged to the George Town airport.

West and southwest of Barraterre is a mini-marls region dotted with small cays that is home to countless bonefish. Good wadable flats lie outside the maze of mangroves and shoreline flats serpentine in every direction. This area is now the home water of the Barraterre Bonefish Lodge. The lodge, near the end of the road north of Fisherman's Inn, can accommodate up to 12 anglers in six double rooms overlooking the water. If you are a hard-core fishing fanatic, the lodge offers an "unlimited" bonefishing package so you can fish from dawn until dusk.

Boaters continuing south to Elizabeth Harbour and George Town will do best by staying outside of the inshore cays. Those looking to explore and do some fishing will find a variety of flats from Black Cay to Steventon and Roker's Point, then from Roker's Point to the Channel Cays. There are anchorages in the lee of Black Cay, about a mile north of Rolleville. The Rolleville settlement has a government wharf for the mail and freight boats. The coastline of Great Exuma is rugged and dramatic in this area. From land, high bluffs present spectacular ocean views over white sand beaches and emerald cays. Kermit's restaurant and tavern is located on one of these bluffs above Rolleville. Lunch and dinner are served, but we suggest calling ahead to check on the menu items available. On weekends, Kermit's usually has a live band with dancing outside.

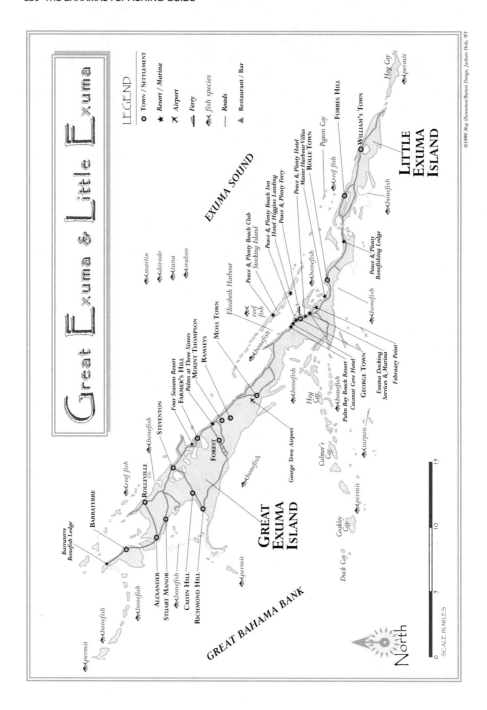

© 1999 Map Illustration/Barton Design, Jackson Hole, WY

The flats in this area usually extend out from the small cays, or from sand bars linked to the main island. There are also a number of bays and coves where you can find bonefish on higher stages of the tide, though the low incoming tide is best overall. Calm weather is the key to fishing success here. When the wind blows from the east you'll need to head to the other side of the island for the best fly-fishing. Reef and cut fishing in the area is good, with jacks and snappers found over the darker coral and grass bottoms.

JJ Dames of the Exuma Bonefish Guides Association.

Steventon also has a government wharf with good anchorages for boaters. The coastline is flatter from Roker's Point to the Channel Cays but the fishing habitat remains the same. Long stretches of white sand beaches combine with lush coconut palms to create a picturesque tropical setting. There are a number of rental houses available throughout this stretch, several on their own private beaches with good bonefishing right out front.

Just north of Farmer's Hill, the Four Seasons Resort Hotel (opened in late 2003) is nestled in Emerald Bay, and the resort has really put this area on the map. The luxury beachfront property has a variety of restaurants and bars, elegant guest rooms and suites, freshwater swimming pool, spa and gym, golf course, and a marina scheduled to open in 2005. The concierges here can arrange everything from bonefishing and offshore guides to rental cars. Exclusive home sites and villas are also for sale.

Three miles south, the Palms at Three Sisters Beach Resort is more of a motel and restaurant than resort. It offers land-based anglers comfortable accommodations and good food along with a prime beachfront location. This is a good spot to stay—you need to rent a car—if you want to explore the northern part of Great Exuma. The resort can arrange for fly-fishing guides or you can book independent guides on your own.

Most people traveling to Exuma specifically to fly-fish, or to stay in the many resort properties, arrive by air at the George Town airport (actually called Moss Town), about a 20-minute drive north of George Town proper. With a population of more than 900, George Town is the largest settlement in the southern Bahamas.

The Palm Bay Beach Resort, on Elizabeth Harbour at the northern end of the settlement, is a 300-acre ownership resort consisting of cottages and villas at the waters edge, lush landscaping, and a popular restaurant.

Next door is the Coconut Cove Hotel, a charming inn that has nine distinctive air-conditioned rooms and three deluxe suites, all with ocean views. The swimming pool and bar are on the beach. The food here is excellent, and the bar comes to life during Happy Hour. You can choose to be on a meal plan, but we suggest not doing this, as there are a number of good restaurants to choose from in George Town. The hotel can arrange for boat and car rentals and for fishing guides. Our suggestion to people staying here is to rent a Boston Whaler, have the hotel pack you a lunch, then take off and explore on your own. Take your fly rod because you'll find many flats interspersed between the ocean-side cays.

Next in line is the Peace & Plenty Beach Inn. The Beach Inn has 16 air-conditioned guestrooms, a freshwater swimming pool, restaurant, and bar, all on a small beach. A mile farther on, in the town proper, is the Club Peace & Plenty Hotel. Built on the edge of the bay, the hotel has 32 air-conditioned rooms and suites, gift shop, restaurant, bar, and swimming pool.

The Club dock is home to the P&P ferry, which shuttles guests back and forth to Stocking Island. The dock is also a dinghy tie-up for boaters stopping by to eat and drink. Both P&P facilities serve excellent Bahamian meals. Reservations are recommended. On many weekends, the Club gets in the party spirit with lively local bands and dancing under the stars.

The Peace and Plenty ferry boat, docked at Stocking Island.

A third Peace & Plenty facility, the Bonefish Lodge, is 20 minutes south of George Town on a waterfront point facing the ferry bridge to Little Exuma. This eight-room facility is headquarters for the bonefishing operation, though anglers can also stay at the Beach Inn. The large air-conditioned rooms all have private baths and balconies with ocean views. The upstairs clubhouse is for anglers only, and contains a bar, dining area, lounge area, satellite TV, and fly-tying area. Downstairs is an artistically crafted bar made of polished hardwood and a large dining room that is open to the public. The grounds are landscaped with young palms, native stone and shrubs, and a sand sunbathing area. The highlight here is the saltwater pond, open to the ocean. At night the sharks have been trained to come in for a feeding worth watching.

The P&P fishing program puts anglers on different waters that run from north of Rolleville to south of Hog Cay. Most bonefishing is done on the western or leeward side of the island, where miles of wadable flats extend out from the island and cut through turquoise channels. It's easy to become distracted by the gorgeous scenery here, which is one of the reasons we recommend Peace & Plenty for couples, and for anglers traveling with non-anglers.

The Doctor of Libation at the Peace & Plenty Hotel Bar.

Guests staying at any of the three facilities can try all the restaurants on the "dine around plan."

P&P operates a beach club on Stocking Island that includes a snack bar for lunch and a couple of miles of deserted beaches to explore. An extensive water sports program is available, including diving, snorkeling, sailing, and windsurfing. Anglers traveling to the island on the ferry might want to take a fly rod because you can catch bonefish in several bays. When the wind is down, the surf and reef fishing on the windward side is very good for jacks, grouper, and snappers.

Elizabeth Harbour, between Stocking Island and George Town, is one of the best anchorages in the Caribbean, and it's the headquarters for boaters exploring the southern Bahamas. Good anchorages lie off the Club P&P dock, and off Stocking Island. It has become extremely difficult to get a spot to anchor off Stocking Island because many boaters drop anchor and just don't leave. Frankly, we can't say that we blame them.

Seven-mile-long Stocking Island has a pristine sand dune-laced coastline facing the Atlantic and tranquil white sand beaches and turquoise coves on the leeward side. Club Peace & Plenty operates a ferry service to their dock here twice a day, where they have a beach club for water sports and a colorful lunch shack renowned for the best burgers in the islands. Out on the point you'll find, Chat & Chill, the "cool" place for locals and boaters to gather for a surprisingly tasty lunch of grilled fish and conch burgers. The Sunday pig roasts are a daylong party.

Also on Stocking Island is Hotel Higgins Landing, a deluxe solar-powered eco-resort. The charming guest cottages have large decks with ocean views. Everything is open and airy and the smell of wildflowers mingles with the salt. The food here is outstanding, and there are good bonefishing flats within walking or sea kayaking distance.

Back on the mainland, there are good anchorages in Kidd Cove protected by a long curved-finger of land called Regatta Point. At the far end of the point is an all-suites inn owned by Nancy Bottomley, also called Regatta Point. This is a convenient spot for serious anglers, couples, or families with non-anglers. The six apartments rest on the water's edge and are fronted by a private swimming and snorkeling beach.

You're just a few minute's walk from George Town, and you can rent a boat and keep it right in front of your place. The apartments are nicely furnished, have full kitchens, ceiling fans, private verandahs, and views of the harbor.

The government wharf is on the northern side of the point. Exuma Docking Services operates the only marina in George Town, located just south of Kidd Cove. There is space there for about 40 boats, and they can take boats up to 140 feet. Many boaters become semi-permanent residents, especially during the winter, so calling ahead for dock space and space at the fueling dock is a must. Use "Sugar One" as the call name on VHF Channel 16.

The marina has full services for boaters, including fuel, water, ice, electricity, laundry, showers, marine products, liquor store, restaurant, and bar. This is the most convenient location for boaters, as you can walk right into the heart of the settlement from the dock. Sam's Place is the marina restaurant, offering tasty Bahamian dishes for lunch and dinner. If you prefer, rental cars can also be arranged through Kim Thompson and Thompson's Car Rentals.

Exuma Docking Services also owns a small resort three miles west of town called Mount Pleasant Suites Hotel. The hotel has 24 air-conditioned suites with full kitchens and a swimming pool. It's just a short walk from your suite to the white sand beach at Hooper's Bay.

George Town fronts Elizabeth Harbour, but it is also built around what locals call "the Pond," a saltwater lake connected to the harbor by a thin neck of water. The main highway bridge passes over this link, and at high tide you need to duck when going under, even in a dinghy. The Exuma Markets, next to the highway bridge, is one of the best grocery stores in the islands. Fresh produce and meats are almost always in stock, as are non-prescription medicines. As a service to boaters, and to people renting houses on the island, Exuma Markets will hold mail and faxes for you.

Minn's Water Sports, a small boat dock where you can rent or buy a Boston Whaler, and have outboard motors serviced, is on the Pond. There are several stores and shops along the road that circles the Pond. You can buy items ranging from Bahamian crafts to books, postcards, and T-shirts. Eddie's Edgewater restaurant, owned by Andrea and Rap Brown, serves breakfast, lunch, and dinner. This is the happening local place to eat, especially for the ex-pat boating crowd. The seafood is outstanding and turtle steaks are a specialty. Reservations are necessary in winter. On Monday and Thursday evening Rap Brown usually has a local rake 'n' scrape band playing, and he serves complimentary bar snacks.

The Two Turtles Inn has long been a favorite spot for budget-minded anglers fishing Exuma on their own. Centrally located in the settlement, the Inn has fourteen air-conditioned rooms, three with kitchenettes, satellite TV, plus a laid-back restaurant and bar. You can eat inside or out, and we suggest not missing the Friday-night barbecues. The Tuesday, and sometimes Monday, seafood nights are also worth a try.

Boaters and land-based visitors will find a full array of additional services available in George Town. Pay telephones are located all around the settlement, including the telephone station just south of Exuma Docking Services marina. Small groceries, liquor stores, and hardware stores usually have decent stocks of goods. The town clinic is up the hill from Club Peace & Plenty. This is one of the better Out Island clinics, with a doctor, a dentist, and nurses working somewhat regular hours. There is also a town library that has an active book swap most often used by boaters. Back on the Pond, Diane Minns has a nice gift shop called Sandpiper where she sells paperback books, postcards, ceramics, jewelry, straw bags, and a pleasing array of original Bahamian artwork.

Just south of George Town is an 80-acre peninsula that is home to February Point, one of the most upscale yet casually delightful Out Island ownership resorts. Ranging from comfortable to elegant, the ocean-view villas are accompanied by private docking facilities, a gorgeous beachfront swimming pool, tennis courts, and one of the best restaurants on the island, the Bistro.

Continuing south of George Town the highway follows the contours of the shoreline, past Master Harbour Villas, to Rolle Town, then on to the Peace & Plenty Bonefish Lodge, and the bridge leading to Little Exuma. The main highway runs the length of the island and is in good condition. There are several dirt roads on the west side of the highway that lead to the leeward flats, most notably to the Airport Flat.

The Airport Flat is one of the most glorious eye-appealing spots in the Bahamas, and one of the most-fished. The white sand bottom makes wading easy and many people wade barefoot. There is a channel between the land and the flats that you can't cross at high tide without a boat, or without swimming. While it's true that the Peace & Plenty bonefish guides try to rotate this flat (not fish it too often), anglers fishing on their own don't follow this etiquette. If you want to fish the Airport Flat just ask any taxi driver to take you. They all know the way.

The bonefish on the Airport Flat are smarter than rocket scientists. To catch these fish you must be stealthy, make long casts, and use long fluorocarbon leaders tapered down to six-pound test. And even then plan on spooking a lot more fish than you catch. A key to fishing this area without seeing any guides is to check the tides and go early or late. Peace & Plenty guides will not show up here before 8:30 A.M. and they won't be here after 4:00 P.M. Some independent guides, on the other hand, do fish the best tides whenever they occur.

Little Exuma brings back the feeling of being up north in the Exuma Cays. Only three settlements—the Ferry, Forbes Hill, and William's Town—occupy the 12-mile long and mile wide island. There are some stunning white sand flats along this stretch that merit the time of anglers who want to fish on their own. Across from the tip end of Little Exuma are O'Brian's Cay, Polly Cay, and Hog Cay. Hog Cay Cut shoots between O'Brian's and Hog Cay to offer boaters a shortcut to the southern part of Long Island, or to the Jumentos Cays and Ragged Island.

A strong current rips through Hog Cay Cut with the advancing and falling tides, making for good jack, snapper, and barracuda fishing. Hog Cay itself is privately owned, and extensively farmed by the residents. White Cay is the last piece of land in the Exumas, and is surrounded by white sand beaches. This area to the south and east of Little Exuma is superb bonefish and permit habitat. There are huge wadable flats that go dry or almost dry at low tide.

Boaters continuing on from White Cay can head east for Simms settlement on Long Island. Boaters who want to fish and explore the leeward side of Little and Great Exuma turn north after passing through Hog Cay Cut. The best flats fishing starts at the northern end of Little Exuma and runs all the way back up to Barraterre.

Fishing Highlights

There are two distinct ways to fish the Exumas. One is with a professional guide and the other is to cruise and fish on your own. Either way, you'll enjoy some of the most spectacular tropical scenery and fishing on the planet.

The Exuma fishery is unique to the Bahamas due to its central location and its length from north to south. The fishery is part of the Great Bahama Bank, which is a migratory area for tarpon and other gamefish species. It is adjacent to the deeper waters of the Tongue of the Ocean and Exuma Sound, and is sandwiched between Andros, Eleuthera, Cat Island, and Long Island. These features combine to produce high numbers of bonefish and quality offshore fishing.

The three main areas of this fishery are the Exuma Cays, the windward flats from Rolleville to Forbes Hill, and the leeward flats from the Little Exuma ferry bridge to Barraterre. Our favorite windward flats run from George Town to Mariah Harbour Cay. Anglers fishing on their own out of George Town can rent a small boat and

explore this area with confidence by using a little common sense and a tide chart. Pack a lunch and take snorkeling gear along. White sand bottoms offer good visibility for bonefish and easy wading. You can also take advantage of some consistently good reef and cut fishing.

The leeward flats are the meat of the fishery, and the area most fished by professional guides and do-it-yourself anglers. Just south of the Little Exuma ferry bridge is an extensive mangrove flats region. There is good protection from the wind here, and high numbers of bonefish. Turning north, you cruise out into deeper water that can be rough in bad weather, but you have to make this run to reach the Airport Flats.

Can flats be any flatter than this?

Between the Airport Flats and Moss Town is a chain of cays with fertile habitat for bonefish, permit, and tarpon. Local knowledge is necessary for boaters to navigate this area. Exploring in a dinghy or small boat is the way to go on your own. Green Turtle Cay, Perpalls Cay, Hog Cay, Tommy Young's Cay, and Jew Fish Cay all have good surrounding flats. Green Turtle Cut is the route most often used by boaters choosing an inshore passage. Jew Fish Cut is used by the Long Island freight boats and by boaters requiring more water.

This area has dark grass flats interspersed with white sand and coral. Mangrove bays and coves are common, providing protection and food for many smaller bonefish. Farther out to the east, Bowe Cay, Coakley Cay, and Duck Cay have flats surrounded by deeper water that hold larger bonefish and some permit. We've also seen some tarpon out here.

Continuing north to Richmond Hill and Rocky Point, anglers will find a fair selection of outside sandy flats and a varied shoreline composed mostly of mangroves. While fishing throughout this area is good, we prefer to focus more north and south.

There are more miles of wadable flats through the Exumas than any other area of the Bahamas. Usually composed of white sand and coral, these flats are fed by countless cuts, creeks, and nearby deeper ocean water. The best time to fish these flats is on the incoming tide. Water depth is especially critical. As soon as bonefish have enough water to wriggle onto a flat they will begin to feed on shrimp and crabs. Gobies and glass minnows are a primary food source near the edges of cuts and creeks. Once water depths rise past mid-calf, fish will disperse, and if mangroves are in the area, that's where they'll head.

For anglers who prefer to wade, we recommend fishing Exuma on a neap tide. This will give you more time during the day to wade your favorite flats. Be sure to check the time of day of the tides also, especially if you fish during a spring tide. On a spring tide you'll want to fish flats that are not lined with mangroves. These outside flats, or flats that extend out from various cays, will not give bonefish a place to hide. You will also find larger fish on average in these areas, plus you'll have a better chance of seeing permit.

Remember that tides are significantly different when moving from the windward to the leeward side of the island. Tides also vary two to three hours when moving from Barraterre to Little Exuma. This means anglers fishing here for a week or longer will have the opportunity to fish the tides they prefer.

The Tropic of Cancer passes just south of George Town, which means the weather in the region is more stable than it is in the northern Bahamas. Anglers looking to increase their chances of good weather, especially from December through February, should seriously consider fishing Exuma, Long Island, or the other islands to the south. Cold fronts often stall before reaching Exuma since winter winds from the southeast are more common than the northeast winds that prevail on Andros, Eleuthera, Abaco, and Grand Bahama.

When bad weather does occur, the number of wade-fishing options here means you'll still have a decent chance of catching fish. Clouds and wind will create difficult

Well, they aren't all trophies! Stephen with one of the world's smallest bonefish.

conditions, but the white sand bottoms will help with visibility, and wading anglers can set themselves up to cast in the direction they prefer. We usually choose to cast into the wind on a tough cloudy day. The wind will straighten out your backcast, help load your rod on the forward cast, and will carry any sounds away from the fish.

Bonefish are by far the number-one gamefish species in the Exumas. Fish range two to six pounds, with three pounds being average. Because of the wading opportunities, and many well-trained guides, this is an ideal location for beginning bonefishers. To improve their skills, beginners need as many opportunities, or "shots," as possible. High numbers of fish, especially in the more remote areas, will provide these shots in conditions that are often favorable.

We generally fish smaller and lighter flies on Exuma than we would on Andros or Grand Bahama. This strategy is very important on the wadable flats that receive the most pressure. A #6-8 Gotcha or Bunny Gotcha are two of the most popular bonefish flies, and this size range holds true for many other patterns as well.

When fishing a low incoming tide we recommend eyeless flies such as a Blind Gotcha, Bonefish Special, or Horror. We also like a #6 Tan Yarn Crab, a #6 Pink Bonefish Puff, a #6 Pink or Chartreuse Hoover, a #6 Bunny Bitter, a #6-8 Mantis Shrimp, and other flies that land softly. Just as important is the way you present your fly, then strip it when the time is right. We like to present the fly a good 20 feet in front of oncoming fish. It is common to see schools of 6 to 20 fish feeding in with the tide. Let your fly sink to the bottom, and then wait for the fish to work toward it. When a fish is close, just twitch the fly with the smallest of strips, and be prepared to set the hook. Don't make too long of a strip because the sudden movement will spook fish more often than not.

As water levels rise to knee-depth, a #4 Bunny Gotcha or a Becks' Sililegs are good choices for sand bottoms. For bottoms laced with grass or coral outcroppings, try a #4-6 Greg's Flats Fly. This fly is tied with a weed-guard so it won't get hung up as you hop it along the bottom. As you move out toward the edges of these wadable flats the fish will be less spooky. You'll also find larger fish, and more singles and doubles. We prefer to fish these areas from a flats boat.

Fishing here for bigger bones is like anywhere else in the Bahamas: You'll find higher numbers of big fish in deeper water. There are many flats dissected by deep blue creeks, and others that bump up against rugged coral cays with deep offside banks. The middle part of the incoming tide is best for these larger fish.

Exuma is one of the few places where we've consistently seen huge numbers of "laid-up" bonefish, fish that will hang together in large schools at the top of the tide. These fish are literally hanging out, milling around, just waiting for the tide to fall. We've seen this phenomenon more commonly on ocean-side flats and bays on other islands, but in Exuma fish displaying this behavior can be found around a variety of cays and in mangrove bays. Usually, laid-up fish are hard to catch. You can cast and cast and cast without spooking them, but they won't eat. Throughout the Exumas, however, we've found these laid-up fish to be aggressive feeders at times. Why? Who knows? Enjoy it when it happens.

Mudding is another bonefish behavior we've observed in the Exumas on a more consistent basis than on some of the other islands. Mudding is when a school of bone-fish moves out into deeper water, usually 6 to 10 feet in depth, and tears up the bottom in search of shrimp, crabs, and clams. Clouds of white mud bloom in otherwise clear water. These muds can stretch for hundreds of yards, making it easy to spot the school's location.

While we prefer not to fish muds, this is a good opportunity for beginning anglers to hook some fish. Casting a Clouser's Minnow into the leading edge of an expanding mud will usually produce repeated strikes. During bad weather and on hot days when fish have left the flats in search of cooler water, fishing the muds can provide action not available anywhere else.

We have not seen tarpon in the Exumas on a consistent basis, but to be honest, we haven't spent much time looking. Based on the habitat, which includes the Grand Bahama Bank, and access to deep water, we have to believe that decent tarpon fishing is available in some areas. Some of the independent guides are now spending more time looking for tarpon, and having some success. They are reluctant, however, to talk about their favorite spots.

We have talked with boating anglers who have seen tarpon at Pipe Creek, Darby Island, Bock Cat Cay, in the passage between Rocky Point and Richmond Hill, at Jew Fish Cay, and near the outside cays off the Airport Flat. We have also seen tarpon in this area, and have caught a few in the 60-pound class. Like elsewhere, May, June, and July are the best months.

An exception to this would be fishing for tarpon in some of the blue holes. The guides do know the holes that hold tarpon, and they are now more willing to take anglers to these spots.

Permit fishing is on par with the tarpon fishing, meaning you can never count on getting consistent shots. The outside flats and cays off the leeward side of the island lure permit out of the deeper channels throughout the year, with April through October being the best months. We have seen permit here on the backs of rays on several occasions. This is the ideal scenario, since these permit are in an eating mood. While our favorite permit flies would be Yarn Crabs, Del's Merkins, or Clouser's Minnows, tossing any fly onto the back of a ray can produce a take.

We have also seen permit hanging out with laid-up bonefish around these same outer cays at high tide. For some rea-

The waters of Exuma abound with gamefish.

son, maybe competition for food, these permit are more likely to eat than in most other situations. Anglers who are seriously on a permit hunt should spend more time in the south, from Hog Cay to White Cay and down across the sand banks to Sandy Cay. We have friends who have fished around Sandy Cay with Docky Smith from Long Island, and they report heart-stopping permit fishing, with good numbers of tailing fish. The largest landed was over 25 pounds. This is an area we look forward to exploring in the future.

Barracuda fishing is good year round over the reefs, and best on the flats from November through May. Fishing for sharks is best from April through the summer months on the flats and in the cuts and creeks.

Reef and cut fishing is outstanding throughout the Exuma Cays, and off the windward side of Great Exuma. Jacks, grouper, and snappers are available year round. Our favorite fly-fishing method is to prospect in the cuts or over the reefs during periods of strong tidal flows. We like to use #2/0 Clouser's Minnows in a variety of colors on a sinktip or full-sinking line, though fishing different types of saltwater poppers on floating lines is lots of fun for bigger horse-eye and bar jacks.

Wahoo is the premier offshore species during winter, though dorado, white marlin, and several species of tuna are available. Fishing for wahoo is great sport and these fish are hard to beat on the dinner table or in a fresh batch of ceviche. January and February are prime months for wahoo, with the best areas running from Hawksbill Cay down to Darby Island.

Fishing picks up for blue marlin, dorado, sailfish, and tuna in May. By June the fishing for these species is at its best, and this is when most offshore tournaments take place. Sailfish are found in good concentrations in the Exuma Sound throughout the summer, as are Allison and yellowfin tuna. Conventional trolling methods will produce the most consistent results, though anglers can have luck with flies as well using the appropriate teasing techniques.

Optional Activities

A variety of upscale resorts, home and villa rentals, casual hotels, good restaurants, and lots of adventure activities make Exuma an ideal choice for anglers and non-anglers to enjoy a vacation together. While boating, both sailing and motor cruising, is number one in the Exumas, diving and snorkeling are a close second. Add in sea kayaking, swimming, exploring, biking, hiking, or just catching rays while reading your favorite book, and you should have enough fun and sun to stay happy.

With the opening of the Four Seasons Resort at Emerald Bay in November 2003, the island can cater to the most discriminating traveler. Golf, tennis, and a world-class spa are just a few of the amenities you can enjoy.

The Exuma Dive Centre, located in George Town, is the premier diving operation in the Exumas. It offers a variety of dives, from working over shallow reefs and coral heads teeming with fish, to wall dives and blue-hole adventures. A resort course is available for first-time divers. Guided snorkeling is the ideal way to spend part of a day exploring the Exuma's underwater splendor, or to spear fish that can be cooked up for dinner at your hotel.

Most reef locations are near George Town, not more than a 20-minute boat ride from the dock. The Peace & Plenty properties also have a full water sports activity desk, including diving, snorkeling excursions, and small sailboat rentals.

The Exuma Dive Centre rents small boats for exploring or fishing. You can even rent a push pole and test out your ability to become a guide.

Remote small hotels such as Higgins Landing on Stocking Island are the perfect choice for eco-minded visitors. This resort has won several awards for its natural construction and use of solar power.

If you don't want to get away from it all, the atmosphere in George Town is festive and upbeat. The people are friendly and helpful. If you're looking for a party, you can usually find one, especially during the many regattas. In April, the National Family Island Regatta lures boaters from all over the world.

Lodges, Guides, and Services

Featured Lodges

Club Peace & Plenty

George Town Peace & Plenty's centerpiece is the Club, a casual 35-room Bahamian inn featuring air-conditioned rooms with private balconies, and six deluxe suites. Excellent meals are served in the dining room, and mixology wizard "Doc" Rolle runs the bar. Guests can also enjoy a freshwater swimming pool, twice-weekly cocktail parties, and live calypso music and dancing on the weekends.

The Stocking Island Beach Club is one of the main attractions for P&P guests. Swim, sail, snorkel, or fish along white sand beaches and off coral reefs. If you're looking for a place to sunbathe in total privacy you'll find it on Stocking Island. The Club operates daily ferry service to the island.

Season: October through July.

Suitable For: Anglers and non-anglers.

Optional Activities: The Club operates a full water sports program, including diving and snorkeling options. Tennis can be arranged, as can car and boat rentals.

What's Included: Complete vacation packages are available, including airport transfers, meals, accommodations, taxes, and gratuities. If you are fishing, you will stay at either the Beach Inn or Bonefish Lodge.

Not Included: Airfare to/from Exuma, optional activities.

Pricing: $$

Contact: Reservations and information, 800-525-2210 or 242-336-2551.

Internet: www.peaceandplenty.com

Peace & Plenty Beach Inn

George Town The Inn features 16 deluxe air-conditioned rooms with tile baths, ceiling fans and large balconies or terraces facing the beach. The airy indoor restaurant and bar are accompanied by a new covered terrace for lunches and dinners. A pier extending into Bonefish Bay includes a waterfront Sponge Bar. Guests can also enjoy the freshwater pool and white sand beach on Bonefish Bay. A complimentary shuttle is available to the club, and guests can eat on the "dine around plan" at the Club or the Bonefish Lodge.

Season: October through July.

Suitable For: Anglers and non-anglers.

Optional Activities: The Inn participates in the Club's full water sports program, including diving and snorkeling options. Tennis can be arranged, as can car and boat rentals.

What's Included: Complete bonefishing packages are available including airport transfers, meals, accommodations, guided fishing, taxes, and gratuities to the lodge staff.

Not Included: Airfare to/from Exuma, alcoholic beverages, gratuities to guides, and any other optional activities.

Pricing: $$-$$$

Contact: Reservations and information, 800-525-2210 or 242-345-5555.

Internet: www.peaceandplenty.com

Peace & Plenty Bonefish Lodge

Little Exuma Ferry Bridge This is the headquarters for P&P's bonefishing operation, though non-anglers will be happy here too. Eight large air-conditioned rooms feature private baths and balconies overlooking the water. An upstairs private fisherman's lounge includes a full bar, card and game room, fly-tying facilities, fishing tackle and clothing pro shop, satellite TV and video library, reading room, and sporting art gallery. Fly-fishers will enjoy more than 60 miles of expansive flats surrounding the island covered with schools of two- to six-pound bonefish, plus larger fish cruising in pairs or alone. Guided fishing is done from skiffs and by wading, with miles of wadable flats the highlight. For the non-fisherman, the Lodge participates in the Club's full water sports program, including all activities on Stocking Island. Guests can also choose to eat at the Club or the Beach Inn on the "dine around plan."

Season: October through June.

Suitable For: Anglers and non-anglers.

What's Included: Exuma airport pick-up and return, accommodations, all meals on the dine-around plan, guided fishing, hotel gratuities, and Bahamian taxes. Trips of any length are available.
Not Included: Airfare to/from Exuma, alcoholic beverages, and gratuities to guides.
Pricing: $$-$$$
Contact: Reservations and information, 800-525-2210 or 242-345-5555.
Internet: www.ppbonefishlodge.net
E-mail: info@ppbonefishlodge.net

Coconut Cove Hotel

George Town Attention to service and details combine with a casually elegant atmosphere to create this relaxing B&B–style retreat. All rooms are distinctively furnished and include queen-size beds, air-conditioning, mini-bars, ceiling fans, toiletries, bathrobes, and optional TV. The Paradise Suite features a king bed, extra-large bath with Jacuzzi, and a private hot tub on the beachside deck. The freshwater pool and bar are on the beach. The dining room serves breakfast, lunch, and dinner, with daily gourmet specialties.
Season: November through August, closed September and October.
Suitable For: Anglers and non-anglers.
Optional Activities: Diving and snorkeling arranged with Exuma Dive Centre, boat rentals for exploring and remote picnicking, sailing, biking, swimming, flats, and offshore fishing arranged with good independent fly-fishing guides.
What's Included: Usually just accommodations and taxes, though a meal plan is available. There are no set packages. Each trip is custom-designed to suit your needs. Trips of any length are available.
Pricing: $$-$$$
Not Included: Airfare to Exuma, airport transfers, alcoholic beverages, and optional activities.
Contact: Reservations and information, 242-336-2659; fax 242-336-2658.
Internet: www.bahamasvacationguide.com/coconutcove

Hotel Higgins Landing

Stocking Island Stocking Island, across Elizabeth Harbour from George Town, is four and a half miles long and half a mile wide, and is lined with numerous coves and white sand beaches and shaded by coconut palms.

Hotel Higgins Landing is on a slender piece of land that stretches from the sea to one of the lagoons. It's the only hotel on Stocking Island. Excellent snorkeling is available over the reefs on the beach side, while sea kayaking and bonefishing are prime activities on the lagoon side in Gaviota Bay.

This eco-property took almost four years to complete and was constructed to be harmonious with its surroundings. The owners of Higgins Landing, Carol and Dave Higgins, want you to know that eco-tourism is "not about giving up luxury." Each of five cottages is furnished with antiques, queen-size beds, ceiling fans, and screened windows, while large private decks present dreamlike views.

Breakfast and dinner are included in the room rate. Meals are excellent, with eggs Benedict a specialty for breakfast, and fresh seafood for dinner. Lunches are optional, and can be packed for a picnic on an even more remote cay.

The hotel is always peaceful, thanks to the resort's 100-percent use of photo-voltaic solar electricity. All cottages are equipped with 12-volt power. There is also standard 110-volt power at several locations for guests who can't give up their hair dryers, or who need to recharge a video camera battery.

Season: October through June.
Suitable For: Anglers and non-anglers.
Optional Activities: Bonefishing, offshore and reef fishing, diving, snorkeling, boat rentals, swimming, and relaxing.
What's Included: Accommodations, breakfast and dinner, evening hors d'oeuvres, transfers to/from George Town, use of snorkel gear, sunfish, kayaks, fishing equipment, windsurfers, paddleboats, beach chaises, and beach towels.
Not Included: Airfare to/from Exuma, airport transfers to/from George Town, taxes. There is no additional tipping.
Pricing: $$-$$$
Contact: Reservations and information, 242-357-0008.
Internet: www.higginslanding.com
E-mail: stockisl@aol.com

Four Seasons Great Exuma

Emerald Bay   Bask in sun and luxury in pristine Emerald Bay. The first Four Seasons resort in the Bahamas has gone all out to create an island paradise—casual and fine dining restaurants, a Greg Norman–designed golf course, Asian-influenced spa, fitness center with private trainers, freshwater pools, water sports, six Har-Tru tennis courts, children's programs, and a new marina scheduled to open in 2005. Generously sized guest rooms, suites, and villas offer sophisticated comfort designed for privacy and include CD players, private bars, high-speed Internet, and furnished terraces or balconies. The concierge desk can arrange bonefishing, reef and offshore fishing, and rental cars.
Season: October through July.
Suitable For: Anglers and non-anglers.
What's Included: Exuma airport pick-up and return and accommodations are most common, but you can book specific packages. Trips of any length are available.
Not Included: Airfare to/from Exuma, meals, optional activities, and gratuities.
Pricing: $$$$
Contact: Reservations and information, 242-336-6800.
Internet: www.fourseasons.com/greatexuma

Barraterre Bonefish Lodge

Barraterre   On the northern end of Great Exuma at the end of the road, this two-story waterfront lodge puts anglers in the perfect location to fish the area's vast remote flats. Southwest of Barraterre is a mini-marls region where anglers can rack up large numbers of bones, especially on the outside wadable flats. The guides here work on the "unlimited" fishing plan, meaning you can fish from dawn to dusk, so this is an ideal location for hard-core anglers. But guests will also be very comfortable. Six double air-conditioned rooms have twin beds, private bath, satellite TV, and ocean views. The lodge has a satellite TV lounge, bar, restaurant, and screened-in waterfront porch. Anglers fly into George Town airport, and then take a 50-minute taxi ride to the lodge. Non-anglers can visit the Four Seasons Resort at Emerald Bay for dining, shopping, and spa services.
Season: October through June.
Suitable For: Anglers.
What's Included: Exuma airport pick-up and return, accommodations, all meals and Bahamian taxes. Trips of any length are available.

Not Included: Airfare to/from Exuma, alcoholic beverages, and gratuities to guides.

Pricing: $$-$$$

Contact: Reservations and information, 772-466-8369.

Internet: www.barraterrebonefishlodge.com

E-mail: info@barraterrebonefishlodge.com

Additional Accommodations

The Palms at Three Sisters

Mount Thompson Twelve air-conditioned motel rooms on one of the prettiest beaches in the Exumas. The restaurant and bar serves a variety of seafood and rum drinks. Excellent snorkeling is right down the beach. Bonefishing guides can be arranged. You should rent a car if you stay here. The Four Seasons Resort is just three miles to the north.

Pricing: $$

Contact: Reservations and information, 242-358-4040; fax 242-358-4043.

Mount Pleasant Suites Hotel

Hooper's Bay Twenty-three one-bedroom suites and one two-bedroom suite include full kitchens, living room, dining area, and satellite TV. The same people who own the Exuma Docking Services own this facility. Hooper's Bay beach is a short walk away. Reasonable rates make this property a good choice for anglers looking to explore the island on their own. You will need a rental car if you stay here.

Pricing: $$

Contact: Reservations and information, 242-336-2960; fax 242-336-2964.

Sampson Cay Club & Marina

Sampson Cay Completely renovated in late 2003, the full-service marina can accommodate boats up to 180 feet. Refurbished rental cottages, along with spacious villas and houses, offer a range of accommodation options. The fine restaurant and swinging bar are the cool gathering places for people touring through the islands. This is a good base for anglers who want to stay in an "off the beaten bonefish path" location with non-anglers. While you can find a fishing guide at times, you can't count on it.

Pricing: $$-$$$

Contact: Reservations and information, 242-355-2034 or 866-497-7766.

Internet: www.sampsoncayclub.com

Musha Cay Resort

Musha Cay One of the most luxurious private island resorts in the world. And this isn't hype. A staff of 32 attends to a maximum of 24 guests. Accommodations range from the 10,000-square-foot Manor House to the romantic beachfront Pier House. Fine dining is in the Landings waterfront restaurant. Groups are not mixed at Musha Cay. When you reserve the cay, it's all yours. Amenities and activities include: use of five luxury boats, Hobie and Sunfish sailboats, windsurfers, jet skis, snorkeling and diving gear, swimming pools, billiard room, spa and gym. Bonefishing, blue-water fishing, water skiing, and other sports are arranged.

Pricing: $$$$
Contact: Reservations and information, 877-889-1100 or 203-602-0300.
Internet: www.mushacay.com
E-mail: mushacay@sanctuare.com

Palm Bay Beach Club

George Town   A delightful full-ownership cottage and villa resort on the waterfront of Elizabeth Harbour. The grounds are beautifully landscaped, with wooden walkways connecting the cottages, and the beach is the finest white sand. From the swimming pool and bar you have splendid views across to Stocking Island. You can keep your rental boat out front. Fishing guides can be arranged.
Pricing: $$$
Contact: Reservations and information, 242-336-2787 or 888-369-0606.
Internet: www.palmbaybeachclub.com
E-mail: info@palmbaybeachclub.com

Two Turtles Inn

George Town   Fourteen air-conditioned rooms with ceiling fans. You can feast inside or out on some of the best Bahamian food on the island. The Flyers Bar is a local hotspot for Happy Hour. Special meal events are held twice a week. Snorkeling and diving and fishing guides can be arranged by the hotel. This is a popular spot due to the friendly atmosphere and economical prices, so we recommend booking well in advance.
Pricing: $$
Contact: Reservations and information, 242-336-2545 or 800-688-4752; fax 242-336-2528.
E-mail: info@twoturtlesinn.com

February Point Resort Estates

George Town   Two- and three-bedroom deluxe oceanfront villas on a private 80-acre peninsula minutes south of George Town. Villas and home sites in this resort community are for sale, but villas are also rented by the night or week. Spacious villas have ocean and beach views, A/C, full kitchen facilities, and are beautifully furnished. Resort amenities include freshwater infinity pool, tennis courts, private docking facilities, and one of the best restaurants on the island. This is a prime luxury location for fishing or vacationing.
Pricing: $$$-$$$$
Contact: Reservations and information, 242-336-2661 or 242-327-1567.
Internet: www.februarypoint.com
E-mail: info@februarypoint.com

Do-It-Yourself Options

Fowl Cay Resort

Fowl Cay   A magnificent private island resort situated between Sampson Cay to the north, and Staniel Cay to the south. The clubhouse and restaurant sit atop the island's highest point, about 40 feet above the water, creating spectacular views of crystalline sunrises and dramatic sunsets. The freshwater pool, restaurant, and bar are located here. The clubhouse also has an exercise room with free weights, treadmill, and elliptical trainer. The guest villas are nearby on a powdery white beach.

Each villa is air-conditioned and furnished in a casually elegant island style. Satellite TV and CD players are among the amenities. Guests also have the use of a tennis court, sea kayaks, outboard runabout, volleyball court, Zuma sailboats, and beach grills. You can fish on your own, or the resort managers can arrange for a professional bonefishing guide.

Season: October through July.

Suitable For: Anglers and non-anglers.

What's Included: Accommodations, meals, all amenities, and equipment on the island.

Not Included: Airfare to/from Staniel Cay, or private boat charter to Fowl Cay. Boat transfers from Staniel Cay. Fishing guides. Gratuities.

Pricing: $$$-$$$$

Contact: Reservations and information, 804-288-1081 or 866-369-5229.

Internet: www.fowlcay.com

E-mail: reservations@fowlcay.com

Staniel Cay Yacht Club

Staniel Cay   Six air-conditioned waterfront cottages with private balconies serve up stunning views of the ocean and the sunset. The restaurant and bar are lively gathering places for the boating crowd. The fresh seafood is excellent. You can rent a boat and explore on your own, or fishing guides can be arranged. Most people arrive here by boat. For flight information, call Executive Air Travel at 954-224-6022, or ask the Club for information.

Season: October through July.

Suitable For: Anglers and non-anglers.

What's Included: Accommodations and meals, or just rent a room.

Not Included: Airfare to/from Staniel Cay, or private boat charter to Staniel Cay. Fishing guides, boat rental, optional activities, and gratuities.

Pricing: $$-$$$

Contact: Reservations and information, 242-355-2024 or 954-467-8920.

Internet: www.stanielcay.com

Regatta Point

George Town   This all-suites property is set on a finger of land almost surrounded by the waters of Elizabeth Harbour. The six suites and cottages, complete with kitchens, have panoramic views of the harbor, the marina, and Crab Cay, and you can walk into town via a short causeway in five minutes. All guests have the complimentary use of a private beach, Sunfish sailboats, and bicycles. Your rental boat can be tied up right in front of your suite. You can hire an independent fishing guide or fish on your own. This location is hard to beat for convenience, price, independence, and charm.

Season: October through July.

Suitable For: Anglers and non-anglers.

What's Included: Accommodations.

Not Included: Airfare to/from George Town, transportation, meals, fishing guides, boat rental, optional activities, and gratuities.

Pricing: $$

Contact: Reservations and information, 242-336-2206 or 888-720-0011.

Internet: www.regattapointbahamas.com

E-mail: mmnoll@earthlink.net

Master Harbour Villas

Elizabeth Harbour/Master Harbour   Located three miles south of George Town on an idyllic beach, the air-conditioned villas (four total villas—one 1-bedroom, two 2-bedroom, one 4-bedroom) are comfortably furnished and have full kitchens, washer, air-conditioning, outdoor grills, and porches. Bonefish flats are within walking distance. For convenience, you need to rent a car if you stay here. Boat rentals can be arranged and a 100-foot dock is available for your use. You can book your own independent fishing guides, who will pick you up here, or fish on your own. Owner Jerry Lewless is a fine host, very helpful and accommodating.

Season: October through July.

Suitable For: Anglers and non-anglers.

What's Included: Accommodations.

Not Included: Airfare to/from George Town, transportation, meals, fishing guides, boat rental, optional activities, and gratuities.

Pricing: $$

Contact: Reservations and information, 242-345-5076, cell 242-357-0636.

Internet: www.bahamasvacationguide.com/masterharbourvillas.html

Independent Guides

There are a number of independent guides throughout the Exuma Cays and on Great and Little Exuma. It is best to book most of these guides through your hotel or a local marina.

The guides we recommend on Great Exuma are *JJ Dames, Garth Thompson, Reno Rolle*, and *Drex Rolle.* They are part of the Exuma Guides Association, and have formed ExumaBonefish.com. Their Web site provides detailed information on each guide, pricing for guide trips, a booking form, information on flies, and more. Visit their site at www.ExumaBonefish.com.

Services

Air Charters: There are many air charter services available from Florida and Nassau.

Fandango Air: Air charter services between Ft. Lauderdale and George Town. Contact: 954-462-2552.

Stella Maris Charters: Air charter services between Nassau, George Town, and Long Island. Contact: 954-359-8236 or 242-336-2106.

Diving and Snorkeling: A number of operators offer equipment and services. With proper caution, there are many areas you can snorkel on your own. You can also book diving and snorkeling trips through most hotels.

Exuma Dive Centre, in George Town offers resort courses for beginners, while advanced divers will enjoy wall and blue-hole dives. Equipment is provided. They also rent small boats and motor scooters. Guided bonefishing can be arranged with the island's independent guides, and offshore boats can be chartered. Reservations and information, 242-336-2390 or 800-874-7213; fax 242-336-2391. E-mail: exumadive@batelnet.bs

Exuma Fantasea specialize in eco-diving and snorkeling, and they also rent boats. Reservations and information, 242-336-3483.

Marinas: *Exuma Docking Services* is the only marina in George Town. Full services for boaters. Monitors VHF Channel 16, call for "Sugar One." Rental cars are available. Sammy's Place restaurant is a nice lunch spot, and well-stocked liquor store is on site. You need to call ahead for slip reservations, and space at the fueling dock. Contact: Reservations and information, 242-336-2578; fax 242-336-2023. Hours: Monday through Saturday 7:00 A.M. to 6:00 P.M., Sunday 8:00 A.M. to 1:00 P.M.

Restaurants: *Eddie's Edgewater* is a must for fresh seafood, turtle steak, and to experience the island "scene." You need reservations. The *Bistro* at February Point serves a variety of delicious dishes in a casually elegant atmosphere. This is a romantic dinner spot. All three P&P properties have good restaurants. Reservations are advised. The *Two Turtles Inn* has specialty nights for barbecue and seafood. *Coconut Cove* offers waterfront dining outside. The *Four Seasons Hotel* is the "in" place to eat as of late 2004. Choose from the chic Italian *Il Cielo*, or the casual *Sea Breeze Grill*. For a Sunday lunch, the pig roast at *Chat & Chill* on Stocking Island is the place.

Car Rentals: You can rent cars through most hotels. In George Town, call Kim Thompson at *Thompson's Rentals* 242-336-2442. Kim will leave rental cars for you at the airport to save you the expense of a taxi in getting to her office in George Town to sign the rental agreement. You can also leave your car at the airport on your way home.

Taxi Service: Lots of taxis on the island and service is reliable. Most hotels will arrange for a specific driver to meet you at the airport, or you can just pick the first driver you see. Always ask about the fare to a specific location before hiring a taxi.

Out Island Regatta: The yachting event of the season, held in April. If you like to party, this is the time to visit George Town. Make your reservations well in advance.

Banks: The *Bank of Nova Scotia* in George Town is open Monday through Friday, 9:30 A.M. to 3:00 P.M.

Clinics: The George Town medical clinic is the best on the island.

Government: *Exuma Tourist Office*: 242-336-2430; fax 242-336-2431.

New Developments

Spurred by the opening (finally) in November 2003 of the Four Seasons Resort at Emerald Bay, development has boomed. Much of the activity is in the upscale home and villa market. February Point began a new phase of oceanfront villas and luxury homes in 2004. Palm Bay Beach Club is projecting a 2005 completion date for their new phase of villas and cottages. Another developer has proposed plans for a golf course resort community just north of George Town.

The biggest news, and the ritziest development, is at Crab Cay in Elizabeth Harbour. Accessible only by water (about 200 feet from the mainland), either by private boat or the Club's Hinkley tender, the cay is ringed with pristine powder-white beaches and quiet coves lined with black coral. A 15-acre private docking facility and arrival center is being constructed on the mainland. Transportation on the cay is by golf cart only.

This exclusive private island community expects to have 58 estate enclaves, 34 villas, and 20 beach club cottages along with a mega-yacht marina, several restaurants, a beach pavilion, and distinctive thalassotherapy spa. Each guest or resident will also be assigned a personal concierge during their time on the cay. Check out the Web site at www.crabcay.com.

We have heard that the Palms at Three Sisters property was being sold (as of August 2004), and that the new owners have plans to upgrade and expand the facilities.

For more updates, see our Web site at www.bahamasflyfishingguide.com.

CHAPTER 11

CAT ISLAND

A commercial boat stands out at the dock. (Brian O'Keefe)

One hundred thirty miles southeast of Nassau, and a little more than 30 miles southeast of Eleuthera, Cat Island is 48 miles long and 1 to 4 miles wide. The island's name probably came from Arthur Catt, the British sea captain and notorious pirate. This boot-shaped island is one of the most beautiful and fertile Out Islands, with miles of unspoiled pink sand beaches set against tall green bluffs and rugged forest-covered hills. Just outside New Bight, Mt. Alvernia's peak reaches 206 feet, one of the highest points in the Bahamas. Atop the peak sits the Hermitage, the final home and burial site of the famous religious leader and hermit, Father Jerome.

Cat Island, like many of its neighboring islands, was once a thriving Loyalist colony. Cotton plantations established during the 1700s prospered until the abolition of slavery. Now, as a reminder of the past, vine-covered ruined mansions and stone walls mingle with tropical flowers, wild grass, and sand dunes. Many of the early settlers ended up moving back to the United States. Others stayed, with their descendants still living in the same towns. Over the past few years some of the original settlers' descendants began moving back to the island. Evidence of this can be seen in the elegant new homes going up on some of the prettiest beaches around the island.

Cat Islanders live by a simple day-to-day philosophy: "What nature and the Lord will provide." People here are known for their ingenuity at using available materials to make or build whatever they need. Musical instruments are a good example. A piece of wood, some fishing line and a worn tin tub are combined to create the bass instrument in a "rake 'n' scrape" band. A conch shell is used as a horn, while an old comb covered with paper works as a harmonica. The saw is a unique instrument played throughout the Bahamas, while a goatskin stretched over a piece of rounded wood makes a great drum. By using all of these instruments together, Cat Island bands produce a unique sound.

If you want to learn about the history of the Bahamas, asking long-time Cat Island residents is one of the most interesting ways to do so. These people love to tell engrossing stories. One of their favorites is about Christopher Columbus. If you think Columbus originally landed on San Salvador, don't mention it. Cat Islanders are vehement in their belief that Columbus landed on their island first. They also believe that Bahamian music, and many Bahamian myths, was spawned from their shores. Superstition here is equal to that on Andros Island. The saying, "I'll be with you in spirit," is put into action. When the last of a generation dies, his or her house is left for the spirit to live in. Surviving relatives then gather stones from the site and build a new dwelling. On many parts of the island, especially up north, locals anchor spindles atop their roofs to ward off danger and evil spirits.

The main highway from Orange Creek in the north to Hawk's Nest and Port Howe in the south is in good shape. While you could drive the length of the island in one day, you'll need two days if you want to do any exploring. There are so many small settlements that you won't average more than 30 miles an hour. And be careful of all the basketball-playing children. Hoops are set up all along the roadsides, with the pavement used as the court.

The population of Cat Island is a little over 2,000. Fishing and farming are the mainstays of the economy. Tomatoes and pineapples are the primary crops, with watermelons, bananas, and peas also exported to the other islands. Tourism is growing as more and more vacationers discover this splendid remote island.

Cat Island does not have as many anchorages and harbors as some of the other islands, which is one of the reasons it has remained on the quiet side of general tourism. Reefs that make anchoring difficult and dangerous until you reach the southern end of the island and Port Howe protect the wild and awe-inspiring eastern coast, called the "north shore" by locals. The beaches along this coastline are the most dramatically inviting stretches of sand in the Bahamas.

Diving and snorkeling are excellent around Cat Island, while hiking, biking, and sea kayaking are also popular. If you're looking for action, however, you'll need to look elsewhere. Cat Island is peaceful, relaxing, and soothing, an ideal place for a honeymoon, a quiet family vacation, and a little fishing.

Bahamasair flies two to three times a week from Nassau to Arthur's Town and New Bight, but Cat Island Air and Southern Air provide the best and most reliable commercial air service. Fernandez Bay Village operates their own air charter service, and it's one of our favorite places to stay. Owned and operated by Pam and Tony Armbrister, this small casually deluxe resort is on a picturesque crescent-shaped beach that's ideal for swimming and snorkeling. Good bonefishing that you can enjoy on your own is a ten-minute bike ride away.

Greenwood Beach Resort and Hawk's Nest Resort & Marina also offer air charter service to New Bight, and to the airstrip at Hawk's Nest settlement. Tom Jones Charters and Island Wings are two other air charter services that fly here on a regular basis.

Around the Island

Most visiting anglers and vacationers fly to Cat Island, arriving either at Arthur's Town or New Bight. Arthur's Town is the government headquarters for the north end of the island. The settlement expands out around a grass park where children play basketball and soccer. A telephone station, police station, and clinic are nearby. Several small grocery stores are well stocked when the freight boat arrives. The best place to eat is Pat Rolle's Cookie House Bakery on the north side of town. We like to eat lunch there when we drive up to Orange Creek to fish for the day.

Orange Creek is the northernmost settlement on the island. The Orange Creek Inn has 16 motel-style rooms, a store, and a telephone. A long white sandbar stretches across much of the entrance to Orange Creek itself, and this bar goes almost dry at low tide. Waves create a white-capped rip especially during the last of the falling tide. A rough dirt road runs up the southern side of the creek, providing wading access to good bonefishing flats, but you have to fish the last of the falling or first of the incoming tide. Once the water gets up, you could become stranded if you've wandered too far to the north side of the creek.

Orange Creek is best fished and explored from a Boston Whaler or dinghy. A number of houses are for rent in this area, a couple of which include a boat and car. If you decide to rent a house here, be sure you have a car and boat or you won't have the land and water access you need to enjoy your vacation.

If you keep driving along the Orange Creek road you'll end up on a secluded white sand beach. Before you reach the beach you'll think you're lost, that the road has ended, but don't worry, just keep driving. This is a wonderful secluded beach for picnicking, swimming, and snorkeling when the weather is good. From here you can hike to the rugged northern point of the island. The view is worth the walk.

About 15 miles south of Arthur's Town is Bennett's Harbour, one of the island's oldest settlements. There are bonefish flats here and there along this drive that can be fished at the lower tidal stages. Once you reach the settlement you need to turn right to get to the mail boat dock and the various rental houses. You might get lost, as the narrow roads are confusing. But don't worry, you'll probably see a few local women on their way to socialize at the dock. In exchange for a ride, you'll get directions and as many interesting stories as you want to listen to.

There is a white sand beach just north of the mouth of Bennett's Creek where several rental houses are located. The tidal flow in and out of the creek moves at river speed. The government dock is on the northeast side of the creek. If you want fresh-baked

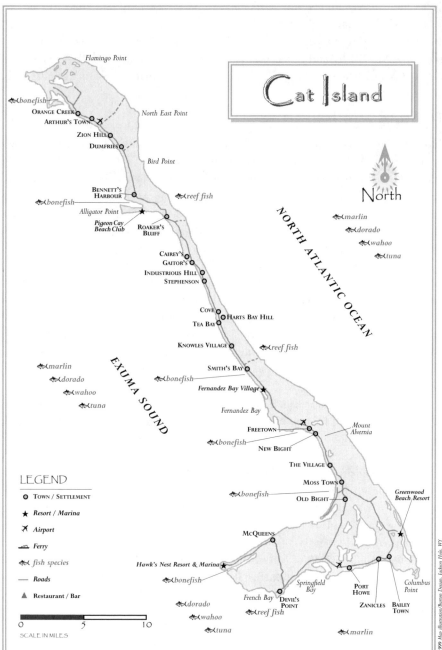

Cat Island

North

NORTH ATLANTIC OCEAN

EXUMA SOUND

Flamingo Point

bonefish

ORANGE CREEK
ARTHUR'S TOWN

North East Point

ZION HILL
DUMFRIES

Bird Point

BENNETT'S
HARBOUR

bonefish

reef fish

Alligator Point

Pigeon Cay
Beach Club

ROAKER'S
BLUFF

CAIREY'S
GAITOR'S
INDUSTRIOUS HILL
STEPHENSON

COVE   HARTS BAY HILL
TEA BAY

KNOWLES VILLAGE

reef fish

SMITH'S BAY

bonefish

Fernandez Bay Village

Fernandez Bay

marlin
dorado
wahoo
tuna

FREETOWN

Mount
Alvernia

bonefish

NEW BIGHT

THE VILLAGE

MOSS TOWN

bonefish

OLD BIGHT

Greenwood
Beach Resort

marlin
dorado
wahoo
tuna

McQUEENS

Hawk's Nest Resort & Marina

bonefish

dorado
wahoo
tuna

French Bay

Springfield
Bay

DEVIL'S
POINT

PORT
HOWE

ZANICLES

Columbus
Point

BAILEY
TOWN

reef fish

marlin

LEGEND

Town / Settlement
Resort / Marina
Airport
Ferry
fish species
Roads
Restaurant / Bar

0   5   10
SCALE IN MILES

© 1999 Map illustration/Burton Design, Jackson Hole, WY

bread for breakfast, or to make sandwiches, you can buy it here every morning. The creek winds inland for over a mile and spreads out through a maze of mangroves. Bonefishing here can be good during the lower stages of the tide, but be careful of the softer bottoms that can suck you in to your knees. This creek is best explored and fished from a small boat.

Boaters tell us that the anchorage is good in Bennett's Harbour in most weather conditions, but caution is advised when entering the harbor due to the strong tidal flows and accumulated sand that is ever shifting. Most boaters prefer to remain anchored outside the harbor over the hard sand bottom.

On the south side of Alligator Point is the Pigeon Cay Beach Club, the best place to stay to enjoy the northern portion of Cat Island. This is an idyllic do-it-yourself resort with seven deluxe cottages set steps away from the powdery beach. You can cook your own meals here or the resort will provide a cook and stock your refrigerator before you arrive. Anglers can fish several miles of beachfront flats, Bennett Creek, or cruise over to the north shore.

From Alligator Point to Smith's Bay the highway serpentines through one small settlement after another. There are a couple of small flats and reef areas where you can catch bonefish, jacks, and snappers, but this is not an area to spend much time fishing, and there aren't many beaches. The real treasure along this stretch of the island is the exquisitely wild and rugged north shore. There are five or six rutted dirt tracks that cut across the island from the highway to reach this magnificent area. Rental car companies will make you sign a release promising not to drive on these dirt tracks, so what you do is up to you. Hiking and biking are alternative methods to reach this must see part of the island.

The track we most often take is just north of Smith's Bay. If you're staying at Fernandez Bay Village, you can pack a picnic lunch and ride your bikes to the north shore. Be sure to wear long pants for the bike ride because some thorny bushes encroach on the track, and don't forget your fly rod. Once you arrive, you can walk for miles along deserted pink sand beaches, at times crossing black coral outcroppings to reach the next beach. White-capped waves wash over the outer reef, while inside are many tidal pools bustling with sea life. You can walk out through these pools on hard sand and coral to reach ocean flats and coral drop-offs. We've caught some big bonefish out here, though we've never seen much in the way of numbers. The best fishing is in the cuts and along the drop-offs for jacks, snappers, mackerel, and grouper. This is great sport with a floating line, long leader, and big Clouser's Minnow. Take plenty of flies because the bigger jacks and snappers will often break you off on the coral. Wire shock tippet is a good idea.

Back on the civilized side of the island, Smith's Bay offers anchorages for boaters that can include fuel delivery. The freight boat makes regular visits to pick up produce being shipped to Nassau. To the south of the dock is a large protected flat that bonefish cruise on the incoming tide, though these fish are spooky due to angling pressure. The flat is mostly hard sand with areas of softer mud to watch out for. The bottom is uneven in the middle, with deeper troughs that might surprise you if you're not careful. The ocean-side shore and back of the bay are lined with mangroves. At high tide, the bone-fish disperse through the mangroves and are unreachable.

To the south is Fernandez Bay Village, one of the most picturesque and laid-back resorts in the Caribbean. The resort was established in 1980 by the Armbrister family, and it's dedicated to warm and welcoming personalized service. Twelve oceanfront villas and cottages are strung along a mile of sugary beach, tucked between shady casuarinas and vibrant red hibiscus. Diving, snorkeling, swimming, exploring, and fishing are the main activities, though just laying on the beach or in a hammock takes up its share of time for many visitors. Guided flats, reef, and offshore fishing can be arranged for guests of the resort. You can also rent the resort's Boston Whaler to reach flats that are only accessible by boat.

Meals are served in the open-air dining room and on the beachside terrace. Buffet dinners on the beach are outstanding, with fresh seafood, beef, salads, and fruits as specialties. Call ahead for dinner reservations if you're not staying at the resort. If you're staying in one of the villas, you'll have a full kitchen that you can stock from the resort's store or from one of the markets in New Bight.

In good weather boaters can anchor off the resort and enjoy the clear aquamarine water. The creek system south of the resort can be explored by dinghy or sea kayak. This looks like perfect bonefish habitat, but we've never seen more than a couple of fish here. You can hook into some big barracuda at the creek mouth, especially on the falling tide.

South of Fernandez Bay is the New Bight airport, then the settlement itself. On the way you'll pass the Bridge Inn, a local motel with a good restaurant and bar. For a few extra bucks you can get a room with air-conditioning. Just north of the motel is a dirt road that runs along the edge of an inland lagoon that is home to bonefish, permit, and tarpon. We've caught bonefish and tarpon here, but have never seen the permit. This is a fun place to fish on a sunny day when you can see into the water. On a cloudy day you can sometimes catch fish blind casting.

New Bight has a good grocery store that is usually well stocked with frozen chicken, produce, and breakfast foods. A liquor store is next-door, and you can rent a car at the service station. This is also the government headquarters for South Cat Island. Adjacent to the commissioner's office is the trail leading up to the top of Mt. Alvernia and the Hermitage.

Four miles farther south is Old Bight. Before you reach the settlement you'll come to a roundabout. Going left, or southeast, you'll head toward the Greenwood Beach Resort and Port Howe. On the southwest side of the roundabout is a narrow dirt track. You can drive onto this track to gain access to a good bonefish flat that is best fished on a neap tide. This flat gets fished on a regular basis, however, so you'll need to use long fluorocarbon leaders and small flies.

Continuing on past the roundabout toward Old Bight you can take the auxiliary road along a nice stretch of beach, and in season you can stop to collect pineapples. A telephone station, laundromat, nurse-staffed clinic, and two small grocery stores are available in the settlement.

If you drive to Port Howe you'll pass a huge landlocked lake on the west side of the road. There are actually many lakes in this area that hold tarpon, jacks, and cubera snapper. A couple of our friends who stay at Hawk's Nest report good tarpon fishing in several of the mangrove-lined bays to the west; tarpon in the 10- to 30-pound range, plus exciting cubera action with fish up to 50 pounds.

The turn-off to the Greenwood Beach Resort is just past the ruins of an old mansion on the left side of the road, but trust us, it's easy to miss, so pay close attention if you're going here. The resort overlooks miles of virgin beach and the deep blue waters of the Atlantic. The 20 rooms are comfortable and clean and cooled with ceiling fans, though some now have air-conditioning. The clubhouse has a restaurant, bar, and quaint library. The main attraction here is the diving and snorkeling. In fact, the resort has the island's best dive operation. Beginner snorkeling and diving courses and outings are available, while advanced divers can enjoy awesome wall diving. The secret here is that there is very good bonefishing throughout the area, especially on the oceanfront flats and in the creeks to the south.

If you drive past Port Howe toward Dolphin Head and Devil's Point, you'll be treated to a mesmerizingly beautiful coastline. Near the settlement of Devil's Point there are glistening coral beaches ideal for shelling. On calm days there is good fishing from various rock outcroppings for jacks, snappers, and grouper. There are also a number of creeks with flats that hold good numbers of bonefish. This area has been somewhat "discovered" by anglers, but is still a nice remote option for those who want to fish on their own.

To reach Hawk's Nest you have to turn right off the highway before Devil's Point. This will take you back north to McQueens, which is on the leeward shore. Hawk's Nest Resort and Marina is on the southwestern tip of the island and is one of the best reef and offshore fishing locations in the Bahamas. The fishing grounds between Hawk's Nest and Devil's Point are excellent, with deep ocean water pushing in close to the shoreline. As you continue south to Tarter Bank, the fishing just keeps getting better. Boaters can also take a line straight north along the bank drop-off for consistent action. Marlin, sailfish, wahoo, tuna, dorado, amberjack, kingfish, and trevally are in abundance in season.

The Hawk's Nest Resort and Marina was renovated and expanded in 2002 and 2003. The marina, nestled across from the resort in Hawk's Nest Creek, now has 28 slips, fuel, electricity, water, and ice. A fully equipped dive shop is located in the marina. Diving and snorkeling excursions can be scheduled for guests of all ability levels. You can also rent bicycles and small boats to explore and fish on your own.

The resort sits on a wide beach facing the Exuma Sound where the tranquil waters are ideal for swimming. Ten cheerful air-conditioned guestrooms have ocean-facing patios, and there's also a two-bedroom house available for rent. A relaxing pool area is adjacent to the beach. The restaurant serves a variety of delicious dishes including grilled wahoo and rack of lamb.

Both Hawk's Nest Creek and Cove Creek have enticing bonefish flats that are rarely fished since most anglers here focus on the blue-water action.

Fishing Highlights

The Cat Island fishing grounds are sandwiched between the Exuma Sound and the blue waters of the Atlantic Ocean. The leeward side of the island does not have the miles of sprawling wadable flats found in the Exumas and on Long Island (see the following chapter). Deeper water pushes in much closer to land here. Most of the bonefishing flats along the west coast are inside protected bays and creeks, or just outside these areas along stretches of white sand beaches. For anglers willing to search out these spots, however, the fishing can be extremely rewarding.

Stephen hooks a hefty bonefish.

Fishing the incoming tide usually produces the best results, though the last of the falling tide is also good. Water depths, along with bottom and shoreline structure, are the keys to setting yourself up to find the most fish. Bonefish will move into feeding areas when water levels reach a certain point and keep moving at that depth. Bones like to follow shoreline structure and trough contours that run through the flats. This is really noticeable in Smith Bay, for example, where the bonefish follow the same pattern every day. Our favorite flies include #4-8 Gotchas, #6 Bunny Gotchas, #6-8 Pink Hoovers, #6 Mantis Shrimp, and #6 Tan Yarn Crabs.

The east coast, or "north shore" of the island, has some of the best wadable reef fishing anywhere. Add in the dramatic rugged setting complete with miles of untracked pink sand beaches and you have a unique location worth a special trip. Hard sand, smooth coral, and rough jagged coral laced with irregular holes make up the bottom structure of the inshore fishery. You are completely "out there" in terms of remoteness, especially if you've walked a mile or two from where you accessed the beach, so be careful walking on the coral. A bad cut or broken ankle here could be a major problem.

Ocean bonefish are usually looking for crabs. A small brown or green Yarn Crab, a Turneffe Crab, or a Bunny Bitters are our favorite flies. When you hook up expect your fish to make a run for the reef. The game here is to keep that silver bullet from making it over the edge.

The best time to fish for bonefish is at the bottom of the tide, when the water is slack, though the last of the falling and first of the incoming are good. This is also the prime time to fish for grouper. You can walk right out to the edges of the reef and cast Clouser's Minnows along the drop-off. Let your fly get down at least 10 feet, then make a jigging retrieve. You should be able to see the take most of the time. We recommend using wire shock tippet.

Amazing numbers of bonefish can be found here.

Along with grouper, you might catch several kinds of jacks or snappers fishing this way, though these fish like a little more tidal flow. The last half of the falling tide is best for the bigger jacks, especially in the coral cuts. We like to fish baitfish imitations like Sea Habits, Sardinas, and Abel Anchovies, though Edgewater Poppers work well at times. For the bigger jacks you might have to take a little pounding from the waves to reach the better spots. Just be careful.

If you're into spin fishing, take a variety of spoons and plugs. With long casts you'll be able to avoid the waves and reach the fish consistently. Carry plenty of lures because you'll definitely break off a number of fish.

The southern coast of the island produces the best boat-accessed reef fishing and the best offshore fishing. Blue water pushes in close here so short runs will get you into the action. Blue marlin and sailfish turn up throughout the year, though the best months are May through July; good numbers sometimes linger through the summer.

Kingfish, blackfin, bluefin, Allison, and yellowfin tuna are also at their peak during this time period, though April can be a good month for yellowfin too. Dorado can be good through the winter but late spring is usually best. The prime winter gamefish is wahoo, with January and February producing the highest numbers.

Reef fishing for jacks, snappers, mackerel, and grouper is good year round, with amberjack best November through May. Trevally fishing is best March through July.

Cat Island's location east of the Exuma Sound means good weather prevails throughout most of the year. Cold fronts moving down from Florida often stall before crossing the Sound. It is not uncommon to be sitting on a beachside terrace facing west under a clear star-filled sky watching dazzling lighting storms over the Exuma Cays.

When the weather is good, the bonefishing is usually good. During storms the fish stay off in deeper water. As for permit, we have never seen one on the western flats. The few guides on the island report that permit rarely turn up in numbers, though the Orange Creek area is fair May through July. If you want to catch a tarpon, you'll have your best chance in the lakes at the south end of the island, or in some of the blue holes. If you're an adventurous angler looking to fish and explore on your own, you ought to explore some of these lake areas that have rarely been fished.

Optional Activities

Snorkeling, diving, swimming, exploring, windsurfing, and sea kayaking are the main make-your-own-fun activities. Bring along several good books and lots of suntan lotion. Many visitors spend two to three weeks on the island. If you want to turn into a vegetable for a while, Cat Island is the place. If you're looking for lots of things to do, including nightlife, you need to go somewhere else.

If you want some structure, staying at one of the resorts is the best plan. At Fernandez Bay Village you can be left completely alone, or you can participate in daily activities such as snorkeling tours and evening buffet dinners. Bicycles, sea kayaks, and Boston Whalers are available to guests. Rental cars are easily arranged. We recommend getting a car for at least a day or two to explore the island. If you're into diving, Greenwood Beach Resort is the best option. Most offshore anglers stay at Hawk's Nest Resort and Marina. If you want to be completely on your own, there are a number of houses you can rent.

Visiting the Hermitage atop Mt. Alvernia is one of the sort-of-mandatory things to do. Father Jerome retired here and spent the last 12 or so years of his life as a hermit. His final religious act was to carve the steps to the top of the mountain, including the carvings of the 14 Stations of the Cross that represent events from the Passion of Christ. Visitors begin the hike to the Hermitage next to the Commissioner's office in New Bight. You will definitely spend some energy climbing to the top, but the panoramic view of the ocean on both sides of the island is spectacular. Don't forget your camera.

Lodging and Services

Featured Lodges

Fernandez Bay Village

New Bight Fernandez Bay Village rests on a crescent-shaped mile of sugary white sand beach. Twelve seaside villas and cottages are just steps away from the water. Villas are equipped with full housekeeping items, so you can cook your own meals if you choose. Fish, snorkel, explore, bike, hike, eat, drink and dance; and if this wears you out, just kick back and relax. Dinners are served on the beachside terrace, usually in front of a blazing bonfire. Shoes are not part of the dress code. The beachfront tiki bar is run on the honor system. Most bonefishing is done by wading. You can go out to fish for two hours, half a day, or a full day, whatever your pleasure. This is an ideal location for couples and families. Any length of stay is available.
Season: October through July.

Suitable For: Anglers and non-anglers.

What's Included: All-inclusive packages are available—accommodations, charter flight Nassau/Cat Island, meals, and Bahamian taxes. Or just book a room.

Not Included: Airfare to/from New Bight, meals, (though a meal plan is available), alcoholic beverages, guided fishing or fishing tackle. You can book guided fishing in advance, or wait until you arrive at the resort.

Contact: Reservations and information, 800-940-1905; fax 954 474-4864. On the island, 242-342-3043; fax 242-342-3051.

Pricing: $$-$$$

Internet: www.fernandezbayvillage.com

E-mail: catisland@fernandezbayvillage.com

Hawk's Nest Resort and Marina

Devil's Point Located at the southwest tip of the island on a white sand beach, this is a truly out-of-the-way resort. Ten rooms and one two-bedroom house are on the waterfront. The 28-slip marina was completely renovated and expanded in 2002 and provides a range of services to boaters. The resort has a good restaurant, bar, swimming pool, and full-service dive shop. Snorkeling around the point is wonderful, and the tranquil beach is ideal for swimming and catching rays. This is the best location on the island for offshore and reef fishing. Bonefish flats and creeks are relatively nearby.

Season: October through July.

Suitable For: Anglers and non-anglers.

What's Included: Accommodations, meals, and offshore fishing can be combined in one package or you can book accommodations only and then fishing, diving, and other activities separately. Bahamian taxes.

Not Included: Airfare to/from New Bight, meals, (though a meal plan is available), alcoholic beverages, guided fishing or fishing tackle. You can book guided fishing in advance, or wait until you arrive at the resort. We recommend renting a car at this location.

Pricing: $$-$$$

Contact: Reservations and information telephone/fax, 242-342-7050.

Internet: www.hawks-nest.com

Greenwood Beach Resort

Port Howe Set on an eight-mile stretch of stunning Atlantic beach, the resort has 20 brightly painted rooms cooled by the ocean breeze and ceiling fans. A few rooms now have air-conditioning. The large clubhouse is the center of activity and it includes a restaurant, bar, satellite TV, and long terraces overlooking the ocean. A swimming pool is set in the gardens near the beach. The Cat Island Dive Center, an independent PADI dive operation, is located in the resort. They offer a variety of diving and snorkeling programs, including some spectacular wall dives. Boat and car rentals can be arranged. We recommend renting a car at this location. Offshore, reef, and flats fishing guides can be arranged.

Pricing: $$-$$$

Contact: Reservations and information, 242-342-3053 or 877-228-7475.

Internet: www.greenwoodbeachresort.com

E-mail: info@greenwoodbeachresort.com

Pigeon Cay Beach Club

Alligator Point   If you're looking for a remote escape, Pigeon Cay Beach Club might be the spot. They are located one mile off the main island road near Alligator Point, close to the settlement of The Bluff. The Beach Club has seven self-catering cottages, all just steps away from the sea. Each cottage is uniquely decorated in a southwestern Caribbean style. Local stone and stucco, tile and wood floors are used throughout. A full-service beach bar and barbecue area are on the white sand beach. You'll find this a great spot to hang out after a day or exploring, fishing, diving, or snorkeling, and you'll be hard pressed to find a better spot to catch a beautiful Bahamian sunset. Rental cars are available. Fishing guides can be arranged.

Season: October through July.

Suitable For: Anglers and non-anglers.

What's Included: Accommodations and Bahamian taxes.

Not Included: Airfare to/from New Bight or Arthur's Town, airport transfers, rental car, meals, alcoholic beverages, guided fishing, or fishing tackle. You can book guided fishing in advance, or wait until you arrive at the resort. You need to rent a car at this location to enjoy the island.

Pricing: $-$$

Contact: Reservations and information, 242-354-5084.

Internet: www.pigeoncay-bahamas.com

Additional Accommodations

Bridge Inn

New Bight   Friendly and family operated, the Inn has six new (2003) two-bedroom apartments in three two-story buildings. Each apartment has a private entrance, full kitchen, dining, and living room. Twelve motel rooms, some with air-conditioning, are in a single story building. If you want air-conditioning, you have to request it and pay extra. The restaurant here is very good, and they often have live music in the bar on the weekends. The Inn is next to the land-locked ponds that hold bonefish, permit, and tarpon. It's a short walk to the beach. A fishing guide can be arranged. Car rentals are available.

Pricing: $-$$

Contact: Reservations and information, 242-342-3013; fax 242-342-3041.

E-mail: robl@starband.net

Orange Creek Inn

Orange Creek   Sixteen motel rooms with satellite TV, some with air-conditioning and some with kitchenettes, are across the street from the beach. If you want air-conditioning, you have to request it. This is a good budget location to hang out and fish the northern part of the island.

Pricing: $

Contact: Reservations and information, 242-354-4110/1; fax 242-354-4042.

Services

Air Service:

Cat Island Air: 242-377-3318

Southern Air: 242-377-2014

Bahamasair: 800-222-4262

Diving and Snorkeling: Cat Island offers some of the best diving in the Bahamas with more than 12 miles of unlimited wall diving sites along the southern coast alone. The *Cat Island Dive Center* in Port Howe is affiliated with PADI and PDIC and offers a complete certification course. Cat Island's southern wall begins at 50 feet and drops vertically to depths up to 6,000 feet. You can explore coral canyons and sandy valleys, and discover caves and tunnels packed with thousands of colorful fish. Just off the Greenwood Beach Resort are shallow reefs ranging from 15 to 40 feet that are ideal for snorkeling. Reservations and information, 242-342-3053.

Car Rentals: You can rent cars through your hotel.

New Bight Service Station: Car rentals are available here. If you're staying at Fernandez Bay, the hotel will drive you over to the station to pick up your car. Rates are based on the number of days you rent the car. We suggest getting a car with air-conditioning. Reservations and information, 242-342-3014.

Restaurants: *Pat Rolle's Cookie House Bakery* in Arthur's Town, 242-354-2027, is a good lunch or dinner spot and an island institution. You need to call ahead to be sure they will be open. The restaurants at the Bridge Inn, Fernandez Bay Village, Greenwood Beach Resort, and Hawk's Nest Resort are all very good. You should call ahead for reservations.

Stores and Supplies: Arthur's Town, New Bight, and Old Bight have well-stocked grocery and liquor stores, but remember that supplies can run low if the mail boat hasn't been to the island recently.

Clinics: Nurse-staffed clinics are in Arthur's Town, Smith Bay, and Old Bight.

Banks: There are no commercial banks on the island.

New Developments

We've heard a few rumors about some large developments on the north shore but nothing solid, and the cost of putting in the necessary infrastructure here doesn't seem to make sense. The fact is that tourism is low key on this jewel of an island. The main development is by individuals building private getaway homes.

Log on to our Web site at www.bahamasflyfishingguide.com for updated information.

CHAPTER 12

LONG ISLAND

Aerial view of Long Island, flats around Cape Santa Maria and Stella Maris.

Cape Santa Maria, Long Island's northernmost landfall, is 27 miles northeast of George Town, Exuma, and roughly the same distance from Devil's Point on Cat Island. From the Cape to South End, the island snakes for almost 80 miles, and is never more than four miles wide.

The island is one of stunning contrasts in geography. The west coast is composed of sandy flats, powdery white beaches, and calm turquoise-colored bays, while the east coast consists of harsh reefs and chalk-white cliffs that plunge into often wild dark-blue waters. Divided by the Tropic of Cancer, the island's terrain varies from the dramatic limestone cliffs in the north and south, to rolling hillsides, swampland, and stark white flatlands where salt is produced. The island is thought to be one of Columbus' early stops, probably his third, after San Salvador and Rum Cay. The Arawak Indians called the island Yuma; Columbus named it "Fernandina," out of respect for his Spanish sponsor.

American Loyalists from the Carolinas settled on Long Island with their slaves in 1790. Plantations were built, and more than 4,000 acres were planted with cotton. Rich soil made cotton-growing more successful here than on any of the other Out Islands. With the abolition of slavery, however, the plantations failed. Today, Loyalist buildings stand in ruin, while agriculture is still a significant part of daily life.

Pothole farming is the most popular method of growing a variety of crops, from peas, squash, and corn, to bananas, pineapples, and other fruits. While many natural potholes are used, locals also blast holes in the rocky soil to create additional "fields." Along with farming, residents make a living from raising cattle, sheep, goats, and pigs.

The traditional economy aside, tourism is the main reason that prosperity is growing on Long Island, and why the population has grown to more than 5,000 permanent residents. The two major resorts—Stella Maris Resort Club and Cape Santa Maria Beach Resort—are attracting more and more visitors to this uniquely beautiful island. Fishing, diving, snorkeling, magnificent beaches, and enjoying the tropical atmosphere are the key ingredients.

More than 100 years ago, settlers built a carriage road running the length of the island. These people understood that commerce and development required good communication and transportation routes. The island's 35 farming towns and settlements are situated along the road and around the harbors and anchorages. Today, the Queen's Highway is in good shape and it provides smooth driving from Columbus Cove to South End. There are many side roads leading to beaches and flats that are, however, nothing more than dirt tracks, so be careful when venturing into these areas.

Renting a car and driving the length of the island is something we recommend. You'll have an opportunity to see Loyalist and Arawak ruins, several monuments to Christopher Columbus, and sample fresh conch salad in any number of roadside stands. You'll also be able to stop off at remote beaches, blue holes, and deserted flats where you can wade in and start casting to tailing bonefish.

The majority of tourists traveling to Long Island stay at either Stella Maris Resort Club or Cape Santa Maria Beach Resort, though there are many other lodging options. You should fly into the Stella Maris Airport when visiting the northern resorts. If you fly into Deadman's Cay Airport the taxi fare to reach the northern resorts will be $120 or more. Bahamasair flies most days from Nassau to Stella Maris. Stella Maris has its own charter flight service from George Town, Exuma, and Nassau. Island Wings is another good charter flight company servicing Long Island.

When you arrive at Stella Maris Airport you'll find taxis waiting to take you to any destination. If you're staying at one of the resorts you won't need a car, but we recommend renting one for at least a day or two to explore the island on your own. Cars and scooters can be rented through the resorts or through Taylor's Rentals.

You will want to fly into Deadman's Cay Airport if you have booked a fly-fishing package to this area, or if you are staying in the Clarence Town area. Taxis are usually waiting for each Bahamasair flight. You can rent a car in advance, or rent one after arrival. If you're not on a bonefishing package, or if you're staying around Clarence Town, you will need a rental car.

Around the Island

There are no services for boaters on the northern end of Long Island, though several good anchorages over sandy bottoms are available just north and south of the Cape

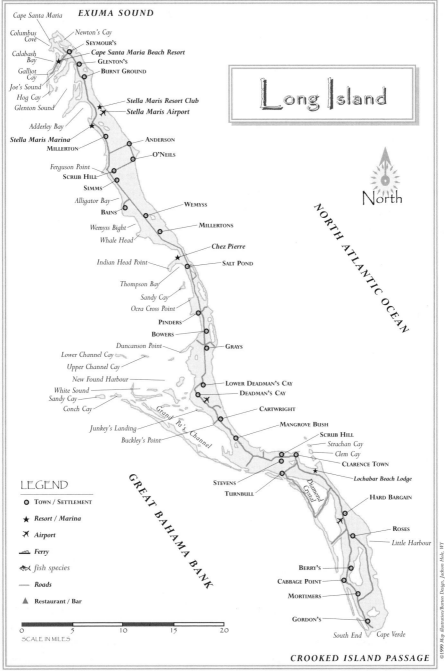

EXUMA SOUND

Cape Santa Maria
Columbus Cove
Newton's Cay
SEYMOUR'S
Cape Santa Maria Beach Resort
Calabash Bay
GLENTON'S
Galliot Cay
BURNT GROUND
Joe's Sound
Hog Cay
Glenton Sound
Stella Maris Resort Club
Stella Maris Airport
Adderley Bay
Stella Maris Marina
MILLERTON
ANDERSON
O'NEILS
Ferguson Point
SCRUB HILL
SIMMS
Alligator Bay
BAINS
WEMYSS
Wemyss Bight
MILLERTONS
Whale Head
Chez Pierre
Indian Head Point
SALT POND
Thompson Bay
Sandy Cay
Ocra Cross Point
PINDERS
BOWERS
Duncanson Point
GRAYS
Lower Channel Cay
Upper Channel Cay
New Found Harbour
White Sound
LOWER DEADMAN'S CAY
Sandy Cay
DEADMAN'S CAY
Conch Cay
CARTWRIGHT
Junkey's Landing
MANGROVE BUSH
Buckley's Point
SCRUB HILL
Strachan Cay
Clem Cay
CLARENCE TOWN
Lochabar Beach Lodge
STEVENS
TURNBULL
HARD BARGAIN

Long Island

North

NORTH ATLANTIC OCEAN

GREAT BAHAMA BANK

Grand Pa's Channel

Diamond Crystal

ROSES
Little Harbour

BERRY'S
CABBAGE POINT
MORTIMERS

GORDON'S
South End   Cape Verde

LEGEND

⊙ TOWN / SETTLEMENT
★ Resort / Marina
✈ Airport
⛴ Ferry
🐟 fish species
— Roads
▲ Restaurant / Bar

0   5   10   15   20
SCALE IN MILES

CROOKED ISLAND PASSAGE

©1999 Map illustrations/Burton Design, Jackson Hole, WY

Santa Maria Beach Resort. The resort itself is located on Calabash Bay, on a four-mile stretch of beach made of the softest powder-white sand that you can imagine.

Facing northwest, the resort is a sheltered paradise for people wanting a peaceful tropical vacation with good food, fishing, diving, and snorkeling. Ten colonial-style cottages feature one- and two-bedroom air-conditioned villas with over-sized baths. Rattan furnishings, marble-tiled floors, and large screened porches create a feeling of casual elegance, and no room is more than 60 feet from the beach.

The main two-story hotel building includes a dazzling marble and tile lobby, equipment rental center, gift shop, satellite TV room, exercise room with modern workout equipment, plus an inviting bar and restaurant with panoramic views of Cala-bash Bay. Additional activities include windsurfing, sea kayaking, sailing, snorkeling, water skiing, bicycling, and hiking. This resort's beach is one of the most alluring and relaxing places we've ever been. The resort can arrange bonefishing, reef fishing, or offshore fishing, and all equipment can be provided, including fly rods and reels.

A mile or so north of the resort is Columbus Cove. On a windswept hilltop over-looking the ocean and the cove is a monument marking Columbus's visit. It's possible to drive to the monument, but you'll need a four-wheel drive vehicle. If you want to hike it will take at least 30 minutes.

The easiest access to the cove is by boat. You can have the resort pack you a lunch, drop you off here, then pick you up later. Don't forget your snorkeling gear and your fly rod. Bonefishing is very good at the lower tidal stages on the flats around the cove.

The northernmost settlement of Seymour's is at the end of the Queen's Highway, though the road continues on to the bay at the southern tip of Newton's Cay. You can park your car in the turn-around, and then hike over the bridge and out to a gorgeous beach where you can swim and snorkel. There are also bonefish along the edges of the inner bay, tarpon in the creeks, and reef fishing options at the mouth of the bay.

The well-maintained community of Seymour's, with a population of around 200, is on ground that's high enough to offer views of Conception Island and the southern Exuma cays on clear days. The locals farm the higher ground around the Cape and export a good portion of their crops to the other islands.

On the western side of Seymour's is Joe's Sound, a mangrove maze of creeks and small flats that merge into a deep blue channel flanked by glistening white sand banks. Boaters line up to anchor in this protected creek that opens to the sea at the north end of Hog Cay, and then serpentines south across more flats that run into Glenton Sound. Wading anglers can gain access to the upper part of Joe's Sound and the smaller north-ern creek that connects to Glenton Sound. A boat is necessary to reach the massive wadable flats further out in Glenton Sound. While bonefish are the most plentiful gamefish in this area, there are tarpon in the creeks and channels, and permit move onto the outer flats in the summer.

Other flats can be accessed by wading anglers just south of Glenton's settlement. Be aware that this area is now well known to anglers staying in the surrounding rental

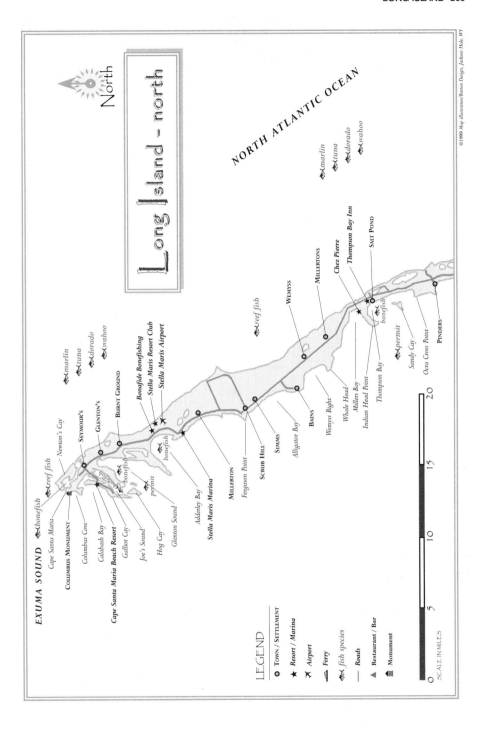

Long Island ~ north

North

NORTH ATLANTIC OCEAN

marlin
tuna
dorado
wahoo

reef fish

SALT POND

Thompson Bay Inn

Chez Pierre

MILLERTONS

WEMYSS

reef fish

bonefish

permit

Sandy Cay

Ocra Cross Point

PINDERS

Indian Head Point

Thompson Bay

Whale Head

Millers Bay

Wemyss Bight

BAINS

Alligator Bay

SIMMS

SCRUB HILL

Ferguson Point

MILLERTON

Stella Maris Marina

Adderley Bay

Glenton Sound

Hog Cay

permit

Joe's Sound

Galliot Cay

Cape Santa Maria Beach Resort

Calabash Bay

Columbus Cove

COLUMBUS MONUMENT

Cape Santa Maria

Newton's Cay

EXUMA SOUND *bonefish*

reef fish

bonefish

SEYMOUR'S

GLENTON'S

BURNT GROUND

Bonafide Bonefishing

Stella Maris Resort Club

Stella Maris Airport

bonefish

marlin
tuna
dorado
wahoo

LEGEND
○ TOWN / SETTLEMENT
★ Resort / Marina
✈ Airport
⛴ Ferry
🐟 fish species
— Roads
▲ Restaurant / Bar
🏛 Monument

SCALE IN MILES
0   5   10   15   20

© 1999 Map illustration/Barton Design, Jackson Hole, WY

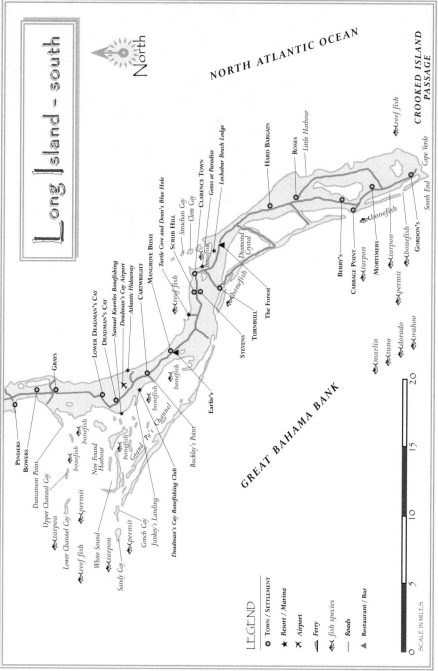

Long Island – south

North

NORTH ATLANTIC OCEAN

CROOKED ISLAND PASSAGE

©1999 Map illustration/Burton Design, Jackson Hole, WY

reef fish

Cape Verde

South End

GORDON'S

bonefish

permit

tarpon

MORTIMERS

bonefish

tarpon

CABBAGE POINT

BERRY'S

Little Harbour

ROSES

HARD BARGAIN

dorado

wahoo

tuna

marlin

The Forest

STEVENS

TURNBULL

Diamond Crystal

Gems at Paradise

Lochabar Beach Lodge

CLARENCE TOWN

Clem Cay

Strachan Cay

SCRUB HILL

Turtle Cove and Dean's Blue Hole

MANGROVE BUSH

CARTWRIGHT

Atlantic Hideaway

Deadman's Cay Airport

Samuel Knowles Bonefishing

LOWER DEADMAN'S CAY

DEADMAN'S CAY

bonefish

bonefish

reef fish

Earlie's

bonefish

bonefish

Buckley's Point

Deadman's Cay Bonefishing Club

Junkie's Landing

Grand Pa's Channel

Conch Cay

White Sound

Sandy Cay

permit

tarpon

reef fish

Lower Channel Cay

Upper Channel Cay

tarpon

permit

bonefish

Duncanson Point

New Found Harbour

bonefish

PINDERS

BOWERS

GRAYS

GREAT BAHAMA BANK

LEGEND

⊙ TOWN / SETTLEMENT
● Resort / Marina
✈ Airport
⚓ Ferry
🐟 fish species
— Roads
▲ Restaurant / Bar

SCALE IN MILES

0   5   10   15   20

houses, so you will usually see other people fishing. And that means the bonefish have become clever and spooky. Stealth and long fluorocarbon leaders are a must for catching the wise fish in this area. A #6 Mantis Shrimp with rubber legs doesn't hurt either.

Max's Conch Bar and Grill.

Continuing south, the highway runs through the settlement town of Burnt Ground. Mangrove swamps spread to the west of the settlement, while high bluffs run to the eastern coast. A mini-peninsula juts out toward the southwest here, separating Glenton sound from Adderley's Bay. The mangrove swamps and shorelines create good bonefish habitat. Anglers can fish the sound or the bay on their own without a boat, though a boat will provide access to more flats. These light-bottomed flats are often glass calm, especially in the mornings and evenings. When the low incoming tide is early or late, you can often cast to tailing fish in ideal conditions.

A little farther south is Stella Maris, which is composed of a marina, airstrip, and plantation-style resort complex. Boaters cruising down from the north, or east from the Exumas, will pass Dove Cay en route to the small man-made harbor and marina. Twelve slips are available for visiting boaters. Calling ahead for space is necessary. Use VHF Channel 16. Full services include fuel, petroleum products, electricity, water, ice, showers, and laundromat.

The airstrip and resort are north of the marina. The resort itself is perched on a hill overlooking the rugged eastern shore. Steep white limestone cliffs arch and bend to the north and south. At the bottom of the hill, the Atlantic Ocean sprawls to the horizon with its aquamarine water washing over dark coral reefs just offshore. The main clubhouse includes a restaurant, bar and lounge, game room, satellite TV area, and gift shop. Spacious air-conditioned hotel rooms and one-bedroom cottages are situated around the clubhouse. Two-, three-, and four-bedroom beach houses, several with private pools, are also available for rent. Three freshwater swimming pools and a secluded beach cove round out the amenities.

The atmosphere at Stella Maris is laid back, but also festive, and the staff, led by general manager Jill Smith, (her large extended family has owned/operated the resort for more than 30 years), is extremely helpful and friendly. Monday nights feature an Out Island Cave Party, a lively event with a barbecue buffet, live band, and dancing. On Wednesday nights, guests party on with special rum punches and another barbecue at the beachside swimming pool. At times, these party nights are switched around and special events are added. Diving and snorkeling excursions are available every day, as is complimentary transportation to Cape Santa Maria and other beaches. All you have to do is sign up. Serious divers will want to try the wall dives off Conception Island, or one of the blue-hole dives.

Anglers staying at Stella Maris can walk or bike to fish Adderley Bay, or take a rod to one of the eastern snorkeling beaches and catch jacks, snappers, and grouper. The resort can arrange for bonefishing guides, or for reef and offshore fishing charters. James "Docky" Smith, Jill's husband, is the head guide and one of the best guides in the Bahamas. If you want to book Docky, you will need to do it well in advance.

Stella Maris/Long Island guide Docky Smith.

The Bonafide Bonefishing Tackle Shop and Café is located just off the Queen's Highway on Stella Maris property across from Adderley Bay. Owned and operated by Docky and Jill, the shop has a good selection of fly-fishing and conventional tackle, flies, tropical clothing, hats, T-shirts, and gifts.

Eight miles south of Stella Maris is Simms settlement, one of the oldest on the island. Neat pastel-colored houses are shaded by casuarinas and often fronted by low stone walls. A nurse-staffed clinic can be found here, along with a telephone station, several small stores, and a couple of restaurants serving Bahamian specialties. Our favorite is Blue Chip Restaurant and Bar, owned by Mario Simms. Mario does the cooking himself, creating wonderful dishes of baked mutton snapper, fried grouper, delicious crawfish tails, barbecue chicken, and an amazing guava duff. It's best to call ahead for reservations, though if you're driving by, go ahead and stop in.

Many boaters traveling from Exuma head straight to Simms, then on south to Salt Pond, which has the best anchorages on the west coast.

Driving from Simms to Salt Pond, about 10 miles, takes you past Millers Bay, Indian Head Point, and the settlement of Thompson Bay. There is a road that heads west toward Millers Bay that will take you to Chez Pierre, a delightful small resort with six elevated cottages set on a wide curved beach. Canadian owners Pierre and Anne have created the perfect place to relax and fish or explore the island on your own. The restaurant, one of the best on the island, serves delicious Italian dishes and fresh seafood.

The shorelines around Millers Bay, Indian Head Point, and on the south side of the point in Thompson Bay have good bonefish habitat and wadable flats though there are mucky areas to watch out for around the mangroves. Larger bones like to cruise these shorelines at the lower tidal stages looking for sea crabs. A small Yarn Crab or a Borski's Bonefish Critter is effective throughout this area.

Church on Salt Pond.

Salt Pond is headquarters for the annual Long Island Regatta that is held in May. Several stores between the main and regatta docks are well stocked with groceries, non-prescription drugs, hardware, and household goods. The mail boat makes regular visits and repair service is available for outboard motors.

The Thompson Bay Inn, a large yellow two-story building, is located north of Salt Pond. Proprietor, Alphonso Bowe, serves breakfast, lunch, and dinner, and the bar is a lively meeting place for friendly locals. Good quality rental cars are available here.

If you drive through this area be on the lookout for a couple of easy-to-miss food stands that serve irresistible fresh conch salad. Also remember that most of the "established" restaurants are not always open for every meal, and some won't take you unless you called ahead to make a reservation. We always carry a cooler in our car with drinks, sandwiches, and snacks when exploring any of the Out Islands.

Another eight or so miles south of Salt Pond is Deadman's Cay, the largest settlement on the island, and site of the main island airport. This is a pleasant community of hard-working, friendly people. There are several restaurants, small motels, and a couple of gas stations. Max's Conch Bar and Grill on the east side of the road on the way into Deadman's Cay is one of the few small restaurants that is hard to miss. Actually, impossible to miss is more accurate.

Max's place is a brightly painted array of small buildings, and colored banners are strung across the property. You can sit at the bar and order a cold Kalik while munching on fresh jerk ribs and chicken, or sit down in the dining area and enjoy a complete meal.

Samuel Knowles's bonefishing operation is just down the road behind the BaTel-Co station. If you turn right onto a dirt track you'll come to the waterside lodge where Sammy has created one of the most popular fishing programs in the southern Bahamas. Jerry and Frank Cartwright are two of the top guides. These guys know the area extremely well and fish out of well-maintained Rahming skiffs with Yamaha outboards. The lodge offers complete bonefishing packages including air-conditioned rooms, meals, and guided fishing.

The Deadman's Cay area is actually several settlements that run together. Continuing south you'll enter Mangrove Bush. Kooters Restaurant is on the water just north of the dock where several independent guides, including Ivan Knowles and his sons, keep their boats. Kooters serves seafood, chicken and ribs, burgers, and more than a dozen flavors of ice cream. You can sit out on the deck overlooking the water while you eat and watch bonefish and baby tarpon cruise in the quiet bay.

A little farther on is Earlie's Tavern, run by Judy Knowles and her family. Judy's husband, Cecil, is a commercial lobster fisherman who is also a bonefishing guide. Earlie's Tavern serves good Bahamian-style food at lunch and dinner, and their bar and outdoor dance floor are hopping on the weekends and during regatta time. They also prepare picnic lunches to go. Judy's sister, Nancy, is the manager of Lochabar Beach Lodge south of Clarence Town. Judy is also a real estate agent. She rents houses in the area that are ideal for travelers interested in do-it-yourself fishing and vacationing.

If you drive south toward Clarence Town, you'll see the pink-walled entrance to Turtle Cove on the ocean side of the highway. If you turn in here you'll have easy access to several nice beaches and Dean's Blue Hole, which has been measured to be roughly 660 feet in depth. The Stella Maris dive shop runs regular trips to explore this fascinating spot. If you decide to go, don't ask the locals to tell you any of the stories attached to the blue hole. If you're superstitious, you'll never dive in any blue hole again.

Turtle Cove itself is a planned resort community that has never really made it due to a number of factors, including problems with clear title to some of the land. If you decide to invest in real estate on Long Island, or any of the other Family Islands, be sure to hire a good lawyer who can verify land titles.

Dean's Blue Hole near Clarence Town.

We know of no good harbors or anchorages for boaters from Salt Pond to South End, though in calm weather you can drop anchor off Calloway Landing, which boasts one of the most spectacular powder-white beaches we've ever seen. Good reef and offshore fishing are just a mile away from here along the edge of the Great Bahama Bank. This is also a prime area for

The beach at Lochabar Beach Lodge.

commercial lobstering. Boaters rounding South End and heading north again will find good anchorages in Clarence Town harbor.

The Fly Fish Marina is also located here. When the marina opened in June 2000 it created a good base for blue-water anglers to fish these virgin waters, and to rest up before moving on to Crooked and Acklins Islands or further south to the Turks and Caicos. The marina has 15 slips and can take boats up to 110 feet. Services include fuel, electricity, water, ice, laundry, showers, e-mail, telephone, and trash disposal. There is a well-stocked store, restaurant, and bar on site. The marina can arrange for sportfishing charters, bonefishing guides, and they can set you up with a room in a cool beachside cottage just up the road.

If you drive into Clarence Town from Mangrove Bush, you will immediately notice the two twin-spired churches. On the left side of the highway, just before town, is St. Paul's Anglican Church with a red roof, built by Father Jerome during his Anglican days. Father Jerome later converted to Catholicism and built St. Paul's Catholic Church with a blue roof, on the right side of the highway farther into the settlement and overlooking the harbor. Both churches have twin spires that can be seen by boaters approaching the harbor from miles away. Father Jerome, as you'll recall, is buried in the Hermitage tomb on the peak of Mt. Alvernia on Cat Island.

The main settlement buildings, including the Commissioner's House, overlook one of the most beautiful harbors in the Bahamas. The harbor bottom, visible through the glass-clear turquoise water, is dark coral and grass laced with hard white sand and dotted with a number of verdant cays. The three largest cays, including Strachan Cay, create better anchorages than anything in the harbor proper. Meat, produce, and other groceries are usually in good supply, but check the mail boat schedule to see the last time supplies were delivered from Nassau. The Harbour Rest Restaurant and Bar is at the mail boat dock. Breakfast, lunch, and dinner are served on a somewhat regular schedule. A telephone station is near the Commissioner's office, as is a nurse-staffed clinic.

Back out on the main highway, and a mile or so farther south, is the turn-off to Lochabar Beach Lodge. The tranquil lodge has two large suites downstairs with full kitchens, private baths, and spacious decks literally steps from the beach and a dazzling blue hole. Upstairs is a one-bedroom suite with a full kitchen, living and dining room, and a large covered verandah. At low tide, you can walk the beach all the way to Clarence Town. Manager Nancy Knowles takes good care of the property and can also arrange car rentals, groceries, prepared meals, and fishing guides. You must have a rental car if you stay here. This is a dynamite spot for do-it-yourself anglers to set up shop.

Back out on the main highway again is the Forest Restaurant and Bar, on the right-hand side of the road, just south of the Lochabar Beach Lodge turn-off. This is the best place to eat in the area, with specialties such as cracked conch, grouper fingers, baked chicken, and barbecued ribs. The bar serves chicken wings, fries, and potato skins throughout the day. The pool table always seems to be in use, especially on Friday and Saturday nights. A live band plays here a few Friday's every month in the large disco that was added to the back of the restaurant. Six motel rooms are also available.

If you continue driving south, you'll pass a good number of ruins, including what looks like an old castle on a high bluff near Dunmore. The view from here gives you the feeling of being alone in a newly discovered place. It's a 10 on the Wow Scale.

South of Hard Bargain you'll be able to take the leeward road to Berry's or Cabbage Point, or stay on the Atlantic side and head down to Little Harbour. Little Harbour is a mini, more remote, version of Clarence Town. You can step out of your car and walk onto flats where big bonefish tail in solitude. This is also a good anchorage for boaters, and off the beaches here, you'll find some of the best snorkeling on the island.

If you take the leeward road you'll have access to miles of bonefish flats, creeks, and land-locked mini-lakes, some of which are easy to reach, and others that will require walking through mucky mangrove terrain.

Gordon's and South End are at the end of the road: the southern tip of the island. If you reach this spot you can experience what it might be like if you could reach the end of the earth. It's awesome. Miles of rarely fished flats sweep around to the west and back up to Cabbage Point and beyond. It is not an exaggeration to say that adventurous anglers could spend years exploring the fishing options between here and Deadman's Cay.

Fishing Highlights

The Long Island fishery is fed by the Exuma Sound to the north, the Great Bahama Bank to the east, and the North Equatorial Current, which originates in the Canary Islands and eventually sweeps along the windward coast. Blue water is only a short run off Long Island's northern, eastern, and southern shores. Good numbers of blue and white marlin, sailfish, dorado, wahoo, and a variety of tuna create excellent offshore fishing activity in season.

The flats habitat off the western coast is home to high numbers of bonefish, plus sharks, barracuda, permit, tarpon, and some snook. Most of the flats are light-colored, composed of hard sand, variable coral, or soft white muck. Shrimp and crabs are the most common bonefish food, with white and gray sea crabs the highlights. When local guides work with spin fishermen, they usually use fresh sea crabs.

The northern part of the island, including Cape Santa Maria and Stella Maris, has a latitude equivalent to the fishing grounds

Strip it, mon, strip it!

of Great Exuma. South of Simms settlement, the island is below the Tropic of Cancer. This relatively southern location means that weather is more stable than in the northern Bahamas. Most cold fronts moving down from the north will stall before they reach the Deadman's Cay area. When combined with miles of protected leeward flats, these weather patterns mean that fly-fishers pursuing bonefish will see favorable conditions most of the year.

Bonefish rank as the number-one flats gamefish. High numbers of fish and relatively little fishing pressure makes Long Island a good choice for beginning fly-fishers. Being able to cast to many fish is the best way to improve your skills. More experienced anglers will have the opportunity to catch lots of fish on days when the weather is good. Fish average 3 to 4 pounds, with 6- to 8-pound fish common, and fish over 10 pounds possible. On the northern part of the island we prefer to fish the incoming tide, especially when wading, though the last part of the falling tide is very good as well. On the Deadman's Cay salt pan flats, wade fishing is excellent at any stage of the tide, though when you move out to White Sound, the incoming tide is best.

Be aware that the salt pan flats now receive a good deal of pressure and the fish here can be spooky. Stealth and long fluorocarbon leaders are a must during the main season, March through May.

Day in and day out, bonefish will be more aggressive on the incoming tide. The length of the island means that anglers fishing on their own, and renting a car, can set up a strategy to fish an incoming tide for most of the day. This can be done by fishing both sides of the island, and by moving on the north/south axis. Tides vary at least two hours from the windward to leeward side of the island, and up to three hours from the northern to southern tips. Our favorite bonefish flies include #4-8 Gotchas, #4-6 Gotcha Clouser's, #4-8 Mantis Shrimp, #4-8 Bunny Gotchas, #6 Pink Hoovers, #4-6 Spawning Shrimp, and #6 Tan Yarn Crabs.

We recommend fishing with a guide at least part of the time. Usually, you will learn more from a guide in a day than you will on your own in a week. Guides can be arranged through professional booking agents, through the island's resorts, or with guides directly. You should always plan on booking in advance, especially from March through May.

Fly-fishing for permit is fair at best, though this is partly due to the fact that most local guides don't understand the permit fishery. (Docky Smith is doing a good job up north of getting anglers into permit during the late spring and sum-

Stephen in Deadman's Cay, Long Island.

mer.) Most guides end up pursuing permit with live crabs and spinning gear. The best months are April through August. Our favorite permit flies include a #4 White Yarn Crab, #2 Del's Merkin, and #2 Spawning Shrimp.

The tarpon story is similar to the permit story, with some of the best fishing grounds overlapping. The main difference is that tarpon fishing is good in many of the blue holes, creeks, and land-locked lakes. We suggest hiring a guide for a day of blue-hole fishing. On the flats, we've seen tarpon from Joe's Sound to South End, with the Sandy Cay and Mortimers Cut flats having the highest number of fish. A number of creeks and mangrove bays around Mortimers lure tarpon into protected feeding areas. In the last couple of years we've enjoyed some fabulous fishing here. Our favorite flies include a #4/0 Shallow Water Cockroach, #4/0 Red/White Dahlberg's Nothing Fancy, and #4/0 Sand Devil LeMay's Big Eye Tarpon.

Sharks and barracuda roam the flats throughout the year, but the best fishing for these species is over the reefs. In general, the reef fishing is outstanding everywhere. If you just want to catch a lot of hard-fighting gamefish take along plenty of chum and enjoy a day of reef fishing with a guide. Jacks, snappers, grouper, and mackerel will join a variety of sharks and barracuda in a feeding frenzy that will give your arms a workout.

The offshore fishing is outstanding most of the year; you just need to pick fishing times based on the species you want. The best months for billfish are May through July. Most billfishing is done with conventional gear. We don't know of any fly-fishing savvy crews operating out of Long Island, but experienced anglers can see enough fish in the prime months to take some shots with flies. But words of warning—most blue marlin around here weigh more than three pounds. Dorado show up in March, with April through June prime. These aggressive fish hit flies with abandon. Fish average 20 to 30 pounds, with some bulls approaching 70 pounds. Yellowfin tuna in the 30- to 150-pound range are best from March through May. Rainbow runners in the 10- to 30-pound range are best March through May. Wahoo, our favorite blue-water fish to put on the dinner table, show up in October and November, and run strong into January, and sometimes into February. Blackfin tuna turn up in good numbers in July, and run through December. These powerful fish average 20 pounds, with larger fish going over 30.

Serious blue water anglers who cruise down in their own boats can have a fishing bonanza basing out of the Flying Fish Marina. Both points right off the marina are sensational bait magnets that draw in huge numbers of wahoo, dorado, tuna, and marlin in season. And of course from Flying Fish Marina you are within striking distance of the best fishing grounds between there and Crooked Island.

Optional Activities

Long Island is the perfect vacation choice for anglers and non-anglers. Diving and snorkeling don't get any better in terms of undersea splendor and a variety of options. For the best combination of fishing, diving, snorkeling, and general relaxing, we recommend staying at either Cape Santa Maria Beach Resort or Stella Maris Resort, though real do-it-yourself folks should consider Chez Pierre, too.

The dive program at Stella Maris is first-class. Beginning divers can learn to scuba in warm clear water without fighting currents. A resort course includes theory and practical instruction, then your first ocean dive. For advanced divers, trips to Conception Island, including overnight trips, offer pristine wall diving equal to the best locations in the world.

Other diving options include hundreds of coral heads and reef sites in the northwest lee of the island in depths of 30 to 85 feet, plus shark diving and diving over the wrecked freighter *Comberbach*. Along the northeast Atlantic coast, coral fields and reef drop-offs create an endless variety of sites. If you want to test your courage, you can dive in one of the two deepest blue holes in the world.

If you like swimming and looking at tropical fish, but don't want to dive, you'll find as many snorkeling locations as you're willing to look for. Snorkeling is good around the major resorts, and along the entire length of the island from Cape Santa Maria to Little Harbour. Stella Maris offers guided snorkeling trips, plus self-guided trips that include the use of their boats to access more remote areas.

Lodging, Guides, and Services

Featured Lodges

Stella Maris Resort Club

Stella Maris A stunning setting on a green bluff overlooking the deep blue Atlantic. Deluxe air-conditioned accommodations include 20 rooms, 12 one-bedroom cottages, 7 two-bedroom cottages, and 4 houses. These accommodations range from spacious and comfortable to luxurious. Houses include full kitchens, and some have private pools. We highly recommend the "Rainbow House," a spacious three-bedroom house with a massive master suite overlooking a large swimming pool, deck, and the ocean.

Resort amenities include a large casual dining room, spacious bar and lounge, satellite TV, three pools, bicycles, sailing, snorkeling, ping pong, boating, water-skiing, a complete dive shop, and complimentary shuttles to area beaches. Guest activities include complimentary island excursions, boat cruises to remote beaches, and special parties several nights a week. General manager Jill Smith and her family (they've owned the resort for almost 40 years) go out of their way to provide the best in guest services. This resort receives our highest recommendation for an all-around beach, sun, and fishing vacation.

Season: October through July.

Suitable For: Anglers and non-anglers.

Optional Activities: The resort offers flats, reef, and offshore fishing. James "Docky" Smith is the head guide, and one of the best guides in the islands. Top-of-the-line Hewes flats boats with poling platforms are used to access the nearby fishing grounds, with wading a priority when the tide is right. It is a short walk or bike ride to good flats for anglers who want to fish on their own. The Stella Maris marina offers most services for boaters. The dive shop is the best on the island, and suited to beginners or experts. The resort arranges for overnight diving excursions to Conception Island.

What's Included: As much or as little as you want. Complete bonefishing packages are available that include deluxe accommodations, meals, guided fishing, and Bahamian taxes. Custom packages can include all types of fishing, mixing flats, reefs, and/or offshore. The resort provides its own air charter service from Nassau and George Town, Exuma.

Not Included: You can book accommodations only, then choose daily activities and meals as you go. Airfare to/from Stella Maris. Taxis meet you at the Stella Maris airport for the short trip to the resort.

Pricing: $$-$$$

Contact: Reservations and information, 800-426-0466 or 242-338-2051; fax 954-359-8238 or 242-338-2052.

Internet: www.stellamarisresort.com

E-mail: info@stellamarisresort.com or smresort@batelnet.bs

Cape Santa Maria Beach Resort & Fishing Club

Cape Santa Maria Looking for an intimate resort with deluxe accommodations in an isolated location on one of the world's most beautiful beaches? This is the place. Enjoy the charm and hospitality of the Bahamian people, calm waters, cooling trade winds, and a variety of abundant gamefish.

The resort has 18 one- and two-bedroom air-conditioned villas decorated in soothing tropical colors. Each large villa is adorned with ornate woodwork, a screened verandah with rattan lounge chairs, marble floors, and private baths. All rooms are within 60 feet of the white sand beach. A reverse-osmosis system supplies abundant fresh water. In the "Beach House" main lodge is the lobby, gift shop, satellite TV room, library, rental shop, and gym. The upstairs restaurant serves fresh seafood with a Bahamian flare and offers soothing views of Calabash Bay. The tropical bar is a relaxing place to sip rum drinks and watch the sunset.

Season: October through July.

Suitable for: Anglers and non-anglers.

Optional Activities: The resort offers flats, reef, and offshore fishing. Bonefish guides work out of Florida flats skiffs, though wading is a priority when the tide is right. The lodge can supply all the tackle for all types of trips, including fly rods and wading booties for flats fishing.

Non-fishing activities include sunbathing, snorkeling, bird-watching, and boating day trips to secluded coves and caves near the lodge. Toys include a windsurfer, Hobie cat, and bicycles to explore the island. **What's Included:** As much or as little as you want. Complete bonefishing packages are available that include deluxe accommodations, meals, guided fishing, and Bahamian taxes. Custom packages can include all types of fishing, mixing flats, reefs, and offshore.

Not Included: Airfare to/from Stella Maris Airport. You can book accommodations only, and then choose daily activities and meals as you go. Round trip taxi service between Stella Maris Airport and the lodge is $40 for two people.

Pricing: $$$

Contact: Reservations and information, 242-338-5273 or 800-663-7090; fax 242-338-6013.

Internet: www.capesantamaria.com

E-mail: resort@capesantamaria.com

Samuel Knowles Bonefishing

Deadman's Cay Samuel Knowles has put together a tremendous bonefishing program with some of the best guides on the island—himself, Jerry Cartwright, and Frank Cartwright. The guides work out of well-maintained Rahming skiffs with center consoles and Yamaha outboards. The comfortable lodge features two-bedroom/one-bath air-conditioned units with kitchenettes and a small living area. The hospitality here is top-notch. The boat dock is just a few steps from the rooms. The vast fishing areas include some of the best wading for bonefish anywhere. While this is not a well-publicized operation, tremendous word of mouth has made it one of the most popular bonefishing programs in the islands. Booking well in advance is required, especially during March through June, and October and November.

Season: October through July.

Suitable For: Anglers only.

What's Included: Accommodations, meals, guided fishing, Deadman's Cay airport transfers, and Bahamian taxes. Package prices are some of the lowest in the Bahamas. Seven-night/six-day packages run Saturday-to-Saturday.

Not Included: Airfare to/from Deadman's Cay Airport, alcoholic beverages, and optional gratuities.

Pricing: $-$$

Contact: Reservations and information, 242-337-1056.

Chez Pierre

Millers Bay Six elevated cottages with generous bedrooms, bath, and airy screened porches line this secluded Millers Bay beach location, halfway between Stella Maris and Deadman's Cay. Canadian owners Pierre and Anne deliver exceptional personalized service. Chef Pierre whips up fresh innovative dishes with homegrown ingredients and daily-caught seafood in the relaxing oceanfront restaurant. Explore nearby cays in sea kayaks, wade the adjacent flats for bonefish, or schedule a diving adventure. Fishing guides, car rentals, and airport transfers can be arranged. This is our top pick on Long Island for "do-it-yourself" fishing. We have heard several good reports from returning anglers who fished with guide Loxley Cartwright. Loxley can be booked through Anne at Chez Pierre.

Season: October through July.

Suitable for: Anglers and non-anglers.

Optional Activities: Swimming, snorkeling, bonefishing, sea kayaking, and beachcombing are right out the front door. Diving can be arranged with Stella Maris.

What's Included: As much or as little as you want. Complete bonefishing packages are available that include deluxe accommodations, meals, guided fishing, and Bahamian taxes.

Not Included: Airfare to/from Stella Maris Airport. You can book accommodations only, and then choose daily activities and meals as you go.

Pricing: $$

Contact: Reservations and information, 242-338-8809 or 242-464-2181.

Internet: www.chezpierrebahamas.com

Additional Accommodations and Do-It-Yourself Options

Atlantic Hideaway

Deadman's Cay   The two-story lodges sits on the bluff overlooking the Atlantic Ocean, and is a five-minute drive from the fishing dock on the lee side of the island. Guestrooms are comfortable and air-conditioned with private baths. The owner goes out of his way to make guests feel at home, and he prides himself on the delicious Bahamian food he prepares, including many seafood favorites. A good group of guides takes anglers to the salt pan flats, plus the best outside areas around White Sound and beyond.

Pricing: $-$$

Contact: Reservations and information, 242-337-1055 or 800-211-8530.

Internet: www.anglingdestinations.com

Lochabar Beach Lodge

Clarence Town   Located one mile south of Clarence Town on the ocean side of the island. Open-air Bahama shutters and double screen doors bring the island right into your suite (two separate downstairs suites), which includes a kitchen and private bath. You can step from your covered deck onto a pristine beach that meanders back toward Clarence Town in one direction, and around a beautiful blue hole and natural cove in the other. A large one-bedroom upstairs suite has a full kitchen, living and dining room, and large covered verandah. Management can arrange anything you need from rental cars to fishing guides.

Pricing: $-$$

Contact: Reservations and information, 242-337-0025 or 800-211-8530.

Internet: www.bahamas.com or www.anglingdestinations.com

Gems at Paradise

Clarence Town   On the hillside overlooking the magnificent beach and bay of Clarence Town Harbour. The resort has one-bedroom condos with kitchens, regular hotel suites, and a mesmerizing view. Guests have the use of a Boston Whaler for cruising around and fishing on your own, plus the resort owns a 31-foot Bertram for offshore fishing. The resort also has a restaurant, meeting rooms, and water sports toys. We recommend that you rent a car if you stay here.

Pricing: $$-$$$

Contact: Reservations and information, 242-337-3016 or 242-337-3019.

Internet: www.gemsatparadise.com

E-mail: gemsatparadise@batelnet.bs

Constantakis Bay View Hotel

Deadman's Cay   Five spacious air-conditioned rooms on the lee side of the main highway. This is a convenient economical location for do-it-yourself anglers. Earlie's Tavern is just a short walk for meals and nightlife.

Pricing: $

Contact: Reservations and information, 242-337-0644; fax 242-337-0217.

Private Rental Houses

Deadman's Cay to Clarence Town   Call Judy Knowles if you want to rent a house in this area. Judy and her husband, Cecil, also put together bonefishing packages that include a private house, meals, guided fishing, and Bahamian taxes. Houses can include air-conditioning, telephones, full kitchens, and satellite TV.

Pricing: $-$$$$

Contact: Reservations and information, 242-337-0329 or 242-337-1555; fax 242-337-6556.

E-mail: barealty@batelnet.bs

Independent Guides

Bonafide Bonefishing Tackle Shop and Cafe is owned and operated by James "Docky" Smith and his wife, Jill Smith. Our pick as one of the best guides in the Bahamas, Docky conducts full- and half-day guided trips in his state-of-the-art 16-foot Hewes flats skiffs, and also runs reef fishing trips. Docky also books several other top independent guides. The tackle shop rents conventional and fly-fishing gear, prepares snacks and box lunches, and sells a range of tackle, clothing, and flies. You don't have to stay at Stella Maris to fish with Docky, but you do have to book him well in advance. Reservations and information, 242-338-2025; Internet: www.bonafidebonefishing.com.

Captain Phillip Cartwright has received high recommendations from readers who have fished with him a number of times and keep going back. He guides mainly out of the Deadman's Cay area. Reservations and information, 242-337-0143.

Captain Colin Cartwright works most often from Simms to Deadman's Cay, and often guides clients staying at Chez Pierre. He has received numerous recommendations from our readers. Reservations and information, 242-337-0443; e-mail: colin@batelnet.bs.

Services

Please Note: All visitors to Long Island will be best served by making rental car and activity arrangements through their hotels, or through sources listed below. There are a number of good restaurants on the island outside of the resorts, though some are not always open. We recommend calling ahead if you can. Also, most restaurants and bars only take cash, no credit cards, traveler's checks, or personal checks.

Air Charter Services:

Island Wings: 242-338-2022 or 242-357-1021.

Stella Maris Resort Air Service: 800-426-0466, 954-359-8236, or 242-338-2051; Internet: www.stellamarisresortairservice.com.

Diving and Snorkeling: Diving and snorkeling gear is available for rent at the major resorts. So are bicycles, sea kayaks, small sailboats, and windsurfers. We recommend renting a car and taking a picnic lunch along to explore the east coast of the island. Countless beaches, reefs, and outside flats provide fishing, snorkeling, and seclusion.

Stella Maris Marina Dive Shop: 242-338-2055

Cape Santa Maria Diving: 242-338-5273

Restaurants: *Earlie's Tavern* in Mangrove Bush: The Knowles family runs this dining room, bar, and poolroom. Try the delicious lobster, grouper, or cracked conch. Burgers, sandwiches, and boxed fishing lunches are made to order. This is a lively nightspot on weekends, and the place rocks with occasional special events, including the Long Island Regatta. Contact: 242-337-1628.

Blue Chip Restaurant and Bar in Simms: Mario Simms serves up great Bahamian dishes at reasonable prices—baked mutton snapper, fried grouper, cracked conch, grilled crawfish tails, barbecue chicken, cole slaw, peas 'n' rice, and guava duff. Contact: 242-338-8106.

The *Forest Restaurant*, a mile south of Clarence Town on Queen's Highway: Proprietor Dudley Dean likes to fish and is a great source of fishing information for southern Long Island. This popular laid-back restaurant serves spicy wings, potato skins, cracked conch, barbecued chicken, and grouper fingers in a large open room furnished with simple tables and chairs. Enjoy a drink at the bar—which is made of seashells embedded in glossy resin—and a game of pool. Every other weekend or so there's live music and dancing. Six spacious motel rooms are in a concrete building behind the bar. Each room has white tile floors and bright wood furnishings, including two double beds, satellite TV, and a private bath. Contact: 242-337-3287.

Kooters Restaurant in Mangrove Bush: Grab a seat on the deck at this casual spot for a splendid view of Mangrove Bush Point, and watch bonefish and baby tarpon cruise the adjacent shallow flat. Enjoy a conch burger, club sandwich with homemade fries, or a cold Kalik. Daily specials range from ribs to seafood. Save room for one of the many flavors of ice cream. Contact: 242-337-0340.

Max's Conch Grill and Bar in Deadman's Cay: You can't miss this brightly painted outdoor restaurant on the east side of the main highway as you approach the settlement of Deadman's Cay. Have a chat with Max while sampling his conch salad, conch dumplings, or daily specials like barbecue ham, steamed pork, or grilled crawfish. The place is usually open every day until 9 P.M., and sometimes later when the bar is rocking. There is a free conch shell-lined miniature golf course behind the bar, and a general store is next-door. Contact: 242-337-0056.

Marinas: *Flying Fish Marina*, Lighthouse Point Road, Clarence Town: Tucked into the northern corner of Clarence Town Harbour, the marina can accommodate boats up to 110 feet. Bathrooms, showers, and laundry facilities are available to marina guests only. The restaurant and bar is open to the public. Bonefishing, reef, and offshore guides can be arranged by the management with advance notice. Reservations and information, 242-337-3430.

Car Rentals: *Taylor's Rentals* has cars and scooters available. You can arrange for this company to deliver your car to your hotel. Reservations and information, 242-338-7001.

Clinics: Nurse-staffed clinics are in Simms, Deadman's Cay, and Clarence Town.

Banks: *The Royal Bank of Canada* in Deadman's Cay and in Grays is open Monday through Thursday 9:00 A.M. to 1:00 P.M., and Friday until 5:00 P.M. *The Bank of Nova Scotia* in Stella Maris is open Tuesday, Thursday, and Friday.

New Developments

The absolutely stunning coastline of Long Island is ripe for a large-scale development like the Four Seasons at Emerald Bay of Great Exuma, but frankly, we hope it never happens. We'll just have to wait and see.

In the meantime, most of the development on the island is happening with small resorts and private homes. The Villas at Cape Santa Maria are a fee-simple investment situated on the resort's prime beachfront property in Calabash Bay, and to keep things exclusive, they only allow two new homes to be built per year.

For the best information if you are interested in purchasing property or renting a vacation home, call Jill Smith at Stella Maris (242-338-2051) or Judy Knowles at Bahamas Realty (242-337-1555).

Log on to our Web site at www.bahamasflyfishingguide.com for updated information.

CHAPTER 13

CROOKED AND ACKLINS ISLANDS

The airstrip at Pittstown Point Landing.

Crooked and Acklins Islands, Long Cay, and Castle Island form an atoll that surrounds the fertile shallow water fishery of the Bight of Acklins. Gleaming black coral reefs, which can be dangerous to boaters, run along the northern and western edges of this triangular-shaped group. The bottom of the triangle covers 45 miles from Portland Harbour and Pittstown Point to Castle Island. Another reef spans from Windsor Point off the south end of Long Cay to Salina Point off southwestern Acklins, protecting the entrance to the Bight. This island group is 225 miles southeast of Nassau and about 35 miles southeast of Long Island across the Crooked Island Passage.

Columbus sailed across the passage, making what historians think was his fourth Bahamian landfall at Portland Harbour. The story goes that Columbus was lured ashore by enchanting fragrances carried on the ocean breeze. Cascarilla bark was one of the herbs creating the aroma, and it remains an important export item today; it is used in certain medicines.

The islands existed in obscurity until 1783 when American Loyalists arrived with their slaves. Unlike on Long Island and Abaco, the soil here could not support the cotton-growing plantations that were built. When the cotton industry failed, the population was forced to earn a living from the sea. Sponging became the lifeblood of the island until the early 1900s when fungus destroyed the sponging grounds. The people continued fishing, plus they eked out a living by farming the few fertile areas available. Not much has changed since then, and in most ways these islands remain as unspoiled and natural as when they were first discovered.

One of the least known islands of the Bahamas, Acklins comprises the eastern and southeastern part of the atoll. The terrain is hilly and desolate, with unusual rock formations and varied plant and animal life, including an occasional swamp turtle. Along the eastern coastline treacherous reefs protect tranquil coves and white sand beaches.

Spring Point, in the middle of the island, is the main settlement. The airport and government headquarters are located here. To say this island is quiet and laid-back is an understatement. Locals like to say, "you make your own sunshine," or in other words, "you're on your own."

Crooked Island, together with Long Cay, forms the northern and western part of the atoll system. Columbus christened the island "Isabella," after his queen, though the Arawaks called the island "Samoete." Somehow, the more functionally descriptive name of Crooked Island took hold and is used today.

This remote island is lined with glistening white beaches that stretch for miles to the east and south. Colonel Hill, on the northeastern end, is the main town and the highest point on the island. The airport and government headquarters are located here. Other settlements include Cripple Hill, True Blue, French Wells, and Gun Point; all are connected by a good paved road.

Albert Town, the only village on Long Cay, is basically a ghost town. Known as Fortune Island in more prosperous times, Long Cay served as a transfer and stopover point for Spanish and British ships sailing between Europe and the Americas.

Castle Island, off the southwest tip of Acklins, was a favorite pirate retreat. A lighthouse was built on the island in 1867. Most of the island is low and sandy, with higher hills along the northern shore. A decent anchorage is available on the south side of the island in Mudian Harbour. The reef protecting the harbor is a great fishing spot for jacks, snappers, mackerel, yellowtail, and grouper.

Both Crooked and Acklins islands have populations of about 400. Farming and fishing continue to be the basis for the local economies, though tourism does have an impact. The mail boat arrival from Nassau is a big weekly event. Paved roads run the length of both islands, and power was made available to all residents for the first time in 1998, though many houses are still not connected. Land-line telephone service is available, and many locals now have cell phones that often work better than the land lines.

Bahamasair usually flies into Colonel Hill and Spring Point on Tuesdays and Saturdays, though the schedule can change at any time. Charter flights are available to these two airports, and to the paved strip at Pittstown Point Landing. We suggest having your insect repellent handy upon landing. If the wind is down, you will need it right away.

If you attempt anything on your own in these islands, be aware that there is no guarantee of services of any kind. Groceries and supplies may or may not be available.

If you rent a car, you may or may not be able to buy gas. If you reach a telephone, it may or may not work. If you take your cellular phone be sure to check with your service provider before you leave home to see if service will be available. VHF radio is still one of the best means of communication. In general, credit cards will do you no good. Same for traveler's checks. Make sure you have cash and a nothing-bothers-me casual attitude, and you'll have no troubles, mon.

Around the Islands

Most visitors fly to Crooked and Acklins with their objectives being fishing, diving, or just relaxing. Pittstown Point Landings and Landrail Point are located on the northwestern tip of Crooked Island. The most convenient travel plan is to take a charter flight to Pittstown's private airstrip. Commercial flights land at Colonel Hill Airport. It is about a 30-minute taxi ride from the airport to the resort area.

Pittstown Point Landings is the best choice available for accommodations and activity programs. The resort complex, composed of 12 guest rooms (some with air-conditioning), bar, restaurant, gift shop, and office, overlooks Portland Harbour and the Bird Rock Lighthouse. An inviting white sand beach is just steps away. The Bahamas' first post office was located here, and its remaining walls are part of the Pittstown Point clubhouse. The resort has an all-inclusive fly-fishing, conventional fishing, and diving program. The fishing program can include flats, reef, and offshore options. The best bonefishing guides on the island work with the resort, though they can also be booked as independents. Trips to the lighthouse and to intriguing nearby caves can be arranged.

A typical sign of Bahamian friendliness.

NORTH
ATLANTIC
OCEAN

North

Bird Rock
Portland Harbour
Gordon's Bluff
Pittstown Point Landing
LANDRAIL POINT
MOSS TOWN
CRIPPLE HILL
FAIRFIELD
CABBAGE HILL
COLONEL HILL
Mackey's Bluff
Major's Pizgah Harbour
Bullets Hill
COVE LANDING
LOVELY BAY
CHESTERS
Artward Harbour
TRUE BLUE
BROWNS
Pestell
Turtle Sound
CHURCH GROVE
COLONEL HILL AIRPORT
MAJORS
CROOKED ISLAND
French Wells
Gun Point
Lovely Bay Cay
Hell Gate
Grey's Point Bonefish Inn
PINEFIELD
Black Rock
Coventry Bight
Jewfish

CROOKED ISLAND PASSAGE

ALBERT TOWN
Long Cay
Covery Bight
ANDERSON
HARD BARGAIN

Windsor Point

THE BIGHT OF ACKLINS

SNUG CORNER
MASONS BAY
GOODWILL
Acklins Island Lodge

North Cay

Fish Cay

Harry Point
GOLDEN GROVE

Guana Cay

Wood Cay

SPRING POINT
Spring Point
DELECTABLE BAY
Bob's Nose
Abraham's Bay
Pompey Bay
Maria Bay
Jamaica Cay
MORANT
BAY
Spring Point Airport
Claret Cove

LEGEND

⊙ TOWN / SETTLEMENT
★ Resort / Marina
✈ Airport
⛴ Ferry
🐟 fish species
— Roads
▲ Restaurant / Bar

ACKLINS ISLAND

BINNACLE HILL
Rocky Point

Spar Creek

Jamaica Bay
Ben's Landing
Salina Point
SALINA POINT
South Bluff
South West Point
Castle Rock
Castle Island

MAYAGUANA PASSAGE

SCALE IN MILES
0   1   2   3   4

Acklins & Crooked Islands

©1999 Map illustration/Barton Design, Jackson Hole, WY

To the south, Landrail Point offers the best anchorage for boaters, though that is a relative statement. In a strong storm surge, this is not a safe anchorage. On the ocean side of the road from Pittstown to Landrail are several brightly painted houses and cottages for rent. This is also the location, on a half-mile stretch of beach, of Casuarina Villas. Four air-conditioned cottages with full kitchens and decks that open onto the beach are for rent.

The public wharf in Landrail is where the mail boat docks. Nice beaches and groves of citrus trees flank the pretty settlement. Gibson's Lunch Room is a good place for a meal, with conch salad a specialty. Most locals are Seventh Day Adventists, so they don't work from sundown Friday to sundown Saturday, and there is no alcohol available in the settlement. The island's only clinic, nurse-staffed, is located here.

Seven miles farther south is French Wells. This is where guides from Pittstown Point begin fishing miles of wadable flats. French Wells Harbour is fairly well protected and provides good anchorages over a sand bottom. The long creek cutting north is accessible by flats boats and other boats with a shallow draft, and is home to lots of tarpon and bonefish. South across the cut are Goat and Rat Cays, then Long Cay. If you continued north of French Wells on the inside you would move toward Turtle Sound, a vast mangrove-lined creek system and bonefish haven. Church Grove Landing is the entrance to the sound. The ferry to Albert Town, which usually runs on Saturdays and Wednesdays, uses the dinghy dock here. It is a two-mile walk from the landing to the Church Grove settlement, which is adjacent to Colonel Hill.

Heading east on the main road out of Pittstown Point you'll skirt the northern part of Turtle Sound on the way to Colonel Hill and the airport. A couple of stores are stocked with necessities that include non-prescription drugs. A few bars, which aren't always open, serve snacks, and a telephone station is open during the week.

Continuing east, the road runs through True Blue and Browns settlements, ending at Cove Landing on the western shore of Lovely Bay. You can take a ferry across the bay to Acklins Island, but the schedule is often erratic, so be prepared to wait an indefinite period.

The Lovely Bay settlement is where the ferry docks on Acklins. A rough road connects to Chesters settlement where the telephones work on occasion and a nurse-staffed clinic operates during the week. From here it's about two miles to Atwood Harbour, one of the best anchorages in the four-island region. Heading south, the road skirts around mangrove swamps and bonefish flats to reach Pinefield Point. Grey's Point Bonefish Inn is located here on a hill overlooking Relief Bay to the west and Gordon's Bay to the east. Both bays have extensive bonefish flats. The Inn, upgraded and renovated a couple of times, has comfortable air-conditioned rooms and a main lodge with bar and restaurant. All-inclusive bonefish packages are offered for up to 12 anglers.

If you drive south, you'll pass through Hard Bargain, which is the highest point on the island. Continuing south toward Spring Point, you'll pass two bonefishing lodges. Top Choice Bonefishing Lodge is on the Bight side just north of Mason's Bay

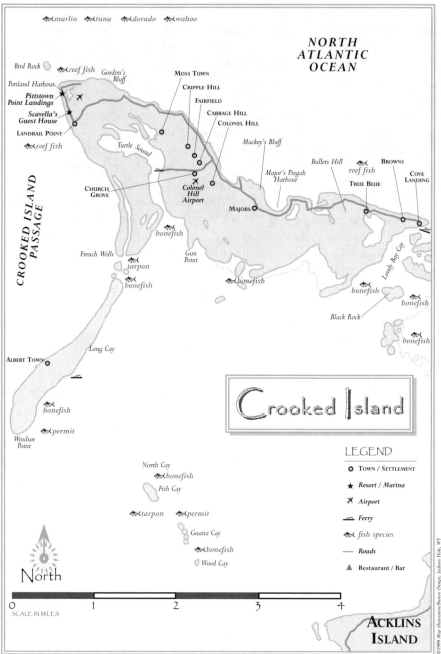

marlin   tuna   dorado   wahoo

NORTH
ATLANTIC
OCEAN

Bird Rock
reef fish   Gordon's   MOSS TOWN
Portland Harbour   Bluff   CRIPPLE HILL
Pittstown   FAIRFIELD
Point Landings   CABBAGE HILL
Scavella's   COLONEL HILL
Guest House
LANDRAIL POINT   Mackey's Bluff
reef fish
Turtle Sound   Bullets Hill   BROWNS
Major's Pizgah   reef fish   COVE
Harbour   LANDING
CHURCH   TRUE BLUE
GROVE   Colonel
Hill
Airport   MAJORS

bonefish

French Wells   Gun
Point
tarpon
bonefish   bonefish   bonefish

Black Rock   bonefish

Long Cay

ALBERT TOWN   Crooked Island

bonefish

permit
Windsor
Point

North Cay
bonefish
Fish Cay

tarpon   permit

Guana Cay
bonefish
Wood Cay

CROOKED ISLAND
PASSAGE

Lovely Bay Cay

LEGEND

◉ TOWN / SETTLEMENT
★ Resort / Marina
✈ Airport
⛴ Ferry
🐟 fish species
— Roads
▲ Restaurant / Bar

North

0   1   2   3   4
SCALE IN MILES

ACKLINS
ISLAND

©1999 Map illustration/Bruton Design, Jackson Hole, WY

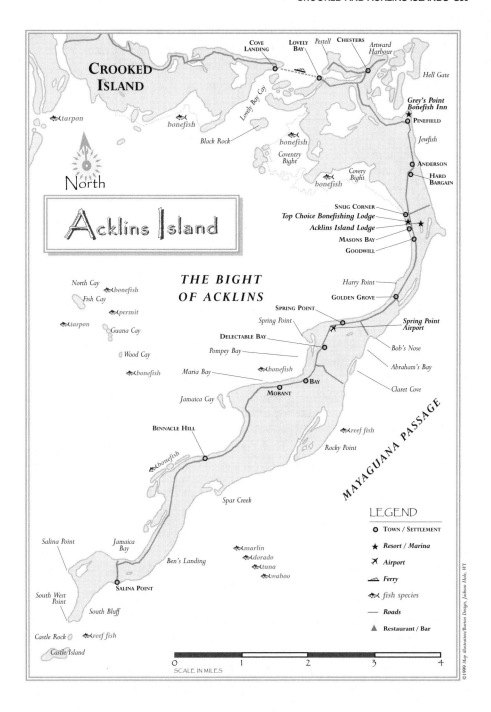

CROOKED ISLAND

COVE LANDING
LOVELY BAY
Pestell
CHESTERS
Artward Harbour

Hell Gate

tarpon

bonefish

Lovely Bay Cay

Grey's Point Bonefish Inn
PINEFIELD

Black Rock

bonefish

Jewfish

North

Coventry Bight

Covery Bight

ANDERSON
HARD BARGAIN

Acklins Island

bonefish

SNUG CORNER
Top Choice Bonefishing Lodge
Acklins Island Lodge
MASONS BAY
GOODWILL

North Cay
bonefish

THE BIGHT
OF ACKLINS

Harry Point

Fish Cay

permit

GOLDEN GROVE

tarpon

Guana Cay

SPRING POINT

Spring Point

Spring Point Airport

Wood Cay

DELECTABLE BAY

Pompey Bay

Bob's Nose

bonefish

Abraham's Bay

Maria Bay

bonefish

BAY
MORANT

Claret Cove

Jamaica Cay

BINNACLE HILL

reef fish

Rocky Point

bonefish

MAYAGUANA PASSAGE

Spar Creek

LEGEND

Salina Point
Jamaica Bay

Ben's Landing

marlin
dorado
tuna
wahoo

TOWN / SETTLEMENT

Resort / Marina

Airport

South West Point

SALINA POINT

Ferry

fish species

South Bluff

Roads

Castle Rock
reef fish

Restaurant / Bar

Castle Island

0   1   2   3   4
SCALE IN MILES

© 1999 Map Illustration/Burton Design, Jackson Hole, WY

settlement. The lodge, operated by Ethlyn and Felix Bain, opened in the fall of 1998, and has four air-conditioned rooms with private baths and satellite TV. Meals are served in the bar/restaurant across the street. The lodge works with three guides using Carolina and Florida skiffs and can take six anglers.

A mile south, at the narrowest point on the island on a bluff overlooking the ocean and the Bight, is a deluxe bonefishing lodge, Acklins Island Lodge. The lodge opened in 1999, went through a number of ownership problems with the locals, closed, and finally reopened in the fall of 2003. The lodge has six air-conditioned rooms in two cottages and a main clubhouse building with a restaurant, bar, satellite TV, and expansive wrap-around decks. The ocean views are spectacular to say the least, and the high-ground location catches cooling offshore breezes, which help to keep the bugs down.

Just down the hill from the lodge is Liza's OK Corral, a local restaurant that serves Bahamian specialties and packs tasty fishing lunches.

Spring Point is the government headquarters for the island. There is a small motel and restaurant near the airport and a nurse-staffed clinic. The friendly locals can provide supplies and fuel, but you might have to ask around. The best means of communication is by VHF radio or cell phone, but you'll have to be sure your cell phone company provides service in the Bahamas.

The low areas along the coastline are mosquito heaven, so make sure you are well coated with bug dope, especially when the wind is down. Continuing south, the road winds around Pompey Bay, Jamaica Bay, and ends at Salina Point. There's not much going on down here except sensational remote fishing. There are innumerable creeks, flats, and bays accessible from the road. On the ocean side there are a number of eye-popping deserted beaches. The few residents in the area are very hospitable and will provide supplies to boaters when available. There is a small restaurant and bar in Salina Point that is sometimes open, and a telephone station that usually operates during the week.

Fishing Highlights

The Crooked and Acklins Islands fishery is one of the best and most varied in the Bahamas, and certainly one of the least fished. With its sweeping interior flats throughout the Bight, surrounding fertile reefs, and deep blue water minutes from shore, this atoll is similar to Andros Island.

Most of the southern shorelines of Crooked and Acklins are composed of mangrove mazes and creeks. Long Cay, which extends straight south of Crooked, and the length of Acklins, which curves back toward the west, have more defined shorelines with coral points and harder-bottomed bays. In the center is the Bight, with a grouping of small cays at the southern end. The bottom structure throughout the Bight varies from hard wadable sand, to irregular coral and grass, to softer mud areas.

This is all prime bonefish habitat, supporting amazing numbers of fish that average three pounds, with plenty of fish in the five- to eight-pound range. These fish are some of the most aggressive in the Bahamas, making this an ideal location for beginners. Fishing the incoming tide is best on the wadable flats, but fishing is good throughout the day at most stages of the tide. Bigger bones, 10 pounds and up, are available here too, but you'll need to spend some time looking for them instead of hooking up so many smaller fish. Our favorite

Stephen and independent guide Mike Carroll.

flies include Gotchas, Gotcha Bunnies, Spawning Shrimp, Mantis Shrimp, Bonefish Puffs, Yarn Crabs, and Clouser's Minnows.

Anglers looking for permit will have a reasonable chance of getting a shot or two during a week's fishing. Some of the best permit fishing is available throughout the southern cays, from North Cay to Wood Cay. This is a long boat ride, so we suggest going on a calm day. Permit also concentrate on the inside of Long Cay, around Black Rock, around Jamaica Cay, and in the channels of Lovely Bay, and south of the Going Through. Our favorite flies are Del's Merkins, Yarn Crabs, Spawning Shrimp, and Borski's Bonefish Critters.

Tarpon move in and out of the various creeks on the tide, with French Wells, Black Creek, and the Going Through, holding decent numbers of resident fish. The guides have really focused on tarpon fishing the past few years and their anglers have been hooking up tarpon consistently. Put that together with the developing permit fishery and this is possible grand slam territory. Tarpon anglers should have a rod rigged with a Shallow Water Cockroach or a Red/White Dahlberg's Nothing Fancy.

The flats fishery is best from March through July, with October and November also good. December through February can be good when the weather is decent, though these are the windier months. This southern location means cloudy cold fronts often stall before reaching the area but the wind still likes to blow in the winter.

The inshore fishery has become very popular, and for good reason. Fishing is done around the reefs in water that's one hundred feet deep or less. Sharks, barracuda, snappers, grouper, jacks, amberjack, yellowtail, and mackerel are the primary species. The reefs are just minutes away from Pittstown and Pinefield Points, plus there is tremendous fishing around Windsor Point and Salina Point. The guides out of Pittstown are practiced in using chum (live pilchards are best) to create a feeding frenzy around their boats. If you want to catch a bunch of hard-fighting fish, this is a blast. We recommend using a 10-weight fly rod with shock tippet matched to the species of fish you're trying to catch (though you can't be sure what you'll hook up at any

Stephen with Carter Andrews and Captain Robbie Gibson.

given time). Sixty-pound mono shock or wire tippet will hold up against most fish. Your fly selection should include Sea Habits, Abel Anchovies, Black Sardinas, Clouser's Minnows, Carter Andrew's Snak Pak series baitfish flies, and Saltwater Poppers in a variety of colors. The reef fishing is good year round, and if you can take rolling seas, fishing is good even in bad weather.

The offshore fishery is equally impressive. Captain Robbie Gibson, out of Pittstown, is fishing areas not touched by any other sportfishing boats. Daily catches of 30 or more fish, including a variety of tuna, dorado, and wahoo of world-record size, are common. October through February is the best time for wahoo, king mackerel, and some tuna. April through July is best for marlin, dorado, yellowfin, blackfin, and skipjack tuna, with wahoo and mackerel still available. Carter Andrews, the owner of *Thunderbird*, a 36-foot Luhrs offshore boat captained by Gibson, has put together an offshore fly-fishing program to go with the already established flats and reef programs. Offshore flies depend on the species you're after, but essentials include Bluewater Mullets, Bluewater Billfish flies, Sea Habits, Snak-Pak flies, and Saltwater Poppers.

If you're looking for an incredible variety of fishing in relatively untouched waters, and are an experienced, mostly self-sufficient angler, we suggest you consider booking a trip to Crooked and Acklins soon.

Optional Activities

OK, we'll add diving and snorkeling to our mantra of "fish, drink, eat, sleep, fish, drink, eat, sleep." If you want anything beyond this, aside from lying on a beach reading a book, don't make the trip to Crooked or Acklins. The Acklins residents' saying, "make your own sunshine" is right on the money.

Pittstown Point Landings has a good diving and snorkeling program that features some of the best wall diving in the Bahamas. Snorkeling and spear fishing are sensational along the northern shore of Crooked, inside the barrier reef.

Lodging, Guides, and Services

Featured Lodges

Pittstown Point Landings

Crooked Island   The isolated location on the northwestern tip of the island is a blend of natural beauty and convenience to the fishing grounds. The 12 guest rooms (6 air-conditioned) are large and bright, with island-style furniture and big windows. The lodge restaurant and bar is the gathering place for anglers and locals. Excellent fresh seafood is a highlight at dinner and breakfasts are made to order. The beachside tiki bar is a perfect spot for an après-fishing beer or rum drink.

The best guides on the island work here, including Elton "Bone Fish Shakey" McKinney, Randy McKinney, Jeffrey Moss, Derek Ingraham, Michael Carroll, and Clinton Scavella. These guys have hot boats—18-foot Action Crafts, Hewes Bonefishers, and Mako Silver Kings, with 90- to 115-hp 4-stroke outboards.

Captain Robbie Gibson and Carter Andrews run the reef and offshore fishing programs. Their 36-foot Luhrs, *Thunderbird*, has a large fishing area, plenty of shade, an air-conditioned cabin, and twin diesels that really move out. Additional reef fishing is done from a 26-foot center-console Boston Whaler.

The resort operates a program for scuba and snorkeling enthusiasts. Beach barbecues are weekly events. The resort can arrange excursions to the caves and to shelling beaches.

It is most convenient to book an air charter directly to the Pittstown Point airstrip. Commercial flights on Bahamasair land at Colonel Hill airport, about a 30-minute drive from the lodge.

Season: October though July.

Suitable For: Anglers and divers.

What's Included: Saturday-to-Saturday all-inclusive bonefish packages with accommodations, meals, guided fishing and Bahamian taxes. Arrivals and departures can also be on Tuesdays, though there is no guided fishing on Saturdays.

Not Included: Airfare to/from Pittstown Point Airstrip or Colonel Hill, taxi fare from Colonel Hill, optional reef and offshore fishing, alcoholic beverages, and optional gratuities.

Pricing: $$

Contact: Reservations and information, 772-546-8299 or 242-344-2507.

Internet: www.pittstownpointlandings.com

E-mail: info@pittstownpointlandings.com

Acklins Island Lodge

Acklins Island   The lodge is perched on a hilltop on the narrowest point of the island overlooking the ocean and the Bight. Six air-conditioned double rooms are situated in three duplex cottages and have tiled floors, twin beds, ceiling fans, satellite TV, and private baths. The large clubhouse includes a bar, dining room, and wide wrap-around decks that provide stunning views of the water. Good food and friendly service contribute to the convivial atmosphere at this remote fishing destination.

The vast fishing grounds cover the area from Lovely Bay on down past Jamaica Cay. There are miles of wadable flats and backcountry creeks loaded with bonefish, as well as deeper channels that hold permit and tarpon. Anglers are driven down the hill each morning to the Bight side of the island. Fishing is from Bay Skiffs with Yamaha outboards. The lodge's hilltop location means you don't have much of a bug problem, but that changes quickly down on the shoreline. Mosquitoes are abundant, particularly after a rain, so insect repellent is a must.

Anglers fly to Acklins on Bahamasair or private charter, landing at Spring Point, where they are met and transferred to the lodge, about a 15-minute drive.

Season: October though July.

Suitable For: Anglers only.

What's Included: Saturday-to-Saturday all-inclusive bonefish packages with accommodations, meals, guided fishing, beer and wine, and Bahamian taxes. Packages can also include reef and offshore fishing. Shorter stays are possible, but depend on the ever-changing airline schedule, or you can book a private charter.

Not Included: Airfare to/from Spring Point, taxi fare from Spring Point, optional reef and offshore fishing, hard liquor, and optional gratuities.

Pricing: $$

Contact: Reservations and information, 800-593-7977.

Internet: www.acklinsislandlodge.com

E-mail: info@acklinsislandlodge.com

Additional Accommodations and Do-It Yourself Options

Casuarina Villas

Landrail Point   The four modern cottages sit on a half-mile stretch of white sand beach between Landrail Point and Pittstown Point Landings. Each has a full kitchen, satellite TV, and western-facing decks. A local market, gas station, and restaurants are two miles away in Landrail Point, or you can eat at Pittstown Point resort. A rental car and fishing guide can be arranged. Diving excursions are led by owner Ellis Moss.

Pricing: $-$$

Contact: Reservations and information, 242-344-2197 or 242-344-2036.

Scavella's Guesthouse

Landrail Point   Accommodations are in a remodeled, air-conditioned guesthouse. Delicious home-cooked meals are served nearby at a local restaurant. Top guides use new boats with 115-hp Yamaha motors and trim tabs to swiftly carry you to the best flats even in rough weather. Complete bonefishing packages are available.

Pricing: $-$$

Contact: Reservations and information, 242-357-9472 or 800-211-8530.

Internet: www.anglingdestinations.com

Grey's Point Bonefish Inn

Acklins Island   Located 19 miles north of Spring Point at Pinefield Point, the Inn has six modern air-conditioned rooms and a main lodge with a restaurant, bar, satellite TV, and large decks, all overlooking the water, beaches, and bonefish flats. The eastern flats areas from Pinefield Point to Hell's Gate are the flats fished most often. The Inn's guides can also fish the Bight out of Snug Corner. Excellent reef and blue-water fishing off the east coast is just 15 minutes from the lodge.

Pricing: $$

Contact: Reservations and information, 242-351-4042 or 344-3210.

Internet: www.greyspointbonefishinn.com or www.anglingdestinations.com

Top Choice Bonefishing Lodge

Acklins Island The lodge is on the bight side of the island just north of the Mason's Bay settlement. Operated by Ethlyn and Felix Bain, the lodge has four air-conditioned rooms with private baths. A bar and restaurant is across the street. The lodge works with three guides using Carolina and Florida skiffs and can take six anglers at a time.

Pricing: $$

Contact: Reservations and information, 242-344-3628; fax 242-344-3550.

Independent Guides

Crooked Island has a number of highly regarded bonefishing guides with quality boats and fly-fishing tackle. Most can be booked through Pittstown Point Landings, but the guides also take direct bookings and house their guests at other locations. Be aware that telephone service to and from Crooked and Acklins Islands is not always operational.

Additional information on fly-fishing Crooked Island, and on the guides listed below is available at: www.crookedislandbonefishing.com.

Derrick Ingraham: 242-556-8769

Jeff Moss: 242-457-0621

Michael Carroll: 242-636-7020

Elton "Bone Fish Shakey" McKinney: 242-344-2507

Clinton Scavalla: 242-422-3596 or 242-344-2197

Randy McKinney: 242-422-3276

Captain Robbie Gibson: Robbie can be contacted through Pittstown Point Landings. He is the most experienced reef and offshore fishing captain on Crooked Island where astounding fishing in virgin waters is the rule. Many wahoo over 100 pounds are landed each season with his assistance. Robbie's personal best wahoo is a whopping 180 pounds. He is also a skilled guide for anglers pursuing tuna, marlin, sharks, barracuda, jacks, snapper, and grouper, and he leads snorkeling and diving excursions as well. Contact him at 242-344-2507.

Services

There is very little available on Crooked or Acklins in terms of established or organized services outside of the accommodation options we've mentioned. You will be much better off to arrange services, including guides and rental cars (if available), through one of the recommended lodges or resorts. Also, the independent guides listed are very helpful and can help you arrange your trip. There are a couple of restaurants in Landrail Point, a gas station, a grocery store, a hardware store, and the mail boat docks there.

Government: The police and commissioners office are located at Colonel Hill on Crooked Island. Contact: 242-344-2197 or 242-344-2599.

Clinics: In case of emergency, nurses are available at Colonel Hill and Mason's Bay. The only doctor on either island lives in Spring Point.

New Developments

There is a major resort and marina development planned for Long Cay, but we've heard the developers have hit a snag with government approvals for an airstrip on the cay. It makes sense that the developers would want their own airstrip because the transfer from Colonel Hill to Long Cay would be a logistical challenge.

Pittstown Point Landings has filed extensive development plans with the government to develop a marina, marina villas, private home sites, and to expand their runway and airport facilities. As of late 2004 the developers were optimistic that they could move forward in 2005.

A few new guesthouses have been built in Landrail Point and near Colonel Hill. There is talk of a new resort at Winding Bay.

For up-to-date news on these and other developments, visit our Web site at www.bahamasflyfishingguide.com.

CHAPTER 14

SAN SALVADOR, RUM CAY, AND CONCEPTION ISLAND

San Salvador—where Columbus made his first landfall in the New World. (Brian Hodges)

October 12, 1492 was the big day. Christopher Columbus made the first landfall in the New World on the island of Guanahani, which he renamed "Holy Savior," or San Salvador. There are four monuments marking the spot where Columbus first came ashore, though it is generally believed that he landed at Long Bay, about three miles south of Cockburn Town. A simple white stone cross, erected in 1956, marks the spot. A little farther south is the gaudy Olympic monument, symbolizing the transfer of the Olympic flame to the New World.

While this is the recognized spot where Columbus first landed, many scholars believe Samana Cay or Grand Turk was really the first landfall. Others have made a case for Fernandez Bay on Cat Island. Whatever the truth may be, this small island, 12 miles long and 6 miles wide, has earned its share of fame. Located about 50 miles southeast of Cat Island, and 108 miles southeast of Nassau, the island remains as splendid and alluring as the day Columbus arrived.

This natural serenity and proximity to the shipping corridor through Crooked Island Passage caused the notorious pirate George Watling to make the island his base. Watling's influence was such that the island was called Watling Island until 1925, when the name was changed back to San Salvador.

The island is also known as the "Island of Lakes," as most of the interior is composed of lakes and creeks. Many forest-covered hills dot the island, with 140-foot Mt. Kerr being the tallest. Coral reefs protect three quarters of the shoreline that is a combination of deserted beaches and black rock.

The pace of life on the island has changed very little over the centuries. Today, Cockburn Town, on the western shore in the center of the island, is the main settlement, government headquarters, and mail boat dock. The Riding Rock Marina & Inn is located just south of the airport. Diving is the main attraction here, with some of the best reef, wreck, and wall-diving in the Bahamas. North of Riding Rock Point is the luxurious Club Med-Columbus Isle, an all-inclusive resort considered by some people to be the most spectacular in the Club Med chain. The resort closed after hurricane damage several years ago, but is now reopened, and is better than ever.

The island's population hovers around 500, with fishing and tourism the economic mainstays. The remote location means you have to make a special effort to travel here. Why do it? It would be hard to imagine a better place to escape daily life: to relax, dive, snorkel, catch some rays or some fish, all in an enchanting, historical, tropical paradise.

Rum Cay, about 25 miles southwest of San Salvador and 20 miles east of Long Island, is surrounded by coral reefs, white beaches, and forested hills that pop up around the coastline. Salt exports to Nova Scotia kept the islanders in rum until the salt flats were destroyed by two hurricanes in the early 1900s.

Port Nelson is the only settlement on the island, protected by Sumner Point on the southeast side of the island. Coconut groves shade this peaceful spot, inhabited by about 50 full-time residents. The Sumner Point Marina has several slips, fuel, electricity, water, and ice. Friends who visited here in May 2004 told us the restaurant and bar serves delicious food and strong libations, and that the people are super friendly.

The interior of the island has a number of blue holes worth exploring. The easiest ones to reach are to the west of the road from Port Nelson to Liberty Rock and Port Boyd. We've been told the road is in good shape and the airport renovations are complete.

Conception Island lies 10 miles northwest of Rum Cay and 14 miles northeast of Cape Santa Maria, Long Island. The island is uninhabited and protected by the Bahamas National Trust. This sanctuary is home to thousands of migratory birds and nesting green turtles. The interior of the island is composed of creeks and a huge lagoon that can go mostly dry at low tide. Friends from Long Island have told they see tailing bonefish in the southwestern creek entrance on a regular basis.

Diving, snorkeling, and beachcombing are the draws here, with the dive resorts on Long Island, Cat Island, and San Salvador all offering trips to these awe-inspiring waters.

Bahamasair flies from Nassau to Cockburn Town, San Salvador, most days. American Eagle flies from Miami. With the runway now extended to 8,000 feet, there is talk of larger jets flying here to service Club Med, but so far this seems to just be talk. Riding Rock Marina & Inn operates charter flights on Saturdays.

San Salvador

NORTH ATLANTIC OCEAN

White Cay

Catto Cay
Hawksnest Cay

Green Cay

reef fish

Cut Cay

Man Head Cay

reef fish

Graham's Harbour

North East Point

Barkers Point

RECKLEY HILL

Rocky Point

UNITED ESTATES

QUARTERS

HARBOUR ESTATE

DIXONS

VICTORIA HILL

BRANDY HILL

Bora Cay

bonefish

Guana Cay

POLLY HILL

Bonefish Bay

Club Med

HARD BARGAIN

Greens Harbour

Riding Rock Point

Riding Rock Marina & Inn

COCKBURN TOWN

Storr's Lake

marlin
tuna
dorado
wahoo

Fernandez Bay

Granny Lake

Great Lake

FORTUNE HILL

HOLIDAY TRACK

LEGEND

COLUMBUS MONUMENT

LONG BAY

FARQUHARSON

TOWN / SETTLEMENT

OLYMPIC MONUMENT

SOUTH VICTORIA HILL

Resort / Marina

SUGAR LOAF

Airport

Creek

Ferry

fish species

Roads

OLD PLACE

Pigeon

Restaurant / Bar

TRIAL FARM

Monument

MONTREAL

marlin

ALLEN

tuna

bonefish

dorado

wahoo

High Cay

Southwest Point

French Bay

Snow Bay

Middle Cay

NORTH ATLANTIC OCEAN

reef fish

Low Cay

North

0 1 2 3 4

SCALE IN MILES

© 1999 Map illustration: Burton Design, Jackson Hole, WY

Around the Islands

If you visit San Salvador chances are you'll stay at either the Riding Rock Inn or Club Med. In either case you can rent a car or bike and tour the island. Riding Rock Inn is adjacent to the marina and just north of the settlement. Club Med is a couple of minutes north of the airport on a velvety white beach. Continuing north you'll pass the Northwest Arm of Great Lake on the way to Graham's Harbour. Columbus described this reef-protected anchorage at the north end of the island as big enough "to hold all the ships in Christendom." It's also a good spot for snorkeling and reef fishing.

The road turns south near Reckley Hill. The Dixon Hill Lighthouse is a mile farther on, about half way down East Beach, which is protected by a continuous reef. This is an ideal spot for swimming and snorkeling. The road cuts inland at Storr's Lake. Crab Cay, which you can only reach by hiking, is the site of the *Chicago Herald*'s monument to Columbus.

The road skirts across a narrow piece of land between Storr's Lake and Granny Lake before emerging along Snow Bay, only to cut inland again at the north end of Pigeon Creek. The creek has picture-perfect bonefish habitat, plus we've caught some baby tarpon here. We've also seen tarpon in some of the lakes that went up to 50 pounds.

There are wadable flats around the mouth of Pigeon Creek that consistently produce quality bonefishing. On the falling tide, we like to wade into the creek and along the creek edges to catch the abundant fish pouring out. This is a wonderful place to fish on your own.

French Bay, at the southern end of the island, is a protected anchorage and another fine spot for reef fishing and snorkeling. The road rounds Sandy Point and then turns north again, traversing three miles of inviting beaches that include Long Bay and Fernandez Bay before ending up back in Cockburn Town.

A leisurely drive around the island will take a few hours, or you can make a day outing of it. In either case, take a picnic basket and a cooler with ice and drinks.

On Rum Cay you can drive or bicycle from Port Nelson to Port Boyd and Liberty Rock, though the best exploring on this little isle is done on foot or in a small boat along the shoreline. There is good reef fishing all around the island, and a number of small flats and creeks for bonefishing. Flamingo Bay on the northwest corner of the island has good snorkeling, sunning, and fishing in a gorgeous, isolated setting.

Conception Island has no roads. You can come ashore from small boats to do some bird-watching, or to take photographs, but remember that the island is protected by the Bahamas National Trust. There is no "taking" of anything. Just look and enjoy.

Fishing Highlights

Offshore and reef fishing opportunities are the stars of this region, but anglers who want to fish on their own will find a surprising number of good flats and creeks with relatively

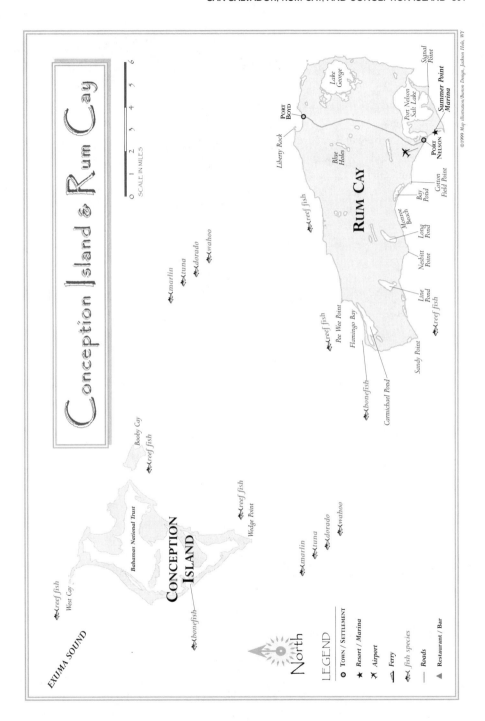

Conception Island & Rum Cay

SCALE IN MILES
0 1 2 3 4 5 6

North

LEGEND
- ⊙ Town / Settlement
- ★ Resort / Marina
- ✈ Airport
- Ferry
- fish species
- Roads
- ▲ Restaurant / Bar

EXUMA SOUND

West Cay

Bahamas National Trust

CONCEPTION ISLAND

Wedge Point

Booby Cay

reef fish
bonefish
marlin
tuna
dorado
wahoo
reef fish
reef fish

RUM CAY

Lake George
Port Boyd
Liberty Rock
Blue Holes
reef fish
Pee Wee Point
Flamingo Bay
Sandy Point
Carmichael Pond
bonefish
Line Pond
reef fish
Nesbitt Point
Long Pond
Monroe Beach
Bay Pond
Cotton Field Point
Port Nelson Salt Lake
Summer Point Marina
Port Nelson
Signal Point

reef fish
marlin
tuna
dorado
wahoo

© 1999 Map illustration/Burton Design, Jackson Hole, WY

easy access. Offshore and reef charters are available through the Riding Rock Marina on San Salvador. Charter boats from Long Island and Cat Island also fish these waters.

Wahoo are best in January and February. Tuna, dorado, and billfish become plentiful in April and May, with excellent fishing continuing into the summer.

Reef fishing is very good year round. Water depths of 20

Baby tarpon.

to 80 feet are most productive. If you use chum you're likely to create a boiling feeding frenzy in most areas. Sea Habits, Snak Pak flies, and Clouser's Minnows are all you'll need to catch jacks, snappers, mackerels, yellowtail, 'cudas, and sharks. If you want to hook up with some monster amberjack, fish over some of the wrecks. Be sure to use at least 80-pound shock tippet, or 30-pound wire tippet, just depending on the species you are targeting. And even then, you'll break off lots of fish.

You can catch bonefish on wadable flats on San Salvador just north of Club Med, and at various other spots around the island, but the Pigeon Creek area is best. Easy access is available from the main road, though you'll have to do some walking to reach the best flats at the mouth of the creek. A Bunny Gotcha or Mantis Shrimp will take fish consistently, but almost any bonefish fly will work, as these bones rarely have to deal with fly-fishers.

In the past couple of years we've had the opportunity to explore the inland lakes and they turned out to be better that we expected, though we had to really "earn" our fishing. The walking is not easy, often through mangroves and thick brush, and the lakes bottoms are sometimes soft and treacherous. We found and caught good numbers of tarpon between 2 and 30 pounds, and we saw fish we estimated at around 50 pounds. We also caught jacks, mangrove snappers, and cubera snapper. The biggest cubera was about 20 pounds, and frankly, we were surprised not to find bigger ones.

We believe this same sort of fishing could be available in the lakes and blue holes on Rum Cay, but haven't been able to get there yet. Someone should give it a try.

Optional Activities

Diving, snorkeling, sailing, biking, hiking, and letting the tension drain from stress-taut muscles are the main activities. The only real vacationing option is San Salvador, unless you're cruising in your own boat, though overnight trips to Conception Island are available through Stella Maris out of Long Island. If you need things to do, stay at Club Med. The staff there has enough energy, and enough toys, to keep most people entertained 24 hours a day.

The diving programs out of Club Med and Riding Rock Marina are world class. Resort and certification courses are available along with courses in underwater photography. Both facilities provide gear rentals. The Club Med facilities include a decompression chamber.

Lodging and Services

Featured Lodges

Club Med

San Salvador Unlike many other Club Med resorts, this location promotes a low-key atmosphere and caters to upscale couples. Set on 80-acres of virgin coastline, the 288-unit resort has elegant rooms with handcrafted furniture, satellite TV, telephones, walk-in closets, spacious bathrooms, and patios or balconies. Amenities include state-of-the-art dive center with three custom-made 45-foot catamarans and a decompression chamber; nine tennis courts, swimming pool, exercise room, bicycles, sailing, windsurfing, massages, beauty salon, and three restaurants. Guided bike tours can introduce you to island life beyond the resort. Non-guests can partake of the sumptuous buffet lunches and dinners with advance reservations. You can walk to good bonefishing flats to the northeast. Car rentals and offshore fishing can be arranged.
Season: October though July.
Suitable For: Anglers and non-anglers.
What's Included: All-inclusive packages are the Club Med way, though they do tack on some extras here and there.
Not Included: Airfare to/from Cockburn Town, taxi transfers, optional reef and offshore fishing.
Pricing: $$$-$$$$
Contact: Reservations and information, 888-722-0697, 800-258-2633 or 242-331-2000.
Internet: www.clubmed.com

Riding Rock Inn & Marina

San Salvador A diver's paradise, this clean two-story motel-style resort offers three dives per day to pristine offshore reefs and a drop-off wall teeming with life. It's also the only place to stay on San Salvador if you want to manage your own activities. The inn's three buildings house rooms facing either the ocean or the freshwater pool. The ocean-side rooms have oak furniture, queen-size beds and sofa beds, sitting areas with a table and chairs, and refrigerators. Poolside rooms lack refrigerators and queen-size beds. Two villas are also available for rent. We suggest the deluxe rooms facing the ocean. The restaurant serves grilled wahoo and tuna right off the fishing boats as well as breakfasts cooked to order. Amenities include telephones, bar, satellite TV, and an okay tennis court. A meal plan is available. Guanahani Dive Limited runs the diving program. Car and bicycle rentals are available. The marina has seven slips, plus fuel, electricity, water, ice, and laundromat.
Season: October though July.
Suitable For: Anglers and divers.
What's Included: Dive packages including accommodations and meals are available. Complimentary airport transfers.

Not Included: Airfare to/from Cockburn Town, optional reef and offshore fishing, alcoholic beverages, and optional gratuities.

Pricing: $$

Contact: Reservations and information, 800-272-1492 or 954-359-8353.

Internet: www.ridingrock.com

E-mail: info@ridingrock.com

Services

Air Service:

American Eagle: 800-433-7300; Internet: www.aa.com

Bahamasair: 242-339-4415 or 800-222-4262

Air Sunshine: 954-434-8900 or 800-327-8900

Taxi Service: Taxis meet arriving flights.

Diving and Snorkeling Excursions: *Riding Rock Marina* will arrange diving and snorkeling excursions for you.

Car and Bike Rentals: Both car and bike rentals are available at Riding Rock Inn.

Restaurants: There are two restaurants in Cockburn Town: *Harlem Square* and the *Three Ships*. Both serve tasty Bahamian dishes, and Harlem Square has a pool table.

Government: There is a government clinic and police station in Cockburn Town.

New Developments

None that we know of. Log on to our Web site at www.bahamasflyfishingguide.com for updated information.

CHAPTER 15

MAYAGUANA, GREAT INAGUA, LITTLE INAGUA, AND RAGGED ISLANDS

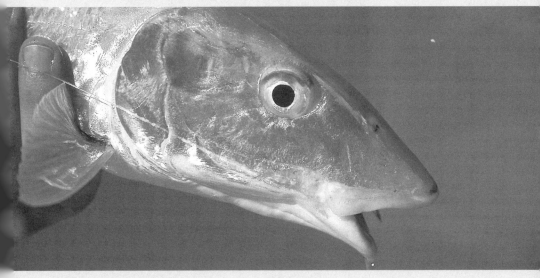

The Bahamas is the destination for fly-fishers seeking monster bones. (Brian Hodges)

O f all the Out Islands, these are the most out, as well as the least developed and visited. Located 350 miles southeast of Nassau, and 50 miles across the Mayaguana Passage from Acklins Island, Mayaguana is the eastern-most Bahamian island. Twenty-four miles long and as much as six miles wide, the island has forests of lignum vitae and other hardwoods, ideal soil for farming, plus miles of wild unspoiled beaches and rich coral reefs.

Mayaguana, which is the original native name, was uninhabited until 1812, when people from the nearby Turks Islands began to settle here. The main settlements and best anchorages are at Abraham's Bay, Betsy Bay, and Pirates Well. These settlements, which retain an authentic Bahamian appearance and mood, received electricity and telephone services for the first time in 1997 and 1998. The population of around 300 makes their living by farming and fishing. The weekly mail boat visits always create a stir among the locals, as do visits by boaters. The friendly people often greet visitors coming ashore with hugs and offers of food and drink.

Deep blue water surrounds most of the island, creating a phenomenal fishery for both commercial and sportfishing interests. Conch is abundant on the flats and in other shallow-water areas. If you want to learn about the pirate days, many of the locals can tell you stories of battles between the buccaneers and treasure-laden Spanish galleons.

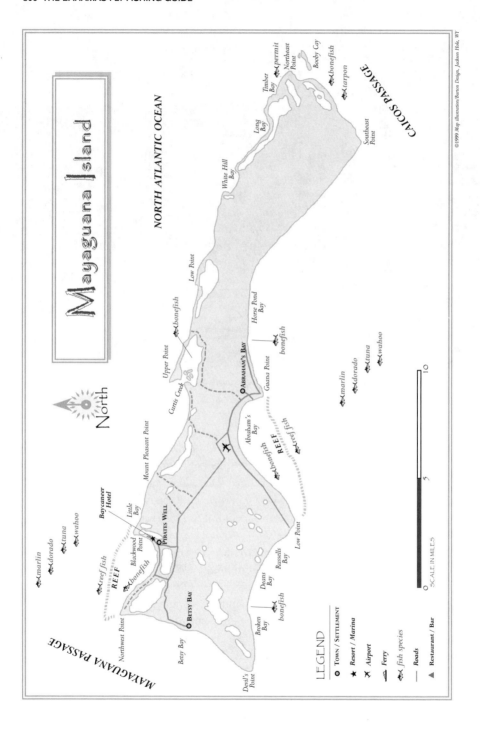

Mayaguana Island

North

NORTH ATLANTIC OCEAN

MAYAGUANA PASSAGE

CAICOS PASSAGE

Devil's Point

Betsy Bay

Northwest Point

REEF

Blackwood Point

Little Bay

Bayaneer Hotel

PIRATES WELL

BETSY BAY

Broken Bay

Deans Bay

Russells Bay

Low Point

Mount Pleasant Point

Curtis Creek

Upper Point

Low Point

White Hill Bay

Long Bay

Timber Bay

Northeast Point

Booby Cay

Southeast Point

Abraham's Bay

ABRAHAM'S BAY

Guana Point

REEF

Horse Pond Bay

amarlin
dorado
tuna
wahoo

reef fish
bonefish

bonefish

bonefish

bonefish

reef fish

bonefish

bonefish

amarlin
dorado
tuna
wahoo

permit
carpon
bonefish

LEGEND

○ TOWN / SETTLEMENT
★ Resort / Marina
✈ Airport
⚓ Ferry
🐟 fish species
— Roads
▲ Restaurant / Bar

0   5   10

SCALE IN MILES

©1999 Map illustration/Burton Design, Jackson Hole, WY

Mayaguana's airstrip is the residual of a U.S. missile tracking station used in the early days of space exploration. Bahamasair flies in a couple of times a week, while private aircraft use the strip on a daily basis. We have heard of several development companies with plans to build 50- to 60-room hotels on the island, but nothing has happened as of late 2004.

Activities at any resort on this island would include excellent diving, snorkeling, and shelling, plus superb untouched reef and offshore fishing. There is excellent bonefishing on numerous flats around the island. John Pinto and Gary Borger are operating the only established fly-fishing program on the island out of the Baycaneer Hotel, a 16-room hotel with a restaurant and bar. The program is based on using canoes (self-paddled) to access the flats, then anglers stalk bones on foot. This is a great opportunity for experienced anglers who are looking for remote fishing, and who don't need a guide looking over their shoulder all the time. Anglers should also be in good physical condition.

Great Inagua is 80 to 85 miles south of Acklins and Mayaguana, and 50 miles east of Cuba. At 45 miles long and 25 miles wide, it is the third largest Bahamian island. "Inagua" is an anagram for the iguana, a common island resident. Together with uninhabited Little Inagua, the islands are simply referred to as the Inaguas.

The lure here has long been the Bahamas National Trust Park and Wildlife Sanctuary, administered by the Bahamas National Trust. The 287-acre park, which includes 12-mile long Lake Windsor, is home to the world's largest population of West Indian flamingos. These birds now number close to 60,000, after approaching extinction. Other birds include the endangered Bahama parrot and white-crowned pigeon, plus thousands of egrets, herons, cormorants, owls, pelicans, hummingbirds, and ducks. There are also populations of wild boar and wild donkeys.

Most of the coastline is sheltered by reefs that make life difficult for boaters looking for an anchorage, while creating sensational dive sites and reef fishing. Inside the reefs, there are miles and miles of flats, most completely inaccessible. On the south side of the island, there are flats and creeks from Lantern Head to MacKenzie Point, also known as Southwest Point.

Around the point and just north is Matthew Town, the island's main settlement. Salt is "gold" on Inagua, with a high percentage of the island's thousand residents working for the Morton Salt Company. The town is made up of a few restaurants and bars, a few guesthouse/motels, well-stocked grocery and liquor stores, hardware stores, a cinema, and the usual array of varied residential dwellings.

Services include a post office, customs office, commissioner's office, bank, and clinic with a resident doctor. The mail boat arrives at the government wharf once a week. The Bahamas National Defense Force maintains a full-time base here that is mainly focused on drug interdiction. There are no good services or anchorages for boaters. The well-maintained airport, usually serviced three times a week by Bahamasair, is a mile north of town.

The Morton Salt Company produces about a million pounds of salt a year at this location, and more when worldwide demand increases. Great Inagua's environment is

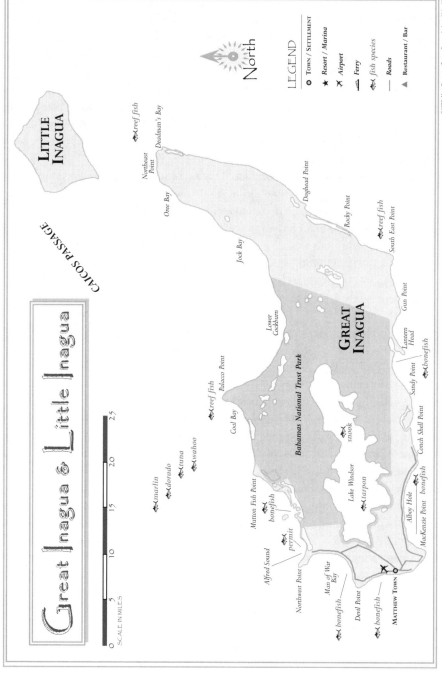

Great Inagua & Little Inagua

SCALE IN MILES

0   5   10   15   20   25

LITTLE
INAGUA

CAICOS PASSAGE

Deadman's Bay
reef fish
Northeast
Point
Oree Bay
Doghead Point
Rocky Point
reef fish
South East Point
Jock Bay
Gun Point

GREAT
INAGUA

Lower
Cockburn
Lantern
Head
bonefish
Sandy Point
Palacco Point
reef fish
Bahamas National Trust Park
Cod Bay
Conch Shell Point
wahoo
tuna
snook
dorado
Lake Windsor
tarpon
marlin
Alboy Hole
MacKenzie Point   bonefish
Mutton Fish Point
bonefish
bonefish
permit
Alfred Sound
Northwest Point
Man of War
Bay
Devil Point
bonefish
MATTHEW TOWN
bonefish

North

LEGEND

⊙ Town / Settlement
★ Resort / Marina
✈ Airport
⚓ Ferry
🐟 fish species
— Roads
▲ Restaurant / Bar

©1999 Map Illustration/Burton Design, Jackson Hole, WY

ideal for salt production. The weather is unusually hot and dry, the terrain harsh and, for the most part, flat. There are more cacti on Inagua than anywhere else in the Bahamas, basically because the salt-soaked soil makes it impossible for other plants to survive. The most striking features of the island are the vast crusty salt beds and the sparkling white mountains of brine you can't miss when you fly into the airport.

Just off the airport are good bonefishing flats you can walk to from town. These flats continue on to Devil Point and resume in Man of War Bay. The road from town runs along the coast making the flats fairly easy to access, though you need to be in shape to walk through the mangroves and deal with areas of muck. This is a rugged region ideally suited to experienced anglers who want to fish in a remote location on their own, and it is beautiful—white sand and turtle grass flats rimmed with mangroves that stretch on and on.

The bonefish here run four to eight pounds, and there is always the chance to encounter a double-digit beast. If you're looking for a guide, there is one on the island: Ezzard Cartwright. Ezzard has a vehicle and a boat he can trailer to various spots around the island, including Alfred Sound. Starting at Northwest Point, the Sound runs more or less east where a series of flats and creeks create perfect bonefish and permit habitat.

This is one of the best areas in the Bahamas to fish for permit, with the higher tidal stages preferable. At lower tidal flows you can fish for tailing bones along the mangroves. And if your dream is a grand slam—there are good numbers of tarpon in Lake Windsor.

Visiting anglers should be aware that Matthew Town is not a tourist destination. While the people are extremely friendly, you will have to fit into their lifestyle, not the other way around. That said, some of the best frontier flats fishing in the islands is waiting for those who are up to the challenge.

Little Inagua is five miles to the north off the eastern tip of Great Inagua. It covers 30 square miles and is uninhabited except for herds of wild donkeys and goats and a variety of bird life, including a rare species of heron.

The Ragged Island chain extends for 90 miles from Ragged Island in the south to the Jumentos Cays in the north. These islands form the southeastern end of the Great Bahama Bank, with most of the islands and cays being uninhabited.

It's only about 20 miles from the Jumentos Cays to Little Exuma, and to Sandy Cay on Long Island, yet this is another universe. Rough windy weather is common in the winter, while spring and summer usually deliver calm seas that are ideal for boating, fishing, and diving. Good reef and offshore fishing is available along the entire chain, and there are flats interspersed throughout many of the smaller cays.

Ragged Island is about four miles long and not very wide. Duncan Town is the only settlement. Less than 100 residents try to make a living from fishing and some farming. A grocery store has decent provisions, and there are a couple of places to eat, drink, and shoot pool. Bahamasair usually services the Duncan Town airstrip twice a week.

permit

Jumentos Cays Wet Rock   Nuevitas Rock
             No Bush Cay   reef fish
        Pear Cay
   Stoney Cay

reef fish
bonefish   Little Water Cay
Melita Cay   Water Cay   bonefish

Lanzadera Cay

Torzan Cay

Flamingo Cay

reef fish   bonefish

Man-of-War Cay

North

Ragged Island Range

reef fish
bonefish   Jamaica Cay
Black Rock   White Rock

Seal Cay   marlin

                            dorado

Sisters Cay   tuna

                            wahoo

North Channel Cay

CROOKED ISLAND
PASSAGE

South Channel Cay
Nurse Cay
bonefish   Little Nurse Cay
Buena Vista Cay

LEGEND

○ TOWN / SETTLEMENT

★ Resort / Marina

✈ Airport

Raccoon Cay   Ferry

reef fish   Johnson Cay   fish species
Double Breasted Cay
Margaret Cay   Roads
bonefish   Maycock Cay
Hog Cay   ▲ Restaurant / Bar

Hog Point   Black Rock Point
bonefish
Ragged Island ○ DUNCAN TOWN

Little Ragged Island   0   5   10   15   20   25
Wilson Point   bonefish   SCALE IN MILES

GREAT BAHAMA BANK

© 1999 Map illustrations/Burton Design, Jackson Hole, WY

To the north, Ragged Island Harbour is located between Duncan Town and Hog Cay. The mail boat calls here weekly, and some services are available to boaters, but don't count on anything in particular. The harbor authorities monitor VHF Channel 16.

The Ragged Island Bonefishing Club is no longer in operation, and the two main guides who worked here have left the island. That means the wonderful flats fishery that exists in this area is just basking in the sun—untouched. We understand that the *Outpost,* the 61-foot Hatteras motherboat operated by Angling Destinations, has plans to call on this area for a week or two each season. If so, that would be a trip worth taking.

Continuing north, boaters can enjoy good fishing off the reefs and in a number of cuts. You'll see more flats starting around Jamaica Cay. Flamingo Cay is relatively high and covered with vegetation. There are idyllic white sand beaches here and good fishing for cruising and tailing bones. Moving on, there is even better bonefishing around the Water Cays and Stony Cay. And permit? Yep, there are schools of permit around many of these cays. To experience all of this—all it takes is time.

Mayaguana Lodging and Services

Featured Lodges

Mayaguana Bonefishing

Baycaneer Hotel, Pirates Well   Experienced anglers looking for a new adventure will find it here. If you can see fish well on your own, and don't require a guide looking over your shoulder, Mayaguana Bonefishing was designed with you in mind. The program, conceived and implemented by John Pinto and Gary Borger, eliminates guides and boats, and focuses on exploring a wilderness environment in search of aggressive unpressured bonefish. During a 10-hour fishing day it is common to see large bones cruising over white sand flats or tailing along deserted shorelines. Anglers need to be physically prepared for intense, full days of up close and personal, one-on-one, wade fishing for big bones. Anglers stay in a comfortable 16-room beachfront hotel. Breakfast and dinner are served in the hotel dining room. Lunch is on the flats. An American manager is on hand to handle all logistics, answer questions, and describe the various wading options for each day.

Season: October through May.

Suitable For: Anglers.

What's Included: All-inclusive packages cover accommodations, meals, use of canoes, airport transfers, and Bahamian taxes.

Not Included: Airfare to/from Abraham's Bay, alcoholic beverages, fishing tackle, and gratuities. To do this totally on your own, you can just book a room at the hotel then work with some locals for transportation to and from the flats. Leroy Joseph takes people out on fishing and snorkeling day trips. You can contact him through the hotel.

Pricing: $-$$

Contact: Reservations and information, call John Pinto, 586-445-8874, or call the hotel directly, 242-339-3605, and ask for Earnell Brown.

Internet: www.garyborger.com/mayaguana.html

Mayaguana Inn Guest House

Abraham's Bay   Five comfortable rooms and good meals. Everything else is on your own.
Pricing: $
Contact: Reservations and information, 242-339-3065 or 242-339-3203.

There are a couple of other guesthouses that are just rooms in people's homes. Same for "restaurants," with food often cooked in someone's home kitchen. People here consider this "the way it is," and they're happy to have you for a meal or a drink. There are a couple of men in town who enjoy taking people fishing.

In Abraham's Bay there is a police station, commissioner's office, and telephone station, plus two small grocery stores that carry some provisions.

Services

Air Service: Bahamasair usually flies to Abraham's Bay three times a week, but this is not guaranteed. Also, these flights are often late, so be sure to leave yourself plenty of time for connections on your way out.

Great Inagua Lodging and Services

Featured Lodges

Great Inagua Flats Fishing

Matthew Town   Imagine a distant island with only one guide, surrounded by wadable flats stretching out from rugged deserted shorelines, flats with bonefish and schools of permit, and then, a large inland lake with rolling tarpon. In the southern Bahamas, 60 miles northeast of Cuba, Great Inagua is this island. The one guide is Ezzard Cartwright. Ezzard greets anglers at the Matthew Town airport and puts them up in a comfortable two-bedroom apartment across from his house. The air-conditioned apartment has a full kitchen and satellite TV. Meals are served at the house, or anglers can eat in town. Each day Ezzard drives his anglers to the flats for a full day of fishing. Some flats can be accessed directly from shore, while other are reached in Ezzard's skiff. Deeper flats, including most of the permit areas, are fished from a poled skiff. The drive to Lake Windsor for tarpon fishing takes about an hour over rough roads. Most tarpon are 20 to 60 pounds, though there are larger fish. It's not uncommon to catch several bones in a day over 8 pounds, and there are shots at double-digit trophies. Anglers can book a package with Ezzard, combine fishing with Ezzard with fishing on their own, or experienced anglers can go it alone and book their own accommodations at various guesthouses.
Season: October through May.
Suitable for: Anglers.
What's Included: Accommodations, meals, airport transfers, guided fishing, and Bahamian taxes.
Not Included: Airfare to/from Matthew Town, and anything else on your own. If you book on your own you need to do your homework, and you need to be completely self-sufficient with your gear and everything else.
Pricing: $-$$

Contact: Reservations and information, 800-211-8530.
Internet: www.anglingdestinations.com

Sunset Apartments

Matthew Town   A good bet for accommodations on Inagua, these two apartments sit right along the water on Matthew Town's southern side. The cement units all have air-conditioning, terra-cotta tile floors, rattan furniture, small terraces, satellite TV, kitchen, a picnic area, and a gas grill. About a five-minute walk away is a small, secluded beach called the "Swimming Hole."
Pricing: $-$$
Contact: Reservations and information, 242-339-1362 and ask for Ezzard.

The Main House

Operated by the Morton Salt Company, the five rooms are large, clean, and air-conditioned. There are telephones in the rooms, and satellite TV. Take some earplugs because the hotel is right across from the settlement power plant.
Pricing: $
Contact: Reservations and information, 242-339-1267/66; fax 242-339-1265.

Walkine's Guest House

Five comfortable rooms with air-conditioning, two rooms share a bath, three have private baths. Meals are served in nearby Topps Restaurant.
Pricing: $
Contact: Reservations and information, 242-339-1612.

Services

Air Service: Bahamasair usually flies to Matthew Town two to three times a week, but flights are not guaranteed. These flights are often late, so you should give yourself plenty of time to make your outbound connections.

Restaurants: *Cozy Corner Restaurant* (locals just call it Cozy's). Cheerful and loud, this lunch hangout is the best on the island. It has a pool table and a large seating area with a bar. Stop in for a chat with locals over a Kalik and Bahamian conch burger. Cozy's also serves delicious Bahamian dinners on request—grilled snapper, steamed or grilled crawfish, baked chicken and fries, macaroni and cheese, homemade slaw, and piping hot johnnycake. Contact: 242-339-1440.

Local Attractions: The Morton Salt Company has more than 2,000 acres of crystallizing ponds and more than 34,000 acres of reservoirs. Over a million tons of salt are produced every year for a variety of industrial uses, including salting icy U.S. streets. (More is produced when the Northeast has a bad winter.) In an unusual case of industry assisting its environment, the crystallizers provide a feeding ground for the flamingos. As the water evaporates, the concentration of brine shrimp in the ponds increases, and the flamingos feast. Factory tours are available. Contact: 242-339-1300.

Inagua National Park and *Union Creek Reserve* are both are managed by the Bahamas Nation Trust. The Caribbean Conservation Corporation on marine turtle research also works in the Union Creek

Reserve. To tour any part of the park or reserve, you must be accompanied by a BNT warden. Contact the Bahamas National Trust's office in Nassau to make a reservation. BNT will send you a visitor form you must fill out and return with your flight information, length of stay, and number of people in your party. You must pay for your tour before you arrive on Inagua. Reservations and information, 242-393-1317; fax 242-393-4978; e-mail: bnt@bahamas.net.bx.

Flamingo and turtle tours (in the Union Creek Turtle Reserve) can also be arranged in advance by calling Warden Henry Nixon on Great Inagua. Contact: 242-339-1616.

New Developments

Hard-core anglers often take extreme measures to get to virgin fishing. If you fit that description, you might be interested in Angling Destinations motherboat program aboard their 61-foot shoal draft Hatteras, *Outpost*. Unexplored and unfished areas are their specialty, though they already have a lot of experience in many areas of the Bahamas such as the West Side of Andros, the southern tip of Long Island, the remote cays of Exuma, and the southern flats of Acklins.

Taking only four anglers at a time, a trip aboard *Outpost* isn't actually roughing it so you don't have to be that hard-core—you just have to want to fish from dawn 'til dusk in remote locations. The yacht has air-conditioning, a reverse-osmosis water system, comfortable beds, a large salon to hang out in, and they serve great meals.

Two bonefish skiffs suited to exploring remote areas are towed behind the motherboat. Bahamian guides man the skiffs and will be on hand to assist you, or to let you wander the deserted flats on your own.

Be advised that these trips aboard *Outpost* are exploratory trips and only anglers willing to accept both the risks and rewards of these type trips should consider this adventure. *Outpost* plans to visit the Ragged Island chain and Great Inagua in 2005, and they may swing over to Acklins as well. For more information, visit the Angling Destinations Web site at www.anglingdestinations.com.

Visit our Web site at www.bahamasflyfishingguide.com for new updates.

CHAPTER 16

TURKS AND CAICOS ISLANDS (TCI)

The beaches of Grace Bay, Providenciales, invite travelers to dive in their blue waters—or just sit back and catch some rays.

A geographical extension of the Bahamas, the Turks and Caicos Islands (TCI) poke up out of the deep blue ocean about 40 miles southeast of Mayaguana, and 100 miles north of Hispaniola. Home to some of the most seductive white sand beaches in the Caribbean, the islands are mostly flat with the highest point being 250 feet—the undulating green hilltops of Providenciales.

The Islands are composed of two groups of islands: the "Turks islands" (Grand Turk and Salt Cay), and the "Caicos islands" (Providenciales, North Caicos, Middle Caicos, East Caicos, South Caicos, West Caicos). The groups are separated by the Turks Island Passage, also known as Columbus Passage, a 22-mile wide, 7,000-feet deep channel. Of the 40-odd islands and cays that make up this British Crown Colony, only 8 are inhabited. The landmass, covering 193 square miles, is surrounded by a continuous coral reef; one of the largest in the world. The deep bodies of water and reefs create the ideal conditions for baitfish, making TCI a blue-water fishing haven. Blue marlin, wahoo, dorado, tuna, and many other species ply these waters in their respective seasons.

Grand Turk, the capital, is the seat of government, and a scuba diver's fantasy, but this is not the main tourist island, and there are no good flats fishing areas here. The blue-water fishing, however, can be exceptional. The architecture is reminiscent of

Bermuda—the Bermudans arrived in the islands in the mid 1600s and began a boom-ing salt business that lasted into the mid-twentieth century. The main settlement, Cockburn Town, has an old-world colonial feel. The island is seven miles long by a mile and a half wide, and the interior is laced with large creeks and lakes.

Providenciales, or "Provo" as everyone calls it, is the center of the TCI tourism industry, and in fact, Provo was created from scratch by developers in the 1980s. Club Med was the first resort to open in 1981. Grace Bay Beach, a 12-mile long strip of pow-dery white-sand perfection, is the center of resort development. The turquoise waters that lap the shore here rival any in the Caribbean for relaxed swimming, snorkeling, or pretty much any water sport you can name. Setting the idea of fishing aside, this is one of the best island destinations anywhere for an overall sand, sea, surf, golf, and tennis vacation for families and couples. It's an idyllic spot for a romantic getaway, too, with a variety of upscale accommodations, fine dining restaurants, and miles of deserted beaches on nearby cays where you'll never see another person.

Toss in the fact that Provo and its neighboring cays are surrounded by bonefish flats, and you've got the ideal combination for anglers and non-anglers alike. If you rent a car you can fish all over the island on your own. The best flats are on the south side. Some of our favorites include Silly Creek, Cooper Jack Bight, Jim Hill Bight, and areas of Long Bay Beach. If you want to rent a boat, a 16-foot Carolina skiff for exam-ple, you can fish flats on your own from the Leeward Marina all the way to Parrot Cay. Or rent the boat and forget fishing—go snorkeling along the reef or stop off in a secluded cove for a swim and a picnic.

For fishing or vacationing, a trip to the TCIs is the absolute best way to play the odds against the normal winter weather patterns of cold fronts and wind. Cold fronts rarely reach these islands. Delightful warm days are the rule during the winter season, although you'll have some wind at times, which is just the way it goes in the world of saltwater fishing. In the spring, summer, and fall, the weather is almost always gorgeous, with the normal hurricane watches focused on August, September, and October.

American Airlines has at least two direct non-stop flights daily to Providenciales International Airport from Miami. Flying time is approximately one hour and twenty minutes via jet service. American also flies three days a week non-stop from New York's JFK Airport. British Airways flies once a week from London, usually with a stopover in Nassau. US Airways flies four days a week from Charlotte. Air Jamaica flies daily from Montego Bay (the TCIs were annexed by Jamaica from 1873 to 1976). Air Canada flies from Toronto, once a week on Saturdays. Bahamasair flies three times a week from Nassau. For the most up-to-date information, check with your travel agent.

Domestic flights are available from Provo to Grand Turk, Salt Cay, North Caicos, Middle Caicos, and South Caicos.

Entry requirements into the TCIs are the same as the Bahamas, though we highly recommend that U.S. citizens use their passports and not rely on a birth certificate with some other sort of photo ID. Things like electricity, water, telecommunications, package deliveries, and other services are similar to the Bahamas. The TCIs are in the

Eastern time zone. The U.S. dollar is the primary currency, though the Treasury also issues a Turks and Caicos crown and quarter, both of which are legal tender. Traveler's checks in U.S. dollar amounts are widely accepted and other currency can be changed at local banks. American Express, Visa, and MasterCard are welcomed at many locations.

Comprehensive details about the islands, government, people, and a myriad of accommodation and activity options can be found on the following two Web sites: www.Provo.net and www.TCIway.tc.

Around the Islands

Most visitors arrive in the TCIs at the Providenciales International Airport. After clearing customs and collecting your luggage, you will find plenty of taxis and resort courtesy vehicles to take you to any destination on the island. Rental cars are also available at the airport.

Boaters have four choices for entry points with customs services—Sapodilla Bay and Caicos Marina and Boatyard on the south side of Provo, Leeward Marina on the east end, and Turtle Cove Marina in the center on the north side of the island. There are numerous other small marinas scattered around Provo and more under construction as of summer 2004. Boaters should be aware that most approaches to these marinas are through National Parks and Nature Reserves. There are very specific rules for anchorages and fishing. It is your responsibility to know and obey these laws.

Anglers and boaters should pay particular attention to the Caicos Bank, a 50-mile-by-60-mile shallow water haven for a variety of gamefish laced with coral heads, shoals, small cays, and vast sandy flats that can go dry at low tide. To the north, the bank is protected by the four largest islands in the chain—Provo, North, Middle (Grand), and East Caicos. West Caicos forms the western edge, while South Caicos is perched on the eastern fringe at the precipice of the Turks Island Passage. Some of the best bonefish flats in the TCIs are on the lee side of South Caicos. The southern rim of the bank runs from Molasses Reef down to White Cay, to Pear Cay, Bush Cay, then up to Little and Big Ambergris Cays, through the Fish Cays, to Long Cay, and back to South Caicos.

Fishing for jacks, barracuda, snappers, mackerel, and grouper is good all across the bank, around the reefs, and in the various inlets. Bonefish feed on the flats, but you'll need relatively calm conditions to catch them with fly gear. Cruising and day boaters should be aware that this is a huge exposed area. The wind can come up in an instant, turning the previously calm water into a vicious choppy sea. When fishing out on the bank you need to be prepared for tough weather to materialize at any time.

West Caicos is uninhabited; it's wild, tranquil, and protected by reefs on two sides. The majority of the west coast is a national park. A dramatic wall that plunges deep into the ocean creates some of the best diving in the islands. The water is so clear you can easily float on the surface and view a variety of fish swimming more than 50 feet below you. Several of the commercial tourist diving companies offer full-day excursions from Provo.

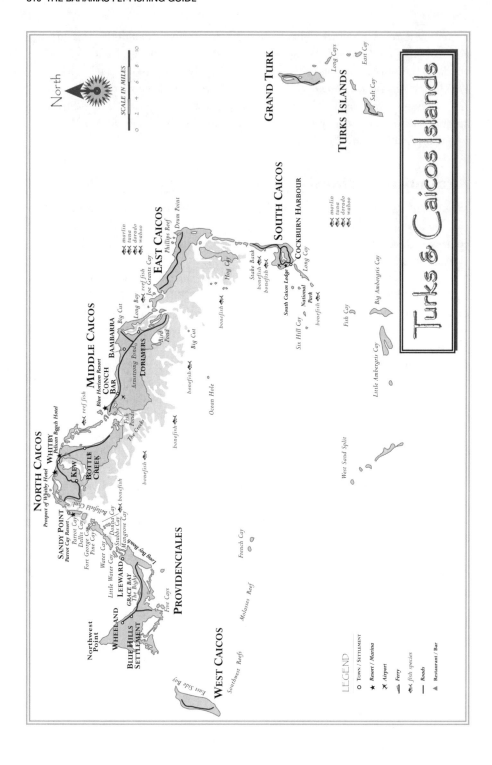

Virgin beaches on the eastern shore await exploration and the area is suitable for swimming as the sandy bottom remains shallow a long way out before reaching the reef. Inland from here is Lake Catherine, where hikers can view flamingoes wading the shallows. There are very few safe anchorages for boaters, though a marina was under construction in the summer

Grace Bay offers water sports galore.

of 2004. The scheduled date of completion is unknown.

Northwest, across the Sand Bore Channel, is Provo. The extensive West Reef protects the western coast of the island, and helps to create sensational bonefish habitat in the Pigeon Pond and Frenchman's Creek Nature Preserve. Outside the reef, trolling anglers can experience memorable fishing for billfish, wahoo, tuna, and dorado in season.

The channel is one of the major entrances to the Caicos Bank, and provides the most direct route for boaters on the way to Sapodilla Bay and South Dock. The shoreline from South Bluff to Silly Creek, a combination of sandy dunes, bluffs, and mangroves, is the beginning of prime bonefish territory that runs the length of this south side of Provo.

There are two water accesses into Silly Creek, one on either side of a small cay. The outside flats are wadable, but the interior flats are often soft and hilly and we don't recommend wading them, though you can walk and fish along the miles of shorelines inside the creek. This is not always easy walking because of the mangroves, and the northern side of the creek is mostly private property.

Silly Creek feeds into Chalk Sound National Park, a massive interior lagoon system laced with cays, inlets, flats, and bays. A long finger of land forms the southern boundary of the park. This finger is accessible throughout its length by a road that pushes in from South Dock and Sapodilla Bay. All-out development of expensive private homes is under way here.

As of summer 2004 it was still relatively easy to fish Silly Creek on your own, and parking a rental vehicle in many locations was not a problem. There are at least three public boat launch accesses along the road where you can park, or better, launch your flats boat. Guides rarely fish this area, so if you have the use of a boat you can reach flats that are not often fished. On the other side of the coin, the flats that can be accessed by anglers on foot are fished hard, so the used-to-be-easy fish are now wary and spooky.

Driving north from South Dock you can take the main highway back past the international airport and through downtown, or you can take a much more enjoyable diversion along the shoreline and up past Five Cays before this road joins the main highway again south of the airport. There are several places to park and fish on your own around the point south of Five Cays.

If you plan to fish on your own, and to have general mobility to enjoy Provo, you need to rent a car. If you're just going to hang on the beach in the Grace Bay area, you won't need one.

Assuming you have a vehicle and want to fish on your own, there are two semi-main roads (you will need to get a road map with your rental car) that lead south from the Leeward Highway in the center of the island. These roads run on either side of Turtle Lake and branch out in various directions. New homes are being built throughout this area.

A wonderful out of the way place to stay in this area is Harbour Club Villas & Marina overlooking Flamingo Lake. This lake, and the others nearby, is loaded with bonefish, and while the bottom is fairly soft, it is wadable, and you can fish to tailing fish most days without worrying about the tides.

A long curvy strip of land, Turtle Tail, continues on out past Flamingo Lake and forms the southern boundary of Juba Sound. This is another area of significant private home development. As of summer 2004 this road was in horrible shape, so you have to drive slowly. Also, this road is a dead end. However far you drive, you have to retrace your path and drive around Flamingo Lake before you can head back north and west. There are very good flats suitable for wading on the south ocean side of Turtle Tail.

Back on the Leeward Highway you can drive east toward downtown and Turtle Cove, or west toward the Grace Bay resort beaches and the Leeward Marina at the end of the island. The residential thumb of Long Bay can be accessed off Leeward Highway to the south. Long Bay has several miles of white sand beaches. The Caicos Marina and Boatyard is at the end of Long Bay at Juba Point.

The main access road to Grace Bay (there are several smaller ones, too) runs down past the Comfort Suites Hotel and runs into the Allegro Resort and American Casino. If you turn left you'll be on your way to the Turtle Cove Marina, and you'll drive along the busiest part of Grace Bay Beach. The major resorts on this stretch include Point Grace, the Sands, Sibonne, Coral Gardens, and Beaches.

The Turtle Cove Marina is a sprawling complex of boat docks and slips, restaurants, shops, and small hotels. The Turtle Cove Inn is a quaint two-story hotel on the marina boardwalk. Comfortable air-conditioned rooms overlook the marina or the gardens and swimming pool. Our favorite restaurants around the marina include Baci Ristorante, Magnolia Wine Bar and Restaurant, and the Tiki Hut. The Tiki Hut is a popular lunch spot right on the water, and they have a theme night barbecue once a week that usually turns into a major party. You'll need reservations if you want to join the fun.

Back out on Grace Bay, if you turn right at the Comfort Suites you'll be heading toward the Leeward Marina. This is the quieter part of Grace Bay Beach with a string

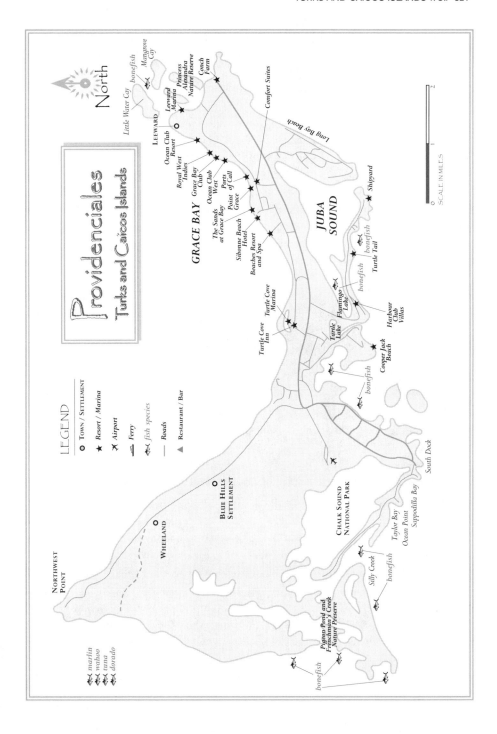

of resorts and restaurants nestled into the sand dunes. It is not an exaggeration to say that this is one of the most awesome resort beaches in the Caribbean. The resort properties are far enough back from the powder-fine beach, and none are more than four stories in this area, so that there is no sense of crowding, with the exception of the beach in front of Club Med.

Resorts along this stretch include Ocean Club West, Grace Bay Club, Royal West Indies, Club Med, and the original Ocean Club. Our two favorite restaurants along the beach are Anacaona at Grace Bay Club, and Mango Reef at the Royal West Indies.

The Leeward Marina faces northeast overlooking Princess Alexandra Nature Reserve and Little Way Cay. A deep blue channel, called Leeward Going Through, sweeps in front of the marina that is home to commercial docks, private slips, a couple of restaurants, and almost every water sports and fishing company on the island. If you want to book a diving or snorkeling trip, arrange a family picnic on a remote cay, book an offshore charter or a bonefishing guide, or sip a beer and have a relaxing lunch, this is the place.

Stephen and guide Arthur Dean of Silver Deep.

Arthur Dean and his guides from Silver Deep meet their bonefishing clients here each morning. So does Captain Barr Gardner. Rental boats are available at the marina and at the Ocean Club for anglers and vacationers who want to cruise the string of cays between here and North Caicos on their own. A more or less continuous reef runs along the ocean side of these cays. Buoys are conveniently placed inside the reef so you can tie up and go snorkeling. Snorkeling enthusiasts will be in heaven along the reef and in the cuts between some of the cays.

There are many white sand flats, and darker turtle grass flats on the leeside of most cays. There are also creeks between the cays that mushroom into mangrove-lined flats, some wadable, and some so soft you'll sink up to your waist if you step out of your boat. There is a fashionable luxury resort, the Meridian Club, on Pine Cay. Across the channel from their boat dock are two good flats that are carved into another smaller cay. Every time we've waded here, we've caught at least a half dozen bones in the four- to five-pound class. We've always used long fluorocarbon leaders and small Gotchas going under the assumption that lots of people must fish here—but we've never seen anyone.

Continuing northeast you'll pass Dellis Cay before you reach Parrot Cay. The deserted beaches on the ocean side of all these cays are perfect for catching rays, relaxing, picnicking, swimming, and snorkeling. We do see some boats pulled up on some of these beaches at times, but you won't have any trouble finding a beach all to yourself.

Parrot Cay has become one of the most exclusive private islands on the planet. The five-star Parrot Cay Resort has managed to create an atmosphere of simple elegance and tranquility that attracts celebrities and jet-setters, and also anglers looking for the ultimate luxury bonefishing excursion. While there are flats you can fish on your own, you might as well hire Arthur Dean to come pick you up at the resort and take you to North, Middle, or East Caicos for a day of pursuing bones on pure white flats that seem endless.

North Caicos is just 12 miles from the Leeward Marina and is the greenest of all the islands because it receives the most rain. This is a large island, over 40 miles in length. Most residents make their living farming and fishing. You can arrive at the island's airport via puddle-jumper from Provo, or by boat at Sandy Point, a settlement just across the channel from Parrot Cay.

It may start to sound redundant but the beaches and snorkeling around North Caicos are beyond belief. There are several small resorts and a number of private rental houses on the island along with a few restaurants. The cays and cuts between North and Middle Caicos can be loaded with bonefish, snapper, jacks, grouper, mackerel, and other species, but at times they can also seem barren. This depends on the locals—as sadly, netting is allowed at times. We've always had at least decent bonefishing in these areas, but the habitat is such that if the locals stopped netting this would be one of the premiere places in the world to pursue the gray ghost.

Middle Caicos is the largest of the seven inhabited islands, but also the least populated with just fewer than 300 residents. Rocky bluffs and rolling hills front the ocean side of the island and create sheltered beaches and coves ideal for sunning and snorkeling. Access is the same as North Caicos, by puddle-jumper to the island's airport at Conch Bar or by boat, including the ferry from North Caicos.

Middle Caicos has more than 15 miles of aboveground caves that were carved out of the limestone by centuries of erosion. Tours are popular because there are many Lucayan/Arawak artifacts in the caves. For hikers there is a five-mile long trail, the Crossing Over Place, that winds along the beach and through the bush. If you want to stay on the island, there are several small resorts and private rental houses. Many flats around the island hold bonefish and, at times, the fishing is sensational, but netting can be a problem here also, especially in the migration routes between the islands.

The 18-square-mile island of East Caicos is uninhabited. The spectacular reefs around much of the island are some of the most dangerous in the Caribbean, and navigation here requires local knowledge. Inland there are extensive savannas suited to ranching, and many lakes and lagoons that are home to flamingos, ducks, and pigeons. Wing-shooting has been popular here for decades.

While dangerous to enter, the harbor of Jacksonville is a stunning anchorage with miles of beaches flanked by Flamingo Hill, which at 156 feet is the highest point in TCI. This area is being considered for a major resort development.

South Caicos is just across the shallow bank from East Caicos, but it is a world apart. Also known as East Harbour, and the Big South, South Caicos has the one of the best natural harbors in the TCI's, Cockburn Harbour. This eight-square-mile island of coral rock has seen it all, from being the hideout for infamous pirates to being part of the thriving turn-of-the-century salt business to now being a bustling community of about 1,200 people who make their living mostly from harvesting conch and lobster.

Visitors will find a charming colonial-style settlement with historic buildings still in use, plus some of the best scuba diving, blue water fishing, and bonefishing in the TCI's. The white sand flats that sprawl from Long Cay up to East Caicos hold high numbers of bonefish, and the nearby deep water drop-offs into Columbus Passage means lots of big bones, too.

All-inclusive bonefishing packages are available with Beyond the Blue Bonefish Charters. Access to the island is via boat, or various puddle-jumpers from Provo.

Another short boat ride, this time across the 7,000 foot deep Turks Island Passage (Columbus Passage), brings you to Grand Turk, the administrative and political capital of the TCIs. Cockburn Town has been the seat of government since 1766. Founded by Bermudan Salt Rakers three centuries ago, this is a classic British colonial town with a colorful Caribbean flare.

Six miles long and maybe a mile wide, Grand Turk is endowed with miles of sugary beaches and some of the world's most enticing dive sites. The warm Atlantic waters are filled with marine life ranging from a tiny sea horse to manta, eagle, and stingrays, green and hawksbill turtles, dolphin, shark, whale shark, and the magnificent humpback whale. Diving is just a five-minute boat ride offshore to the 7,000-foot vertical wall. On top of the wall, divers can enjoy exploring magical coral formations and sand gullies.

There are a number of places to stay, from the elegant and exclusive Turtle Head Mansion to the comfortable and casual Salt Raker Inn and Osprey Beach Hotel on Front Street, the main drag overlooking the ocean. Many good restaurants are also sprinkled along the beach. Angling opportunities focus on the world-class blue-water fishing for marlin, wahoo, tuna, and dorado.

Fishing Highlights

At the risk of being redundant, we'll say again that a trip to the TCIs is the best way to play the odds against the normal winter weather patterns of cold fronts and wind. Cold fronts rarely reach these islands. It seldom rains on Provo, and there is no rainy season in the TCIs, though there is a fair amount of rainfall on North Caicos.

Delightful warm days are the rule during the winter season. The average daily temperature is 83°F (28°C). The hottest months are September and October, when temperatures can reach 90° to 95°F (32° to 35°C). The almost-constant easterly trade winds keep things cooled down and comfortable. OK, so there is wind, but that is a

Stephen on a flat in Provo.

given in the world of saltwater fly-fishing. What's more important is that it's almost always sunny, so good visibility usually prevails year-round. The hurricane season is the same as the Bahamas, with August, September, and October the most likely months for a tropical storm.

Like Andros, the TCIs are blessed with a varied fishery. This means there are vast flats that support large numbers of bonefish, nearby deepwater cuts and drop-offs that support good numbers of big bones, and reef and blue water fishing that rivals any place in the Caribbean.

Flats that have deep water nearby are not only good for big bones, they usually also have water temperatures that all bonefish favor, and tidal flows that nurture shrimp, crabs, and baitfish. Because this is the case for a majority of the flats in the TCIs—from Provo to South Caicos—the islands enjoy good year-round flats fishing.

We don't have a preference here in fishing spring tides or neap tides, but anglers who enjoy wading usually prefer neap tides. If you're in hot pursuit of a trophy double-digit bone, you'll be better off fishing a spring tide. In any case, remember that fish are creatures of habit. You need to be observant and patient for maximum success, especially if you choose to fish on your own.

And fishing on your own in the TCIs can be fantastic. There are many easily accessible—by car and by boat—wadable flats suited to experienced anglers. In general, the most important factors to consider are the tides, tidal flow, water temperatures, plus tactics, leaders, and flies. It is best to obtain accurate tide information once you arrive on Provo. Then you can develop your plan for where and when you want to fish.

Because many of the accessible flats do get fished on a regular basis, you should use long (12-foot) fluorocarbon leaders tapered to 8-pound tippet in these areas. In more remote areas, out around Middle (Grand) Caicos or South Caicos for example, you can go with shorter leaders and heavier tippet. A Gotcha is a killer fly just like it is almost everywhere else, and rubber legs are a key ingredient on many of the bright white sand bottoms. That means a Beck's Sililegs or a Mantis Shrimp are two flies you should always have in your box. When it doubt about size, start with a #4-6, then make adjustments for water depth and how spooky the fish are behaving.

We always highly recommend fishing with a professional guide, and that is definitely the case in the TCIs if you want to fish the best remote flats. Be prepared for a shock in terms of the cost of guided trips out of Provo, as they are almost double what they are in the Bahamas. The TCI government imposes brutal import duties and everything that arrives in the islands, and that means everything costs more.

Most guides offer half-day options (usually about the price of a full day in the Bahamas) in the morning or afternoon. If it fits your schedule, we suggest going in the morning. Half days can be great, but be aware that you will be limited in how far you can go, and you will not be able to fish the more remote flats. That makes full-day trips definitely worth the money if you can afford it.

The reef and offshore fishing is excellent year round, and you won't have to run very far to do either. If you just want to catch a lot of fish, reef fishing is a wonderful option. Jacks, snapper, grouper, yellowtail, mackerel, amberjacks, sharks, and barracuda are the primary reef species.

For monster wahoo, November through April is prime time. These are good months for white marlin, sailfish, yellowfin tuna, and an occasional blue marlin.

May to September is the best time to focus on blue marlin, and several companies "guarantee" blues June through August. These are also the prime months for numbers of yellowfin tuna, sailfish, and white marlin. Wahoo fishing remains good, as does fishing for dorado.

While we do not know of any offshore boats or crews that specialize in fly-fishing, if you are an experienced blue-water angler with your own equipment, there are boats that can get you into fish. Boats can be hired out of Turtle Cove Marina or Leeward Marina.

Optional Activities

For our money, the TCIs offer the best overall vacation options combined with quality fly-fishing anywhere in the islands. The drawback is that you're going to pay more than in the Bahamas in most cases. If you do your homework, you can work out some value options in the TCIs but that probably won't include fishing with a guide.

As for everything else—you can choose from every conceivable water sport and beach activity, from over-the-top exclusive resorts to laid-back inexpensive cottages, from fine gourmet dining to a cookout or picnic on a remote beach.

Diving and snorkeling enthusiasts have more quality options here than in the Bahamas. Many resorts, including Club Med, have all-inclusive diving packages.

The general atmosphere in terms of people and things to do on Provo is similar to Grand Bahama. For some people this will be a drawback, as the experience is more of a "resort" as opposed to the experience on the Out Islands. An Out Island experience can be enjoyed on Pine Cay, Parrot Cay, North, Middle, and South Caicos.

The choices are yours, mon.

Lodging, Guides, and Services

Featured Lodges

Most resorts on Provo are condominium resorts as opposed to hotels. This means accommodations are studio suites to four-bedroom units, usually with full kitchens, though there are some smaller hotels.

Ocean Club West

Grace Bay This resort, and its sister resort down the beach—the Ocean Club— receives our highest recommendation in terms of combining value and an overall casual vacation experience. The resort has beautiful gardens, nicely furnished condos (ask for an end unit on the beach), tennis courts, fitness center, diving and water sports programs, and good restaurants. Ocean Club West is perfectly located in the center of Grace Bay.

Season: October through July.

Suitable For: Anglers and non-anglers.

Optional Activities: Beach, pool, snorkeling, diving, boating, sailing, windsurfing, spa, tennis, golf, fine dining, shopping, fishing, and more.

What's Included: As much or as little as you want. Use of all facilities including the pool, tennis courts, fitness center, and business center.

Not Included: Airfare. You can book accommodations only, and then choose daily activities and meals as you go. For guided bonefishing, we suggest booking in advance.

Pricing: $$$

Contact: Reservations and information, 800-457-8787 or 649-946-5880.

Internet: www.oceanclubresorts.com

E-mail: res@oceanclubresorts.com

The Sands at Grace Bay

Grace Bay Sand and sea meet at this 118-suite luxury beachfront property. Oversized balconies complement large, graceful suites and offer space for quiet relaxation, fine dining, and family play. The suites have sensational views, plus their beachside pool area is the best on the island. Hemingway's Bar and Restaurant is right on the water.

Season: Year round.

Suitable For: Anglers and non-anglers.

Optional Activities: Beach, pool, snorkeling, diving, boating, sailing, windsurfing, spa treatments, fine dining, shopping, fishing, and more.

What's Included: As much or as little as you want. Everything is a la carte.

Not Included: Airfare, ground transfers. You can book accommodations only, and then choose daily activities and meals as you go. For guided bonefishing, we suggest booking in advance.

Pricing: $$$-$$$$

Contact: Reservations and information, 877-777-2637 or 649-946-5199.

Internet: www.thesandsresort.com

E-mail: vacations@thesandsresort.com

Point Grace

Grace Bay On the "point" of Grace Bay Beach, this intimate and elegant resort offers magnificent two- and three-bedroom suites on the water. Just ask and they'll send their Rolls to pick you up at the airport. Their restaurant, Grace's Cottage, is one of the best in the Caribbean, featuring gourmet Caribbean-Asian cuisine. Their spa is one of the most luxurious on the island.

Season: Year round.

Suitable For: Anglers and non-anglers.

Optional Activities: Beach, pool, snorkeling, diving, boating, sailing, windsurfing, spa, golf, fine dining, shopping, fishing, and more.

What's Included: As much or as little as you want. Everything is a la carte.

Not Included: Airfare. You can book accommodations only, and then choose daily activities and meals as you go. For guided bonefishing, we suggest booking in advance.

Pricing: $$$$

Contact: Reservations and information, 649 946-5096.

Internet: www.pointgrace.com

E-mail: reservations@pointgrace.com

Grace Bay Club

Grace Bay A short walk down the beach from Point Grace, the resort has exquisite Mediterranean-style suites with breathtaking views of the turquoise water, a relaxing pool area, tennis courts, and our choice as the best and most romantic restaurant on the island: Anacaona. What else do you need?

Season: Year round.

Suitable For: Anglers and non-anglers.

Optional Activities: Beach, pool, snorkeling, diving, boating, sailing, windsurfing, spa, tennis, golf, fine dining, shopping, fishing, and more.

What's Included: As much or as little as you want. Airport transfers, continental breakfast, bicycles, tennis courts, use of business center.

Not Included: Airfare. You can book accommodations only, and then choose daily activities and meals as you go. For guided bonefishing, we suggest booking in advance.

Pricing: $$$$

Contact: Reservations and information, 800-946-5757 or 649-946-5050

Internet: www.gracebayclub.com

E-mail: info@gracebayclub.com

Royal West Indies Resort

Grace Bay "Indulge in a little tropical therapy" is their slogan, and it is more than suitable for this beachfront resort on Grace Bay. Low-key and casually elegant, with all-suite accommodations, lush gardens, a delightful pool, and one of our favorite restaurants on the island, Mango Reef.

Season: Year round.

Suitable For: Anglers and non-anglers.

Optional Activities: Beach, pool, snorkeling, diving, boating, sailing, windsurfing, spa treatments, fine dining, shopping, fishing, and more.

What's Included: As much or as little as you want. Everything is a la carte.

Not Included: Airfare, ground transfers. You can book accommodations only, and then choose daily activities and meals as you go. For guided bonefishing, we suggest booking in advance.

Pricing: $$$-$$$$

Contact: Reservations and information, 800-332-4203 or 649-946-5004.

Internet: www.royalwestindies.com

E-mail: reservations@royalwestindies.com, info@royalwestindies.com

Parrot Cay Resort

Parrot Cay One of the finest private island resorts in the Caribbean—a retreat for total relaxation and complete pampering. Several miles of private beach, an infinity swimming pool, tennis courts, a gymnasium, and a wonderful spa are highlights. Meals are served in the refined dining room, on the pool deck, or just order room service. Accommodations are in hotel rooms, one-, two-, and three-bedroom suites and villas. Guests fly into Provo, then are transferred to the Leeward Marina, where they board the Parrot Cay tender for the 20-minute ride to the island. All activities can be arranged, and fishing guides will pick you up and drop you off each day at the island dock.

Season: Year round.

Suitable For: Anglers and non-anglers.

Optional Activities: Beach, pool, snorkeling, diving, boating, sailing, windsurfing, spa, gym, golf, fine dining, shopping, fishing, and more.

What's Included: Minimum three-night stay. As much or as little as you want. Airport transfers, ground, and boat. Use of tennis courts, gym, spa, business center.

Not Included: Airfare. You can book accommodations only, and then choose daily activities and meals as you go. For guided bonefishing, we suggest booking in advance.

Pricing: $$$$

Contact: Reservations and information, 649-946-7788.

Internet: www.parrot-cay.com

E-mail: res@parrotcay.como.bz

Beaches Resort and Spa

Grace Bay One of the best family all-inclusive resort in the Caribbean. Accommodations range from deluxe air-conditioned hotel rooms to two- and three-bedroom suites. If you're looking for a place to take the family so you can get in some fishing, this is the place for you. Fully supervised kids' facilities and programs. This location is extremely popular. We recommend booking as far in advance as possible.

Season: Year round.

Suitable For: Anglers and non-anglers.

Optional Activities: Beach, five pools, water slides, Pirates theme park, snorkeling, diving, boating, sailing, windsurfing, golf, fitness center, spa, nine fine dining choices, shopping, fishing, and more.

What's Included: All-inclusive—accommodations, all meals and snacks, liquor, use of all facilities including pools, fitness center, spa, water sports, scuba diving, child care, tips/gratuities, and airport transfers.

Not Included: Airfare, spa treatments.
Pricing: $$$-$$$$
Contact: Reservations and information, 888-BEACHES or 649-946-8000.
Internet: www.beaches.com
E-mail: info@beaches.com

Harbour Club Villas

Venetian Road   Owners Marta and Barry Morton are gracious hosts at this uniquely styled small villa resort overlooking Flamingo Lake and the club's private marina. Six deluxe one-bedroom villas include dining areas, living rooms, and full kitchens. Good bonefish flats are right in front of the property, and others are a short walk away. Still, we advise guests staying here to rent a car to access the island's best beaches, restaurants, and shops. This is a wonderful do-it-yourself option, and it's a great value.
Season: Year round.
Suitable For: Anglers and non-anglers.
Optional Activities: Pool, snorkeling, diving, boating, sailing, windsurfing, spa, gym, golf, fine dining, shopping, fishing, and more.
What's Included: Accommodations.
Not Included: Airfare. You book accommodations only, and then choose daily activities and meals as you go. For guided bonefishing, we suggest booking in advance.
Pricing: $$
Contact: Reservations and information, 649-941-5748.
Internet: www.harbourclubvillas.com; www.bonefishing.tc
E-mail: harbourclub@tciway.tc

Additional Accommodations

Comfort Suites

Grace Bay   Across the street from Grace Bay Beach, this is one of the best accommodation values on the island. The resort has 98 spacious suites, a swimming pool, and Internet access. Guests here are in easy walking distance to the best beaches, and some of the best restaurants and shops.
Pricing: $$-$$$
Contact: Reservations and information, 649-946-8888
Internet: www.choicecaribbean.com

Sibonne Beach Hotel

Grace Bay   This small casual hotel has only 29 air-conditioned rooms, and it's nestled onto one of the most tranquil sections of Grace Bay Beach. Their restaurant, the Bay Bistro, is one of the best on the island, and it overlooks the pool and lush gardens. The bar is a favorite place to enjoy sunset cocktails.
Pricing: $$-$$$
Contact: Reservations and information, 649-946-5547 or 800-528-1905.
Internet: www.sibonne.com
E-mail: info@sibbone.com

Turtle Cove Inn

Turtle Cove Marina Casual, comfortable, and affordable, this two-story marina-front hotel is popular with divers and boaters. Rooms have A/C, telephone, cable TV, mini-refrigerator, and private balconies overlooking the water. It has a swimming pool, plus a convenient location in the marina with lots of good restaurants and shopping nearby.

Pricing: $$-$$$

Contact: Reservations and information, 800-887-0477 or 649-946-4203.

Internet: www.turtlecoveinn.com

E-mail: info@turtlecoveinn.com

Prospect of Whitby Hotel

North Caicos Set on a secluded section of Whitby Beach, the resort has a wonderful Italian restaurant overlooking the water, a swimming pool, and tennis court. The casually elegant atmosphere is apparent in the 27 bright air-conditioned rooms with tile floors, island furniture, minibars, spacious bathrooms, and terraces, all overlooking the seemingly endless white sand and turquoise sea. The all-inclusive resort has an on-site dive shop, plus lots of water sport toys for guest use. Fish on your own or a guide can be arranged.

Pricing: $$-$$$

Contact: Reservations and information, 649-946-7119.

Internet: www.prospectofwhitby.com

Pelican Beach Hotel

Whitby Beach, North Caicos They call this casual laid-back hotel the "un-resort." Nothing fancy here—just 14 spacious air-conditioned rooms facing the beach, a good restaurant and bar, and all the time in the world to relax and enjoy the natural beauty of the island. Bicycles are complimentary to guests. Fish on your own or a guide can be arranged.

Pricing: $

Contact: Reservations and information, 649-946-7112.

E-mail: pelicanbeach@tciway.tc

Blue Horizon Resort

Middle Caicos Bright island-style cottages and villas on 50 secluded acres overlooking a picture postcard beach and cove. All seven units have kitchens or kitchenettes, and some have air conditioning. The on-site owners will stock your kitchen with groceries before you arrive. You can fish on your own, or a guide can be arranged.

Pricing: $$

Contact: Reservations and information, 649-946-6141 (8 A.M. to 6 P.M. Eastern) or 866-828-4874

Internet: www.bhresort.com

South Caicos Lodge

South Caicos Twenty-four standard air-conditioned hotel rooms are set on the water's edge. The large decks are the best place on the island to enjoy dramatic sunsets. The restaurant serves three meals a day, with fresh seafood a nightly specialty. Complete bonefish packages with Beyond the Blue Bonefish Charters are available, or you can book a room and fish on your own. Diving packages are available through South Caicos Divers.

Pricing: $-$$
Contact: Reservations and information, 649-231-1703 or 321-795-3136.
Internet: www.beyondtheblue.com
E-mail: bonefishbtb@aol.com

Marinas

Turtle Cove Marina

Turtle Cove   One hundred slips, 65 of which are deepwater slips, full service for boaters including fuel, water, ice, electricity, cable TV, decompression chamber, and showers. Diving, snorkeling, fishing, and other activities can be arranged on site. Tide and weather information is available. Hotels, restaurants, and shops are a short walk from the docks.
Contact: Reservations and information, 649-941-3781.
Internet: www.turtlecovemarina.com
E-mail: turtlecovemarina@provo.net

Leeward Marina

Leeward   The marina is part of a 425-acre residential resort community on the northeast tip of Provo. The property is bordered by Grace Bay, stunning coral reefs, and the Leeward Going Through Channel. The community has an array of private home sites on the beach and on the canals. The marina has services for boaters that include fuel, water, ice, electricity, and laundry. Many of the island's best diving, snorkeling, fishing, and tour companies are located here. Gilley's is a good restaurant for lunch and dinner.
Contact: Reservations and information, 649-946-5553 or 649-946-5000.
Internet: www.leewardtci.com

Independent Guides and Charters

Captain Arthur Dean, Silver Deep, Leeward Marina. Arthur is a superior guide, one of our favorites in the islands. He has intimate knowledge of the flats, natural boat-handling skills, and amazing eyes. He's also an excellent casting instructor, lots of fun to be with, and a great singer. Kim loves to hear guides sing island songs on the flats, and Arthur is one of the best in the business. He fishes out of an immaculate 18-foot Action Craft with a 115-hp Yamaha 4-stroke, a comfortable boat, and super fast for reaching the remote locations around North, Middle, and East Caicos. Arthur also has several other very good guides; Darin, Shervin, and Godfrey. Don't hesitate to fish with them if Arthur is booked—which he usually is, so you need to call well in advance to make your reservation. Silver Deep will give you a discount for advance bookings. Silver Deep offers full- and half-day bonefishing trips. Be aware that half day trips limit where you can go. Try not to be shocked by the prices! TCI is very expensive and import duty on boats, parts, etc. is brutal for the locals. Reservations and information, 649-946-5612; Internet: www.silverdeep.com; e-mail: silverdeep_dean@tciway.tc.

Captain Barr Gardner, Bonefish Unlimited, Leeward Marina. Barr is a great guy to be out with, very well liked, knowledgeable, and professional. He fishes out of a well-maintained flats skiff with a poling platform. He offers full- and half-day trips. Reservation and information, 649-946-4874 or 649-231-0133; Internet: www.provo.net/bonefish/; e-mail: Bonefish@provo.net.

Beyond the Blue Bonefish Charters, South Caicos. Operated by Bibo Jayne and Granger Lockhart, Beyond the Blue offers some of the most exciting bonefishing anywhere. The flats around South Caicos are like those in Christmas Island and in the Seychelles—easily wadable white sand that seems to stretch on forever. And the numbers of bonefish are impressive; large schools of three- to six-pound fish, plus larger fish in singles and double. Glass-clear water makes the bones easy to see, even on cloudy days. You can book an all-inclusive fishing package or a day trip. Reservations and information, 649-231-1703 or in the U.S. 321-795-3136; Internet: www.beyondtheblue.com; e-mail: bonefishbtb@aol.com.

Gwendolyn Fishing Charters, Turtle Cove Marina. Captain Geoff Adams and his crew have more than 29 years combined experience fishing the islands. All conventional tackle and gear are provided on full-day, multiple-day, and half-day charters. Fly-fishers are welcome (you have to bring your own fly gear), and the crews are adept at chumming and teasing techniques. Capt. Adams operates a deluxe 45-foot air-conditioned Hatteras sportfishing yacht. The fishing grounds are close, less than two miles from the shore, so no long boat rides. Fishing is excellent year round, depending on the species. Blue marlin are guaranteed from June to August, with May and September great months as well. Monster wahoo are in season November through April, and are available year round. White marlin, sailfish, yellowfin tuna, and dorado are best May through September, and available most of the year. Reservations and information, 649-946-5321 or in the U.S. 866-990-3474; Internet: www.FishingTCI.com; e-mail: Gwnedolyn@Provo.net.

Services

Diving, Snorkeling, and Water Sports: *Windsurfing Provo* is the best place to rent a boat to cruise the cays, picnic, snorkel, or fish on your own. The owner, Mike Rosati, is super helpful and friendly, and he's an excellent sailing and windsurfing instructor. Mike will rent you a 16-foot Carolina skiff with a cooler and any other gear you may need—(no fly-fishing gear though, you have to bring your own), including a waterproof map—for a day of exploring, snorkeling, fishing, and beaching. Mike also rents Hobie Cats, windsurfers, and sea kayaks. Windsurfing Provo is on Grace Bay Beach, with two locations—in front of the Ocean Club and the Ocean Club West. Contact: 649-241-1687; www.windsurfingprovo.tc; windpro@tciway.tc.

Provo Turtle Divers, Ltd., established in 1970, is the oldest and one of the most experienced dive operations in the TCIs. They are a PADI gold palm–rated dive operation. They are based in the Turtle Cove Marina with satellite locations at the Ocean Club and Ocean Club West. They work all the major dive sites, and they're always looking for new sites, as well. They invite you to explore the reefs and walls in amazingly clear waters. Contact: 800-833-1341 or 649-946-4232; Internet: www.provo turtledivers.com; e-mail: provoturtledivers@provo.net.

Private boat charters, fishing charters, scuba and snorkeling trips, beach excursions, water ski-ing— *J & B Tours* does it all. Owners and operators, Jill and Brian Swann, work hard to put extra fun in every outing. They are located at the Leeward Marina. Contact: 649-946-5047; Internet: www.jbtours.com; e-mail: jill@jbtours.com.

Owned and operated by Arthur and Paola Dean, *Silver Deep* operates the best overall fishing programs in TCI (bonefishing, blue-water, reef, and bottom fishing). Diving, snorkeling, beach, and barbecue excursions are also available. They are located at the Leeward Marina. Contact: 649-946-5612; Internet: www.silverdeep.com; e-mail: silverdeep_dean@tciway.tc.

Restaurants: There are several free restaurant and shopping guide books available at the international airport in the baggage claims area, and these books are also available at most hotels, and in various other spots.

Some of our favorites restaurants include the intimate, elegant, and romantic *Anacaona* at the Grace Bay Club, which serves outstanding Mediterranean dishes that are beautifully presented, provides excellent service, and is our favorite spot for a special dinner. *Mango Reef* at Royal West Indies Resort is casual and fun, with a variety of dishes from rack of lamb to fresh wahoo with guava sauce. *Coyaba* at Coral Gardens offers casually elegant outdoor dining. They serve inventive Caribbean fare accompanied by an extensive wine list. *Grace's Cottage* at Point Grace is elegant and sophisticated, serving a delicious blend of Caribbean and Asian cuisine. *Bay Bistro* at Sibonne offers casual oceanfront dining. This popular spot serves everything from tasty tapas to conch fritters, pork dumplings, and the freshest grilled seafood. *Fairways Bar and Grill* at the Golf Club is a pleasant and laid-back place for a relaxing lunch or dinner. *Coco Bistro* on Grace Bay Road serves a dazzling variety of Mediterranean dishes under a lush canopy of coconut trees.

At the Turtle Cove Marina there are a number of casual restaurants serving a variety of food. Our favorites are *Tiki Hut Cabana Bar & Grill*, a favorite lunch spot (don't miss the Wednesday night barbecue), *Magnolia Restaurant and Wine Bar*, and *Baci Ristorante*. For those who need an Italian fix, go for the veal parmesan.

Note: These restaurants range from dress nice elegant to shorts and T-shirts, and run the price range.

Car Rentals: *Avis* has everything from sub-compacts to SUVs and minivans. Reservations and information: 649-946-4705.

Budget Rent a Car: Competitive rates on all types of cars. They offer discount car/hotel packages. Reservations and information: 649-946-4079.

TC National Car Rental offers 24-hour service and competitive prices. Free airport pick-up and return. Rent for a week and get one day free. Other discounts available at different times of the year. Reservations and information: 649-946-4701.

Shopping: Provo is not a shopping mecca by any stretch of the imagination, but there are several outdoor malls and a smattering of stores around the island and in the marinas and hotels. The *Bamboo Gallery* and *Caribbean Island Art* have worthwhile selections of fine art, silk paintings, local oil and watercolors, and island crafts.

Banks: Banking is big business in the TCIs so there are lots of banks with regular business hours Monday through Friday. *Scotiabank* and *Barclay's Bank* are the two most prominent.

Medical Services: There are hospitals and clinics on Provo and Grand Turk. Clinics are available on North, Middle, and South Caicos. Emergency medical services are available only on Provo and Grand Turk. *Island Pharmacy* (649-946-4150) on Provo has a full prescription drug service.

For specific details and contact information for these services, government offices, police, and other services, visit: www.wherewhenhow.com or www.tcimall.tc.

New Developments

The TCIs and Provo, in particular, are booming these days with resort and private home development. Visit the real estate section at www.wherewhenhow.com for more information.

Scheduled to open in 2004, the Palms Grand Resort and Spa will be one of the finest luxury resorts in the TCIs.

The Turks & Caicos Sporting Club at Ambergris Cay, an exclusive private island resort, is preparing to offer 100 home sites, every amenity you can think of, and an extraordinary level of service. This may sound like the usual line of promotional propaganda, except the Club will be operated by the Greenbrier Resort & Club Management Company. They are a proven leader in planning and managing premier club services and amenity programs. Their expertise will extend to every aspect of the Turks & Caicos Sporting Club, including hiring and training staff and instructors. This is the company that is developing and managing the Deep Water Cay Club on Grand Bahama. Visit their site at www.ambergriscay.com.

We've heard rumors that East Caicos may be up for sale by the Turks and Caicos Government. Considering that's essentially what happened to Provo, we don't doubt they're thinking it over. Our local friends have their fingers crossed that this won't happen.

INDEX

S

Saddle Back Cays, 52
Salt Pond, 268, 269
Salt Raker Inn, 324
Sampson Cay, 221–22
Sampson Cay Club & Marina, 221–22, 241
Sam's Place, 230
Samuel Knowles Bonefishing, 269, 277
San Salvador
  activities, 302–3
  around the islands, 300
  fishing highlights, 300–302
  lodging, 303–4
  new developments, 304
  overview, 297–99
Sand Bar, 137
Sand Bar Grill and Bar, 137
Sandals Royal Bahamian Resort &
  Spa, 212
Sandpiper, 231
Sands at Grace Bay, The, 327–28
Sandy Point, 138–39
Scavella's Guesthouse, 294
Schooner's Landing Resort, 150
Scorpio Inn, 224
Sea Crest Hotel and Marina, 156, 163
Sea Shell Beach Club, 137–38
Sea Spray Resort Villas & Marina,
  134, 151
Seascape Inn, 62, 86–87
Senses Spa and Fitness Center, 100
services
  Abacos, 152–53
  Andros Island, 90–91
  Berry Islands, 172
  Bimini, 163–64
  Cat Island, 258–59
  Crooked and Acklins Islands, 295–96
  Eleuthera, 194–95
  Exuma Cays, 244–45
  Grand Bahama Island, 114–15

  Great Inagua, 313–14
  Long Island, 279–80
  Nassau, 213–15
  San Salvador, 304
  Turks and Caicos Islands, 333–34
Settlement Point, 98
Seymour's, 264
Shark Hole, 59
sharks
  Abacos, 143–44
  Andros Island, 80
  Bimini, 160
  Eleuthera, 188
  Grand Bahama Island, 105
  Long Island, 274
Sheraton Grand Hotel, 205
shopping, 16
  Abacos, 153
  Grand Bahama Island, 115
  Nassau, 215
  Turks and Caicos Islands, 334
Shroud Cay, 221
Sibonne Beach Hotel, 330
Silly Creek, 319
Silver Deep, 322
Simms, 268
Simms Cay, 56–57
Small Hope Bay, 54, 90
Small Hope Bay Lodge, 54, 56, 83–84
Smith's Bay, 251–52
Snake Cay, 135
snorkeling
  Abacos, 145, 152
  Andros Island, 90
  Berry Islands, 172
  Bimini, 164
  Cat Island, 259
  Eleuthera, 194
  Exuma Cays, 237, 244–45
  Grand Bahama Island, 107, 114–15
  Long Island, 275, 280